Globalisation, Leisure and Social Change

Globalisation, Leisure and Social Change

Essays in Honour of Professor Ishwar P. Modi

Edited by

B.K. Nagla

Vinay Kumar Srivastava

RAWAT PUBLICATIONS

Jaipur • New Delhi • Bangalore • Guwahati • Kolkata

ISBN 978-81-316-0818-0

Published by
Prem Rawat for **Rawat Publications**
Satyam Apts, Sector 3, Jawahar Nagar, Jaipur 302 004 (India)
Phone: 0141 265 1748 / 7006 Fax: 0141 265 1748
E-mail: info@rawatbooks.com
Website: www.rawatbooks.com

New Delhi Office
4858/24, Ansari Road, Daryaganj, New Delhi 110 002
Phone: 011 2326 3290

Also at *Bangalore, Guwahati* and *Kolkata*

Typeset by Rawat Computers, Jaipur
Printed and bound in India

Contents

Preface

Globalisation, has existed for many centuries, as a process by which cultures are influenced by one another and become more alike through trade, immigration, and exchange of information and ideas. However, in recent decades, the degree and intensity of the connections among different cultures and different world regions have accelerated dramatically because of advances in science and technology particularly through telecommunications. With modern development around the world, the contemporary era of globalisation has brought changes in all aspects of life. Indeed, globalisation is simply the scale and growth of development which affects the trends and patterns of social interaction. The effect of globalisation is not only faster data transfer but also the dispersal of lifestyles and activities, all contributing to irrevocable changes. A question that now arises is how people spend their leisure time, or what do they do in their spare time. In other words, the future of the new world of entertainment and leisure activities is an alternative to the traditional condition through TV, music, internet, cyberspace leisure, and computer games in the private spheres of homes.

Leisure time and its spending through technology is the new subject, after industrial revolution, which has become an important subject in sociology. In industrial society, life and work of human beings have become mechanical. They are influenced by the technological changes which reflect the social and cultural lives of people who have limited time now than their traditional leisure time. Hence, globalisation has brought about huge changes in people's lives. One of the important matters is the spending of the leisure time, e.g. in what way the youths and teenagers are playing and talking to each other. Today, due to rapid technological advancement, the new generation is spending a major part of their leisure time in solitude using new tools and gadgets. Against this backdrop, the architects have to create identity residence and create places for answering the needs of leisure time.

In this context, this volume has been planned to honour Dr. Ishwar Modi, celebrating his contribution to the discipline of sociology in general and to the study of leisure in particular. It is with an immense sense of pleasure and pride that we are editing a volume honouring Dr. Ishwar P. Modi. B.K. Nagla's association with him goes back to 1972 when he came to the Jawaharlal Nehru

University (JNU) from Jaipur. He has a vivid memory of their first encounter. They met frequently at the Centre for the Study of Social Systems and the JNU hostel during breakfast and dinner time. They got to know more of each other's interests, academic as well as extra-curricular.

Dr. Modi started his career in the discipline of sociology at the University of Rajasthan, where he taught for more than twenty-seven years. It was an illustrious career, for his department at that time, was known for the stalwarts of sociology. It was internationally reckoned as one of the leading centres of sociology. In fact, it was this department that had sent prominent sociologists to the other upcoming universities where each one of them founded a new department that in course of time grew into an international centre. The JNU is a prominent example of this.

It was in this department that Dr. Modi received his training and later on joined the teaching faculty, supervising a large number of doctoral dissertations. He devoted himself to the incisive understanding of the Indian society. Right in the beginning of his research work, he realized the immense diversity in India. He closely examined the processes that contributed to this diversity. In his writings on villages, he made it clear that although a village appeared to be homogenous from the outside, internally it was divided into different cultural clusters, each caste having its own distinct culture. In addition to these distinctions, where each caste was a distinct unit, there were forces which were keeping the village unified. Both these processes of segregation and unification were working hand in hand. Dr. Modi explored the dialectics between unity and identity, both at the empirical and theoretical levels. In his writings, he made it clear that the concept of homogenisation was utopian. It has neither happened nor will it happen in future that differences would get wiped out. Yes, of course, there are cultures that make concerted efforts to create homogeneity, as happened in China, but even in these cultures the differences could not be effaced. They would be buried of till the time the oppressive measures continued to act, but once the measures would be relaxed, the differences would come up.

In other words, difference is the rule of nature. Working on this idea, Dr. Modi examined these processes in India. In his writings he has opposed the dichotomy of rural and urban societies. He was in favour of the continuities between the village and the town, and thus instead of the two ways of living, there were several forms of social life, and howsoever hard one may try, one would not fit in either the village or the urban life. Such shades of different forms of living need to be closely studied. Because we are so enamoured with the dichotomy of rural and urban that we are unable to see the different shades of living which lie in between the two. The study of such patterns was the hallmark of Dr. Modi's work, for which he will always be remembered.

Above all he has been continuously taking interest in the study of leisure, an area that was hardly explored in sociology. He wrote his doctoral thesis on 'Social Structure and Leisure'. Most of the sociologists gave importance to the study of work, an activity which takes place away from home for which the individual is paid. The activity is time-bound and in case the individual continues to work beyond the schedule, he is paid an extra amount. This definition of work generated a lot of debate with respect to the work of the housewives, for it followed that they did not do any work. Against this backdrop, sociologists did not pay any attention to leisure. Dr. Modi showed the importance of leisure in the lives of people and succeeded in founding the discipline of 'leisurology'.

Dr Modi made remarkable contribution to this field. Not only did he write a lot on this topic but also organized a number of national and international seminars. Considering this as one of the seminal contributions of Dr. Modi, this volume is dedicated to the study of leisure. The editors of this volume and the contributors wish long life to Dr. Modi and look forward to reading his contributions to sociology.

The present volume is an effort to put across the ideas of scholars in varied disciplines on the issues of globalisation, leisure and change. These essays have been written in the honour of Dr. Ishwar P. Modi. As a friend and professional colleague, we have found him sincere to the purpose and a committed scholar. We received a tremendous response to our request to various scholars to contribute a paper to this volume. As we were insistent to have fresh papers for this volume, the process of completion took a long time. But it was worth waiting for, as novelty has always been more invigorating than banality in scholarship.

We are grateful to all the fellow contributors for their kind gesture to honour Dr. Modi. We are also taking the liberty of including in the volume certain articles and papers published elsewhere after due updating. In anticipation, we extend our sincere thanks to the editors of the journals and books in which these had appeared. Last but not least, we are thankful to Professor Madhu Nagla who deserves admiration for helping us in this exercise. Finally, we extend our special thanks to Rawat Publications, Jaipur, for publishing this volume in a short period of time.

Vinay Kumar Srivastava
B.K. Nagla

Short Profile of Professor Ishwar Modi

Dr Ishwar Prasad Modi (born 12 December 1940) did his master's degree in sociology and Ph.D. in social sciences from the University of Rajasthan, Jaipur, where he taught for twenty-seven years. He was a Visiting Professor to the prestigious Indian Institute of Health Management Research, Jaipur for two years after retirement. He has vast academic and organisational experience.

Dr Modi has travelled extensively (to more than forty countries across all the continents), and has participated, chaired, and delivered keynote addresses at several international conferences and spoken in the areas of leisurology, tourism, youth and mass media at several universities and conferences in Asia, Europe and the Americas. Many important universities in Canada and USA have invited him to speak on his pioneering work on leisurology.

He was the President of the Rajasthan Sociological Association (2005–08); Secretary (2008–09); and President of the Indian Sociological Society (2012–13). He was also an Executive Committee Member of the International Sociological Association (2010–14) and President of its Research Committee on Sociology of Leisure. Dr Modi was elected thrice (1991–99) on the Board of Directors of The World Leisure Organization (WLO) which has consultative status with the United Nations and the UNESCO. The WLO conferred its rare distinction of Honourary Life Membership on him in 1994. Dr Modi has also made invited presentations at the conferences organized by the Chinese Academy of Social Sciences, South African Sociological Association, Russian Society of Sociologists, Polish Sociological Association and Bangladesh Sociological Association. Of late, he has been speaking on the various dimensions of BRICS. He was the guest editor of a special issue on India of the official journal of the Polish Sociological Association, the *Polish Sociological Review*, 2 (178) 2012, and also recently edited a special issue on India, of the journal *Politics and Religion* published by the Center for Study of Religion and Religious Tolerance, Belgrade, Serbia as guest editor. Dr Modi is also currently on the Editorial/Editorial Advisory Boards of the journals: *SOCIOPEDIA.ISA, World Leisure Journal* (Journal of the World Leisure Organization), *Leisure Studies* (Journal of the British Leisure Studies Association), *Indian Journal of Gerontology, Sociological Bulletin* (Journal of the Indian Sociological Society), *Politics and Religion* (Journal of the Center for Study of Religion and Religious Tolerance, Balgrade), and *Health Sociology Review*. He was also a member of the Editorial Board of the ISA Journal *Current Sociology/SSIS Monographs* (2006–10). His major publications (authored, co-authored and edited) include: *Leisure, Mass Media and Social Structure* (1985); *Emerging Trends in Indian Sociology* (1986); *Drugs: Addiction and Prevention* (1997); *Human Values and Social Change* (2000); *Ageing and Human Development* (2001); *Themes in Social Stratification and Mobility* (2009); *Leisure and Civilization: Interdisciplinary and International Perspectives* (2010); *Modernization, Globalization and Social Transformation* (2012); *Education, Religion and Creativity* (2013); *Mapping Leisure Across Borders* (2013); *Polity, Civil Society and Development* (2014); *Gender, Identity and Multiple Marginalities* (2015); *India between Tradition and Modernity* (2014); *Politics and Religion in Contemporary India* (2014); *Leisure, Health and Well-Being* (2016): *Mapping Leisure* (2016).

Prof Modi is also the series editor of a ten volume set on *Readings in Indian Sociology* (2014).

Prof Modi was honoured with the Lifetime Achievement Award (2015) by the Indian Sociological Society for his valuable service and contribution to enriching the discipline of Sociology and Sociological Profession in India.

Contributors

Aretha Oluwakemi Asakitikpi, Osun State University, Ikire Campus, Osun State, Nigeria.

Habil Zsuzsanna Benkõ, University of Szeged, Juhász Gyula Faculty of Education, Institute of Applied Health Sciences and Health Promotion, Szeged, Hungary.

Bhagwan S. Bisht, Professor of Sociology, Kumaun University, Nainital, Uttarakhand.

Michael Burawoy, Department of Sociology, University of California, Berkeley, USA.

Eduardo Burgos-Suazo, Graduate Student of the Department of Sociology, University of Puerto Rico, Rio Piedras Campus.

Sukant K. Chaudhury, Professor, Department of Sociology, University of Lucknow, Lucknow.

Angellyn Santon Gonzalez, Doctoral Student of the Department of Psychology, University of Puerto Rico, Rio Piedras Campus.

Vishesh Kumar Gupta, Associate Professor and Head of Sociology Department, M.H. (PG) College, Moradabad, U.P.

Ma Huidi, Director and Distinguished Research Fellow, Center for Leisure Studies, Institute of Chinese Culture, Beijing City, China.

Rashmi Jain, Associate Professor, Department of Sociology, University of Rajasthan, Jaipur.

Neha Kala, Assistant Professor, Department of Sociology, Banaras Hindu University, Varanasi.

Habibul Haque Khondker, Professor of Sociology, Zayed University, Abu Dhabi, UAE.

Francis Lobo, School of Marketing Tourism and Leisure, Edith Cowan University, Perth, Australia.

Fabio Massimo Lo Verde, Associate Professor of Sociology and Sociology of Consumption, University of Palermo, Italy.

Shalini Modi is Founder, Nishkam Trust and Deputy Director, India International Institute of Social Sciences, Pune.

B.K. Nagla, Former Professor of Sociology, M.D. University, Rohtak.

Madhu Nagla, Professor of Sociology, M.D. University, Rohtak.

Scott North, Professor of Sociology, Graduate School of Human Sciences, Osaka University, Japan.

Laura L. Ortiz-Negron, Sociologist and Director of the the Social Science Research Center, Social Sciences College, University of Puerto Rico, Rio Piedras Campus.

Ken Roberts, Professor of Sociology, University of Liverpool, UK.

Anayra O. Santory Jorge, Philosophy Professor at University of Puerto Rico, Rio Piedras Campus.

K.L. Sharma, National Fellow, Indian Council of Social Science Research, New Delhi.

S.L. Sharma, Former Dean, Faculty of Arts, Panjab University, Chandigarh.

Yogendra Singh, Emeritus Professor, School of Social Sciences, Jawaharlal Nehru University, New Delhi.

Vinay Kumar Srivastava, Professor, Department of Anthropology, Delhi University, New Delhi.

Robert A. Stebbins, Professor Emeritus, Department of Sociology, University of Calgary, Canada.

Klára Tarkó, University of Szeged, Juhász Gyula Faculty of Education, Institute of Applied Health Sciences and Health Promotion, Szeged, Hungary.

Lech W. Zacher, Economist, Sociologist and Futurist, Director of the Center of Impact Assessment Studies and Forecasting, Kozminski University, Warsaw, Poland.

1

Writing About Leisure

KEN ROBERTS

Writing is different than talking. In conversation, even in a monologue such as a lecture or conference presentation, a speaker can simply make points and be well received if the remarks are experienced as stimulating, provocative, making the listener think. Writing a book or article is different. The author needs a narrative. There has to be a start-point – a problem or question – then a body of evidence or argument, which leads to a conclusion. In other words, the writer needs a good story, and it now seems that throughout the history of leisure studies we have been searching for really good stories. There have been five main types of leisure narrative and I have tried four of them. There are 'full frontal' stories about leisure; then stories about different types of leisure (sport, other games, tourism, crafts, hobbies and so on). This latter type of story is the one that I have never tried to master. The third type of story is about the leisure of a specific group – a gender, age or ethnic group or a social class, for example. The fourth story is about the different types of providers of leisure goods and services. Fifth and finally, there are stories about leisure as seen through the prisms of different social theories. We can debate, and there is no need to agree on, which kind of story is best. However, we may conclude, and the story in this paper is that we can conclude, that some stories have better endings than others.

Full Frontal Big Leisure Stories

There is a 'birth of leisure studies' story, and also an earlier tale which is still told occasionally. The older tale is basically that 'the devil makes work'. This phrase was used in the title of John Clarke and Chas Critcher's 1985 book, but by then it was a throwback. There were plenty of leisure books in the pre-leisure studies era. There was a spate in Britain between the World Wars (reviewed in Snape and Pussard, 2013). These books told a leisure story with 19th century origins when European countries and America began to become industrial and urban. Family and community social controls were weakened when households and individuals moved into urban areas. Industrial workers had a new kind of (limited) leisure time and money (again limited) to spend at their discretion, on luxuries. Young people were considered especially susceptible to temptations, but all age groups could be tempted by the evils of alcohol and gambling.

Migrants from the countryside brought uncouth habits into the cities. This was the background to efforts by local authorities and (usually middle class led) voluntary associations to promote rational recreation (Bailey, 1978). Urban parks, public galleries, museums, libraries, concert halls and meeting rooms were intended to foster 'civilised' ways of life (Meller, 1976). Recreation became one of the great social crusades of the era. It accompanied first wave of feminism. Voluntary associations, public authorities and some trade unions and employers coordinated their efforts. 'Good wholesome' leisure was advocated as a safeguard against social breakdown which would take the form of crime, disorder on the streets and out of control mobs. However, from the 1920s onwards there was another fear. This was associated with the spread of (at that time) new media – radio, movies, recorded music and subsequently television. It was also associated with the construction of 'soul-less' suburban housing estates. The danger was ennui, boredom, passivity. After the Second World War, television ownership spread rapidly. Television immediately became the default leisure time option, and accentuated these fears. Leisure was said to be an unplanned and unwanted (in the sense that it had no uses) by-product of industrialism (Anderson, 1967). It would be a penalty unless people could be educated to use their leisure in constructive ways (Glasser, 1970). This story has been repeated whenever there have been fears of new technologies reducing demand for human labour (for example, Jenkins and Sherman, 1981). The basic narrative is still available for leisure scholars.

However, since the mid-20th century 'threat' has been replaced by 'promise' in the dominant leisure narrative. This change coincided with the formation of leisure studies as an academic subject, first in North America, then in the UK, then Australasia and then more thinly throughout the rest of the world. Leisure scholars in the post-1945 era knew that leisure had been growing throughout the previous century. This applied however leisure was measured – time, money spent or participation rates in leisure activities. This growth was expected to continue. Why not? The rolling-back of paid work-time was expected to continue. The four-day work-week was forecast confidently (Poor, 1972). As real incomes continued to rise, there would be more money for discretionary spending. Leisure scholars drew on the work of psychologists, especially Abraham Maslow (1943, 1954) who claimed to have identified a hierarchy of human needs. Once basic needs for survival and security had been met, people were to pursue higher-level needs such as social status and eventually, Maslow claimed, they would seek self-actualisation or self-fulfilment, which (according to leisure scholars) leisure was to deliver. Paraphrasing John Kelly (1987), leisure offered 'freedom to be' or perhaps he should have said 'freedom to become' persons whose potential was developed and expressed fully. Paraphrasing Fred Best (1978), leisure was to give more and more people 'the time of their lives'. Tony Blackshaw (2010) has recently revived this promise in our current 'liquid' modern era. However, by the 1980s Maslow had been joined or replaced by Mihalyi Csikszentmihalyi as leisure scholars' favourite psychologist. Csikszentmihalyi (1990) claimed that optimal experience, which he called 'flow', arose when people encountered challenges that stretched their abilities to the utmost. So they would become totally absorbed, lost in the activity. Robert

Stebbins (1992, 2001, 2005), the Canadian sociologist, has written a series of books and papers which, in effect, advocate 'serious leisure' as the route to the benefits that are available through leisure. Instead of self-actualisation, self-fulfilment or flow, in recent decades leisure scholars have adopted life satisfaction, wellness, happiness and enjoyment, which can be measured in quantitative surveys, as preferred indicators of the benefits of leisure. With the exception of watching television, every leisure activity that has been studied, in every socio-demographic group, has been found to enhance 'well-being', now the preferred all-embracing term (Haworth and Hart, 2007; Haworth et al., 1997; Iso-Ahola and Mannell, 2004). Early in the history of leisure studies, it was envisaged that the continuing growth of leisure would lead to some kind of 'society of leisure' or 'leisure society', superseding the industrial societies in which people's lives were work-centred. Joffre Dumazedier (1967), the French sociologist, will forever be associated with 'the society of leisure'.

The problem with all full frontal big leisure stories is that neither the threat nor the promise have been fulfilled. Since the mid-20th century leisure time, spending and activity rates have risen in all the economically advanced societies, but the populations have not become more satisfied with their lives (Layard, 2003). Cross-sectionally, all active and social leisure is associated with enhanced well-being. Longitudinally, at a societal level, the association disappears. Leisure scholars need an explanation or a different full frontal story. Well-being has not risen but neither has the threat materialised, which would be indicated by a decline in well-being.

Most leisure scholars were always sceptical about a future leisure society (Veal, 2011, 2012). Some built careers criticising the narrative (for example, as in Rojek, 2010). Unfortunately, the sceptics and critics do not have a full frontal alternative. I have made successive attempts at full frontal treatments of leisure. The first was in 1970 and the last was in 2006 (Roberts, 1970, 2006). There were three attempts in between (Roberts, 1978, 1980, 1999). Leisure scholars need a fresh narrative. In practice most have withdrawn from full frontal engagement.

Types of Leisure

Since the 1980s in Britain, the number of leisure studies courses and students have declined. This may or may not have been the trend elsewhere, but in Britain a tendency has been for leisure studies to split into types of leisure, mainly sport or tourism, but more recently events. The courses often have 'management' affixed to their titles. The arts and media studies have always been outside, independent of leisure studies, and this largely applies to sport in North America. The big story of leisure never became strong enough to keep the field united, and it also appears, unsurprisingly, that students are more likely to be enthusiastic about a type of leisure, especially sport, than about leisure in general. Moreover, 'practitioner' careers tend to be within a particular type of leisure, not serving the entire field, except when there are public sector departments or agencies responsible for leisure or recreation services.

The narratives in the specialist leisure fields, which themselves have tended to splinter into types of tourism and sport (dark tourism, cultural tourism, eco-tourism, sport tourism, youth sport and so on) have been basically the same as in stories about leisure in general. All types of leisure are able to claim growth and, in a post-industrial era, they can stress their contributions to job generation and (in many cases) a country's exports. Most leisure activities can claim to enhance well-being. The exceptions are investigated in media studies. New media is a relatively new field. In economic terms its growth rate has been spectacular, but as yet there have been no claims that well-being is enhanced.

The weakness in the narratives for specific kinds of leisure is that they mostly make exactly the same claims. They are all undistinguished in terms of outcomes for individual participants and their wider societies. Whether or not people play sport, or a particular sport, is important to the providers, and the activity will be important to its enthusiasts. However, in terms of outcomes, the leisure choices that individuals make are largely inconsequential. None has distinctive outcomes (Roberts, 2011). Being inconsequential is important but this does not make a good climax to the narratives. The leisure specialties yield little. They may make sense in terms of vocational training but not as social science. It is impossible to add together the findings of research into various specialties and reach conclusions that are more than the sum of the parts. Textbooks and courses that progress through the arts, crafts, sport, tourism, hobbies, media and so on are simultaneously repetitive and fragmented. There is no strong, credible narrative. If leisure is split, it is best divided by types of people who participate or types of providers.

Types of People

Instead of dividing leisure into types of activities, the division can be into types of people – age groups, ethnic groups, social classes, men and women and so on. Up till now this has provided leisure scholars with their most successful narratives. The examples are far too numerous to list. Every leisure scholar could cite scores. I have used this story-line frequently, usually in studying the leisure of young people, or a specific group of young people such as the unemployed (Roberts, 1983; Roberts et al., 1991). Ideally, all the uses of leisure of the relevant group are scanned. The explanation of their leisure is in terms of the constraints and opportunities, the typical socialisation and resulting tastes, of the group in question. The outcome is a privileged port of entry into what it means to be a woman or a man, transitioning a life stage which may be youth or later life, a migrant or a member of an ethnic minority in a particular place and at a particular time.

Leisure scholars who undertake this type of enquiry thereby become part of a multi-disciplinary field, or may enter leisure studies from the relevant multi-disciplinary field which may be women's studies, youth studies or ethnic relations or whatever depending on the group. This approach to leisure has been so successful in supplying plausible narratives that leisure studies experiences a high rate of turnover of scholars who enter then leave the field for the conferences, networks and journals that focus on their chosen groups. Leisure scholars find it far easier to raise funds to study a specific social group, especially a group that is deemed to be a problem or to have problems, than to gather leisure data purely for the sake of better understanding leisure.

This research genre is never exhausted because societies change and so do women's lives, the youth life stage, the character of different social classes and so on. There are always groups whose leisure has been relatively neglected. Gender scholars usually focus on women's leisure. Men's leisure has been relatively neglected not in the sense of men being excluded from social surveys but by the treatment of their lives, including their leisure, as simply normal rather than peculiarly masculine. The attention that has been paid to young people's leisure throughout the history of social research is now being rivalled by a focus on seniors. The leisure of mid-life child-rearing families is now relatively neglected. Social researchers habitually, by force of circumstances, have their hand-up, hoping for research funding from above, and eyes down on the groups who are deemed to be problems. Hence, we know more about the leisure of the poor and other disadvantaged groups than about the leisure of voracious middle-class omnivores not to mention the seriously rich. There are many more good leisure stories about types of people waiting to be researched and told.

Types of Providers

Instead of, or as well, dividing leisure into types of activities and/or people, it can be divided by types of providers. Ideal-typically, providers decide what is offered and people decide what to purchase and/or use. In practice, of course, the relationship is interactive. Different sections of any population are subject to different constraints and have access to different leisure opportunities, and they also possess different tastes depending on their prior socialisation and experience. All this applies in all other 'markets'. However, leisure is different from most markets in that, in many countries, and specifically Western countries, there has never been a dominant type of provider. Elsewhere the dominant leisure provider has been the local community, a church, the state, or whatever local authority or magnate to whom the power to provide has been delegated. In the West, leisure goods and services have been supplied by commercial businesses, voluntary associations and the public sector. Up till now none of these providers has been clearly dominant. Each of the providers has been driven by its own 'engine'. Commercial businesses seek profit. Voluntary associations are driven by the enthusiasm and tastes of their members. The public sector will provide whatever politicians prescribe. Ideal-typically, in democracies, elected representatives reflect the wishes of the people and legislate to provide leisure opportunities accordingly. In practice, however, politicians' own enthusiasms and tastes may take charge. Or it may be the public sector professionals, the bureaucrats, who are the controllers. Inertia, simply continuing to support services that were introduced long ago, for reasons long forgotten, is likely to play a powerful role. The different providers have different capabilities. Profitability need not be decisive for voluntary associations or with public services. Each sector relates to users in a distinctive way. Commercial businesses cater for consumers. The voluntary sector serves members and clients. The public sector caters for citizens.

Leisure scholars may concentrate (for one project or longer-term) on a particular type of provider just as they may specialise on the leisure of children, the unemployed or seniors. Those who study a type of provider usually have one 'foot' in leisure studies and another in politics, the public sector or social policy, or the 'third sector', maybe more specifically its volunteers (see Jones, 2002; Treuren, 2014), or market economics. However, in practice leisure scholars have been more likely to study types of people or types of activities than types of providers, and there have been relatively few economists or political scientists who have ventured into the leisure field. The links between types of providers and what is provided have been under-researched despite the availability of good stories about the achievements, capabilities and limitations of each sector (see Roberts, 2004, 2016a).

However, the blockbuster narratives are about historical change. Western first-wave industrial societies have histories when most leisure provision was by the public and voluntary sectors. The explanation is simple. In the early decades of industrialism most people had precious little cash available for leisure spending. Over time the commercial sector has grown in absolute and relative importance and has now become the leading leisure provider whose commercial cultures have seeped into public and voluntary sector provisions They have all become leisure businesses (Roberts, 2016a). Simultaneously, leisure has become a major source of new jobs and is the main hub of economic regeneration in many local economies that have de-industrialised. Alongside widening economic inequalities within countries, this has implications for the leisure goods and services that are accessible by different kinds of people. Leisure provisions are stratified by price, but an even clearer division is created between voracious omnivores, a relatively well-off minority who are responsible for most spending on out-of-home leisure, and the majority whose leisure is mostly mediated, that is, provided by old and new media (Bennett et al., 2009; Roux et al., 2008).

Former communist countries have a different but equally enthralling historical leisure story. Under communism all formal leisure provision was under the auspices of state or party. The aim was to nurture a socialist way of life that would be superior to the 'high' and 'popular' cultures of Western capitalism (Vitanyi, 1981). Since the end of communism there has been rapid commercialisation. Public funding for leisure services was slashed in the first wave of market reforms. The countries have no long-established genuinely voluntary associations. Change has been rapid and sweeping (Butenko, 2005; Clark, 2002; Gvozdeva, 1994; Jung, 1994; Kloetze et al., 1998).

What used to be called Third World, developing or underdeveloped countries have now become the world's emerging market economies (the BRICS). They have a different historical story. For large sections of their populations leisure provision remains mostly informal, based in families and local neighbourhoods, but now served by the modern mass media (old and new), and branded products have stolen the markets for many locally produced goods and services. Meanwhile the countries have new urban middle classes with hyper-modern lifestyles (Donner, 2011; Ganguly-Scrase and Scrase, 2008; Lukose, 2009; Rolandsen, 2011; Varma, 1998). Tourism has been a key business sector and economic dynamo in some of these countries where, for many people, up till now, leisure has been something enjoyed by rich visitors and locals, while for the rest of the locals it has been mainly a source of jobs.

Types of people and types of providers offer powerful leisure narratives but tend to fragment the study of leisure in the absence of convincing, full-frontal, really big leisure stories.

Social Theories

Maybe leisure scholars who have sought their own subject-generated full frontal theories about leisure have been misguided. Does leisure studies really need to develop its own grand narratives? There are ready-made narratives in the general social theories that have been based mainly in sociology for a century and more. Sociology is the natural home for leisure studies since all leisure activities are social inventions. A common mistake when reaching for a general social theory that will suit leisure has been to imagine that just one of the available theories must be correct. The theories offer complementary narratives about leisure. Most of the theories (those of Durkheim, Marx, Weber, the Frankfurt School, Elias, Habermas, Foucault) have been about trends in European societies since the Middle Ages, but the theories can also be used analytically (as can Parsons and Bourdieu) to examine leisure at particular times and in particular places.

Everything is functional in the mathematical sense in that change on one part of any system (including social systems) will produce changes in others. Different leisure practices can be examined in so far as they are functional, dysfunctional or functionally neutral for societies and their sub-systems. The mistake of functionalism's occasional advocates in leisure studies (Gross, 1961; Pronovost, 1998) has been to claim supremacy or exclusive truth for their Durkheimian or Parsonian versions of functionalism. Marxists have been able to detect ways in which sport and other uses of leisure can both undermine and kindle class solidarities and resistance. These tendencies have certainly been detectable at particular times and places (Clarke and Critcher, 1985; Carrington and McDonald, 2009, Gruneau, 1999), but right now the feature of Marxist thought that seems most relevant is its account of how capitalism is necessarily an expanding system. Max Weber's concept of status, probably as developed in Pierre Bourdieu' sociology (Bourdieu, 1984), enables us to perceive how all leisure activities can be strategic acts of social positioning which contribute to the actors' social identities (Wacquant, 2004). Michel Foucault has the theory that seems best able to explain why so much leisure resembles hard labour as Rojek (2010) has noted (but see also Markula-Denison and Pringle, 2006). Jurgen Habermas is useful in detecting how instrumental and communicative speech and action compete with one another (Spracklen, 2009, 2011). Norbert Elias's thesis on the civilising process can be applied to certain features of and trends in sport, and possibly other leisure activities (Elias and Dunning, 1986).

All the major social theories offer narratives about leisure. They can all be used to develop possible explanations of leisure differences between types of people and the distinctive provisions of different types of providers. The theories that are necessarily still in development, and to which leisure scholars can contribute, are about current trends in societies variously described as post-industrial, post-modern, post-welfare, neo-liberal, information and knowledge societies, in a global age. Simultaneously, world systems theory is being developed through debates about globalisation (increased flows and inter-dependencies between countries). Are all societies now being set on the same modernisation trajectory as claimed in different ways, and for different reasons, by Inglehart (1977, 1997) and Fukuyama (1992)? Or are older clashes of civilisations being rekindled (Huntington, 1996) or something else? I have decided belatedly to try many of these potential leisure stories (Roberts, 2016b).

Conclusions

It is good to talk, but what makes good talk does not necessarily make good writing or good social science. This needs narratives that can link different types of events, groups of people, types of behaviour and life patterns. It is interesting to talk about specific kinds of leisure – our favourite sports, teams and players, the places that we have visited, the films that we have seen and the music that we enjoy and on which we have opinions. Leisure scholars are like everyone else in being able to enjoy talk on these topics. So are students and hence the ease with which they can be attracted to courses with their favourite leisure activities in the titles.

Leisure scholars can find common ground in theories which are really just speculations (which can be useful) about the meaning of leisure, and the possible and likely end products of leisure's growth. The paradox is that when we write about leisure these narratives become cul-de-sacs: there are no conclusions to the narratives, and the narratives do not become progressively stronger with better-and-better explanations.

Fortunately we can tell better stories. These begin with types of people and their leisure, types of providers and what they provide, and the trends and tendencies highlighted by macro-social theories. If leisure studies is to progress it needs to focus on the issues that provide narratives which have endings though these conclusions are always interim. This is a strength, because the conclusions can always be challenged by better stories or built into stronger versions of their former selves. The stories that work best are the right base for developing leisure studies into an ever-stronger, more firmly grounded body of knowledge, and this development will always remain unfinished business.

References

Anderson, N. (1967). *Work and Leisure,* London: Routledge.

Bailey, P. (1978). *Leisure and Class in Victorian England,* London: Routledge.

Bennett, T., Savage M., Silva E., Warde A., Gayo-Cal M., and Wright D. (2009). *Culture, Class, Distinction,* London: Routledge.

Best, F. (1978). The Time of Our Lives, *Society and Leisure,* 1, pp. 95–114.

Blackshaw, T. (2010). *Leisure,* Abingdon: Routledge.

Bourdieu, P. (1979b, 1984). *Distinction: A Social Critique of the Judgment of Taste,* London: Routledge.

Butenko, I.A. (2005). Russia, in Cushman G, Veal A J and Zuzanek J, eds, *Free Time and Leisure Participation: International Perspectives,* Wallingford: CABI Publishing, pp. 221–232.

Carrington, B. and McDonald I. (eds.) (2009). *Marxism, Cultural Studies and Sport,* London: Routledge.

Clark, Z. (2002). Goulash and Solidarity, *The Guardian,* November 2, p. 18.

Clarke, J. and Critcher C. (1985). *The Devil Makes Work,* London: Macmillan.

Csikszentmihalyi, M. (1990). *Flow: The Psychology of Optimal Experience,* New York: Harper and Row.

Donner, H. (ed.) (2011). *Being Middle Class in India,* Abingdon: Routledge.

Dumazedier, J. (1967). *Towards a Society of Leisure,* New York: Free Press.

Elias, N. and Dunning E. (1986). *Quest for Excitement: Sport and Leisure in the Civilizing Process,* Oxford: Blackwell.

Fukuyama, F. (1992). *The End of History and the Last Man,* London: Penguin.

Ganguly-Scrase, R. and Scrase T. (2008). *Globalisation and the Middle Classes in India: The Social and Cultural Impact of Neoliberal Reforms,* London: Routledge.

Glasser, R. (1970). *Leisure: Penalty or Prize?* London: Macmillan.

Gross, E. (1961). A Functional Approach to Leisure Analysis, *Social Problems,* 9, pp. 2–8.

Gruneau, R. (1983, 2nd edition 1999). *Class, Sports and Social Development,* Amherst: University of Massachusetts Press.

Gvozdeva, G. (1994). Changes in Free Time Utilization by Rural Residents in West Siberia Under the Ongoing Economic Reform, paper presented at *International Sociological Association Congress,* Bielefeld.

Haworth, J. and Hart G. (eds.) (2007). *Well-Being: Individual, Community and Social Perspectives,* Basingstoke: Palgrave Macmillan.

Haworth, J.T., Jarman M. and Lee S. (1997). Positive Psychological States in the Daily Life of a Sample of Working Women, *Journal of Applied Social Psychology,* 27, pp. 345–370.

Huntington, S.P. (1996). *The Clash of Civilizations and the Remaking of World Order,* New York: Simon and Schuster.

Inglehart, R. (1977). *The Silent Revolution,* New Jersey: Princeton University Press.

Inglehart, R. (1997). *Modernization and Postmodernization,* New Jersey: Princeton University Press.

Isao-Ahola, S.E. and Mannell R.C. (2004). Leisure and Health, in J.T. Haworth and A.J. Veal (eds.), *Work and Leisure,* London: Routledge, pp. 184–199.

Jenkins, C. and Sherman B. (1981). *The Leisure Shock,* London: Methuen.

Jones, R. (2002). Partnerships in Action: Strategies for the Development of Voluntary Community Groups in Urban Parks, *Leisure Studies,* 21, pp. 305–325.

Jung, B. (1994). For What Leisure? The Role of Culture and Recreation in Post-Communist Poland, *Leisure Studies,* 13, pp. 1–15.

Kelly, J.R. (1987). *Freedom To Be: A New Sociology of Leisure,* New York: Macmillan.

Kloetze, J.W. te, ed (1998). *Family and Leisure in Poland and the Netherlands,* Leuven-Apeldoorn: Garant.

Layard, R. (2003). *Happiness: Lessons from a New Science,* London: Allen Lane.

Lukose, R. (2009). *Liberalization's Children: Gender, Youth and Consumer Citizenship in Globalizing India,* Durham, North Carolina: Duke University Press.

Markula-Denison, P. and Pringle, R. (2006). *Foucault, Sport and Exercise,* London: Routledge.

Maslow, A.H. (1943). A Theory of Human Motivation, *Psychological Review,* 50, pp. 370–396.

Maslow, A. (1954). *Motivation and Personality,* New York: Harper.

Meller, H.E. (1976). *Leisure and the Changing City 1870–1914*, London: Routledge.

Poor, R. (1972). *4 Days, 40 Hours*, London: Pan.

Pronovost, G. (1998). The Sociology of Leisure. *Current Sociology*, 46, 3.

Roberts, K. (1970). *Leisure,* London: Longman.

Roberts, K. (1978). *Contemporary Society and the Growth of Leisure,* London: Longman.

Roberts, K. (1980). *Leisure,* Second Edition, London: Longman.

Roberts, K. (1983). *Youth and Leisure*, London: Allen and Unwin.

Roberts, K. (1999). *Leisure in Contemporary Society,* Wallingford: CABI.

Roberts, K. (2006). *Leisure in Contemporary Society*, Second Edition, Wallingford: CABI.

Roberts, K. (2011). 'Leisure: the importance of being inconsequential', *Leisure Studies,* 30, pp. 5–20.

Roberts, K. (2016a). *The Business of Leisure*, Basingstoke: Palgrave Macmillan.

Roberts, K. (2016b). *Social Theory, Sport, Leisure*, London: Routledge.

Roberts, K., Parsell G. and Chadwick C. (1991). Unemployment and Young People's Leisure in Liverpool and Swindon, *Society and Leisure*, 14, pp. 513–530.

Rojek, C. (2010). *The Labour of Leisure*, London: Sage.

Rolandsen, U.M.H. (2011). *Leisure and Power in Urban China: Everyday Life in a Chinese City,* London: Routledge.

Roux, B. Le, Rouanet H., Savage M. and Warde A. (2008). 'Class and Cultural Division in the UK', *Sociology,* 42, pp. 1049–1071.

Snape, R. and Pussard H. (2013). Theorisations of Leisure Inter-War Britain', *Leisure Studies,* 32, pp. 1–18.

Spracklen, K. (2009). *The Meaning and Purpose of Leisure: Habermas and Leisure at the End of Modernity,* Basingstoke: Palgrave Macmillan.

Spracklen, K. (2011). *Constructing Leisure: Historical and Philosophical Debates,* Basingstoke: Palgrave Macmillan.

Stebbins, R.A. (1992). *Amateurs, Professionals and Serious Leisure*, Montreal: McGill-Queens University Press.

Stebbins, R .A. (2001). The Costs and Benefits of Hedonism: Some Consequences of Taking Casual Leisure Seriously', *Leisure Studies,* 20, 305–309.

Stebbins, R.A. (2005). Project-based Leisure: Theoretical Neglect of a Common Use of Free Time, *Leisure Studies,* 24, pp. 1–11.

Treuren, G.J.M. (2014). Enthusiasts, Conscripts or Instrumentalists? The Motivational Profiles of Event Volunteers', *Managing Leisure,* 19, pp. 51–70.

Varma, P. (1998). *The Great Indian Middle Class,* Delhi: Penguin.

Veal, A.J. (2011). The Leisure Society I: Myths and Misconceptions, 1960–1979, *World Leisure Journal,* 53, pp. 206–227.

Veal, A.J. (2012). The Leisure Society II: The Era of Critique, 1980–2011, *World Leisure Journal*, 54, pp. 99–140.

Vitanyi, I. (1981). *The Goals, Methods and Achievements of Cultural Policies as Reflected in the Social Development of Countries,* Budapest: Institute for Culture.

Wacquant, L. (2004). *Body and Soul: Notebooks of an Apprentice Boxer,* Oxford: Oxford University Press.

2

Leisure and Social Change

Emerging Issues in India

YOGENDRA SINGH

It is curious to note that sociology of leisure forms a neglected area of sociological research in India. The reason for this probably rests in the social conditioning of priorities of research and historical development of our society. We had to fight for our freedom from a colonial regime and from institutional and cultural malpractices within our society to construct a project for our future. In this process sociology orientated itself more closely to issues of social, economic, political and cultural developments. It focussed on studies of villages, castes, tribes and on processes of their change and continuity. Cultural sociology, which could have had closer affinity with studies of leisure, also had its priorities determined rather historically. The national movement, need to articulate principles of national unity, the urge to contest distorted western portraits of Indian culture, and society which enlarged *centrifugal tensions* to the neglect of *centripetal linkages* of society which were more urgent. It became necessary to look at culture from the perspective of linkages rather than identities. The sociologists, social scientists and public men found it imperative to analyse cultural features, and styles and forms in their varieties of cultural traditions to articulate national identity.

Consequently, studies of leisure, sociology of time, fashions, styles, media forms, communication systems, art, aesthetics and literature, etc. which have been widely researched in the West, have only haltingly started in India. This is evident from the trend reports on sociological researches composed together under the auspices of the Indian Council of Social Science Research. It seems that sociology in India is now at a new turning point. The processes of change during the past four decades have set into motion social, cultural and economic forces that make it imperative for sociologists and social scientists to examine closely the relationships among factors like work, social structure, ecology and cultural styles. Sociology of leisure constitutes a vital element in this matrix.

Sociological studies are located in a paradigm of thought and methods which emerged historically through the rise of societal self-awareness. This was made possible by the Enlightenment ideology of equality, freedom and human brotherhood – a unique contribution to humanity. When we talk of leisure and social change, we may have to identify the phases of social transformation before and after this historical revolution in ideology. It is intrinsically related to the patterns of leisure, work, cultural styles and social and techno-economic structures of society.

Patterns of Leisure in Traditional Indian Society

It would be simplistic to talk of the pattern of leisure in the singular even for the traditional Indian society. This society had its own periodic phases of cultural and structural differentiations. Instead of one there were many *traditional* patterns in society. Nevertheless, one could heuristically talk of certain common elements in the traditional society of India which contributed to the patterning of leisure. Cultural ideology and social structure of this society closely defined leisure activities. Ideologically, the concepts of time and history as they shaped the definition of self and society also influenced the notions of leisure and work. All traditional societies, even simpler ones, had their own cosmology and metaphysics of time, birth and rebirth which patterned their rhythms of work and leisure. Sacred and profane, pragmatic and transcendental, utilitarian and non-utilitarian levels of symbolisation of work deeply influenced their perception of leisure and leisure time. The notion of leisure in states of being and becoming as creative self-affirmation possibly emanates from this metaphysical dualism of time and work.

Modes of production, technology and division of labour, caste and class played important roles in patterning of leisure. The division between agrarian and industrial modes of production in traditional India contributed to social differentiation and forms of leisure. The commercial, cultural and political linkages among villages, small towns and capital cities articulated these patterns of leisure in different but interrelated forms. The overall distinction was between folk and the elite forms of leisure and work. The slow pace of technological innovations gave a measure of continuity to these forms. The folk pattern was located in oral traditions of culture. The elite tradition was manifested in the written textual forms. This distinction was, however, partial as many overlaps between the two patterns in the concrete situation existed, such as the family, the brotherhood and the community. The folk and elite forms of leisure were socially manifested in the lifestyles, culture and work patterns of peasants, petty artisans and labourers on the one hand and the merchants, literati and feudal lords on the other. The distinctive feature of leisure in traditional society was probably its organic communitarian character, its integration with work and its ritualisation at selected levels of manifestation. Its deeper linkages with ecology and modes of production were reflected in its patterning on calendaric rhythms and lifecycle rituals.

The relationship between leisure and work, gender, community and social stratification had indeed evolved an orderly pattern. The hierarchical principle of ordering of economic and social relationships also operated in the domain of leisure activities. The patronage to several forms of leisure activities such as dance dramas, Ramleela, Krishna Lila, musical meets and a variety of ceremonies which served as leisure time activities was given by the feudal nobility or local *zamindars* (landlords). The village temple, the seat of many artistic and cultural festivities, was under their control. In other parts, the entire community or panchayat exercised this control. Leisure, as a behavioural and cultural phenomenon, was not entirely dissociated from community life or its repretoire of social sanctions. Leisure with the exception of some institutional manifestation was also not dissociated from work. It was common in traditional society for people to go to work and combine with work their expressive leisurely urges, individually and collectively, randomly and in stylised forms. This was particularly so in villages on the occasions of sowing, harvesting, threshing and disposal of crops. The village *chaupals* or urban street-corners were men and women came together to exchange notes, to gossip, to sing and celebrate, and also to complete work, such as weaving, knitting, basket-making and other types of jobs. The village wells or ponds were celebrated places for women to combine work with leisure. The alienation of work from leisure results from breakdown of the traditional society and its worldview. This should not mean that in traditional society no domains of leisure dissociated from work existed. Such domains, however, had their place among the privileged class of society.

This pattern of leisure held sway for centuries in India due to stagnation of modes of production, technology and social organisation of society. The technology of production, communication and transport remained unchanged over a long period of time maintaining the old pattern of leisure. This began to change with India's encounter with modern industrial society during the colonial and independent phases of development. New processes initiated during the freedom movement were consolidated after independence.

Emerging Patterns of Leisure

This emerging pattern of leisure is deeply influenced by changes in social structure, economy, technology and cultural and political processes in society. Significant social and economic changes were initiated in the traditional society soon after Independence. Caste-based village panchayats were abolished, land reforms were introduced abolishing feudalism, *zamindari* and intermediaries. Adult franchise was introduced for national local elections. New technologies, both in sectoral and institutional terms, were brought in for improvement of agriculture and industry. The print and electronic media, which had a halting start during the colonial period, got massive fillip after Independence. These emerged as a strong arm for diffusion and orchestration of information, cultural symbols and recreational packages of various kinds. The political processes of democratic participation set into motion among social groups such as classes, castes, tribes and ethnic groups new movements for consolidation of consciousness. Its emergence has radically, though not wholly, disturbed the traditional pattern of leisure and leisure institutions in society.

In rural India, which constitutes the dominant segment of society, introduction of land reforms and new technology in agriculture has triggered a process of social restructuration. Modern agriculture dictates its own time-schedule independent of traditional calendaric cycle of work and leisure. It has, thus, rendered traditional work codes in agriculture redundant. The oral saying encoding rules of agricultural work cycle have been replaced by a work schedule determined by science laboratory, irrigation technology and market forces. The new agriculture which has ushered in 'green revolution' in India robs people of their old styles of work-leisure relationships and its ritualisation. It also displaces several categories of workers, especially women, older folk and children, from traditional roles in agriculture. Thus, the communitarian participation in agriculture has been increasingly segmentised. Market has penetrated where once community used to rule. The urban-rural nexus has become stronger and in a new qualitative form, not for participation in a common worldview at different but compatible levels as in the past, but as arenas of market, behaviour, bargain for resources and shelter for migration.

The abolition of feudalism and the decline in the role of religious literati have caused the decay of many leisurely pursuits which were patronised by these classes. In some regions village councils keep a few of them going. The role of village *chaupals*, community wells, temples or other sacred or cultural places has been weakening due to penetration of mass media, cinema and video system of entertainment. The communities which made a living by entertaining people by dances, dramas, acrobatics, mimes or other recreational activities are fast losing their vocation. On festive occasions such as marriage, birth or social festivities, videos are replacing these traditional entertainers. The *chaupals* are being replaced by roadside tea-stalls where people assemble to supplement their tea with newspaper information, gossips, and exchange of notes with local and outside members. The institutionalised etiquette of *chaupal* has disappeared in the random mode of behaviour at the tea-stall.

These changes have introduced new dimensions to the rural pattern of leisure and its mode of work. Institutionalised forms of culture to which leisure in the past was orientated, is now increasingly exposed to forces of what is known as 'mass culture' or 'popular culture'. This is happening both at the rural and urban settings of our society. In rural society, this process is reinforced by disenchantment from village life. The green revolution has not only altered the social coordinates of leisure, but it has also sharpened the consciousness of social inequality and raised the level of aspiration. The emerging changes being non-egalitarian and ideologically conservative, large sections of rural working classes, artisans and youth are feeling alienated from village economy and its cultural and social institutions. This has led to massive migration of rural folk from villages to cities and metropolises across the country. Depending on regional characteristics, this migration is also to foreign lands, such as the Gulf countries, Europe and North America. Increasing intensity of migration has introduced heterogeneity in lifestyle and patterns of leisure.

The relationship between migration and leisure has to be analysed at several levels of social stratification. There is massive migration from rural to urban centres mainly of the working classes or rural poor. The migration to foreign lands has socially a more differentiated character, being of the artisan and lower middle-classes to the Gulf nations and of middle and upper classes to Europe and North America. There is also a degree of ethnic selectivity in this process. A new form of internal migration within the rural region itself is also taking place in some parts of the country, mainly of the agricultural labourers who go from place to place in search of contract labour in agriculture. This movement of population, together with growing volume of internal and foreign tourism, has extended the process of social restructuration to the domains of leisure and style of life.

These changes also coincide with other developments in society. Rise of entrepreneurial, professional and mercantile classes, enlargement of administrative, political and cultural elites, etc. set new standards for leisure time activities. These sections also selectively incorporate alien elements of leisure and culture which has demonstration effect on the style of life. It affects culture and leisure in our country due to their social and economic domination over society. More than 150 million members of the middle and upper classes in India have generated a new market for print and electronic media entertainment and a high profile consumerist lifestyle. A small section among these also resembles what Veblen has called 'a leisure class indulging in conspicuous consumption and waste'.

The forces of social mobility, migration, class restructuration and intensity of culture contacts, from within and outside the country, have resulted in changes in the pattern of leisure. The motor forces for this comes from the market forces and capitalist mode of production. This process acquires a new edge due to high rate of population growth in society. It raises the proportion of the youth in society being intensely motivated towards new orientations in leisure and recreation. However, these changes introduce several contradictory tendencies in the forms of leisure. The traditional pattern still subsists even though changes have begun to take place in the form and functions of leisure. Increasingly, radio, television, videos, audio, magazines and newspapers are eroding the interpersonal communitarian mode of communication and leisure. Due to expansion of market forces, a large part of artifacts, symbols, styles and forms related to traditional leisure and recreational pattern, are being incorporated in the mass media forms. A class of 'culture entrepreneurs' has emerged which undertakes systematic marketing of leisure and culture goods within the country and outside. It encourages new waves in fashion and lifestyle such as emphasis on ethnic designs, artifacts and instruments of leisure. Tourism from abroad, both of foreigners and non-resident Indians, reinforces this process.

The cultural base of these changes exists in values of utilitarianism, acquisitiveness, individualistic rationalism and quest for pleasure. When translated into leisure behaviour it tends to deviate basically from the worldview of society and leisure as envisaged by our nation. Elements of humanism, free self-expression, participatory communication, institutionalised collective sharing and participation, or in other words, the social and human character of leisure is eroded by these developments. The symbiotic relationship between work and leisure is gone. It is replaced by more individualised, hedonistic and alienative relationship between leisure and work. The person is replaced by audience. The way for the emergence of a mass culture or popular culture with commensurate forms of leisure is ensured. Leisure ceases to be a mode of self-expression, self-affirmation and celebration of universal human consciousness. It becomes a commodity or is subjectively reified as something to be acquired or maximised. Instead of affirmation of one's humanity, leisure becomes a distinctive mark of consumption and social domination.

The indicators of social and economic development in our society have this dual character. On the one hand, there is growth in technological and material base of society, there is more prosperity, less disease or deprivation for a growing section of population. On the other hand, there is poverty, deprivation and disease. Serious value displacements are, therefore, generated by the rise of the new acquisitive class. The dualism between the rich and poor, traditional and contemporary and communitarian and alienative modes of leisure get sharpened. These generate a social as well as a cultural crisis in society. Even though traditional forms of leisure continue to persist or have worked out adaptive changes, yet, in more crucial areas of leisure, the alienative forms are growing strong. Despite efforts to establish academies of art, culture and theatre, the progress made towards creative integration remains feeble. Their growth potential is encapsulated by the interests of the urban, industrial and professional elite. In the rural areas, where about 70 per cent of our people live, the folk theatre groups, the artists and traditional entertainers are being rapidly displaced and impoverished by new agrarian developments and social transformation.

The mass media, particularly the television which is rapidly penetrating the domains of leisure, are envisaged to project images of person, culture and society to reinforce humanistic social and economic development of society. Its symbols and messages are expected to help in developing a modern, just, prosperous and harmonious society. The richer elements of India's traditional heritages drawn from all regions, communities and groups are to be articulated to show their ever-lasting relevance. Despite there being some evidence that these objectives remain on the agenda of television, the encroachment of consumerist values and market culture in its programmes generates scepticism. It is evident that uneven social development has enhanced the power of the rich to control the institution of mass culture and its pattern of leisure. Relying heavily on mass media for promotion of leisure would logically mean increasing the control of these classes on leisure and culture of society. It would threaten and rupture the cultural and social objectives of modernisation of our society.

An important problem in evolving a policy on leisure and its institutional pattern in India relates to the mix between local and cosmopolitan manifestations of culture and forms of leisure. Strange though it may appear, as the process of economic and educational development advances in a society, correspondingly there is increase in the awareness of people of their own identities in terms of a local group, ethnic, regional culture, etc. Science and technology, on the one hand, promotes massificaton, homogenisation or globalisation of practices and values of leisure and on the other hand, generates forces of encapsulation of consciousness in the form of localism, neo-traditionalism and fundamentalism. This problem is inevitable, particularly in India with its plural traditions. Two points may be recognised in this context. First, localism or neo-traditionalism may not be antithetical to cosmopolitan culture if these are used as a medium of self-affirmation as a community or people. Leisure and culture in order to be meaningful social phenomena have to be rooted in community and local/regional social formations. It protects them from the onslaught of mass culture and market forces. Secondly, the localisation or regionalisation of cultural awareness and forms of leisure may also result from feeling of exploitation and injustice perpetrated by structures of social and economic domination. In this form, the problem assumes urgent policy dimension. It is linked with issues of promoting a just and democratic development of Indian society.

Vision of a Future Society

It is obvious that an Indian model of culture and leisure would have to be an organic part of our vision of a future society. This vision has evolved over several centuries but more concretely in courses of our national struggle for freedom. It is the vision of India as a just, humanistic, prosperous and technologically and rationally progressive society. It is also a society where the dichotomy between leisure and work and work and culture is not accepted since it rejects the materialistic and alienative view of human condition. The dichotomy is not between work and leisure. It is between leisure as consumerism or leisure as communication, sharing human sociability through free expression, participation and empathy.

It is near possible that new society would be in a position to overcome problems of existential deprivations such as of hunger, shelter, illness and drudgery of work, etc. This could be achieved with the help of modern science and technology. The time lag in achieving these goals may vary depending upon the initial condition in each society, its human resources, social structure, distribution of power and reflexivity of power elite. A society even though it achieves these goals would be up against a more formidable enemy – human alienation. There is alienation even in poor society but its roots are existential. It does not totally blunt the feeling of human sociality and need for togetherness or communication. The alienation of a materially advanced society, an information society or a mass society is of a qualitatively different kind. Here, alienation is emotional, spiritual and for a person self-isolating. The culture of consumerism, mass advertising and market control of human responses robs humans of their power of communication, sociality and empathy. This also alters the meaning of leisure. Instead of being active principles of human self-expression, spontaneous communication and social participation, leisure becomes a passive experience, or a sensation to be 'enjoyed' in the isolation of one's living room. Leisure is dissociated from vital human condition.

Indian society is far from reaching this stage in near future. We are, however, forewarned in formulating an agenda on the future perspective on leisure. A sensitivity to this problem has been a part of our national heritage and tradition. Gandhiji and Pandit Nehru – the two architects of modern Indian society – long recognised the need for India to develop a balance between materialism and humanism. They also recognised how one-sided development may contribute to brutalisation of society. A balanced development would imply not only economic growth but social justice and development of human personality, skills and sense of freedom also. An adequate economic and educational policy thus becomes organic to a relevant policy on leisure and culture.

3

Globalisation and its Impact on Indian Society

B.K. NAGLA

Context

Globalisation is as fascinating a term these days as modernisation, development and change have been for the last 20th century. To think of the world as a global village was once a day dreamer's delight. Not any more instead the end of the 20th century will be remembered for bringing the dream of globalisation to reality. On the one side, several outcomes of this transformation are within the reach of a large number of human beings, availability of fax machines and internet facility are its examples. Who could have thought of its widespread availability in India three decades ego? Globalisation as a trend would create its impact on each area of human activity.

On the other side, the process of globalisation has generated universal disenchantment. Those who applaud its arrival are fewer. Disenchantment prevails both in the developing and developed nations. It needs to be analysed as to what lies at the root of such disenchantment.

In this context, the present paper will examine, first, historical perspective of globalisation. Second, it will examine the notions or concepts of globalisation and localisation and how this can be conceptualised as well as its relationships with the global and the local. Third, it will look at the theories of globalisation. Fourth, it will examine the implications of looking at the impact of globalisation on Indian society. Finally, it will discuss the key issues related to globalisation.

Globalisation: Historical Perspective

Globalisation is an outcome of the universal logic of modernity. Giddens (1990) assumes that globalisation is the corollary of modernity. The implication of the modernity/globalisation view is that the history of globalisation begins with the history of the west. But it is not precisely the point of globalisation as a perspective that globalisation begins with world history.

There is no agreed starting point, but understanding of globalisation is helped by considering the following:

- The first great expansion of European capitalism took place in the 16th century, following the first circumnavigation of the earth from 1519 to 1521.
- There was a big expansion in world trade and investment in the 19th century. This was brought to a halt by the First World War and the bout of anti-free trade protectionism that led to the Great Depression in 1930. Some see this period as an interruption to the process of globalisation commenced in the late 19th century.
- A sense that world was united was generated by the establishment of the International Date Line and world time zones, together with the near global adoption of the Gregorian calendar between 1875 and 1925. During this period, international standards were also agreed upon for telegraphy and signalling.
- The end of the Second World War brought another great expansion of capitalism with the development of multinational companies interested in producing and selling in the domestic markets of nations around the world. The emancipation of colonies created a new world order. Air travel and the development of international communication enhanced the progress of international business.
- The fall of the Berlin Wall and the collapse of the Soviet Union ended the Cold War between the forces of capitalism and socialism with capitalism triumphant. The development of the internet made possible the organisation of business on a global scale with greater facility than ever before.

However, the time frame of some of the perspectives is as follows:

Time of Globalisation

Author	*Time period*	*Perspective*
Marx	1500s	Modern capitalism
Wallerstein	1500s	Modern world system
Robertson	1870–1920s	Multidimensional
Giddens	1900s	Modernity
Tomlinson	1960s	Cultural Pluralisation

Source: Nederveen Pieterse, J.P. (1995). 'Globalization as Hybridization' in M. Featherstone et al., *Global Modernity*.

Thus, globalisation is an objective, all embracing historical process which began with the breakthrough of capitalism in some countries of Western Europe, notably England, in the early decades of the 19th century. From almost its inception, it developed along with colonialism and later in the century, blossomed fully as imperialism.

The globalisation process of the period aggravated inequality through exploiting the socio-technical inferiority of the pre-capitalist systems is prevalent in the larger part of the world. An important part of that exploitation was the literal ruination of the productive forces of the countries which were its objects, including the direct producers. It was against such globalisation that the national revolutions of the colonial, semi-colonial and dependent countries were directed. Even before the victory of these revolutions, the globalisers had to beat a retreat and make compromises.

The Myth of Globalisation

Allen and Massey (1995: 3) have demonstrated that images of globalisation are often compelling and suggestive, emphasising certain aspects while neglecting or underplaying others; they are, in effect, distorted.

> [T]here appears to be a number of globalization, a number of worlds, taking shape. There is the globalization of telecommunication, the globalization of finance, the globalization of culture ... the globalization of environmental concerns, and that of the struggles of indigenous peoples. Moreover, the networks of connections that each lays down do not map one to the other, some parts of the world are densely highlighted in some accounts, but not in others.

Allen (1995: 110–117) discusses the following types of globalisation:

The 'story' of *economic globalisation* focuses on the global market where borders are crossed and distances travelled with minimal effort by firms, currencies and commodities.

The rhetoric of political globalisation is that of the continuing erosion of the nation–state's powers and abilities to control or regulate an increasingly volatile and uncertain global world in the face of many changes – for instance, environmental risks or the rise of transnational organisations on the world stage.

Cultural globalisation refers to the homogenisation and hybridisation of worldwide culture. The basis for this is supposedly the new technologies of communication. These are said to further unsettle and loosen traditional cultural ties, influences and established lifestyle codes, thereby exposing localities to different consumer styles, with the message that to consume is to be a pat of one (western) world. Demand is produced by the global marketing of cultural styles and symbols and is met by global standardisation of products. But such a homogenising view of a global culture is false in two main ways. First, it is presented in a monolithic manner: we do not understand and value consumer products or American entertainment in the same way (Allen, 1995: 117). Second, rather than eroding local differences, global consumerism has to work through them, exploring local differences in order to market them on a wider scale. Additionally, a global culture based on the consumption of western styles and symbols is one that has to be bought into, which for a substantial part of the world's population is not possible. Such a view also under-explores the influence of migration on culture and the creation of multicultural societies.

The Concept of Globalisation

The origin of the concept of 'globalisation' is usually traced to Marshal McLuhan (1960), who first introduced the idea of what is today called 'global village' – a notion that implied a sort of compression of the world and intensification of consciousness of the world as a single entity. Therefore, many individuals, organisations and countries consider the world in this new millennium as the 'global village'.

In order to talk about globalisation and its impact on developing societies and their culture, we need to understand the entire canvas of the term 'globalisation'. Globally, globalisation, globalism – these are all ambiguous words that have come into common usage since 1980s, but have been part of the social science vocabulary since the early 1980s. Despite the relative newness of this language, it abounds in the literature on the international relations, sociology and human geography and is creeping into the lexicon of social scientists studying the nature of global environmental change.

Globalisation refers to various multidimensional socio-economic and political processes by which the people of the world are incorporated into a single world society, a global village. It tends to homogenise the cultures as well as popularise even unknown cultures of the world. It acts as hetrogeniser with a possibility of pluralism. Globalisation strives to make the world as its market where all the people are being brought as buyer and seller on unequal terms.

Globalisation refers to the multiplicity of linkages and interconnectedness that transcend the nation–state and by implications the societies which make up the modern world system. It reflects a process through which events, decisions and activities in one part of the world would have significant consequences for individuals and communities of quite distant parts of the globe. However, for Giddens, globalisation embraces much more than a notion of simple interconnectedness. For him, 'globalisation concerns the intersection of the presence and absence, the interlocking of social events and social relations at a distance with local contextualities.'

It may be understood as a dialectical phenomenon in which events at one pole having distance relation often produce divergent or even contrary occurrence at another. While communication and information are increasingly diffused on a global scale, the individuals locally appropriate these, inherently in contextual and hermeneutic way. Thus globalisation becomes glocalisation.

Globalisation and Localisation

Tim O'Riordan and Chris Church (2001) discuss the perspective of globalisation and localisation. Globalisation and localisation unite at all spatial scales. In the text that follows, we distinguish between globalisation and localisation, and globalism and localism. Globalisation and localisation are processes of change that impact economies, cultures and environments in ways that are both global and local. Such changes may take place at any scale and at any level of social organisation. Globalism and localism are socially and politically framed interpretations of these changes that have meaning through processes of personal experience, patterns of trust, connectivities of reciprocity, and social networks of interest and bias. These two discourses entwine to form social identity, the basis for self-actualisation and the bedrock of any transition to sustainability. Globalism and localism are processes of responsiveness and adaptability that are mediated and defined by various institutional arrangements and swirling patterns of expectations.

Theories of Globalisation

The concept of globalisation has been flaunted. Generally, development theorists and development workers consider it as the major ideology for all kinds of development programmes and activities. To large number of policy makers, it means a phenomenon of today's world, and not a choice. Theoretically, there are many precursors to the concept of globalisation. Three of the main approaches are: world-systems theory, globalisation is an outcome of modernity and globalisation as a dual process which centres on culture.

World Systems Theories

Globalisation from the perspective of a world system is associated largely with the work of Immanuel Wallerstein. His world-systems theory is involved principally with the global capitalist economy and combines a sociological and historical look at its development and maintenance, arguing that it is created by a single 'division of labour' – more complex, extensive, detailed and cohesive than ever before. This body of work posits that the world system consists of three worlds: a centre or core, a semi periphery and a periphery. There are many criticisms of this approach but the most pertinent is that it represents only a mono-causal explanation of globalisation.

Modernisation and Globalisation

In a general way, the concept of globalisation is best understood as expressing fundamental aspects of time-space distinction (namely, the condition under which time and space are organised). Globalisation concerns the intersection of presence and absence, the interacting of social events and social relations 'at distance' with local contextualities. We should grasp the global spread of modernity in terms of an ongoing relation between distanciation and the chronic mutability of local circumstances and local engagements ... globalisation has to understood as a dialectical phenomenon (Giddens, 1991: 22–23).

Globalisation can, thus, be defined as the intensification of world-wide social relations which link distant localities in such a way that local happenings are shaped by events occurring many miles away and vice versa ... Local transformation is as much a part of globalisation as the lateral extension of social connections across time and space (Giddens, 1990: 64).

Giddens (1990: 7) puts social relations at the centre of his analysis, which comprises four areas:

1. the world capitalist economy
2. the nation–state system
3. the world military order
4. the international division of labour

These relate to his four institutional dimensions of modernity within which the processes of globalisation take place:

1. capitalism
2. surveillance
3. military power
4. industrialism

Giddens (1990: 55–56) sees capitalism and industrialism as two different dimensions. Capitalism relates owners to capital wage labour; industrialism applies to the link between people and the natural world, including the environment. In this analysis, it is modern institutions, such as money, that are globalising as they dissembled mechanisms, lifting relations out of local contexts enabling them to take place across the globe in a manner that was previously regarded as inconceivable.

Criticism of this approach centre on the complexity of this multidimensionality, as well as its failure to provide any specific implications that arise from these globalising processes, rendering it a 'descriptive, nominalistic definition approach to global-level phenomenon' (Yearley, 1996: 16). For Robertson (1992: 145), globalisation is not just an outcome of the western project of modernity as Giddens claims. Giddens is also criticised for not taking cultural matters seriously enough.

Culture and Dual Processes

Milton (1996: 215) has examined the theoretical approaches from the perspective of culture, defined as 'consisting of everything we know, think and feel about the world'. She distinguishes between those who refer to globalisation as the way world is seen or imagined, defined as cultural phenomenon, and those who refer to events going on in the world, which although dialectically related to culture are not part of it. The two approaches already discussed are the latter, where Robertson (1992: 8) treats globalisation as occurring both outside and inside culture: 'Globalization as a concept refers both to the compression of the world and the intensification of consciousness of the world as a whole.' In this sense globalisation is a dual arrangement, not just events taking place in the world, but also through cultural transformations.

The Global Transformation of Culture

The increased frequency of communications across the globe has been a recurrent theme of the 20th century. Empirically, globalisation has broken down cultural boundaries through the wide availability of air travel, the accessibility to telecommunications and the promotion of mass tourism. The term 'global culture' now implies both the development of a cultural cosmopolitanism spanning the globe and the redeployment of cultural consciousness for accentuating specific identities in global conflicts.

In the first instance, the worldwide dissemination of modern values and practices has taken its toll on the traditionalisms of many non-western societies. In the second instance, globalisation has reinforced boundaries through the politicisation of specific group interests.

In the contemporary West, there is a growing sense that culture, as traditionally understood, has lost its anchors. There are at least two senses to this crisis. The *commodity form* that Eagleton (1992: 33) speaks of in the first place of the global spread of western capitalism and the consequences of its cultural hegemony. An irony of this development is that the relentless drive of western capitalist interest around the world has not only left a trail of territorial conquests and exploitation, but also an indelible imprint of western culture in many foreign lands. For example, English and its cultural expressions are no longer the exclusive property of the British; their variations are found in those parts of the world which were once under British imperial rule.

In the second sense, imperialist culture becomes an agent of its own levelling. It falls victim to the commodity form that spearheads the marketing of modernity. It is this form that belittles cultural referents, even swallowing them up to the extent that culture can only exist as sign in reference to other signs, a simulacrum without origin (Baudrillard, 1983). We see this in the cultural experiences engendered by the spread of fast food chains and amusement theme parks around the world. Ritzer (1983: 100) calls it the McDonaldisation of society which 'encompasses such disparate phenomena as fast food restaurants, TV dinners, packaged tours, industrial robots, plea bargaining and open heart surgery on an assembly-line basis'. This type of consciousness is becoming more widespread with the development of mass tourism.

Global Consciousness

Global consciousness has begun to down on the world community. People are getting more and more familiar with others staying in different parts of the globe. In larger countries, they now know more about their fellow citizens, their customs, traditions, cultures, etc. they are getting familiar with different heritages, trends, practices and also faiths and beliefs. Peoples world over are becoming more conscious of their rights. They are familiar with situations where human rights are respected. They also know where these are being violated and by whom. With more and more getting educated, even those who have suffered for ages on social and economic or cultural fronts would not take these violations lying down. Even the media does not keep quite when human rights are violated in different situations. More than preserving one's own rights, one has to ensure that the rights of others are not treaded upon.

Global consciousness would imply respect for others. One has every right to consider one's community, religion, and culture as 'numero uno'. At the same time, one must concede that others also have a familiar right. Each culture and each religion has a basic right to treat itself as the very best. Such an approach should not lead to conflicting situations, if the approach is reasonable and considerate. We all know that there are difficulties in following such an approach in actual practice. With the gradual internalisation of global consciousness these would hopefully, vanish in near future.

Globalisation has given rise to apprehension of various types. There are cultures which are trying to remain insulated from the information super-highways and media explosion. There are instances where TV sets have been thrown out of the windows to prevent the young and impressionable from getting corrupted by the evil influence of alien cultures. How far that would succeed is debatable. It is, however, clear that global consciousness would never favour single culture, one religion or a unitarily way of life. Life would be pretty dull and colourless if this 'unimaginable' unification actually takes place at any stage. Human beings need to see the full spectrum of all cultures, traditions and religions. Each one of these should have its distinct place and identity. Only that would make this globe a fascinating place.

Globalisation and its Impact on Culture

There are multi-levels, theoretically, at which the relationship between the process of globalisation and the responses of the local cultures can be analysed. In the post modern era, the new approach focuses on local, particularistic and reflexive dimensions of culture (Lyotard, 1987; Dilthy, 1988; Ernst, 1992).

The system of communication has affected or surpassed the boundaries of nation–state at the same time they have affected local culture and social forms such as family, neighbourhood and community, and created forms of social anomie. The system of the folk culture and folk societies due to *marketisation of economy* and *commodification of production* in agriculture convert 'peasants' into 'farmers' eroding the traditional cultural patterns.

Globalisation: The Indian Perspective

Globalisation in India started with the new economic policy in July 1991. Then onwards, India has made tremendous progress in information technology, media sectors and banking. In this context, globalisation, competitiveness and liberalisation came to India as a booster and through the backdoor of 'economic reforms'. The sanctity of economic reforms had been derived from it. It was argued that the progress is taking place through globalisation and economic reforms.

Vinakayam (1995) highlights that India, out of globalisation, could enjoy lots of benefits as follows:

(a) *Leads to free trade:* Globalisation through collaborations and software exports is the password today in the sunrise industry of computers where intense domestic competition and cheaper technology has triggered off a price fall. The Tatas set a good example that how an industrial house could diversify in all directions. Indeed, globalisation foreign collaboration, which impede full flow of free trade.

(b) *International competitiveness:* The cutting edge of international competitiveness is world trade in manufactured goods, where most of the new competitors have specialised to take advantage of their low labour cost. The important aspects of competitiveness are:

   (i) A country's ability to create new products or processes.

   (ii) Worldwide market to consider the entire world as one market and to do a really professional job. In this context, one has to deliver like a 'world class player' matching international quality standards and fighting out the profit sanctuaries of the competitors' right in their home countries.

(c) *Selection of industries:* Globalisation facilitates the selection where there is competitive advantage. Different countries have competitive advantages in different industries. Some of the industries in which India has competitive advantage in the international market are: textiles, jewellery, leather, software, precision engineering products, movie production and so on.

Globalisation, as a phenomenon, involves access to two different entities:

1. Finance capital through MNCs.
2. New technologies such as computers and tele-communications.

It was viewed that the growth and internationalisation of finance capital is good and desirable for projects because it promotes growth of technology. Globalisation provides a useful means to develop technologies, which are necessary for the production of goods and services that improve our well-being.

We are becoming Netizens, making friends with unknown persons across the world neglecting our next door neighbour. Globalising panic like AIDS has affected our psyche. A hybridised culture, without any root, is reshaping us to fit into the globalisation process. Whether we want or not, the powerful globalisation process has been encircling us.

In political sphere, an international managerial bourgeoisie or transnational capital class, often referred as 'comprador', has been solidifying the power of consumerist culture. They are the cohorts of the MNCs. Cocacolisation or McDonaldisation has brought in their world market.

The communication media has fuelled a growing awareness of the inter-connectedness and interdependency. It is nourishing a sense of responsibility, however, fragile for a humanity that is commonly shared.

The process of globalisation and its impact on culture, both local and national, gives it a new urgency. In most studies of cultural change in India, the significance of locality and local culture and its relationship with the nation–state and the national culture has been widely recognised.

When the process of economic development and social development has been extended, the importance of local culture and the particularistic expression of ideology and sentiments have been taken note of in formulation of the public policies as well as in the analysis of nation–state.

The new institutional innovates that globalisation may bring about in society are:

1. Market, trade and finance.
2. Communication and media.
3. Science and technology.
4. Migration and inter-cultural transactions.

These are related issues of tourism, migration of professionals, and the emergence of diasporic sub-culture.

In structural terms, globalisation is a historical process of transition from agrarian to industrial, post industrial and finally the stage of information society (Dissananyake, 1988). Globalisation strives to make the world as its market where all the people are being brought as buyers and sellers in unequal terms.

The Impact of Global Trade and Market on Culture

The scope of trade and market which was accelerated by the processes of globalisation poses formidable cultural problems in developed and developing societies. In India, which traditionally had quite a developed base of trade and market, the impact of the changing role of these institutions has been gradual. The market and trade relations continue to be located in local cultures even today (Ostor, 1980). The economic policy of India up to 1980s has also been that of import-substitution and protectionism in trade and market.

The full momentum of globalisation started in 1990s onwards, but many checks and balances continue to persist. Globalisation brought changes which altered the traditional mode of cultural expression, usage of language and communication, media at the local, regional and national levels.

These have also created new sub-culture in urban areas. The rise of popular culture is a new phenomenon with linkages both in rural and urban centres. Most of these changes have long been in the process of emergence and crystallisation. The forces of industrialisation and developments in agriculture had impact on the consumption style of people.

Green revolution during 1970s gave spurt to changes in the consumption style of villagers. The NSS data shows noticeable decline in consumption of cereals both by rich and poor. The shift is towards consumption of milk, poultry and meat products. The electrification in the villages has changed the energy pattern. The use of kerosene oil is widespread. 'Gobar' gas plant and solar energy is also making dent in villages. The expansion of road networks and means of communication has brought about some homogenisation in tastes and consumption patterns, such as increased popularity of tea, coffee, egg, meat and fish.

A remarkable change in the styles and pattern of women's wear has taken place. It is marked by a shift from *sarees* to *salwar-kameez*. Culturally speaking, the new changes may not have had deeply subversive effect upon the core traditional values or the world-view of the people.

Yet, one witnesses periodic incidence of consumer resistance against multinationals promoting new consumer goods or agro-products, e.g. sporadic movements against products McDonald's and KFC. Farmers are resisting the penetration of agro-multinationals in production of seeds, herbs and new cereals, etc.

The average number of occupations per community stands at 5.3, of which 1.8 are in traditional and 3.5 in the newly acquired occupation (Singh, 1992). Economists have also observed substantial rise in non-agricultural occupations in the countryside.

Globalisation is, however, just in the beginning stage in India. Some of its effects upon the local cultures, for example, globalisation of markets have led to conversion of traditional objects of art and aesthetic having mostly ritual use in the local communities into marketable commodities.

This has not only rapidly disrupted the autonomy of folk culture, but also destabilised the life of the artisans by creating new networks of competition and price war and a new class of exploitative middle-class. In other areas, such as access of local communities to forest resources, land and rivers, hills and lakes, all of which were bound together in a long enduring cultural ecology of rituals and customs, the penetration of market for profit has started a rapid subversion of ecology.

It has disrupted the balance in cultural, social, economic life of tribals, artisans, traditional cultural performers, etc. Being in minority and economically vulnerable, these communities suffer loss of their cultural identity.

Globalisation of Communication, Media and Culture

The electronic media and communication such as radio, television, computer network via satellites, paging services, telephonic, electronic mail and internet web, etc. are modes of communication which are revolutionising the banking, trade and management practices, uses of culture and leisure, and most other modes of inter-cultural and inter-group communicative actions.

Most of these media transcend the territorial national cultural boundaries. They may function beyond the sovereignty of the nation–state, and offer individuals enormous amount of choices and freedom in matters of cultural and ideological performances.

The notion of time, space and symbolism of culture undergo new transformation of meanings under the impact of these new tele-communication technologies. Its impact on cultures – local, regional and national – is multi-faceted and can be integrative as well as disruptive.

Science and Technology

We are being encircled by some visible and invisible powerful global forces day by day. Its hegemony empowered with hyper-technology and enormous economic resources. From alpines to computer chips, we are using many global products produced by MNCs. In this context, a pervasive global culture as the ideology of consumerism has been knocking every moment on our door. It has occupied a substantial space in our society. A powerful media has been trying to negate our identity to hallow or alter our daily life pattern.

Migration and Inter-Cultural Transactions

Globalisation also accelerates the process of migration, tourism and travel. Its cultural and social homogenising effects the process along with creation of pluralism and cultural diversity. Tourism in India is more oriented to religious pilgrimages combined with sightseeing and leisure. Over a period of time, it has strengthened the festive and celebrative activities of various religious groups and communities. And its diffusion effect has been strong.

Key Players of Globalisation

Now, lets have a look at some of the key players of globalisation. Those players have been able to regulate all the actions that accompany the phenomenon of globalisation. These players are: World Trade Organization (WTO), International Monetary Fund (IMF), World Bank, United Nations, Organization for Economic Cooperation and Development (OECD), United Nations Conference on Trade and Development (UNCTAD), World Economic Forum (WEF), multinational companies, etc.

Globalisation and Change: Polity, Integration and Identity

The process of globalisation has triggered off forces of change which have set people's rethinking about the political institutions such as state, the democracy and civil society. In their functioning, the role of cultural pluralism and protection of local cultures is now particularly recognised both in towns of institutional mechanism and as an element of political morality or value system. New thinking is taking place about the changing role of nation–state, its sovereignty and the role of political party, etc. under the growing forces of globalisation (Kothari, 1995).

Global Culture

Appadurai (1990) explains three things for the understanding of global culture. (i) ethnoscope, (ii) technoscope and (iii) mediascope.

1. Appadurai talks about *ethnoscope* which is *landscope* of persons that constitute the shifting world in which we live. For example, tourists, immigrants, refugees, exiles and other moving groups and persons.
2. Appadurai also talks about *technoscope*. *Technoscope* is the global configuration of technology that moves at high speed across various kinds of boundaries.
3. Finally he talks about *mediascope*. *Mediascope* refers to the distribution of the electronic capabilities to produce and disseminate information which are now available throughout the world.

Appadurai says that the combination of *ethnoscope, technoscope* and *mediascope* leads to the globalisation of culture.

Globalisation: Key Issues

Globalisation is now a fait accompli in Asian region including India. Hence, its proponents describe it as irreversible, whereas the opponents, especially social activists have been opposing it for its adverse impact in the region, especially on the disadvantaged sections of the society. Therefore, the basic challenge is: how to humanise globalisation and harmonise it with regional, national and local situations, needs perceptions and aspirations, leading to a happier Asia or world?

Let us now describe some of the key issues related to globalisation.

Does Globalisation Cause Poverty?

Many people who are concerned about the fate of the world's poor now attribute their plight to globalisation. They argue that globalisation has weakened the position of poor countries and exposed to poor people to harmful competition. Their concern is understandable, especially since the gap between rich and poor has, indeed, become more glaring in recent decades.

Mahadevia (2003) sharply points out the inequalities that can be created by globalisation. He says: 'Globalization creates a class of Globalized World Population, who in a sense attain global citizenship, and they flock to a few global cities. The rest of the population does not attain global citizenship as this form of globalisation does not offer global citizenship to all. Hence a dichotomy emerges among those who attain global citizenship and those who do not. Also dichotomy emerges within global cities, where the globalised citizens flock and rest of the urban settlements in all countries, and much more in the developing countries where the gap in levels of living between two sections of population is quite stark.'

Mahadevia further views: 'Increase in inequality in the cities does lead to issues of internal security in the cities. This pushes the rich to live in enclaves that are well protected. There may not be total segregation but some segments of the city would have concentration of the rich and some others of the poor as observed in case of Mumbai. In case of Mumbai, privatisation of basic service could exclude the poor dominated areas from receiving adequate level of services.'

Globalisation or Capitalism

To Marx, as capitalism develops, there is a tendency towards centralised concentration of capital. In the era of globalisation, this has turned out to be absolutely true as there is a very high degree of concentration of capital in a few hands.

In this context, all of us are aware about the growth of the multinational companies and dominations that they have over the world. It is noted that many corporations are larger that nation–states – more than half of the 100 largest economies in the world are corporations. The sales of Ford and General Motors combined are greater than the combined GDP of sub-Saharian Africa while those of the six largest Japanese trading companies are almost as big as all the nations of Latin America combined (Yachuri, 2001).

Critics of globalisation say that the rising inequality is the inevitable result of market forces. Given free reign, market forces give power to the rich to add further to their wealth. Hence, large corporations invest greater profits from low wage levels or because they can get access to their natural resources. The free market out of globalisation does nothing to address re-distribution of wealth.

Does Globalisation Affect Culture?

There are many reasons to think that globalisation might undermine cultural diversity:

(i) Multidimensional corporations promote a certain kind of consumerist culture, in which standard commodities, promoted by global marketing campaigns exploiting basic material desires, create similar lifestyles. In today's advertising world, if you see what is actually being created, they are creating human beings who are capable of consuming certain products. The emphasis is no longer on creating the products that are required by the human beings rather creating human beings that are required for the products. This is essentially the defining feature of the culture under globalisation. Human beings are reduced to the status of products who will consume every other products that capitalism produces. Now we need 'Fair and Lovely', our traditional methods for fairness will work no more.

(ii) Western ideals are falsely established as universal, overriding local traditions. The United States exerts hegemonic influence in promoting its values and habits through popular culture and the new media. Now, we have mobile culture. We watch Hollywood movies, and wear western clothes and listen to rock and hip hop which have become our modern culture. English has become the language of globalisation.

(iii) In a way, we have been mentally and psychologically colonised by 'cultural imperialism'. Not only with regard to products, even the medicines we use are the western products – allopathic medicines. Though better, we hesitate to use our traditional therapies, herbs and ayurvedic medicines. Whereas, western minds use our natural herbs for production of those medicines.

Our mentality is such that we prefer all imported things, including medicines.

(iv) Globalisation has enhanced the culture of corruption.

Oommen (1998) refers to the birth of a New World society by the impact of globalisation on culture. He posits that the consequences of globalisation could be discerned through four interrelated and interacting processes – *homogenisation, pluralisation, traditionalisation* and *hybridisation.*

1. *Homogenisation:* The more visible aspect of homogenisation is that cultural context which manifests in evolving a common lifestyle and consumption pattern, i.e. attire (jeans), food (McDonald's), music (Michael Jackson). These are confined to urban population living in metropolitan cities. However, homogenisation is more popular in certain other contexts of nuclear family, monogamous marriages, parliamentary democracy, private property and western technology. These institutional arrangements were initiated in colonial era but got momentum in the process of globalisation. The homogenisation process is characterised by *displacement syndrome* that is movement towards homogenisation is taking place through the process of displacement. For example, south Indians are wearing *pyjama* instead of *lungi.*
2. *Pluralisation:* Pluralisation is accompanied by *accretion syndrome*. Pluralisation concedes and commends the co-existence of a variety of consumption and institutional patterns. For example, alongwith McDonald's, other modern varieties of junk food and alongwith Michael Jackson's music other recent styles of pop music came to be accommodated. This partial change and partial persistence gives birth to pluralisation.
3. *Traditionalisation:* The *hegemonising* tendency of globalisation gives birth to a loss of meaning and an erosion of identity to the non-West. This leads to the resurrection of roots, a search for identity which reflects a process of traditionalisation accompanied by *revivalistic syndrome*. However, this tendency is not confined to the non-West. *Americanisation* is resisted even by Europeans, particularly the French. Sometimes, the response for modernity takes the form of cultural revival. This also results in the reinvention of tradition. This emerges not only as religious fundamentalism but also religious freedom.
4. *Hybridisation:* The process of hybridisation refers to the *mutation syndrome*. The crossbreeding of traditional and modern, the local and the global give birth to hybridisation. Hybridisation creates new cultural elements and social patterns which are neither traditional nor global. Hybridisation is different from pluralisation in which it is neither co-existence nor elaboration. It is an effort to innovate to breakout of cultural and social dead ends. It is simultaneous engagement with both the tradition and modernity and the local and the global. This is evident of contemporary institutional arrangements and consumption pattern. The mutation between the local and the global leads to hybridisation as is evident in music, art forms and food items; for example, vegetarian hamburger, Indian rap music, European curry, Japanese pasta, and

numerous other examples suggest the relentless march of hybridisation. But affluent and dominant polities dominate over the weak and small cultural sections.

Globalisation as Boon

In his book, *Globalization and its Discontents,* Joseph Stiglitz (2001), winner of the Nobel Prize for Economics, argues: 'Globalization is not a fault but the way it has been managed is faulty.' The spread of globalisation will undoubtedly bring changes to the countries it reaches, but change is an essential part of life. It does not mean the abolition of traditional values. Indeed, new global media, such as the internet, has proven to be a powerful means of projecting traditional culture. To the extent that globalisation does imply some integration of culture, this may not be a bad thing.

But there are good reasons to think that globalisation will foster diversity:

1. Interaction across boundaries leads to the mixing of cultures in particular places and practice of pluralisation.
2. Cultural flows occur differently in different spheres and may originate in many places.
3. Global norms or practices, global values, promoted through international organisations and movements, have been institutionalised. Human rights issues have been internationalised, and we do have international court to take action against its violation, and thus get international support. Global norms have insisted all the nations to consider terrorism as an international issue. In this context, it has been making global efforts to contain the issue at the best.
4. Besides, globalisation benefits both big and small businesses, together with the citizens of those countries that embrace international trade. There are no grounds for asserting, however, that large companies are bent on subverting government. Large corporations generate employment, tax revenues and wealth for the nations in which they operate.
5. Capitalism has brought unprecedented advances in living standards. As the economist, Brad DeLong, views that at the end of the 19th century, average life expectancy in the world was 40 years, a quarter of all babies died in their first year and barely a quarter of adults could read and write. Today, the world population's average life expectancy is 67; only 6 per cent of babies die in the first year, and more than 80 per cent of the world's adults can read and write. Supporters of globalisation say: 'There is mounting evidence that inequalities in global income and poverty are decreasing and that globalisation has contributed to this turnaround. For example, the World Bank points out that China's opening to world trade has brought it growth in income from $ 1,460 a head in 1980 to $4,120 by 1999. The gap between rich and poor is also shrinking in most nations in Asia and Latin America. The poorer countries are those which are not open to world trade, notably many nations in Africa. Poor countries have lowered their tariff barriers and have gained increase in employment and national income because labour and capital shift from import-competing industries to expanding, newly competitive export industries.'

Conclusion

In the discussion, we find that globalisation refers to the expansion of global linkages and the growth of global consciousness, hence to the consolidation of world society, all and all for the development of entire world system.

We can agree upon the fact that 'globalisation is not a choice.' It is an acceptable reality that globalisation has both positive and negative impacts. It's high time to manage this phenomenon by developing framework for humanised globalisation, which could be harmonised with local, regional and national situations. It will hopefully lead to a developed and happier country, region and world as a whole. However, it would be worthwhile to explore two things: (i) challenges of globalisation, and (ii) alternative vision.

Challenges of Globalisation

There are two types of challenges as also discussed by Singh (2004):

(a) Challenges of Economic Development
(b) Challenges of Identity

   (a) *Challenges of Economic Development:* The tensions and anxieties on account of globalisation are primarily economic which spill over to the anxieties about culture and identity. Economic development in a balanced manner holds the key to our ability to meet with the challenges of globalisation and accommodate the upsurge of identities.

   (b) *Challenges of Identity:* Globalisation almost everywhere has given rise to a newer and sharper self-consciousness of identity. Such consciousness tends to be pervasive; it is not confined to the cultural minorities, local cultures, ethnic groups, tribes or weaker sections. The sure of identity consciousness and anxiety about preservation of cultural identity extends also in the relationships between nations.

For reasons of history, pluralistic social structure, culture and the democratic path of development that we have adopted, we enjoy tremendous resilience to meet with the challenges of globalisation.

Alternative Vision

The foregoing review in this paper reflects that effects of globalisation are taking away from people, in local communities, even their basic rights to life and livelihood. For India, it took her nearly half a century since the adoption of the Republican Constitution to turn people's entitlements into rights. These very basic human rights now appear to be threatened by a totally market and commodity-centred globalisation. In this context, Dhanagare (2003: 25) views that the situation calls for a debate on the possibility of an alternative vision of globalisation. In his view such an alternative can be traced and rediscovered in the Indian tradition. Indian philosophical traditions, spiritual resources and civilisational wisdom contain a global vision – a vision that is neither commodity nor market-centred, nor is it focused on material calculus of gains and losses, profits or deficits purely in material-monetary terms. Such an alternative vision is best encapsulated in ancient sayings like: *vasudhaiva kutumbakam* (Let the whole globe be our family), *aa no bhadraha kratavaha yantu vishwatah* (Let noble thoughts come to us from every side), etc. To realise this vision neither any commercial nor any military war has to be fought, nor the conquests of other's territories are necessary, nor external markets need to be captured through media aggression and offending advertisements. It is a humanistic vision that predicates autonomy to individuals, groups, communities and nation–states, freedom of choice of a development path and is also founded on the principles of brotherhood, peace and coexistence.

References

Appadurai, A. (1990). 'De-juncture and Difference in the Global Cultural Economy', in Mike Featherstone (ed.) *Global Culture: Nationalism, Globalization and Modernity*, London: Sage.

Allen, J. (1995). 'Global Worlds' in J. Allen and D. Massey (eds.) *Geographical Worlds*, Oxford: Oxford University Press, pp. 121–143.

Allen, J. and Massey, A. (eds.) (1995). *Geographical Worlds*, Oxford: Oxford University Press.

Baudrillard, J. (1983). *Simulations*, New York: Autonomedia.

Day, G. and Murdoch, J. (1993). 'Locality and Community Coming to Terms with Place', *The Sociological Review*, Vol. 7, pp. 82–111.

Dhanagare, D.N. (2003). 'Globalization: Towards an Alternative View', in *Sociological Bulletin*, Vol. 52, No. 1.

Dilthy, W. (1988). *Introduction to the Human Science* (tr. R.J. Bentazos), London: Harvester Wheatsheaf.

Dissananyake, W. (1988). 'Communication, Knowledge and a Post-Industrial Society: The Need for Values-centred Approach', in Christian Academy (ed.), *World Community in Post-Industrial Society*, Seoul: Wooseok Publishing Co.

Eagleton, T. (1992). *Theory and Cultural Value*, Oxford: Basil Blackwell.

Ernst, D. (1992). Network, Market Structure of Technology Diffusion: A Conceptual Framework and some Empirical Evidence, Report prepared for the OECD Secretariat, OECD, Paris.

Featherstone, M. (ed.) (1990). *Global Culture: Nationalism, Globalization and Modernity*, London: Sage.

Giddens, A. (1990). *The Consequences of Modernity*, Cambridge: Polity.

Giddens, A. (1991). *Modernity and Self-Identity: Self and Society in the Late Modern Age*, Cambridge: Polity.

Kothari, R. (1995). 'Globalization and Revival of Tradition: Dual Attack on Model of Democratic Nation-Building', *Economic Political Weekly*, Vol. 30(12), March 25.

Lyotard, J.F. (1987). *The Postmodern Conditions: A Report on Knowledge* (tr. G. Bennigtomn and B. Massumi), Manchester: Manchester University Press.

Mahadevia, D. (2003). *Globalization: Urban Reforms and Metropolitan Response*, New Delhi: Manak Publications.

McLuhan, M. and Carpenter, E. (eds.) (1960). *Exploration in Communication*. Boston: Beacon Press.

Milton, K. (1996). *Environmentalism and Cultural Theory: Exploring the Role of Anthropology in Environmental Discourse*, London: Routledge.

Oommen, T.K. (1998). 'Emerging Diversity: Birth of a New World Society', *Times of India*, October, 30.

O'Riordan, T. and Church, C. (2001). 'Synthesis and Context' in O'Riordan, (ed). *Globalism, Localism and Identity*, London: Earthscan.

Ostor, A. (1980). *The Play of the Gods: Locality, Ideology, Structure and Time in the Festivals of A Bengali Town*, Chicago: Chicago University Press.

Ritzer, G. (1983). 'The McDonaldization of Society', *Journal of American Culture*, Vol. 6, issue, pp. 100–107.

Robertson, R. (1992). *Globalization: Social Theory and Social Culture*, London: Sage.

Singh, K.S. (1997). *People of India: An Introduction*, Calcutta: Anthropological Survey of India.

Singh, Y. (2004). *Ideology and Theory in Indian Sociology*, Jaipur: Rawat.

Smith, A.D. (1990). 'Towards a Global Culture', in Featherstone, M. (ed.) *Global Culture: Nationalism, Globalization and Modernity*, London: Sage.

Stacey, M. (1969). 'The Myth of Community Studies', *British Journal of Sociology*, Vol. 20, pp. 134–147.

Stiglitz, J. (2003). *Globalisation and its Discontents*, New York: WW Norton.

Vinakayam, N. (1995). *Globalization of Indian Economy*, Delhi: Kanishka.

Voisey, H. and O'Riordan, T. (2001). 'Globalization and Localization', in O'Riordan, Tim (ed.) *Globalism, Localism and Identity*, London: Earthscan.

Waters, M. (1995). *Globalization*, London: Routledge.

Yachuri, S. (2001). 'Globalization' in the National Seminar on Globalization and its Impact on Indian Society, SV Kendram, Hyderabad.

Yearley, S. (1996). *Sociology, Environmentalism, Globalization*, London: Sage.

4

Caste, Class and Globalisation

Continuity and Change

K.L. SHARMA

Though caste has been questioned from time to time as a holistic system of stratification, however, it has functioned more or less as an encompassing arrangement of social groups (castes and sub-castes). Dynamics and ramifications of the caste as a system indicate that it has neither been uniformly rigid and elaborate in different parts of India nor has it been so with regard to specific caste groups. A scale of 'elaboration' or 'rigidity-fluidity' dimension of caste suggests the possibility of change in the system, and that too not of the same magnitude. As we know that economic and political considerations have penetrated into the caste system from times immemorial, and therefore, at times this has made the ideology of 'pure' and 'impure' with regard to caste – 'weak' and 'upside down' in certain respects. Even though 'individual' is not quite significant and visible in the caste system, but due to onslaught of certain economic and political factors, 'group' as the basis of caste ranking has received a setback, and 'individual' has made his presence felt. Such a situation explains the incorporation of class and power in the core of the caste system. One can also say that ritual status implies power. Crystallisation of social (caste), economic and political domains calls for a study of change and mobility in the caste system. Our concern here is to understand the extent and magnitude (both internal and external factors) of social mobility in the Indian society. We have noticed an increased presence of 'individual' in the patterns of migration, mobility, decision-making, etc.

While analysing the dynamics of social stratification, we would like to locate middle castes and classes in contemporary India to see how colonialism, education, social reforms, land reforms, green revolution, adult franchise, etc. have brought about social mobility (including downward mobility). Some questions may be posed here: Is there a middle-class? Is there a new middle-class? What is the nature of clash of interests among different castes and classes? What is the nature and extent of migration from rural to urban? Which are the areas of new spaces for the traditionally deprived people? Is a new social formation in the offing? In the light of these questions we intend to understand the role of 'globalisation' in transformation of India's social stratification. What is 'globalisation'? What is 'just globalisation'? How does it affect different social groups (castes and classes)? An attempt to know 'globalisation' in the context of peasants, workers, artisans, castes, and rural and urban people is also warranted.

II

'Social stratification means the differentiation of a given population into hierarchically superposed classes. It is manifested in the existence of upper and lower layers. Its basis and very existence consist in an unequal distribution of rights and privileges, duties and responsibilities, social values and privations, social power and influences among the members of a society. Concrete forms of social stratification are different and numerous' (Sorokin, 1959: 11). Sorokin's conceptualisation applies to the caste system to a great extent. While analysing members of a society economically, politically and occupationally stratified, Sorokin observes: 'A real picture of social stratification in any society is very complex. In order to make its analysis easier, only the most fundamental traits must be taken. Many details must be omitted, and the situation simplified, without, however, disfiguring it' (ibid.: 12). One more statement from Sorokin's classical work – *Social and Cultural Mobility* – is quite relevant here. He writes: 'Any organised social group is always a stratified social body. There has not been and does not exist any permanent social group which is 'flat' and in which all members are equal. Unstratified society, with a real equality of its members, is a myth which has never been realised in the history of mankind' (ibid.: 12–13).

How does a society get stratified? Who is the main unit/basis of social stratification – individual or group? Take the example of Karl Marx (1888: 12), who pronounces class (group) as the basis of high and low positions. Marx observes: 'The history of all hitherto existing society is the history of class struggles. Freeman and slave, patrician and plebeian, lord and serf, guildmaster and journeyman, or in a word, oppressor and oppressed, stood in constant opposition to one another, carried on an uninterrupted, now hidden, now open fight, a fight that each time ended, either in a revolutionary re-constitution of society at large, or in the common ruin of the contending classes. Thus, group is the basis of formation of society and it has never been stable. Industrialisation, for example, has transformed the earlier structure into two classes, namely, bourgeoisie and proletariat. No fixed and frozen relations exist because the bourgeoisie constantly revolutionise the instruments of production, and with them whole relations of society. Though the proletariats are an instrument of production, and yet they alone are a revolutionary agent of social change. No significant middle class exists. The lower of the middle class – the small tradespeople, shopkeepers, and retired tradesmen generally the handicrafts men and peasants-all these sink gradually into the proletariat ...' (ibid.: 12–32). The proletariat is special and essential product of the capitalist society because it stands face-to-face with the bourgeoisie, and the lower-middle classes do not survive in the fight against the bourgeoisie, and therefore, manufacturer, shopkeeper, artisan, peasant, etc. are not revolutionary but conservative.

A different view is proposed by Max Weber. He observes: 'A class is any group of persons occupying the same "class status"' (Weber, 1948: 429). A class could be: (a) a 'property class', (b) an 'acquisition class', and (c) a 'social class'. Individual is the axis of class. An aggregation of individuals based on common traits may constitute a particular class. Like Marx, Weber also recognises a 'positively privileged property class' and a 'negatively privileged class' ('outcastes/proletarians'). However, Weber recognises the 'middle classes' more significantly than Marx. Between the two – the upper and the lower classes – stand the 'middle' classes. They have all sorts of property or marketable abilities through training. Some of them may be 'acquisition' classes. Entrepreneurs fall in this category. Merchants, shop-owners, industrial and agricultural entrepreneurs, bankers and financiers, members of the 'liberal' professions, and workers with special skills commanding a monopolistic position may constitute the middle classes (ibid.: 424–29).

In French literature the English middle-class corresponds with the bourgeoisie, whereas Marx considers the middle-class as petty bourgeoisie. However, Marx and Engles did not make a systematic distinction between the 'old middle class' of small producers, artisans, independent professional people, farmers and peasants, and the 'new middle class' of clerical, supervisory and technical workers, teachers, government officials, etc. (Bottomore, 1983: 333). Two other considerations in the understanding of the middle-classes are: (1) political orientation – conservative or radical, and (2) size or growth in numbers. In the wake of the recent global developments and also in the context of Indian society in particular, these two points may be worthy of discussion.

The middle-class is a heterogeneous social layer. Income, property, natural or physical inequality, civil and political inequality are the main criteria for defining commonality of a group of people as a (middle) class. Education, standard of living, nature of occupation and wealth determine varying quality of social prestige and power. The growth of the middle-class in England was initially characterised by differentiation of the industrial and commercial functions. Production and trade became distinct activities. Entrepreneurship and management vis-à-vis factory production were required. This heralded a new social order replacing the feudalism in England. Industrial workers emerged from the differentiation of industry and trade. Thus, a number of new groups and categories emerged from the expansion of trade and industry, education and professions (Misra, 1961: 1–7). Further, capitalism made the middle classes an integral part of a unitary social order (ibid.). The old trading middle-class was called 'middle' because it was situated in-between the baronage and the peasant or artisan class (ibid.). The new middle-class was not simply the capitalist and the worker; it had a wide range of occupational interests and was bound together by a common style of living and behaviour pattern. The new middle-classes stood for certain liberal, democratic values which they expressed in their social and political conduct (ibid.). There was respect for the individual, intellectual freedom and social mobility, liberal individualism and political democracy. Thus, the new middle-classes reflected a new standard of values (ibid.).

Before the British advent, the immobility of the caste organisation and the despotism of bureaucracy precluded development of a middle-class bourgeois. Even Buddhism, Jainism and Bhakti movements could not reduce the rigidity of the caste system to a noticeable extent (ibid.: 9). The caste system remained static because it was related to the law of property, land, economy, inheritance, etc. These were fixed status groups and intermediate categories and there were no middle-classes. The British rule also saw an emergence of a middle-class in India. Administration, education, business and occupation played a significant role in the rise of a new middle-class. The British-born Indian middle-class exhibited in great measure an element of behavioural uniformity and style of life, and similarity in their mode of thinking and social values. The middle classes comprised the members of the educated professions, namely, government servants and lawyers, college teachers and doctors in general. The merchants and industrialists were a minority and limited to big cities (ibid.: 12–13). Excluding the top people like owners of industries and corporations and top political leaders, and the people at the bottom like small peasants, agricultural workers, all the people such as merchants, agents, proprietors, salaried executives, officers, civil servants, judges, professionals, peasant proprietors, rentiers, shopkeepers and hotelkeepers, rural entrepreneurs, full-time higher education students and senior level school teachers and officials of the local bodies were included in the middle classes during the British rule in India. A confluence of official hierarchies, professional hierarchies and caste hierarchy was quite evident at the end of the 19th century in most parts of the British India. Despite reactionary revivalism, liberal reformism was quite visible in the Indian society. What has happened to such a formation after India's independence? How do we analyse Indian society today?

III

We may discuss briefly also about the caste system and particularly about the empowered castes with a view to know the role of the Indian state, education and exogenous forces. For a long time caste has been perceived as an overarching ideological system of status determination. Two logical queries would be: In what way caste is a normative system? And, how is it a system of social relations? Louis Dumont (1970) considers more specifically caste as a special type of inequality as ideas and values are basic to know actual and observable behaviour of the people. As such, caste is certainly a means of identity. But, then, the question is: Can caste not be an interest group? We have discussed (Sharma, 1996: 130–46; 1994: 50–78; 2001: 45–74) that caste and class are not polar opposites and antithetical to each other. Caste and class are nearly inseparable as one can be transposed into other by way of appropriating caste status for class gains and the latter for social superiority and cultural enhancement. Bourdieu's concept of 'capital' (1991: 14–15) is in tune with our understanding of the caste-class nexus. The two refer to intertwined processes along with their internal differentiations. 'The caste-class divide was never as rigid as reported in various writings, and hence Indian society was also not as rigidly structured as depicted in several accounts of the caste system' (Sharma, 1998: 1). The 'ideal' and the 'actual' statues were never the same. The inter-caste marriages produced 'mixed castes'. There were status incongruities in ancient India. 'Production' rather than kinship was given premium in shaping of the social formation in olden times. Thus, neither homo hierarchicus nor homo equalis was the absolute system of hierarchy and equality in India and Europe, respectively.

Contradictions within the caste system and influence of external forces of social change on it rule out the possibility of it being homo hierarchicus. A long history of discontinuities, breakdowns, contradictions and changes in the caste system negates its absolutist, unchanging and holistic nature as perceived by some scholars (Dumont, 1970; Srinivas, 1998). Both inequality and equality are built into the ideology and practice of the caste system, and both have changed from time to time, providing scope for continuity, change and nexus of the two aspects, namely, 'social' and 'economic' in India's social formation. It is the caste system, which provides priest and contra-priest, inequality and equality, and as such a semblance of the 'unity of opposites'. Because of such a confluence caste has always acquired a new form and functioning in Indian history. It has not been a static (closed) system of social relations. Changes in the caste system have resulted into changes in class, structure and power relations. 'The emergence of a new middle-class, disproportionate to the forces of production and the size of the upper and the lower classes, has forged a new nexus between caste, class and power' (Sharma, 1998: 2). The principal agricultural castes have given a new direction to the nexus between, caste, class and politics. Economic and political power has become a focal theme today of the study of the caste system. Incongruities between caste, class and power clearly hint at the diminution of caste as an all-encompassing system and the emergence of a new nexus of caste with economy, polity, migration and religion as interlocking sub-systems. Agrarian relations, economic transactions and service relations have set in a process of role reversal in the caste system. Several studies have emphasised the role of migration, education, occupation, political power, style of life, ownership, control and use of land, inter-caste feuds, competition and bargaining for higher wages as the new criteria of status determination and the caste-class nexus. Agrarian relations and green revolution have affected caste, class and land relations by creating divides of gainers and losers.

Today, processes of pauperisation, proletarianisation and downward social mobility on the one hand, and upward mobility and embourgeoisiement on the other, are found simultaneously among different castes and sub-castes. In such a situation caste cannot be a precise equivalent or opposite of class and vice versa. Castes are 'discrete' (Gupta, 1992, 2000), and therefore, they are flexible and segmentary.

The changing nature of nexus between caste and class not only refers to the multifaceted form and substance of social stratification, but it also implies that there is considerable departure from the hierarchical model of consensus, resilience, and summation of roles and statuses in the context of caste. Various social segments and families have witnessed visible change in their social standings. Beteille (1966a, 1966b) has observed 'caste-free areas' of social activities. We have also observed (Sharma, 1973: 59–77) 'downward social mobility' and incompatibility of the pollution-purity principle as a result of the entrenchment of the middle and the lower castes in politics and modern jobs. The problems such as exploitation, domination, poverty, alienation, distributive injustice, suppression of human rights, etc. call upon a reconceptualisation of the caste stratification (Sharma, 2001). We can say that caste is transforming itself rapidly finding out a place for itself in new and secular domains of social, political and economic life.

Caste gives coherence and meaning to actual social relations and as such it is both an actual structure of social relationships and an ideology (Harriss, 1982: 42–56). It is realised that today a dominant caste is also a dominant class. However, there is no uniform pattern of caste-class congruence. Assam and Kerala, for example, show resemblance between caste stratification and corresponding class positions. Bihar has a different pattern as it is characterised by the forwards (the twice-born), the upper backwards, the lower backwards, the minorities, the Scheduled Castes (SCs) and the Scheduled Tribes (STs). West Bengal has considerable radical mobilisation due to an overwhelming presence of the lower caste people, who are extremely poor. We may like to infer here that the emergence of a well-off peasantry belonging to the intermediate castes, white-collar groups from amongst the upper castes and enhanced migration and mobility of these groups (country-town nexus), politicisation of caste identity, differentiation among the SCs and the STs, considerable presence of the class of capitalists, entrepreneurs, professionals, white-collar workers, a select group of elites from amongst the SCs and the STs, etc. are some of the recent actual developments. A continuous change in the caste-class nexus and levels of occupational and social mobility have contributed to the survival of caste as a means of mobilisation for economic and political goals.

IV

In a very forthright manner Nicholas B. Dirks (2001: 3–18) starts with a statement: 'When thinking of India, it is hard not to think of caste.' But there is a paradox. Dirks observes: 'Caste defines the core of Indian tradition, and it is seen today as the major threat to Indian modernity' (ibid.: 3). However, according to Dirks, caste is not in fact some unchanged survival of ancient India, not some single system that reflects a core civilisational value, not a basic expression of Indian tradition (ibid.: 5). More important point in Dirks' analysis is that caste is a modern phenomenon, the product of a historical encounter between Indian and western colonial rule. The British (Risley, 1969; Hutton, 1946) made 'caste capable of expressing, organising a above all 'systematising' India's diverse forms of social identity, community, and organisation' (Dirks, 2001; 5). Thus, colonialism made caste what it is today. Castes were transformed into middle-classes as B.B. Misra observes in *The Indian Middle Classes* (1961). Dirks writes: 'Caste itself was seen as a form of colonial civil society in India, which provided an ironic and inferior, anthropological analogue for the colonized world' (2001: 12). Caste served the interests of a private domain at the instance of the British. As such, caste was opposed to the basic premises of individualism, voluntarism and reinforcement of the modern state. Its functioning remained restricted to social and ritual spheres, rather than political domain and individual and social mobilisation. Thus, during colonialism, caste was a more pervasive, totalising and uniform than it had ever been before (Dirks, 2001: 13). There were other multiple identities other than caste during the British period. However, caste was always a political phenomenon by a way of classifications of people in terms of high and low, superior and inferior, and pure and impure ranks.

Caste has not disappeared despite the claim of having enhanced urbanisation and industrialisation. The constitutional stroke regarding its annihilation has also been falsified. Challenges to dominant caste(s) have been frustrated. Caste violence occurs frequently. Reservations have generated a lot of violence and animosities. Despite all this, 'caste did not die, it did not fade away, and it could no longer be diagnosed as benign' (ibid.: 16). 'At the same time, caste remains the single most powerful category for reminding the nation of the resilience of poverty, oppression, domination, exclusion, and the social life of privilege' (ibid.: 16). Caste provides the basis for new forms of social mobilisation and progressive politics. At the same time, 'it has become the subject of national shame' (ibid.: 17). Today, as in the past, caste is imagined and then appropriated for social and political mobilisation; hence *Castes of Mind* as Dirks rightly names his book to explain caste as a political creation. At the empirical level, castes are segments and not organically interlinked units of a holistic system. Dipankar Gupta (2004: 77–78) observes: 'The distinguishing characteristic of the caste order is the discrete character of its constituent units that resist being forced into a single hierarchical frame. As these castes are discrete and semaphore their separation on multiple fronts, caste competition is built in at various levels. It is only by accepting the reality of multiple hierarchies that we can conceptually make room for the existence of caste politics. If one were to go by the traditional understanding of a single hierarchy of purity/ pollution, with Brahmins at the top, then any evidence of caste conflict should have meant the dissolution of the caste order.' A similar view was articulated by Edmund Leach (1960: 1–10) that as soon as castes began to compete with each other, they ceased to be castes. However, castes have not only been competing with each other, they have had intense fights and violence, and never ceased to be castes, nor they transformed themselves into antagonistic classes in the Marxian sense.

A caste is in mind, a means of identity of the people and so is class based on certain criteria/indices (Sharma, 2001: 45–74). Landowners, landless labourers, traders and moneylenders are not abstractions or conceptual constructions; they are existential structural entities of India's class structure. Both conflict and cooperation refer to life-situations of different classes. One can see interconnectedness of the mode of production and production relations in caste, kinship, family and marriage (Gough, 1980: 337–64). Class relations have been seen as a 'domain assumption' in the treatment of caste and kinship in India (Namboodiripad, 1979: 329–36; Ranadive, 1979: 337–48). Thus, to a large extent, caste and class represent the same structural reality. 'Classes operate within the framework of castes' (Singh, 1968: 31). Since the hiatus between the upper and lower castes is the same as it is between the upper and the lower classes, caste conflicts tantamount to class conflicts. At times castes function as classes with a view to realise their economic (class) interests. Caste associations serve economic interests of their members.

V

What about the middle-classes? The middle-classes are not necessarily the middle castes. On the contrary, they may be from amongst the upper castes to a great extent, and only a minority of them may belong to the middle and the lower castes, minorities and the STs. As such, correspondence between caste and class remains quite unrealistic as well. Broadly speaking, there are three main classes – the bourgeoisie/capitalist class; the middle-classes; and the working class. No doubt, all the three are internally differentiated and they cannot also be seen independent of each other. In the first category, we may include the property-owning, entrepreneurial, capitalist-employer. Secondly, in the recent times, capital and industry are controlled by professional salaried management. Thirdly, in the developing countries like India, due to the new state formation, middle classes have grown enormously. Finally, the material standards of workers have also improved considerably.

We have made a brief reference to the middle-classes relating to the pre-independence period. After Independence, the middle-classes have changed in terms of their size, role and functions mainly due to the nature and character of the Indian state. Ghanshyam Shah (1986: 149–83) reports that the middle class has grown in size disproportionately with economic growth in Gujarat. In the new middle-classes, the members are from amongst the upper and the middle castes on the one hand and the lower castes on the other. Since the middle classes are a product of both the capitalist development and the state, there would be a conflict situation between the entrenched middle-classes and the lower classes aspiring for the status of the middle-classes by having access to lucrative white-collar jobs.

Satish Deshpande (1997: 294–318) observes that in the post-Independence years, the ideology of development helped to create and sustain a strongly synergistic relationship between the developmental state, a relatively small but significant middle class, and the nation. However, in due course of time, due to decline in the development ideology, a new middle-class has emerged with different interests and desires. The new middle-class can be characterised by transnationally dominant ideologies of globalisation and structural adjustment. This has resulted into the growth and differentiation of the Indian middle-class. The developmental state of the Nehruvian era resulted in swelling the ranks of the middle classes. The era of 'globalisation' has marked a new phase in the growth and differentiation of the middle-classes, and this calls for an examination of continuity and change in development, state and middle-classes in India.

However, it is not an easy task to ascertain the exact nature and contents of the 'middle-class'. In everyday life, the term 'middle-class' is referred in a very vague sense. Satish Deshpande (2003: 125–50) observes that it is more of a symbolic term than a factual description. Now, the question is: Can we conceptualise 'middle-class' based on the capita consumption? What about the assets possessed by the people? Deshpande says that consumer as the basis of the middle-class is too narrow to capture the critical multidimensional role of the middle-class in post-colonial societies. A couple of observations by Deshpande may be useful in the conceptualisation of the middle class: (1) The middle-class is the class of the people that articulates the hegemony of the ruling bloc by way of the language of legitimation and mediation between the ruling bloc and other classes. (2) The middle is most dependent on 'cultural capital' and on the mechanisms of its reproduction. (3) The middle-class specialises in the production and dissemination of ideologies.

Despite the ideological base and moorings as the strongest point of the Indian middle-class, the consumerist thirst of the present middle-class cannot be overlooked, and it is a clear indicator of the Indian market. Pawan K. Varma (1998: 170–214) talks of three middle-classes based on a survey by the National Council of Applied Economic Research (NCAER) in 1994. These are: (1) the consuming class (150 million people); (2) the climbers (275 million); and (3) the aspirants (275 million). Besides these middle-classes, at the top are the very rich (6 million people). However, Varma does not endorse the consumerist view of the new middle-class in India. The middle-class in India has a 'history' and its specific characteristic features and relations with the higher and the lower classes. Hence, the middle-class is a socio-economic and political phenomenon because mere economic standing does not make a class a middle-class. As such, the middle-class is a systemic construction and an action entity.

A study of elite formation in India (Navlakha, 1989) shows that select positions are usually taken by persons from select social strata. Such a group controls the positions of prestige, power and responsibility. Higher education is under the grip of upper castes, hence, it is 'status stabilizer' (Jayaram, 1977) or it results into social/cultural reproduction (Bourdieu, 1996: 50–51) rather than an increase in status rigidities. A couple of studies of lawyers, university teachers, technocrats, scientists and managers have brought about social-structural and organisational aspects of the upper-middle class professionals (Sharma, 1997: 124–29; Lal, 1988). The members of the middle-classes have their origins in agriculture and industry (Rudra, 1989). Besides these, there is the class of intelligentsia, who have co-opted a number of members and the two classes having their social origins in agriculture and industry (ibid.). The intelligentsia include all white-collar workers, all office workers, teachers, writers, journalists, artists and skilled workers, professionals, journalists, politicians, trade union leaders, etc. The intelligentsia do not themselves produce any values in the material product sense of the value. Members of this middle-class (intelligentsia) depend for their economic gains on the largesse of the other two ruling classes as well as the state. Middle-classes are not direct rulers nor are they economic producers like the industrialists, workers and peasants. At the same time, there is a marked lack of homogeneity among different middle-classes (Sharma, 1997: 129).

The foregoing account of the middle-classes shows that the upper castes constitute the middle classes in Indian society. Widespread political consciousness and democratisation of politics and land reforms and massive irrigation scheme, education and migration have resulted into an attack on the age-old hold of the upper castes on high-status positions. India's independence has created various contradictions and conflicts of interests between the better off and the deprived sections of Indian society (Kamat, 1980: 1673; Das, 1984: 1616–19; Prasad, 1979: 1955–58 and 1980: 215–19). The entire gamut of social change and mobility centres around caste, class and state (power). Social change could be gauged in terms of gain and loss between groups of people, and by both persistence and emergence of tensions, contradictions and conflicts (Sharma, 1998: 159). For example, in Bihar, the middle castes have registered a stiff opposition to the upper castes and have further legitimised their meteoric rise in the class and power hierarchies leading to rapid decline of the persisting 'semi-feudalism'. Caste-based mobilisation by the middle castes in favour of the policy of reservation of jobs has further sharpened and intensified the class contradictions. Capitalist transformation in agriculture in Tamil Nadu, for example, has created a middle-class, though caste and kinship have blocked the process of change to reach at the top level. The process of modernisation needs to be viewed in relation to caste, family and village community.

No doubt, 'new status groups' or 'new castes' (Beteille, 1969) have emerged due to role differentiation and occupational diversification, which can be characterised by both upward and downward social mobility (Sharma, 1973). Such a situation of differentiation and diversification has arisen due to interpenetration of caste into class and vice versa, and also due to change in the perception of caste, which can be characterised by 'micro-ideology and micro-utopia' (Kolenda, 1989: 1831–38) and by functioning of varna ideology merely as a social practice, rather than an effectual praxis (Franco, Chand and Sarvar, 1989: 2601–12). K.L. Sharma (1997: 161) observes: 'Social mobility in the caste system is evident in the ever-increasing violations of the traditional criteria of status, namely, hereditary occupations, jajmani obligations, observance of certain rituals, and in the acceptance of modern secular occupations, education, migration and positions of power in formal political bodies. At times, competition between different castes accentuates into conflicts and violence.' I.P. Desai (1984: 1106–16), in the wake of the problems arising out of the Mandal Commission (1978–80), recognises type of society, role of political power and social mobility movements as significant factors to understand social and educational backwardness, and does not consider these as an offshoot of the ascribed status of a community/collectivity. Desai observes that today contractual relationships and performance matter a lot in the occupational field. Caste plays a minor role in it. However, this view is contradicted by Ghanshyam Shah (1985: 132–36) by way of persistence of caste consciousness and ineffectiveness of the state in annihilation of the caste system. Immobility generates contradictions and tensions; and such a situation brings about mobility, hence equality. Today, we are talking of the Harijan and the tribal elites and the Kulaks among the upper backward castes.

The state in India has consciously encouraged participation of the backward sections of the society in the polity and economy. Equality and participation are positively correlated. From social participation of a cross-section of society comes out equality and genuine citizenship. 'Equality of outcome' is very difficult to achieve and to sustain over any length of time. Bryan S. Turner (1986: 120) observers: 'The historical origins of equality are bound up with the preconditions for the development of rational capitalism – the occidental city, Roman law, system of monetary exchange, administration by officials and a this-worldly religious ethic. Equality requires equity in terms of the delivery of a service and the achievement of desirable standards of efficiency and reliability requires bureaucracy.' Turner follows strictly the Weberian approach on rational development of capitalism as a sure means of equality. Without reaching a certain level of capitalist development, equality cannot be achieved in Indian society. However, Turner (ibid.: 123) is right in his observation when he says, 'equality emerges out of the active and conscious struggle of social groups to achieve social participation through citizenship rights'.

Earlier, I have observed (Sharma, 2001: 61) that inter-caste and intra-caste relations are no more the basis of caste hierarchy, division of labour, and asymmetrical power relations. Today, people identify themselves as very rich, rich, well-off, not-so-poor and poor. In a different sense, they perceive themselves as 'powerful' and 'weak' families or as 'superior' and 'inferior' people. And yet in another sense, people identify themselves as engaged in lucrative and prestigious jobs, and in middle and lower level occupations. Thus, economic status, esteem and power are clearly the underlying criteria in the current evaluative expressions. Today, people prefer to have equal etiquette and equal rights. Inter-caste marriages and communal violations are no more a taboo, and inter-caste relations have become rarest of the rare. Caste is increasingly becoming a matter of interpretation rather than a pre-given substantialisation. Caste refers to purposive rationality, and therefore, it provides a description, and an explanation of the pathologies of modern polity and economy. Occasional caste outbursts and ostracisations on the basis of the so-called violations of caste ethics may not be taken as an actual pattern of inter- and intra-caste relations. Inter-caste relations are no more the bedrock of the caste system. Family and individual have largely replaced caste in everyday life. Caste is becoming a desideratum, a state of mind, a plastic and malleable institution. There is no more caste hypersymbolisation to express caste differences and typifications.

Despite the process of delegitimisation of the 'essential' of caste, the sporadic appearance of caste-based decisions, articulation of religion and metaphysical interpretations of caste and its divinity pose a serious challenge to the secularised understanding of social reality. Historically speaking, politico-economic interpretations of caste indicate its significance as the system of class exploitation, social distance and rivalry, an instrument of power and social injustice. Clustering of castes in the form of categories for political mobilisation, employment and resources has also been there with a view to question the supremacy of the superior castes. In everyday life, caste has become quite feeble. Summation of statuses at the levels of individual and family implies weakening of the caste system and strengthening of the extra-caste considerations in Indian society.

Because of the incorporation of the economic and political considerations into the caste system, social mobility has become somewhat easy. Development in the post-Independence era has brought about a substantial middle-class in India and this class dominates the power structure of the society. Yogendra Singh (1993: 11–21) states that the Indian middle-classes are a very articulate, active and powerful segment of our society. Expansion of market and trade, information networking and media exposure of the people, expansion of services and strengthening of the integrative impulses selectively are some of the economic, cultural and political consequences of the strong new middle-class in India. At least four points may be noted as reported by Singh with regard to the role of the new middle-classes: (1) structural cleavages in its composition; (2) a lack of harmony with the national ideology/ social change; (3) dominance of the upper and middle castes among the middle-classes; and (4) creation of cleavages between the upper-middle and the lower caste groups within the reserved categories.

Further, Singh states that the middle-classes tend to have a mindset, which decries values of liberalism, social justice, and principles of sharing or sacrifice. The middle class is rapidly taking to consumerism and short-run utilisation values. Such a situation creates conflict of values and expectations and misdirected radicalism alongwith ethical and social opportunism. In Singh's view, Indian society is faced with a situation of double crisis – one of success and the other of failures. No doubt, there is an ascendancy of a new middle-class, and it implies both social and economic change and resilience. The middle-class strengthens market, trade and media and provides a huge base of the skilled manpower. But this is negated by the self-centred ideological moorings and narrow social base of the middle-classes. This is the double crisis – crisis of success and crisis of failures.

VI

While analysing 'the future of equality', Rudolphs (1967: 111) observe: 'Four processes are making Indians more alike and, in doing so, are laying the necessary but not sufficient conditions for national integration: ascriptive boundaries are expanding; the culture and status of the twice-born varnas are spreading to the Sudra castes; westernisation is affecting the ideas and occupations of broader sections of society; and secularisation is dismantling ritual barriers and disarming sacred sanctions.' This is how 'the modernity of tradition' was observed by the Rudolphs in the late 1960s. However, we also know very well that legally group identity has been recognised in India by way of reservations. This is a case of controlled transformation of central social and cultural arrangements. The policy of the compensatory discrimination amounts to substantive equality added to the formal equality. But so long as 'group' (caste) remains the basis of such a policy, tradition-modernity nexus persists (Galanter, 1984: 547–67). Dipankar Gupta (2000: 225–64), while interrogating caste in terms of the pre-given construction, observes that instead of group 'at the root of man is man himself'. 'Social forces must work through the human agent, the social actor, who is essentially, a reflexive cognito. This person contemplates and thinks, rationalises and maximises, such that no social force is left entirely in its pristine form once it has undergone such active human mediations' (ibid.: 263–64). Thus, we may infer the following points:

1. Group alone has never been the basis of social action in Indian society.
2. 'Social' dimension has always existed with economic and political considerations.
3. Social mobility with varying degrees and magnitudes has always been there in Indian society.
4. Internal contradictions and constraints on the one hand, and the external forces and factors on the other, have transformed the Indian society; hence, continuity and change have co-existed.

VII

Let us see now how 'globalisation' is impinging upon the Indian society in general and with regard to specific segments and sections in particular. However, before we map out the impact of globalisation, it is necessary to define this concept, which is still somewhat hazy and ad hoc. In the Indian context, the concepts of westernisation, modernisation, development, etc. are being sidelined by the concept of 'globalisation' since 1990s. In fact, the increasing internationalisation of trade and investment in the developing countries by the developed world has put face-to-face the developed and the developing countries as superior and inferior entities in today's situation. The process of globalisation goes beyond transnationalisation or internationalisation of capital. It is a profound reorganisation of manufacturing, trade and services within a globally encompassing system. Globalisation thus refers to mega corporations and transnational corporations (TNCs) which operate worldwide (Martinussen, 1997: 119–22). Besides accomplishment of economy globally, globalisation refers to a globalising knowledge and global consciousness based on its historical and social contexts. To restrict the concept of globalisation to rapid harmonisation of the world in terms of the power and influence of the transnational corporations is only one side of this reality. The other side refers to destruction of diversity and marginalisation of democratic rights, culture, environment, etc. by way of external implosion. Thus, according to Robbie Robertson (2003: 3–13), 'globalisation is more than just McWorld or Westernisation'. Robertson further observes: 'It is about human intercommunications that have assumed global proportions and transformed themselves' (ibid.: 3).

No doubt, globalisation is a modern strategy of power; it is to be seen also in terms of its historical and social depths. Robertson talks of 'three waves of globalisation', namely, the globalisation of the regional trade, industrialisation, and the new world order after 1945. The three waves cover a span of nearly 500 years. In a way, this applies to the Indian situation as well. The first wave was the pre-British period dominated by the East India Company, the second may refer to the British rule, and the third naturally would be the post-Independence period. All the three periods imply epochal structural changes characterised by internal dynamics and external influences. Trading groups and white-collar workers were the creation of the first two waves. The third wave partly transformed the earlier groups and partly created new groups in terms of India as a newly independent nation. Robertson puts more emphasis on 'human interconnectiveness' in the discussion about the three waves of globalisation and its historical and social dimensions. Another way to look at the concept of globalisation is freedom for investment, production, supply and sale without any constraints whatsoever. Such a conception, if actualised, may result into a ruthless dominance of the strong MNCs over the people of the developing countries.

Globalisation is a process that changes sites and levels of economic decision-making. Christian Comeliau (2002: 96–108), while analysing 'the contradictions of globalisation', observes that it (globalisation) brings new players onto the scene, and transform the relationship of forces among those present on it. Three points are important today in the globalisation of economy: concentration of power in a small number of 'multinational' and 'transnational' corporations and their national branches; emergence of a small number of international public organisations at global and regional levels; and a significant change in the place and role of national public authorities. The new power relations with unequal power of decision-making are an obvious result of globalisation.

Pulapra Balakrishnan (2003: 3166–72) considers globalisation as policy, as process and as justice in an interconnected manner. In the context of India, keeping in view these general features of globalisation, Balakrishnan observes that the economic constraints that bind its economy are very likely internal ones rather than anything external. 'The current bout of globalisation is unlikely to affect her fortunes dramatically either way' (ibid.: 3171). Poverty, health and education have continued to improve in the 1990s. The 1990s have not witnessed either 'unprecedented improvement' or 'widespread impoverishment'. Some segments of economy have integrated with the rest of the world and some cannot be affected adversely because most Indians have either very low incomes or very low skills to be affected by globalisation either way (ibid.). Since integration of the possession of low incomes and low skills with the world economy is not possible, adverse effects are simply not there. The report of the World Commission on the Social Dimension of Globalisation (2004) insists on conducting social dialogues within a democratic framework, at the local, national and international levels, to create a 'fair globalisation' that is inclusive. The Commission calls for 'fair globalisation' that will 'create opportunities for all'. Emphasis is on ethical, economic and social dimensions of globalisation, hence, a strong plea for human development.

A Marxist critique of globalisation is in Samir Amin's recent work (Harshe, 2002: 1407–12). Rajan Harshe, the reviewer of Amin's seminal work, looks at globalisation as an offshoot of capitalism and modernity. Marxism, capitalism and globalisation have been seen as inextricably interrelated developments. While tracing the history of the world capitalist system (1945–90), according to Harshe, Amin looks at globalisation as a fresh crisis and a challenge in the management of the world capitalist system. Three limitations may be noted in this process: (1) a lack of evolution of compatible institutions beyond nation–states to effect global transactions; (2) a failure to take the newly industrialising countries of Asia and Latin America (including India) along with the developed ('global') countries; and (3) absence of the process of competitive industrialisation. Further, with continuing strong 'ethnic complexities' and 'ontology of nation–state' and hegemonic capitalism of the USA, Western Europe and Japan, globalisation remains a new form of monopoly and dominance in the hands of the countries of the First World.

Recently, D.L. Sheth and others (*EPW*, 2004: 45–116), in a series of 11 articles, have discussed different aspects of globalisation. In a nutshell, globalisation has created 'new politics with old dilemmas'. Opposition to globalisation has resulted into micro-movements with a view to check onslaught on the interests of farmers, women, artisans and poor sections of Indian society. This has raised a new discourse on democracy, beyond the conventional institutions of elections and political parties. Participatory democracy is being reinvented through such a discourse of politics and micro-movements challenging globalisation as a new hegemonic development. Transnational activities are touching almost all aspects of India's social fabric, including religion, media, migration, economy, polity, women, labour, family, community, etc. India is confronted with the dilemma of joining the global race on the one hand, and to retain its national distinctive character, on the other. Besides this, the differential nature of gains and losses of the globalisation process for the nation as a whole and for specific socio-economic entities in particular cannot be overlooked. But 'localisation' or insulation of a nation from the global order is no way as it would obstruct modernisation of economy and migration and mobility of the people. How does localism benefit the poor? Or, how does globalisation harm the people at the bottom? It depends upon the strength of the indigenous economy in providing employment and security to the members of a given country, and the nature of globalisation may also affect the poor, but not necessarily, and may affect the middle-classes alone.

To understand globalisation in the Indian context we may have to know clearly the concepts such as 'individual', 'development', 'freedom', 'opportunities', 'market', 'state', etc. as formulated by Amartya Sen (2000). Sen looks for the 'social' behind all human endeavours. The concept of 'social opportunity' proposed by Sen becomes relevant for us as it covers a wide range of societal dimensions having implications for Indian polity, economy and culture. Development is freedom, and freedom is social opportunity, and it is constrained by social arrangements. Thus, freedom is 'social' and unfreedom is inequality. The removal of unfreedom is constitutive of development. Effective social arrangements alone can ensure freedom leading to development. Sen talks of 'substantive freedoms'. Is globalisation weakening the social arrangements? What happens to the marginalised groups due to globalisation? Does globalisation result into reproduction of the old middle-classes and continuation of the dominance of the upper and the upper middle-castes?

Bihar, Uttar Pradesh, Gujarat, Maharashtra, etc. have witnessed 'caste wars' which tantamount to 'class wars' between the landless and the landed people. 'Attacks' and 'counter-attacks' have become quite frequent in Bihar in particular. Susan Bayly (1999: 355–59) observes that 'caste war'/violence has tended to become a conflict between urban centres and the rural hinterlands as many students and factory workers are drawn in such a situation. She observes: 'Such outbreaks are not then to be seen as a reversion to the 'feudal' or 'traditional' past. 'Modern' institutions, especially the courts, the universities and the mass media, have figured prominently in the so-called caste-feud phenomena' (ibid.: 355). The anti-Mandal agitation in the wake of 27 per cent reservation in jobs for the OBCs was geared by the urban middle-class youth and students who normally looked for government jobs, which even today provide security and social status to the incumbents. Caste divides among students and staff have become a common feature in colleges and universities in India. Even hostels are dominated by students of specific castes/sub-castes. Recent decision of the Government of India to implement 27 per cent reservation for the OBCs in the central universities and institutions has once again evoked protests, particularly by students of medicine, JNU and Delhi University.

Since the 1970s, the English-speaking intelligentsia have watched the growth and diversification of the Indian middle-classes with considerable alarm (ibid.: 360). This particular class of people was engaged in government jobs, professions and middle-level entrepreneurship. However, with the expansion of trade and industry and the commercialisation of agriculture, new aspirants for the jobs, cornered by the old middle-class, have come up to claim their shares in professions and other white-collar jobs. Reservations have also added to the aspirations and claims of the formerly deprived groups. However, the gap remains unbridged between the upper and the middle castes or between the traditional middle-classes and the newly aspiring groups of people for white-collar jobs because the old middle-classes have been looking for new pastures and possibilities in the wake of globalisation. The newly aspiring groups at this juncture are not in a position to compete with the traditionally privileged groups. More or less this was the case a few decades ago when the lower castes tried to move up by way of sanskritisation and the upper castes opted to de-sanskritise their cultural pantheon and decided to take up new and secular jobs and practices. A similar situation prevails today. Globalisation calls for new adjustments and alterations in our society and culture. The intensity of the hiatus between the upper and the lower social segments would remain there despite very basic changes in economy and social milieu. This is how resilience of Indian society becomes a perpetual focal point.

Indian society is characterised by a semblance of tradition and modernity, continuity and change having differentiated effects on individual, family and group. Hence, no uniform pattern of change and its impact on different social units. The pre-British period had witnessed large-scale transformation as a result of the agrarian policy and administrative structuring. The British created a new class structure to serve its colonial interests and along with a reconceptualisation of caste and inter-caste relations. Constitutional provisions, Five Year Plans, adult franchise, reservation policy and social movements have brought about a new consciousness and transformation of the pre-Independence society and culture.

At any given epochal phase no complete overhauling of the structure of Indian society has occurred. Part continuity and part change have characterised the Indian society. Such resilience is peculiar to Indian society. The upper castes might have partly lost their traditional high status after Independence, but at the same time, they remained as the main middle-classes for quite sometime. Since, for sometime, new middle-classes from amongst the middle and lower castes have been showing their presence challenging the continuing middle-classes in their new reincarnation, the latter are busy in search of greener pastures in India and abroad. Initially, when a challenge was thrown to the upper castes living in the villages, by the politically upcoming middle and lower castes, the former moved out of their villages to settle down in towns and cities. Today, they are either looking for those avenues in India which are not accessible to the upcoming mobile groups and individuals, or they are moving out of India. In a note, Rajesh Kochhar (2004: 20) rightly observes: 'Globalisation has prevented Indian upper castes from accepting a diminished role and status consistent with their actual numbers. Aspirations of an Indian middle-class that reveals in emulating the west are costing India dear and glorifying trivia in an unprecedented fashion.'

A sort of 'cultural lag' persists between the formerly privileged middle-class and the new class of people aspiring for middle class status. Globalisation has created a new 'space', which is taken by the entrenched middle class being in an advantageous position. The 'space' vacated by this class is occupied by the aspiring class. The trajectory of the class structure demonstrates such a dynamics all over the world. However, one has to see the class of people who get adversely affected or who remain stagnant due to global/local factors of social change. The question is: What is 'just globalisation'? How does it help or does not help the poor, peasants, artisans, labourers, petty shopkeepers and women? Primordial structures in India have not obstructed the processes of social change and globalisation. Adaptive capability of Indian society is evident in its continuity and change even in face of both external and internal threats.

References

Balakrishnan, Pulapra. (2003). 'Globalisation, Growth and Justice', *Economic and Political Weekly*, Vol. XXXVIII, No. 30.

Bayly, Susan. (1999). *Caste, Society and Politics in India from the Eighteenth Century to the Modern Age*, Cambridge: Cambridge University Press.

Beteille, Andre. (1966a). *Caste, Class and Power*, Bombay: Oxford University Press.

—. (1966b). *Castes: Old and New*, Bombay: Asia Publishing House.

—. (1969). 'Closed and Open Social Stratification in India', *European Journal of Sociology*, Vol. VII, pp. 224–46.

Bottomore, Tom. (1983). *A Dictionary of Marxist Thought*, Oxford: Basil Blackwell.

Bourdieu, Pierre. (1991). *Language and Symbolic Power*, Cambridge: Polity Press.

—. (1996). *The State Nobility*, Cambridge: Polity Press.

Comeliau, Christian. (2002). *The Impasse of Modernity*, London: Zed Books.

Das, A.N. (1984). 'Caste in Itself, Caste for Itself: Social Articulation in Bihar', *Economic and Political Weekly*, Vol. XIX, No. 37.

Desai, I.P. (1984). 'Western Educated Elites and Social Change in India', *Economic and Political Weekly*, Vol. XIX, No. 15.

Deshpande, Satish. (1997). 'From Development to Adjustments: Economic Ideologies, the Middle Class and 50 Years of Independence', *Review of Development and Change*, Vol. 2, No. 2, pp. 294–318.

—. (2003). *Contemporary India: A Sociological View*, New Delhi: Penguin.

Dirks, B. Nicholas. (2001). *Castes of Mind*, Princeton: Princeton University Press.

Dumont, Louis. (1970). *Homo Hierarchicus: The Caste System and Its Implications*, London: Weidenfeld and Nicholson.

Franco, F., Sherry Chand and V. Sarvar. (1989). 'Ideology as Social Practice: The Functioning of Varna', *Economic and Political Weekly*, Vol. XXIV, No. 47.

Galanter, Marc. (1984). *Competing Equalities: Law and the Backward Classes in India*, Delhi: Oxford University Press.

Gough, E. Kathleen. (1980). 'Modes of Production in Southern India', *Economic and Political Weekly*, Vol. XV, Nos. 5–7, Annual Number.

Gupta, Dipankar. (1992). 'Continuous Hierarchies and Discrete Castes', in Dipankar Gupta (ed.), *Social Stratification*, Delhi: Oxford University Press.

—. (2000). *Interrogating Caste: Understanding Hierarchy and Difference in Indian Society*, New Delhi: Penguin Books.

—. (2004). 'Caste Is Not Race: But, Let's Go to the UN Forum Anyway' and 'Caste, Race, Politics', in Sukhadeo Thorat and Umakant (eds.), *Caste, Race and Discrimination*, Jaipur and New Delhi: Rawat Publications.

Harshe, Rajen. (2002). 'Marxism, Capitalism, Globalisation', *Economic and Political Weekly*, Vol. XXXVII, No. 15. This is a review article on Samir Amin's Book, *Capitalism in the Age of Globalisation: The Management of Contemporary Society*, London: Zed Books.

Harriss, John (1982). *Capitalism and Peasant Farming*, Delhi: Oxford University Press.

Hutton, J.H. (1946). *Caste in India*, Oxford: Oxford University Press.

Jayaram, N. (1977). 'Higher Education as a Status-Stabliser: Students in Bangalore', *Contributions to Indian Sociology* (New Series), Vol. II(1).

Kamat, A.R. (1980). 'Politico-economic Development in Maharashtra: A Review of the Post-independence Period', *Economic and Political Weekly*, Vol. XV, Nos. 39 and 40.

Kanan, K.P. (2004). 'For a Fair Globalisation', *Economic and Political Weekly*, Vol. XXXIX, No. 38. A brief account of the report of the World Commission on Social Dimension of Globalisation is given in this note by Kanan.

Kochhar, Rajesh. (2004). 'Denationalised Middle Class: Global Escape from Mandal', *Economic and Political Weekly*, Vol. XXXIX, No. 1.

Kolenda, P. (1989). 'Micro-ideology and Micro-utopia in Khalapur: Changes in the Discourse on Caste over Thirty Years', *Economic and Political Weekly*, Vol. XXIV, No. 32.

Lal, S.K., (ed.) (1988). *Readings in the Sociology of Professions*, Delhi: Gian Publishing House.

Leach, Edmund R. (1960). 'Introduction: What Should We Mean by Caste', in Edmund R. Leach (ed.), *Aspects of Caste in South India, Ceylon and North-West Pakistan*, Cambridge: Cambridge University Press.

Marx, Karl. (1888). *Manifesto of the Communist Party*, Chicago: Charles H. Kess.

Martinussen, John. (1997). *Society, State and Market: A Guide to Competing Theories of Development*, London: Zed Books Ltd.

Misra, B.B. (1961). *The Indian Middle Classes: Their Growth in Modern Times*, Delhi: Oxford University Press.

Namboodiripad, E.M.S. (1979). 'Caste Conflicts Versus Growing Unity of Popular Democratic Forces', *Economic and Political Weekly*, Vol. XIV, No. 7 and 8, Annual Number.

Navlakha, Suren. (1989). *Elite and Social Change: A Study of Elite Formation in India*, New Delhi: Sage Publications.

Prasad, Pradhan H. (1979). 'Caste and Class in Bihar', *Economic and Political Weekly*, Vol. XIV, Nos. 7 and 8.

—. (1980). 'Rising Middle Peasantry in North India', *Economic and Political Weekly*, Vol. XV, No. 4.

Ranadive, B.T. (1979). 'Caste, Class and Property Relations', *Economic and Political Weekly*, Vol. XIV, Nos. 7 and 8, Annual Number.

Risley, H.H. (1969). *The Peoples of India* (2nd ed.), Delhi: Orient Books.

Robertson, Robbie. (2003). *The Three Waves of Globalization: A History of a Developing Global Consciousness*, London: Zed Books Ltd.

Rudolph, L. and Susanne Hoeber Rudolph. (1967). *The Modernity of Tradition: Political Development in India*, Chicago: The University of Chicago Press.

Rudra, Ashok. (1989). 'Emergence of the Intelligentsia as a Ruling Class in India', *Economic and Political Weekly*, Vol. XXIV, No. 3.

Shah, Ghanshyam. (1985). 'Caste, Class and Reservation', *Economic and Political Weekly*, Vol. XX, No. 3.

—. (1986). 'Social Stratification among the Scheduled Tribes in the Bharuch and Panch Mahals Districts of Gujarat', in S.C. Malik (ed.), *Determinants of Social Status in India*. Shimla: Indian Institute of Advanced Study.

Sen, Amartya. (2000). *Development as Freedom*, New Delhi: Oxford University Press.

Sharma, K.L. (1973). 'Downward Social Mobility: Some Observations', *Sociological Bulletin*, Vol. 22, No. 1.

—. (1977). *Essays on Social Stratification*, Jaipur: Rawat Publications.

—. (1989). *Caste, Feudalism and Peasantry: The Social Formation of Shekhawati*, New Delhi: Manohar.

—. (1994). *Social Stratification and Mobility*, Jaipur and New Delhi: Rawat Publications.

—. (1996). 'Conceptualisation of Caste-Class Nexus as an Alternative to Caste-Class Dichotomy', in A.R. Momin (ed.), *The Legacy of G.S. Ghurye: A Centennial Festschrift*, Bombay: Popular Prakashan.

—. (1997). *Social Stratification in India: Issues and Themes*, New Delhi: Sage Publications.

—. (1998). *Caste, Feudalism and Peasantary: The Social Formation of Shekhawati*, New Delhi: Manohar.

—. (2001). *Reconceptualising Caste, Class and Tribe*, Jaipur and Delhi: Rawat Publications.

Sheth, D.L. (2004). 'Globalisation and New Politics of Micro-Movements', *Economic and Political Weekly*, Vol. XXXIX, No. 1. Other special articles in this number are by Abhay Kumar Dubey, Ravi Sundram, Aditya Nigam, Shail Mayaram, Madhulika Banerjee, Ashis Nandy, Nivedita Menon, Supriya Roy Choudhary, Rahul Mukherji and Vivek Kumar.

Singh, Yogendra. (1968). 'Caste and Class: Some Aspects of Continuity and Change', *Sociological Bulletin*, Vol. XVII, No. 2.

—. (1993). *Social Change in India: Crisis and Resilience*, New Delhi: Har Anand Publications.

Sorokin, Pitirim A. (1959). *Social and Cultural Mobility*, New York: The Free Press.

Srinivas, M.N. (1998). *Village, Caste, Gender and Method: Essays in Indian Social Anthropology*, New Delhi: Oxford University Press (Paperback).

Turner, Bryan S. (1986). *Equality*, New York: Tavistock Publications.

Varma, Pawan K. (1998). *The Great Indian Middle Class*, New Delhi: Penguin Books.

Weber, Max. (1948). *From Max Weber: Essays in Sociology*, Translated, Edited and with an Introduction by H.H. Gerth and C. Wright Mills, London: Routledge and Kegan Paul Ltd.

5

Leisure in Indian Tradition

Looking Beyond the West

S.L. SHARMA

The field of leisure studies has long been dominated by the western perspective. This perspective views leisure as typically a western phenomenon and seems to imply that non-western societies have had no tradition of leisure nor any conception of it. The protagonists of this perspective contend, 'Leisure is not a term that can be applied to societies of the archaic period. Nor was leisure, in the modern sense, to be found in the agrarian societies of recorded history' (Dumazedier, 1967: 248). They view the phenomenon of 'modern leisure' as product of industrial civilisation (de Grazia, 1962; Dumazedier, 1967). In the words of Dumazedier, '... leisure has certain traits that are characteristic only of the civilisation born from the industrial revolution' (1967: 298). Textbooks on leisure are also full of similar observations, as is clear from the following statement of Murphy: 'Three out of these (four) texts viewed leisure as stemming primarily from industrial revolution' (1981: IX). A number of other leisure scholars, however, traced the origins of leisure philosophy to the writings of Aristotle in the city-state of Athens in ancient Greece (Goodale and Godbey, 1988; Cross, 1990; Kraus, 1990; Arnold, 1991). In either case, the western scholarship locates the origins of leisure and its philosophy in the West.

Having prevailed for long, the western viewpoint has come under serious interrogation in recent years. Even in earlier literature one comes across certain moderating notes that acknowledge the practice of leisure in some non-western cultures. Huizinga, for instance, in his work published in 1955, makes a passing reference to the evidence of play in non-western cultures of ancient China and India. Similarly, Csikszentmichalyi in 1975 cites evidence of the practice of zen yoga and some other forms of meditation in eastern cultures which the finds akin to the ancient Greek philosophical notion of leisure. In much the same way, in 1975 again, Kaplan perceives a close affinity between the eastern and the Greek human ideals of leisure. Accordingly, he observes, 'The conceptualization of leisure as an end has ... historical roots in both East and West' (Kaplan, 1975: 21). However, such notes have remained largely marginal to the mainstream domineering western view.

More recently, some scholars have advanced systematic evidence of leisure from the non-western societies to further contest the claims of the western perspective. Based on the empirical studies of leisure patterns of some Indian tribes, Bhattacharya (2003) and Singh (2007), among others, have called into question the contention about the origins of leisure in industrial societies and its non existence in pre-industrial societies. Likewise, Raychaudhari and Samdahl (2005) have contested the assumption of the Greek origins of the philosophy of leisure and argued that Aristotle's notion of *Schole* (leisure) itself is influenced by the Indian Vedic vision of leisure. Similarly, citing significant evidence of leisure philosophy in the Taoist thought, Hultsman (1995) states: 'At the least, it appears evident that there are opportunities to expand our dialogues about concepts of leisure by turning to sources other than those traditional western texts we have typically used as foundations for our discussions. Perhaps by considering Taoism and other eastern philosophies, we can, in the future, open new windows through which to view leisure' (p. 98).

Carrying forward the trend of looking beyond the West to expand the frontiers of leisure studies, the present paper provides a case study of the Indian tradition of leisure. The study shows that India has had a tradition of leisure as well as of leisure philosophy, as vigorous and vibrant as the West, and that it is marked by certain cultural distinctions. The paper brings out its implications for moderating the claims of the western perspective. The purpose is not to claim 'me first' for India for the origins of leisure or its concept or its philosophy. Instead, it is to 'expand our dialogues about the concepts of leisure' so as to help develop a more comprehensive and balanced perspective. To this end, the paper is organised into three parts. Part one provides a brief note on the concept of leisure in order to facilitate the account of leisure patterns in India. Part two offers an historical sketch of leisure in India through the ages. Part three brings out the implications of leisure in India to provide for a more nuanced and inclusive understanding of leisure.

Concept of Leisure

A discerning look at the existing leisure literature reveals three conceptions of leisure: (a) as a lifestyle, (b) as free time, and (c) as a state of mind. These have emerged in that order. The first conception dates back to the times of Aristotle in ancient Greece. Aristotle envisaged leisure as an ideal state of being and a lofty goal to be achieved. In his view, leisure connotes a cultivated lifestyle marked by refined qualities of body and mind, free from the drudgery of labour. This conception gains in meaning in the light of the then prevailing background of slavery. In this usage, leisure signifies an attribute of elite class vis-à-vis the labour class.

Another conception of leisure is cast in terms of 'free time'. Having had its traces in ancient Rome, this usage of leisure got formally articulated with the rise of formal organisations in the wake of industrial revolution. The category of time got formally dichotomised between work and off-work time. As a result, the term leisure acquired a formal connotation as 'free time'. While questions have been raised about the fuzzyness of the distinction between work and off-work time as well as about the use patterns of the latter, this conception remains one of the most common kinds.

Recent years have witnessed rise of a new conception of leisure. It is now defined as a state of mind, a disposition signifying 'disinterested' pursuit of leisure. It is a 'disinterested' pursuit in the Aristotelian sense of the term which excludes considerations of economic and social gain. It is essentially a pleasure-seeking pursuit in that it seeks to meet the needs for 'rest, entertainment and self-transcendence', in the words of Dumazedier (1967).

In my view, leisure represents a combine of three elements: free time, favourite delight and a joy-seeking state of mind. Leisure contains an attribute of free time as free time is necessary for it. But it is not just about free time. For, leisure as free time isn't always fun. It may be a boring experience to many. It is, therefore, not what you have but what you make of it. Similarly, leisure also involves an attribute of certain kinds of activities that are usually associated with pleasure-seeking such as relaxation, recreation and amusement. However, it is not just about the kind of activity. For, the same activity may be drudgery for some and pleasure for others, depending upon their bent of mind. Take, for instance, reading a fiction. It may be drudgery if one is doing it for purposes of examination. It may be leisure if one is reading it as a hobby or pastime. It thus refers to one's favourite delight. Above all, leisure signifies a joy-seeking state of mind. In essence, then, leisure is not so much a case of free time as of 'me time'. It is not so much about a particular activity as about an activity that one seeks to do for no other reason except that one enjoys doing it. In the ultimate analysis, leisure is a state of mind seeking pleasure, fun, contentment or bliss just for its own sake.

Leisure in India Through the Ages

India has had a rich tradition of leisure through the ages: ancient, medieval and modern. Authentic evidence of it can be cited from various sources, including the archeological, indological, philosophical, historical, literary, ethnographic and sociological. For example, the archeological excavations of Indus valley civilisation provide significant evidence of it in the precious find of a bronze statue of a dancing girl. Similarly, we also have the big find of the *great bath* in Mohenjo-daro which is believed to be a community centre for relaxation and recreation. Further, the ancient Vedic literature is replete with revealing indological evidence of leisure, both sensuous and contemplative. It also provides evidence of leisure philosophy as much. For the medieval period, the history books are full of accounts of leisure as a lifestyle of royalties and aristocracies. In much the same way, philosophical and literary sources offer ample evidence of contemplative and expressive leisure and its creative manifestations. Likewise, ethnographic studies advance solid evidence of leisure patterns of tribal communities. Above all, sociological studies focus on the leisure patterns of modern urban communities, including the changing profile of leisure in contemporary times.

Ancient Age (3,000 BC – 10th Century AD)

There are numerous hymns and verses in the Vedas, particularly the Rigveda, that provide evidence of the popularity of leisure activities. There are references to the game of *pasa* (dice), hunting excursions, chariot-race, horse-race, music and dance, apart from contemplative leisure. During the early Vedic period dancing was associated with hunting excursions and much as with celebration of joyous and festive occasions. Unlike the Indus valley period when indoor games were more popular, the Vedic period provides evidence of popularity of outdoor games.

More importantly, the Vedic period witnessed rise of what may be called Indian philosophy of leisure. It is enshrined in the Vedic philosophy of *Purusarthas*. *Purusarthas* represent ultimate goals of human life. These are envisaged to be four: *dharma, artha, karma, moksa*. *Dharma* signifies normative order; *artha* stands for wealth; *karma* for desires; and *moksa* for liberation from bondage. According to some commentators, by the Epic period *kama* indeed came to mean pleasure. In postulating *kama* as one of the four principal goals of life, the philosophy of *purusarthas* underscores the prime importance of leisure for human life. It thus provides a theory of philosophical foundations of leisure. The goals of *kama* and *artha* have to be achieved within the framework of *dharma* (the moral order) with the goal of *moksa* as an end-in-view. There has come up a great deal of debate on the point whether relationship amongst the four goals is hierarchical or interactional. But that is not of primary importance for the present purposes. What matters here is the fundamental importance accorded to *kama* as a major goal of life. For, that is what is germane to the idea of leisure.

The philosophy of leisure in ancient India acquired a reflective dimension in the Upanishads which represent discourses on the Vedas. In the *Upanishads*, there developed the concept of *sat-chit-ananda* meaning pure spiritual bliss. The notion of *ananda*, i.e. bliss is central to the Indian vision of leisure. There is a subtle difference between pleasure and bliss. While pleasure refers to sensuous enjoyment, bliss connotes sublime joy that transcends sensuous confines. One of the important means to attain *ananda* is the art of *yoga*. The theory and practice of yoga is propounded by *Patanjali* in his *Yoga Sutra* which appeared in the 2nd century AD. *Yoga* signifies holistic harmony of body, mind and soul for attaining a state of bliss. For all practical purposes, *yoga* is a form of meditative leisure. Patronised by hermits and seers earlier, *yoga* has now become a common man's delight.

Besides patronising meditative leisure, ancient India also provided for celebration of sensuous leisure. This is evident from Vatsyayan's classic text *Kamasutra* – a treatise on the art and aesthetics of love and sex. There is no agreement on the exact date of its composition. However, in the light of the references that it entails scholars consider 4th century AD as a probable time of its appearance. Incidentally there sprang up six other works on the art of sex and love, but Vatsyayan's *Kamasutra* is regarded as the authentic of them all. The book comprises seven parts running into 36 chapters. It begins by commending *kama* as a fundamental human craving and provides an instructive account of the science and art of love making. It tells about the various kinds of women and their psychologies, their manners and morals, the art of seduction, the various facets of sexual union, including kissing, embracing, foreplay, postures, and as many as 64 forms of sexual union.

Kamasutra also provides authentic evidence of the tradition of leisure as lifestyle of the elites. Providing a vivid account of the leisure life of *nagarik* (men of town, elite), it observes: his 'morning is spent in amusements, the afternoon with friends, cock-fighting or teaching parrots to talk, and in the evening there is singing'. In addition to the above leaf from the daily life of an elite, Vatsyayan further commends the following as usual diversions and amusement for him: celebrating festivals, holding musical concerts and keeping company of public women or courtesans. The institution of public women was an important institution of early Hindu society. She used to possess education and intellect superior to that of the women of the household. Such women were especially trained for association with man. All this provide telling evidence of the practice of leisure in the day-to-day life of the elites.

The royalties of the latter part of ancient period, i.e. from the age of Buddha to that of Harsa, patronised the sports of hunting and the game of dice as their favourite delights. Harsa, for example, was known as a fawn-eyed hunter and Candrapida as a veteran hunter. Hunting expeditions used to be organised with all palatial comforts and luxuries. Wild boars, lions, carabao, yolks and deer were the favourite preys of hunting parties. Little wonder that Kautilya commends hunting as one of the royal sports. The game of dice, another royal delight, is as old as *Mahabharat*. Its popularity in the 6th century AD is evident from the classic works of Bana Bhatta – *Kadambari* and *Harsacharita*. Bana Bhatta refers to a town called *Sthaneshwara* which was known as a gambling hub. *Chaturang* (Chess) was another popular game which is believed to have appeared in the 7th century AD.

Like the kings and aristocrats, commoners had their leisure activities too. Wrestling, acrobatic, archery, animal fights, cart-race, horse-race, swimming, water sports and swinging were some of the popular pastimes of the commoners. Drinking, music, magic, fairs, folktales, painting, etc. were some other merriments of the common man. The popularity of painting can be gauged from the fact that Bana Bhatta refers to a city known for its *Citrasalas* (Picture galleries). Pilgrimage was as well an important leisure activity of this period.

Ancient period is also known for the development of artistic and aesthetic leisure. Dwivedi provides a perceptive account of the development of various art forms and their cultural philosophies. Dance, according to him, was the first and the earliest art form that developed in ancient India. Reflecting on the philosophy of dance, he projects it as a case of transcendence of human consciousness and emotions beyond the confines of the body. It symbolises expression of joy or bliss that human body cannot hold. For the same reason, it was spontaneous and effortless in its earlier manifestation. Little wonder that it is a common leisure activity found in abundance among the tribals as well. Like dance, drama (theatrical performance), according to Dwivedi, has also had a long history in India. It attained an advanced stage in the ancient era itself, which is evident from Bharat Muni's famous classic *Natyashastra*. Similarly, music also had an amazing development during this period which is apparent from the lyrical recitation of Vedic verses as well as development of the divine music and its classical forms. According to Dwivedi, even other art forms including painting and sculpture are also indicative of the expressive craving of human consciousness beyond the confines of human body. They are viewed in Vedic literature as a manifestation of self-transcendence.

Medieval Period (11th–17th Century AD)

History books are replete with accounts of leisure life of the royalties of medieval period. It is clear from historical accounts that the royalties of early medieval era were known for their love for activistic leisure, including hunting and adventurous sports like *polo* (a game played with stick and ball riding over horse). Sultan Qutb-ud-din Aibak and Sultan Sikanadar Lodi were known for their love for polo. In fact, so fond of polo was Sultan Qutb-ud-din Aibak that he died of having fallen from horse back while playing polo. Huning and hawking were the other great delights of royalties and aristocracies. A number of sultans, including Shams-ud-din Iltutmish, Razia Sultan, Balbu, Ala-ud-din Khilzi, Mohammad-bin-Tughlaq and Feroz Shah Tughalaq took keen interest in hunting excursions. It may be noted here that Razia was the only female sultan known for her distinction as a great hunter. So important was hunting as a sport that according to Aamir Khusrou, the sultans used to appoint *Amir-i-Shikar* (Tiger of the Hunt or Chief of Hunting portfolio). The position of *Amir-i-Shikar* was so coveted that the emperor would entrust this charge only to his/her close confidant. One of the reasons for the fall of the rule of Razia Sultan (1236–40AD) was her historic folly of appointing a *hubshi* (black African) as *Amir-i-Shikar*. This led to rebellion against her resulting in the overthrow of her rule. A graphic account of hunting excursion is provided by Amir Khusrou in his book *Ijaz-i-Khusrav*. Apart from the royal pomp and show of the hunting party, Khusrou mentions about separate sites of hunting called *Shikaristaan* and *Shikargah*, the former a site for hunting birds and the latter for hunting wild animals. Other outdoor games included archery, horse-race, *dholphari* (rural hockey), *geru* and wrestling contests.

Among the indoor games of royalty, chess occupied the pride of the place. According to Amir Khusrou the game of chess originated in India and was the greatest delight of the Muslim rulers. *Chausser/Chaupa* (ludo) was another popular indoor game of the medieval period. In the palaces of emperor Akbar at Fatehpur Sikri, the *chaupat* board is inbuild into the floor adjacent to the place called *Panchamahel* (five-storyed palace). *Gamarbazi* (game of hazard), *nard, girahbazi* and *kabutarbazi* (pigeon flying) were some of the other favourite games of the royal families.

Another distinctive feature of the leisure life of the Mughal rulers was the maintenance of *harems* (palatial quarters of women and courtesans). Known for their colourful life, several Mughal rulers were polygynous and had the royal privilege of having large number of wives and concubines. Jahangir, for example, had in his *harem* as many as hundred wives, more than 300 concubines and more than 1,000 courtesans. The size of *harem* used to be a measure of the royal status of the ruler: the larger the number of women in *harem* the higher the status. In addition, the Mughals were also fond of places of relaxation, including *hamams* (great baths) and gardens. Babar was the first Mughal ruler who promoted garden culture here. No wonder that all historical monument of the Mughal period are surrounded by gardens.

Yet another feature of the leisure life of the Mughals was their patronage to aesthetic and artistic leisure. They were known for their personal interest in and patronage to music, dance and painting. Akbar, for example, gave patronage to Tansen who was the greatest singer of his times. Akbar himself was a great dancer and he specialised in performing *kathak* – a classical dance form. As for painting, Emperor Jahangir earned distinction as a great painter.

Not a preserve of royalties, common men had their leisure life too. Their leisure activity included indoor games like *ganjeefa* (playing cards) and *chaupar* (ludo); outdoor games like *hawking, wrestling, animal fights* and *kite-flying*; pastimes like *folktales, story-telling* and *puppet shows*; amusements like *festivals and fairs*; entertainment like *gymnastics, acrobatics, juggling,* and *magic shows*; and the performing arts like music and dance including *folk songs* and *folk dances*. Pilgrimage (religious tourism) was yet another occasional leisure time activity of the people in this period.

Modern Era (18th Century AD Onwards)

With the advent of the British rule here, the Indian leisure scenario got exposed to Western games, music and dance. Accordingly, *volleyball, football, hockey, cricket and badminton* made their appearance on Indian playgrounds. Western music and dance also became popular in elite circles. All this notwithstanding, the traditional games, music and dance did not loose their popularity altogether. It is only after the surge of pop culture, thanks to expansion of mass media, that the traditional patterns of leisure have begun to decline. A notable change in the texture of Indian leisure came about with the recent advances in information cum communication technology (ICT). Reporting about some of these changes, a study on the 'India Leisure and Entertainments Trends 2008' cites TV viewing as the most favourite pastime of as many as 75 per cent respondents. Film music is reported as another favourite leisure time activity. Cell phones have emerged as a popular source not only of entertainment but also socialising. Add to them, the new age net-based leisure activities including chatting, gaming, romancing, etc. The study also reveals the popularity of religious activities like visit to temples and engaging in prayer and worship which is evident from 60 per cent respondents reporting to have done so in the past one year. Travel and tourism, physical fitness, reading and shopping are also reported to be catching the fancy of the respondents. Most important of all, the study reveals that respondents indulged in leisure activities not only on weekends but throughout the week and are shelling out more for entertainment (Sachdeva, 2008).

While the above reported trends of leisure provide good account of leisure in the urban setting, they need to be complemented with the leisure patterns obtaining in the countryside. The leisure patterns of rural folks include traditional games such as *kabaddi, kho-kho, gulli danda* and *wrestling contests; folk songs, folk dances, folktales* and *folk theatre, including nautanki* and *Ramleela; visiting friends, socialising, gossiping.*

Participation in *bhajans* and *kirtans* (devotional songs) and pilgrimage. The folk forms of leisure have come under severe strain of the modern means of leisure like TV and films. Nevertheless, they are still popular among the rural folks though with diminishing interest.

The leisure pursuits of high class elites differ significantly from those of the common man. They patronise games like golf and lawn tennis, have their exclusive clubs and prefer foreign and exotic tourism. In fact, some of them own their private islands and yachts as a mark of their superior status. It is all very special for them. In short, their leisure life is marked by three distinctive features: privacy, exclusivity and superiority. These features are the markers of their distinction not only from the commoners but also among themselves. While the leisure life of elites in the past had an element of majestic touch and show off for the public, today's elites privilege privacy in that they favour private space, private luxury (including private planes and yachts) and private entertainment. Earlier, it used to be exclusive in the sense of being out of bounds of the common man, but now it has become exclusive in the sense of making it extraordinary. Earlier, it used to smack of superiority over the leisure patterns of common man, but now it's a case of competing for superiority over the members of their own class.

The character and complexion of leisure in modern India has changed in some significant ways. One, it has undergone a technology-inspired shift whereby it has acquired an electronic character. In technical parlance, therefore, a significant portion of modern leisure is aptly characterised as virtual leisure. Two, tourism has emerged as a significant leisure activity with more people opting for it. Three, leisure has moved from community place to market place, its contours being shaped largely by entertainment industry. Four, a way of life earlier, leisure has now become a mark of emerging lifestyle of the new middle-class.

Implications for Leisure Theory

It is abundantly clear from the above that tradition of leisure in India is as old as 5,000 years and that it has certain culture-specific characteristics. It is premised upon a philosophical foundation in that it envisages *kama* (pleasure pursuit) as one of the fundamental goals of life. Further, it is known more for its meditative and contemplative character than for sensuous and erotic. It has also had a splendid component of aesthetic, expressive and artistic leisure. Its contours have begun to change today from traditional to modern with the rise of pop culture, virtual leisure and new-found love for tourism.

It will be in order at this point to bring out the implications of the Indian tradition for the existing theory of leisure. Since the existing theory is largely based on western experience, it is necessary to outline some of the broad features of the western paradigm. West, for sure, is not a homogenous region, nor it is devoid of internal diversities. Yet, it shares a common core of ideas and activities that set it apart from the rest of the world. The tradition of leisure in the West is fairly old and developed which is evident from the formal discourse about it in the works of Plato and Aristotle. Plato viewed idle society as ideal society as it provides for attainment of highest stage of evolved mind. Like Plato, Aristotle too commends leisure as a resource for the advancement of art, literature and culture. In the same vein, Bertrand Russell highlights the virtues of leisure in his perceptive essay 'In Praise of Idleness'. The discourse is also marked by some critical reflections on leisure. Marx, for example, deplores leisure on account of it being a product of exploitation of slaves and labour class by the leisure class. Similarly, Veblen indicts leisure class for its pompous and wasteful lifestyle.

Along with the tradition of discourse on leisure, West has also had a great tradition of leisure activities. The archaeological excavations in various parts of Europe have recovered grand stadia signifying enormous popularity of games and sports. Similarly, artistic and expressive leisure has as well blossomed a great deal in the West. But the most distinctive feature of leisure in the West has been the tradition of tourism and camping. Grand tour is the historic mark of it. It all happened during 1600–1800 AD when some educated young men of elite background from England, Netherlands, Germany and Scandinavia took to border crossings to explore the world 'out there'. These young men brought back with them pictures of the places, people, cultures and later on of the palaces, monuments, universities, etc. They were fascinated by the splendour of nature, sea beeches and other romantic sites. Eventually these explorations turned into opportunities of discovering their own identity and distinction vis-à-vis the exotic others. That is how tourism in all its diverse forms developed as an outstanding feature of leisure in the West.

The tradition of separation of work and leisure is another distinctive mark of the Western paradigm of leisure. It began with the development of two parallel traditions – *Vita activa* and *Vita contemplativa*. The tradition of *Vita activa* developed in ancient Rome and it accorded priority to work while *Vita contemplativa* developed in ancient Greece and it valued enlightenment. This age-old dichotomy between work and leisure got reinforced into the dichotomy of work time and free time following the rise of formal organisations in the course of industrialisation. In effect, leisure got formally conceptualised as free time and it came to be called modern leisure by Dumazedier.

The above is a highly selective and synoptic view of the Western scenario of leisure. But it does provide a broad idea of the salient features of the Western paradigm about leisure in the West, it is understandable that the leisure theory reflects the Western bias. No quarrel with that. However, there are certain things about the traditions of leisure in other cultures, in the present case Indian culture, from the study of which leisure theory can gain in comprehensiveness. Here are a few such features of the Indian tradition of leisure. One such feature is the theory of *purusarthas,* especially the concept of *kama* (desire for pleasure), that provides for philosophical foundations of leisure. While India has had no tradition of a formal discourse about leisure, it certainly has had a great philosophy of *purusarthas* which is of seminal significance for understanding the prime importance of leisure in human life. Its further elaboration in *kamasutra* and later in other works of literature and arts, including painting and sculpture, is indicative of a splendid tradition of sensuous as well as contemplative leisure. It has had a contemplative dimension in terms of its aesthetic orientation. The notion of aesthetics elevates it to a higher plane. Aesthetics is a graded construct. According to Longinus, it encompasses five vertical stages, i.e. charming, pretty, beautiful, grand and sublime. While the western tradition stays put at the idea of beauty 'as a thing of joy forever', the Indian tradition goes beyond beauty and regards the sublime joy as its highest stage.

The concept of *ananda* (bliss) is another element of the Indian tradition that has crucial importance for enlarging the concept of leisure. Leisure is not just about pleasure as postulated in the western tradition. It is also about *ananda*, a state of bliss, which is a higher order experience. Bliss signifies a state of sublime joy. It differs from pleasure in three significant respects. One, unlike pleasure, which is dichotomous, bliss is non-dichotomous. Pleasure is dichotomous because it is premised upon the dichotomy of subject and object. Subject derives pleasure from the object. Once the object is lost that leads to pain. Therefore, pleasure is dialectically related to pain. Bliss is non-dichotomous in that in it the dichotomy of the subject and object gets dissolved. In other words, the subject attains a higher plane of consciousness where both the subject and the object get merged into each other. Two, pleasure is transitory; it is a fleeting experience. Bliss, on the other hand, is perpetual. Three, pleasure denotes a sensuous experience while bliss signifies sublime joy, an ultimate joy. As such, it calls for rethinking the concept of leisure to incorporate within it the notion of *ananda*. A third feature of the Indian tradition is its practice of meditative leisure. Meditative leisure is about inward journey into the realm of consciousness. *Yoga* is a classic form of it. There have developed various forms of *yoga* but all of them aim at attaining bliss by means of inward voyage through disciplining breathing and achieving concentration, along with some other exercises. Unlike the western tradition of leisure which has grown on tourism as a mode of exploring the outer world, the Indian tradition of leisure has cultivated meditative leisure as an art of exploring the world within.

Fusion of leisure and work into each other is another feature of Indian leisure that warrants rethinking the leisure theory. Its present premise of sharp segregation between leisure and work is an untenable preposition in the light of the Indian experience. This is further reinforced by the emerging trend of fun engineering (provision of recreation) at the workplace by some of the leading formal organisations so as to intersperse work and leisure with each other for their employees. Thus, the dichotomy of the leisure and work seems to be fallacious, as leisure just not a temporal but an experiential phenomenon.

Finally, it is necessary to situate the Indian tradition of leisure in the broad context of Indian culture in order to grasp its full import for the existing theory of leisure. Indian culture is known for its three defining traits: spirituality, transcendence and harmony. Spirituality is about belief in the self and connectivity with oneself as well as with the cosmic self. Transcendence is about looking beyond the existing confines of the body and the mind. Harmony is about interdependence and resolving the dichotomies, the differences and the contradictions. In a word, it is about looking for synthesis. It is these cardinal principles that account for the earlier delineated distinctive features of the Indian tradition of leisure.

From all accounts it is clear that there are some categorical differences between the Indian and the western traditions of leisure. While the western tradition is oriented more towards exploring the universe, the Indian tradition cares more for exploring the self within. Since the existing theory of leisure is based largely on the western experience, it may gain in generalisability by incorporating some of the insights yielded by the present study.

References

Arnold, S. (1991). The Dilemma of Meaning, in T.E. Godbole and P.A. Witt (Eds) *Recreation and Leisure: Issues in an Era of Change (3rd ed.)*, State College, Pa.: Venture, pp. 5–20.

Bhattacharya, Kumkum. (2003). Aspects of Leisure Among Tribes, *Journal of Tribal Studies*, New Delhi, Vol. 1.

Cross, G. (1990). *A Social History of Leisure Since 1600.* State College, Pa.: Venture.

Csikszentmihalyi, M. (1975). *Beyond Boredom and Anxiety.* San Francisco: Jossey-Bass.

De Grazia, S. (1962). *Of Time, Work, and Leisure*, New York: Twentieth Century Fund.

Dumazedier, J. (1967). *Toward a Society of Leisure.* New York: The Free Press.

Dwivedi, Mukund (1981), *Hazari Prasad Dwivedi Granthavali.* New Delhi: Raj Kamal Publication.

Goodale, T. and Godbey, G. (1988). *The Evolution of Leisure.* State College, Pa.: Venture.

Huizinga, J. (1955). *Homo Ludens: A Study of the Play Element in Culture.* Boston: The Beacon Press.

Hultsman, John. (2004). *Playful Pursuits: Games from Asia to the West.* Humanities. July–August.

Kaplan, M. (1975). *Leisure: Theory and Policy.* New York: John Wiley and Sons.

Kraus, R. (1990). *Recreation and Leisure in Modern Society* (4th ed.) Glenview, Il.: Scott Foresman.

Murphy, J. (1981). *Concepts of Leisure* (2 ed.). Englewood Cliffs, N.J.: Prentice-Hall.

Raychaudhuri, Uttiyo and Diane, M. Samdahl. (2005). 'Leisure Embodied: Examining the Meaning of Leisure from Greek and Vedic Perspectives, in Tom Delamere, Carligh Randall, David Rabinson (eds) Abstracts of Papers Presented at XI Canadian Congress on Leisure Research.

Sachdeva, Sujata Dutta. (2008). 'Indians Shelling Out More for Entertainment'. *The Times of India.* May 1, Chandigarh.

Singh, Sagar. (2007). Conceptualising Leisure, Recreation and Tourism from an Anthropological Perspective. *Tourism Recreation Research.* 32.

6

Some Reflections on Technology and Values Nowadays

LECH W. ZACHER

Such categories as technology and values are understood and interpreted in the social thought in many different ways and depend on a multiplicity of factors and conditions (be it philosophical, religious, political, etc.). The history of social science and social practices shows the growing complexity of these categories and their ongoing evolution. So there is a need for the pertinent novel approaches considering these tendencies. Contemporary understanding of technology and values must overcome historical and academic disputes, especially if we want to appreciate the real processes and phenomena in which technology is rooted. In addition to scientific and public debates concerning both categories, in social practice the real problems of innovations, their creation and application, diffusion, costs (not only financial, but also environmental and cultural, for example), their effectiveness, risk evaluation and negative side effects, and a shaping of the future because of the present choices, decisions and actions also exist.

Technology is a vital domain of human and social practice that has accompanied people since the prehistoric times in our imagination, behaviour, consumption patterns, culture, and lifestyles. Enormous performativity of technology disclosed its power mostly in the leading countries. Its breakthrough meaning became visible on a large scale in the form of the Great Industrial Revolution (18th–19th century) and the subsequent still-ongoing industrialisation in many regions. Revolutions in science and technology (investigated by Kuhn) and the 20th-century scientific and technological revolution (announced by Bernal) make us inclined to new evaluations of the role and impact of technology (its extreme form was technological determinism enhanced by such a concept as technological fix, technological imperative, technological optimism, technological future, technological man, etc.) and to a new systems approach to technology together with a systems approach to society (also in a global scale). The latter is responsible for more and more wide use of such a term as a socio-technical system, which indicates increasing linkages and feedbacks between technology and society.

The vital role of technology, especially in modernity, is also documented by such terms as technological civilisation, technological man (homo technicus in philosophical discourse), global technological capitalism (coined by G. Soros), among others. Similar etiquettes, also technologically-originated, are ascribed to societies (advanced above all), for example: technological society, cyber-society, information society, network society, digital society, virtual society, bio-info-society, etc. Of course, in the real world there are societies are characterised by the prefix pre (e.g. pre-informational) or by such terms as dualistic, hybrid or multitrajectorial development. However, ideal types are being implemented in the technologically leading countries, which impose the type of narrative in academia, media and politics.

The growing 'density' of technical artefacts, objects, methods and procedures, concrete effects, risks and detrimental impacts and their enormous diversity in time and space induce us not to discuss technology in the abstract (technology signed with capital letter T), but to investigate and evaluate its practical forms, applications and specificities. Generalisations concerning technology, its role and meaning are in practice not very conclusive. People are impacted by specific and real technologies, by their usages, notoriously ambivalent results and consequences. It is difficult to sum them up in order to state something about technology in general. Beyond it, its scale and effects of applications increase greatly, its systemic complexity grows, it penetrates and co-shapes practically all spheres of life of the individual, groups, societies, mankind and future generations, as well.

It is difficult to steer technology, though there are efforts to influence it by policies, law, finances, religious bans and the like. In a broad understanding, technology consists of technical objects (various technical artefacts such as factories, bridges, buildings, cars, airplanes, missiles, computers, tomographs, cell phones, etc.), operational ways and regulations of their use (i.e. recipes, programs, instructions), technical research (or scientific/technological investigations, presently increasingly practical and called techno-science), technical models, prototypes, also technical thinking, technological culture (i.e. technological consciousness and skills), technological knowledge and technological rationality, as well as organisations and institutions connected with technology development, promotion of innovations, technical regulations (as norms, standards, bans, sanctions, etc.). Such a deconstructed sphere of technology creates the real possibilities of an influence on its shape, structure, internal linkages, costs, effects, and evaluations. So it is possible to evaluate technologies and their effects from the point of view of the sets of certain criteria (be it moral, psychological, social, political, economic, environmental, international, global, long term, etc.). Such an approach was invented in the 1960s in the United States and was called technology assessment (later generalised as impact assessment). Impact assessment has become not only an expanding practice (in governments, parliaments and businesses) but also a platform for the discourse on values which are generated, supported, modified and changed by technology.

Publications devoted to the aforementioned themes often refer to the classic approaches, and to the philosophy of technology, to sociology, to civilisational and cultural studies and reflections (one can recall many important, already classic names such as, i.e. Heidegger, Gehlen, Mumford, Jonas, Ellul, Marcuse, Schumacher, Postman, Hareway). Revolutionary changes in technology in the last decades have promoted inventors and visionaries, technologists, innovators, entrepreneurs, often connected with ICT, robotics, computer science, bio- and nano-technology (e.g. Dertouzos, Negroponte, Jobs, Lanier, Gates, Assange, Zuckerberg, Kurzweil, Rheingold, Venter). Such people, often treated as *gurus*, have created not only new technologies, but also visions of the future, new futuristic ideologies, and axiology. They create the future by their creative activity and messages in mass media. However, anything that is novel or new, different, breaking tradition, creating challenges and generating risks brings about controversies and occasionally violent resistance. There are many historical cases of this phenomenon, such as in the medieval times drowning innovators in a well, destructing factory machines (Luddite movement during industrial revolution in England at the turn of 18th and 19th centuries; the counter-culture and hippie movements in the 1960s in the US and Western Europe, the spectacular actions of the 'Unabomber,' Theodore Kaczynski (justified in his Manifesto); recent manifestations and protests of internauts and hackers (Anonymous group, Anti-ACTA, Occupy Wall Street, Wikileaks and Assange message, the Snowden case, 'green' movements (also international, e.g. Greenpeace). All these examples were directly or indirectly connected with technology and its negative consequences, risks and dangers. Their moral and political grounds varied substantially from protests against invigilation and the 'surveillance society,' against present post-political manipulations, against environmental devastation by industry and business as a whole, to being against growing world inequality also in access to modern cutting-edge technologies (digital divide is an example), against replacing man with machines, technocratic governance (so called netocracy), and technocratic management (neglecting democracy and citizens' participation in decision-making).

The philosophy of technology or, rather, the ideology of technology exerts significant influence on our Weltanschauung (worldview – to recall the term used often by K. Mannheim) because of the acceptance of superiority of so-called technological imperative (what is possible in technology should be done) and technological determinism (in a strong or weak form – reducing factors of social and cultural development to technology), not to mention technological optimism or triumphalism assuming that technological fix will solve all human problems. Thus, technological values, technological rationality and technocracy constitute a one-dimensional vision of the future. However, one must admit that many factors and phenomena form theoretical and material grounds for such views. For example, the progressing process of de-naturalisation (or in other words – artificialisation) of human surroundings and humans themselves due to use of various implants, prostheses, heart pacemakers, to expose to advanced medical technologies due to living in smart buildings and working in an automatic office, to make use of artificial intelligence (AI) and navigating in cyberspace. Moreover, technologisation of human life and even human culture has evolved quickly (Postman called the dominance of technology over culture – a technopoly). Additionally, we face the globalisation of technology and its multiple, detrimental as well, effects. So such terms were coined as McWorld (by Barber) and

McDonaldization of society (by Ritzer), for example. All this would not be possible without technology and its massive production and use (predominantly in the advanced countries) including military, industry, transportation, ICT, etc. Needless to prove that de-traditionalisation of values and 'clashes of civilizations' (Huntington's term) are endowed with a powerful material (technological) tools. Thanks to technology, the Orwellisation of the world becomes more and more possible and real.

In spite of all the risks, negative side effects and other dangers, technophobia does not surpass technophilia with its optimistic hopes. People's expectations revolve around the promising technological advances in healthcare, biomedicine, regenerative medicine, pharmacology and the resulting treatment of formerly incurable diseases, not to mention the possibility of prolonging human life. Such advances already have led to a trans-humanism era, in which these technological processes such as artificialisation, machinisation of man, automation, computerisation, and AI, progressing cyborgisation radically change the man-technology relation in favour of technology. These are not just visions of a far reaching future, but the already visible signs of accelerating dynamics of technological progress, its massive applications, and their profound consequences. Needless to say, new technologies, products and applications appear frequently. To mention a few: cloud computing, Big Data, 3D printers, Google glasses, wearable ICTs. Moreover, new demands are generated by the mostly advanced and well-off and ageing societies. The growing number of old people, many disabled, often lonely, creates a demand for various devices facilitating living (e.g. caring or assistive robots, which have progressed significantly in Japan). Social robots (or socially interactive robots) are the next generation robotic technology to arouse safety and ethics issues. There are also intensive research and experiments with autonomous (driverless) cars and smart management of house, for example. So technology's role, meaning and value are perceived and treated in terms of utility and its strongly commercial value (of course with not the same access). At any rate such a commercial utilitarianism broadens moral limits of technology development and applications (e.g. in genetic engineering, GMOs, surveillance technologies). These limits are not only extended but also violated in the present 'risk society' (to recall Beck's term).

Visionaries, such as the futurist and inventor R. Kurzweil, have forecasted that man will reach and overcome biological limits – not really distant in time. Such situation will result de facto in a systemic feedback of man and machine. Moreover, in many respects, machines will be more effective in such activities as data processing, storage capacity and the speed of work. So, will man integrate with machine and what will be the proportion of the biological to the artificial? Such integration also will include man's surroundings which already is an intelligent ambiance. The question is whether a new specie – machinekind will replace humankind? If so, what will happen with man, to human values, and to morality? The answer is not known. However, such a vision – in the face of ongoing trends and determinisms – should not be neglected. Hopes of traditionalists that the world and man (and man's nature) will remain generally the same are rather wishful thinking.

However, in a shorter time horizon, before the Singularity point (described by Kurzweil), there are other expectations such as technology socialisation, humanisation and democratisation. These are great practical and moral challenges. These expectations require humans to be proactive on all levels – the individual, local, national, international, global. Moreover, it is not yet clear whether these activities – even if they are persistent, coordinated, massive and on time – can outweigh risky megatrends of technology and its impacts on man, society, economy, environment, politics, culture, etc.

Technology studies and future studies are closely linked because technological breakthroughs produce their effects with sometime lag; moreover some impacts are really long term. This problematique is a subject of increasingly intensive research called STS – Science, Technology, Society Studies. Scientists of various disciplines constitute 'epistemic communities,' analysing and debating new techno-social challenges (i.e. in such journal as 'Science, Technology and Human Values'). It seems doubtful, however, that the activity of this community will be able to stop or to delay fatalistic prophesies of mankind's dehumanisation. At any rate intensive intellectual efforts have taken place in recent decades to ameliorate our understanding of technology and its multifaceted effects and impacts. They have also practical dimension in a form of technological innovations and their applications. New concepts and ideas are put into practice and new practices promoted, including non-technological activities such as citizens' deliberations and participation in technological decision-making. Another important trend is connected with searching for new patterns and paradigms of development. In recent decades, the idea of sustainable development was crucially strengthened not only in theory, but also in countries, strategies and policies, not to mention international organisations and institutions (e.g. the European Union, and the United Nations promoting the new program called Sustainable Development Goals following the former Millennium Goals). Moreover, this idea has developed from environmental protection issues and eco-development to an overall multisectorial and comprehensive concept of a paradigm change. Nowadays, this concept comprises not only advances, problems, relations, and impacts of technology (and of technologies) but also production, industry, transportation, urbanisation (megacities in particular), agriculture, quality of life, healthcare, social well-being, consumption models, care for the future generations, also biodiversity, climate change, ecologisation of local communities, renewable energy applications and so on. Hence, many new ideas and terms have appeared including eco-technologies, eco-efficiency, environmental human rights, sustainable consumption, and environmental citizenship. They concern not only ecological values but also civil, political, global, and human ones. They illustrate and at the same time reflect the new research interests and professional and public debates. Moreover, the practical implementation of these ideas has materialised to the form of governmental and business strategies and policies, and various innovations. These ideas and connected with them practical activities have begun to function on a local community and household level, such as citizens exploitation of renewable energy sources – solar, water, wind, biomass. A new business model and a model of life (behaviour, attitudes, values, consumption patterns, customs, etc.) if supported by governments and international organisations can greatly ameliorate societal welfare worldwide. Needless to say, a multidimensional aid is required in case of less advanced and poorer countries in a form of global programme of sharing and co-operation. New cutting-edge technologies such as ICTs, bio- and nano-technologies, robotics, automation, AI seem to be difficult because of their novelty and competition to fulfil postulates of sustainability in all dimension. Their future is still open-ended.

In the discourse concerning the relationship of technology and values, it is rather not easy to evaluate whether and to what extent technology (and particular technologies) change and generates values or reflect them in artefacts. Values and value systems are constitutive elements of any culture. Referencing them indicates what is good and what is bad, what is desirable and what undesirable. However, in practice, the situation is not so simple because there is a great diversity of cultures (e.g. European, American, Asian), they do not integrate, they evaluate, they clash (multicultural politics in Europe, for example, has failed). So probably the old idea of a federation of cultures (A. Mazrui) would be more appropriate. Therefore, the global task sometimes formulated within the international community to make culture universal and common seems not feasible. There are many obstacles in making values objective and universalised in the epoch of 'liquid modernity' (Z. Bauman's term). These include uncontrolled market mechanisms, significantly autonomous technology, cultural diversity in the world (and within societies), growing chaotics and uncertainty of socio-technical systems (substituting traditional forms of societies), hybridity of the real and virtual world, and the structural ambivalence of technological effects and human activities, along with people's conflicting ideals, norms, principles, goals, needs and expectations.

Thus, it is difficult to identify honestly what and whose values serve technology in general – businesses, the military, human? Who should evaluate and judge – investors, sponsors, government agencies, the military, citizens (and what about the interest of yet unborn, the future generations?)? Which values (and their distribution) are the most crucial for certain groups of people *hic et nunc*? Who is interested in their change and why? Answers are very difficult to determine and are notoriously biased. Moralistic discourse does not help much in solving such dilemmas that exist in practice and are incessantly challenges of our technological civilisation. Pragmatised values gain different meanings than traditionally ascribed. This refers to interpretations of such traditionally perceived values as liberty, equality, human dignity, democracy and global order (stability). In Asia, Africa or even on the Internet, these values are understood differently than they were and are in Europe. Of course, changes, modifications, reconfigurations, interactions, linkages, etc. of values are not the only result of technology. They are effects of multiple mechanisms of the 'social fabric' and increasingly of socio-technical systems. Evaluation of the applications and the multidimensional effects of technology indicates a significant ambivalence in understanding and performance in such fields as security, quality of life, sound environment, human rights, economic development, political stability, social justice, basic human needs (especially in poor societies or in case of exclusion), treatment of animals (called by P. Singer 'non-person subjects' deserving respect and care).

Technology should not be demonised. Technology, because of its powerful performativity, can devastate anything, not intentionally but by its side effects, unexpected technical catastrophes, excessive risks (in medicine, pharmacology, genetic engineering), destroy the environment (due to its extensive existence everywhere), also can contribute to technological unemployment, to McDonaldisation of societies, to support military conflicts, and facilitate crime (formerly connected mostly with guns, today also with computers).

Morality should not be expected from technology per se, but rather from people who choose, make decisions, and behave. The present state of morality does not seem very optimistic and hopeful in a face of declining human values, the relativisation of social norms, the erosion of moral consensus, fragmentation of moral convictions, etc. We do not know whether this state is a transitory turbulence or an effect of clashes of cultures rapidly being transformed by technology and the market. Or will it lead to a kind of a 'new stability' – more humanitarian, rational, enlightened and at the same time human? Perhaps such a situation will be a permanent dimension of the present and future conditio humana? Anyway, domination of machine over man does not augur well. That is why a constitution of a kind humanistically profiled stability becomes probably the most important and the most difficult challenge of our epoch.

References

Adas, M. (1989). *Machines as the Measure of Men: Science, Technology, and Ideologies of Western Dominance*. Ithaca, NY: Cornell University Press.

Aronovitz, S. et al. (ed.). (1996). *Technoscience and Cyberculture*. New York: Routledge.

Barber, B.R. (1995). *Jihad vs. McWorld*. New York: Times Books.

Batteau, A.W. (2010). *Technology and Culture*. Long Grove, Illinois: Waveland Press.

Bauman, Z. (2000). *Liquid Modernity*. Cambridge, UK: Polity Press. Cambridge Berger P., Huntington S.P.: Many Globalizations – Cultural Diversity in the Contemporary World. New York: Oxford University Press.

Berger, P., Huntington S.P. (2002), *Many Globalizations: Cultural Diversity in the Contemporary World*. New York: Oxford University Press.

Bernal, J.D. (1939), *The Social Function of Science*. London: Macmillan.

Breton, Ph. (2011), *The Culture of the Internet and the Internet as Cult: Social Fears and Religious Fantasies*. Duluth, Minn.: Litwin Books.

Dinello, D. (2005), *Technophobia! Science Fiction Visions of Posthuman Technology*. Austin, Tex.: University of Texas Press.

Featherstone, M. (2000): Technologies of Post-human Development and the Potential for Global Citizenship, in J.N. Pieterse (ed.) (2000*) Global Futures: Shaping Globalization*. London and New York: Zed Books.

Fuller, S. (2011), *Humanity 2.0: What It Means to Be Human Past, Present and Future*. London: Palgrave Macmillan.

Hanks, C. (ed.) (2010), *Technology and Values: Essential Readings*. Blackwell: Wiley, Mass.: Malden.

Harbers, H. (ed.) (2005). *Inside the Politics of Technology: Agency and Normativity in the Co-Production of Technology and Society*. Amsterdam: Amsterdam University Press.

Hughes, T.P. (2004). *Human-Built World: How to Think about Technology and Culture*. Chicago, Ill.: Chicago University Press.

Huntington, S.P. (1996). *The Clash of Civilizations and the Remaking of World Order*. New York: Simon and Schuster.

Johnson, D.G. and Wetmore J.M. (ed.) (2009). *Technology and Society: Building Our Sociotechnical Future*. Cambridge Mass.: The MIT Press.

Kurzweil, R. (2005). *The Singularity Is Near*. New York: Viking.

Maines, R.P. (2009). *Hedonizing Technologies: Path to Pleasures in Hobbies and Leisure*. Baltimore: John Hopkins University Press.

Mazrui, A.A. (1976). *A World Federation of Cultures: An African Perspective*. New York: The Free Press.

Miller, V.A. (2011), *Understanding Digital Culture*. London: Sage.

Morgan, K. et al. (ed.) (2004). Human Perspectives in the Internet Society: *Culture, Psychology and Gender*, Vol. 4, Wessex, England.

Nye, D.E. (2006). *Technology Matters: Questions to Live With*. Cambridge, Mass.: The MIT Press.

Oudshoorn, N. and Pinch T.J. (ed.) (2005), *How Users Matter: The Co-Construction of Users and Technology*. Cambridge, Mass.: The MIT Press.

Postman, N. (1992). *Technopoly*. New York: Vintage.

Rheingold, H. (2002). *Smart Mobs: The Next Social Revolution: Transforming Culture and Communities in the Age of Instant Access*. Cambridge, Mass.: Basic Books.

Ritzer, G. (2000). *The McDonaldization of Society*. New York: Sage.

Rycroft, R.W. and Kaph D.E. (1999). *The Complexity Challenge: Technological Innovation for the 21st Century*. London: Pinter.

Schroeder, R. (2007). *Rethinking Science, Technology, and Social Change*. Stanford, Calif.: Stanford University Press.

Schumacher, E.F. (1973). *Small Is Beautiful: A Study of Economics as if People Mattered*. New York: Harper and Row.

Seidensticker, B. (2006). *Future Hype: The Myths of Technology Change*. San Francisco: Bernett-Koehler Publishers.

Singer, P. (1975). *Animal Liberation*. New York: Harper Collins.

Smith, M.R. and Marx L. (1994). *Does Technology Drive History? The Dilemma of Technological Determinism*. Cambridge, Mass.: The MIT Press.

Stivers, R. (2004). *Shades of Loneliness: Pathologies of a Technological Society*. Lanham, Md.: Rowman and Littlefield.

Taylor, P.A. and Harris J.L. (2005). *Digital Matters: Theory and Culture of the Matrix*. London: Routledge.

Vanderburg, W.H. (2005). *Living in the Labyrinth of Technology*. Toronto: University of Toronto Press.

Wajcman, J. (2004). *Technofeminism*. London: Polity/Blackwell.

Zacher, L.W. (2007). E-Transformations of Societies, in A.V. Anttiroiko (ed.) (2007), Electronic Government: Concepts, Methodologies, Tools and Applications, *Information Science Reference* (IGI Global), Vol. 6, Chapt. 8.5, New York: Hershey.

Zacher, L.W. (2008). Some Repetitive Reflections on Visioning the Future, in S. Sharma, P.K. Sharma (eds.) *Transformative Pathways: Attainable Utopias*. Jaipur: Prateekasha Publications.

Zacher, L.W. (2009). Information Society Discourse, in: *Encyclopedia of Information Science and Technology*, Hershey, Pa: IGI Global.

Zacher, L.W. (2012). Society, Market and Technology Nexus as Contexts of ICT Policies and Applications: Some Issues and Reflexions, *International Journal of Information: Communication Technologies and Human Development*, July–September, Vol. 4, No. 3.

Zacher, L.W. (2012). Technological vs. Political Modernization: Interactions and Feedbacks, in I. Modi (ed.) *Modernization, Globalization and Social Transformation*, Jaipur: Rawat Publications.

Zacher, L.W. (2012). Toward Democratization of Science and Technology Spheres: Some Opportunities and Problems, in A. Bammé et al. (ed.) *Yearbook 2011 of the IAS-STS*. München-Wien: Profil.

Zacher, L.W. (2013), Human and Societal Potentials for Transcending the Crisis of Civilization, in A. Targowski, M.J. Celiñski (ed.) (2013) *Spirituality and Civilization Sustainability in the 21st Century*. New York: Nova Science Publishers.

7

Leisure, Happiness and Development

A Global Perspective

FRANCIS LOBO

This paper deals with the relationship of leisure and happiness to development. It does so in stages from happiness in societies to individuals. Our world is illustrated as having different shades of happiness among nations. A key variable of income and its relationship to well-being is reviewed generating a hypothesis to the income-happiness relationship. The paper then focuses on levels of happiness in China. Later the discourse shifts to an individual level. Happiness is viewed from an artist's perspective and compared to leisure. Finally, dimensions of feeling and experiences are highlighted in order to improve the quality of life of individuals.

Happiness and Leisure

Happiness has been defined as feeling good, enjoying life and wanting the feeling to be maintained (Layard, 2005). In this paper, the term happiness has been used interchangeably with subjective well-being and enhanced quality of life. A good feeling which psychologists call positive affect may be experienced at different times of the day. It may fluctuate from moment to moment and so may be short term. When individuals are in good health, reasonably prosperous and content they are generally happy over a long-term. The Veenhoven Database measures happiness among nations periodically over several years. These are measures of long-term happiness. Happiness may be experienced in different realms of life – at work, with the family or during free time.

Leisure has three dimensions – time, activity and experience (Jackson, 2006). It is generally defined as activity pursued usually in free time from which one derives pleasure and enjoyment. Stebbins (2011) states that leisure is not happiness. It plays a pivoting role in generating short-term happiness through casual leisure (Stebbins, 1997) and long-term well-being through serious leisure (Stebbins, 1992).

Relationship of Income to Happiness

Research into the relationship of income to happiness has suggested that: wealthier countries are happier than poorer ones; economic development is conducive to rising happiness; happiness in nations remains constant and stable over time; as countries become richer, relative gains and losses neutralise each other; biological factors are closely linked with a sense of well-being; aggregate happiness is shaped by social comparison theory and social and cultural factors affect happiness. Each of the foregoing statements is discussed in the following paragraphs.

Wealthier countries are happier than poorer ones. Adrian White (2007) produced *The World Map of Happiness* with colour coding of nations on a continuum from 'most happy' to 'least happy'. Five colours were used with dark blue indicating 'most happy', followed by light blue, pale green, orange, and red. The colour red indicated countries that were 'least happy'. Colour-coded data were interpreted as wealthier countries being happier than poorer ones. Data from national surveys from 1981 to 2007 show that happiness rose in 45 of the 52 countries for which substantial time-series data was available (Inglehart et al., 2008). Further analyses suggested that since 1981, economic development, democratisation, and rising social tolerance had increased to an extent that people sensed that they had free choice, that could lead to higher levels of happiness (Inglehart et al., 2008).

Inglehart (1990) suggested that economic development is conducive to rising happiness. Analysing data from 24 countries over a range of economic levels, he found a favourable correlation (0.67) between Gross National Product (GNP) and life satisfaction. Statistics from the United States showed that richer people tend to be happier than poorer ones. According to Firebaugh and Tach (in press), evidence from the General Social Survey (GSS) in 2006 that depicted the association between happiness and family income found that richest people ($150,000 or above) were 13 times more likely to report being 'very happy'. In distinct contrast, those at the lowest end, families in the poorest category ($20,000 or below), were most likely to be 'not too happy'. Happiness rose monotonically, between the two extremes, with increases of income.

Happiness in nations remains constant and stable over time. Scientists of many persuasions have examined human happiness over a long period of time. One claim has found general acceptance: Happiness remains constant. Research by several investigators (Brickman and Campbell, 1981; Diener et al., 1999; Kahneman et al., 2004) has revealed that rising prosperity on the one hand and severe misfortune on the other hand do not permanently affect happiness. After a period of adjustment, nations return to their baseline levels of well-being. For more than three decades contemporary Japan has experienced mean happiness levels from 'happy' to 'very happy'. Economically, the Gross National Product (GNP) was third on the planet. After the March 2011 earthquake and tsunami, the high happiness levels would be expected to dip. But if the theory that happiness remains constant stays true, then Japan should revert to customary levels of happiness once economic stability is restored.

Since records on national happiness have been kept for many decades in the United States, they provide stable longitudinal data. Firebaugh and Tach (in press) report that Americans are much richer now than they were in 1972. Despite these increases in wealth, the reported happiness has remained constant and even declined slightly over the past three decades. The question arises: Why does happiness remain constant despite increases of income? The answer is that individuals and humanity ride on a 'hedonic treadmill'.

The 'hedonic treadmill' is seen as a barrier to raising a level of happiness (Seligman, 2002). It causes one to rapidly and inevitably adapt to good things by taking them for granted. As individuals accumulate more material possessions and accomplishments, their expectations rise. The deeds and things that individuals worked so hard for, no longer make them happy. They need something better to boost levels of happiness in upper reaches of a set range. Then once one gets to the next possession or achievement, one adapts to it as well, and the adaptation goes on and on. Hence the term 'hedonic treadmill'.

As countries become richer, relative gains and losses neutralise each other. Authors such as Easterlin (1974) and Kenny (2004) have stated that rising prosperity in countries has not resulted in overall increases in happiness of the citizens. Layard (2005) provided evidence that in the United States and Britain people were no happier, although living standards had more than doubled – the same held true for Japan. Forty-five per cent of Americans were very happy compared to 33 per cent in the poorest quarter. These figures had barely changed over three decades. Incomes of the richest people had more than doubled but they were no happier. The poor had also become richer but were no happier. A similar story was true of Britain (Layard, 2005). This led the author to conclude that as whole societies in the West became richer, they did not become happier.

Studies (Ebstein et al., 1996; Hamer, 1996) suggest that biological factors are closely linked with a sense of well-being. Investigations of twins reveal that happiness is heritable to a significant extent (Lykken and Tellegen, 1996; Lyumbomirsky et al., 2005). Findings reported by Layard (2005) on identical and non-identical twins have shown higher proportions of problems with identical than non-identical twins. Ninety-one per cent of identical twins (IT) were more likely to be juvenile delinquents than 73 per cent of non-identical twins (NT). For other human problems the proportions were as follows: criminal conviction (adults) (IT – 52%, NT – 23%); alcoholism (men) (IT – 41%, NT – 22%); manic-depression (IT – 65%, NT – 14%); and schizophrenia (IT – 48%, NT – 17%).

A widely accepted view is that happiness fluctuates around fixed set points (Headey and Wearing, 1989; Larsen, 2000; Williams and Thompson, 1993). Seligman (2002) explained that some people have a lot of positive affect and it stays with them over a lifetime. High positive-affect people *feel* great over a lot of times. Good things in abundance bring about pleasure and joy. There are, however, many people who have low-positive affect. They do not feel great or good most of the times and when success comes their way they do not jump with joy. Accordingly, Seligman suggested that our emotional life is chartered between set points and if the course does not run through times of good feeling there is not much one can do.

Aggregate happiness is shaped by social comparison theory. Layard (2005) linked income to happiness and said it was influenced by the social comparison theory. He maintained that people use their income compared to those of others to measure how they are valued (by others). Relative income is also used to measure how we value ourselves when people compare their income with that of their colleagues or compare the way they live in relation to others, personal satisfaction is affected. People caught up in such relationships with others seem to care about relative rather than absolute income. Layard (2005) concluded 'they want to compete with the Joneses or if possible outdo them' (p. 45).

Graham (2009) found that average, wealthier nations (as a group) are happier than poorer countries (as a group). Yet even among less happy, poorer countries there was a clear relationship between average income and average happiness levels suggesting that many other factors, including cultural traits, are at work. Latin American countries show high levels of life satisfaction although per capita incomes are a lot less than in Western developed economies.

The Firebaugh and Tach (in press) study on Americans confirmed that income of age peers mattered. For given age levels, peers who enjoyed higher incomes tended to be happier than poorer peers. They concluded that richer peers tended to reduce the happiness of their less income-endowed peers. Besides income, Firebaugh and Tach also found that health, marital status and race influenced relative happiness. The predicted probability of being very happy was also reduced when one's peers are richer. Research on the income-happiness relationship has led to the development of a hypothesis.

The Income-Happiness Hypothesis

In 1997, Inglehart hypothesised that economic development brought society-level shifts from maximising economic growth to subjective well-being. He maintained that the transition from a society of scarcity to one of security brought dramatic increases in subjective well-being. But there was a threshold at which economic growth no longer seemed to increase happiness significantly. Starvation was no longer a threat and survival was taken for granted. Inglehart (1997) illustrated how this worked by plotting a curve along two dimensions. The vertical dimension increased from low to high on a survival and well-being continuum. The horizontal dimension ranged from low to high on a GNP/per capita continuum. The hypothesis, therefore, illustrated that as economic gains increased, lifestyles were proportionally enhanced. How does the income-happiness relationship hypothesis apply to occupations?

The Effect of Occupation on General Happiness

In the foregoing paragraphs, income size has been used to indicate the extent of happiness people experience. But drawing on data from the General Social Surveys (GSS), 1972–2006 (Davis et al., 2007), it was found that job satisfaction and general happiness were affected by engagement in occupations. Referring to the latter, general happiness was assessed on a Likert scale – very happy, pretty happy or not too happy. Mean scores ran from 1 for someone who was not too happy to 3 for someone who was very happy (Bryner, 2007).

Bryner (2007) reported that most of the occupations ranking high in general happiness were professions involving helping others, technical and scientific expertise or creativity. The 12 occupations that scored high on the happiness scale – mean scores and percentages of being very happy were: clergy (2.61m, 67.2%); fire-fighters (2.57m, 57.2%); transportation, ticket and reservation agents (2.55m, 56.5%); architects (2.52m, 56.5%); special education teachers (2.51m, 52.6%); actors and directors (2.49m, 51.0%); science technicians (2.47m, 51.0%); mechanics and repairers (2.47m, 53.6%); industrial engineers (2.47m, 48.4%); airline pilots and navigators (2.45m, 49.1%); hardware/building supplies salesperson (2.45m, 55.9%); and housekeepers and butlers (2.45m, 57.7%).

The occupations with the least happy people were unskilled and service positions (Bryner, 2007). At the low end were: garage and service station attendants (1.78m, 13.2%); roofers (1.88m, 14.2%), moulding and casting operators (1.92m, 11.1%), construction labourers (1.94m, 18.8%), construction trades (1.97m, 22.1%), welfare service aides (1.98m, 18.4%), amusement and recreation attendants (1.98m, 15.7), maids and housemen (1.99m, 22.8%), pressing machine operators (1.99m, 23.5%), electronic repairers (2.00m, 15.7%), kitchen workers, food preparation (2.00m, 20.8%), machine operators (2.02m, 17.3%).

It was noted that some very high prestige jobs did not finish at the top. Physicians who are high on occupational prestige scored well above average in general happiness (2.39m, 43.9%) but were not in the top 12 occupations. Similarly, lawyers high on occupational prestige were out of the top 12 with scores of 2.39 on the mean and 43 per cent being very happy (Bryner, 2007). Quoting Tom Smith, the Director of the General Social Service, as to why work affects contentment levels the following is said:

> Work occupies a large part of each worker's day, is one's main source of social standing, helps to define who a person is, and affects one's health both physically and mentally. Because of work's central role in many people's lives, satisfaction with one's job is an important component in overall wellbeing. (p. 1)

The spillover of mood from work to other realms of life such as family and leisure must also be of interest to researchers and would create a meaningful area of research for budding scholars. If income is not seen as a major variable affecting happiness, one may well ask what other variables affect happiness and how they relate to individuals.

Labelled as the 'Big Seven' factors, Layard (2005) named the following as affecting happiness: family relationship; financial situation; work; community and friends; health; personal freedom; and personal values. The US General Social Surveys listed the first five factors in order of importance. According to Helliwell (2006), well-being and life satisfaction were supported by a framework of influences that included four key factors. First, the wellsprings of happiness flowed from trustworthy relations with family, friends, neighbours, colleagues and communities in which people live. Second, although high incomes and consumption had significant positive effects on life satisfaction in relative terms (comparing with neighbours), it diminished as countries and individuals got richer. Third, incomes and consumption had negative spillovers on others, while all important family and community involvements tended to have positive spillovers for others. Fourth, people systematically overestimated the life satisfaction they would get from material aspects of their lives and underestimated the value of investments in human aspects. International indices of income and happiness have recorded Chinese happiness over two decades. The results show that happiness does not increase with higher Gross National Income.

The Relationship Between Income and Happiness in China

China's population is over 1.3 billion. It is the largest of any country in the world. Those under the age of 14 comprise 17.6 per cent of the population. Between the ages of 15 and 64, the numbers comprise 73.6 per cent. Just under 9 per cent (8.9%) are between the ages of 65 years and over. Because of the one-child policy, the proportion of young people is small. In 2010, 47 per cent of the total population resided in urban areas. The estimated male/female sex ratio was 1.06 male/female (Indexmundi, 2011).

The National People's Congress (NPC) of China that had completed its annual session in early 2011, recognised that increasing happiness was more important than increasing Gross Domestic Product (GNP) (*The Economist,* 2011). The Himalayan Kingdom of Bhutan pioneered the idea of 'gross national happiness' (GNP) index to rival GDP as a way to measure a country's well-being (Thinley, 2006). The British government announced plans in 2010 to measure well-being and GDP as did the French President in the previous year (Yapp, 2011). Brazil a country renowned for its beaches, samba and carnival, plans to make the pursuit of happiness as a constitutional right (Yapp, 2011). The idea of promoting happiness in China has been embraced by some provincial governments as they lay down their five year plans. Guandong province declared it would become 'happy Guandong'. Beijing said it wanted its citizens to lead 'happy and glorious lives'. Chongqing municipality wanted its people to be the happiest in the country. Setting up 'happiness indices' is seen as a way government performance is assessed (*The Economist,* 2011).

The vast population of China is not homogeneous in their behaviour patterns. These behaviour patterns are shaped by the social environment and conditions. Goffman (1971) referred to them as 'social regions'. He defined a region 'as any place that is bounded to some degree by barriers of perception' (p. 109). Social regions apply to generations. Erickson (2009) referred to four generations in China: Traditionalists, individuals born from about 1928 to 1945; Boomers, individuals born from about 1946 to 1960/1964; Generation X, individuals born from about 1961/1965 to 1979; and Generation Y, individuals born from 1980 to 1995. The Traditionalists witnessed major transitions of the second Sino-Japanese War, the civil war between Nationalist and Communist parties and the establishment of the People's Republic of China (PRC) on the mainland. The socialist 'Big Push' was initiated to industrialise China from landlord ownership to peasant workers set to develop heavy industry and construct new factories. The 'Great Leap Forward' initiative saw the collectivisation of rural areas designed to shift the nation from an agrarian to an industrial economy. Adolescents witnessed the change of traditional ways of life in the pursuit of modernisation. The boomers grew up through the years of the Great Proletariat Cultural Revolution. After 1976, the culture devolved leaving now young adults disillusioned and angry. They were referred to as the 'Lost Generation'. Generation X grew up in a period or Economic Reform and Openness. The flood of new information, academic opportunities and world knowledge was highly appealing. Lifelong learning was embraced from multiple sources. Economic opportunity was available to those who studied and worked hard. Generation X developed a mental model that was highly pragmatic and facts-based. Generation Y shared many common characteristics of young people around the world. They are technologically savvy and have witnessed a wave of national pride with the return of Hong Kong, Macau, admission to the World Trade Organization, hosting the 2008 Summer Olympics, and 2011 World Swimming Championships. The Ys in China share a global sense of immediacy, coupled with the excitement of being part of the country's wave of economic prosperity and growing national pride (Erickson, 2009). Those born after 1995 have been referred to as the Re-Generation.

China is a regular contributor of information to the World Database on Happiness (Veenhoven, 2009). Data from four selected years: 1990; 1995; 2001; and 2007 was available. The question asked was: How happy do you feel as you live now? Respondents had five options: Very happy; quite happy; not very happy; not at all happy; don't know. The results are listed in Table 1. Chinese were happiest in 1995 when 22.7 per cent said they were 'very happy' and 60.9 per cent were 'quite happy'. The total on the happy/unhappy dichotomy was 83.6 per cent being happy and 15.8 per cent being unhappy. The proportions of Chinese being 'very happy' in 2001 (11.5%) and in 2007 (21.1%) diminished compared to earlier years. But proportions of those feeling quite happy were strong with 66.3 per cent in 2001 and 55.1 per cent in 2007.

Table 1

How Happy Do You Feel as You Live Now?

Selected years 1990–2008 (%) – China						
Year	*Very happy*	*Quite happy*	*Not very happy*	*Not at all happy*	*Don't know*	*N*
1990	27.1	35.7	31.1	2.5	3.7	1,000
1995	22.7	60.9	14.1	1.7	0.6	1,500
2001	11.5	66.3	19.1	2.8	0.4	1,000
2007	21.1	55.1	19.2	4.0	0.0	2,015

Source: Veenhoven, R. World Database of Happiness Findings in Nations, People's Republic of China, Erasmus University, Rotterdam – Last revision: 1–10–2009.

Table 2

Relationship of Income to Happiness

In selected years – China		
Year	*Per capita income$*	*Mean Happiness*
1990	330	2.91
1995	530	3.05
2001	1,000	2.87
2007	2,490	2.94

Happiness range: Very happy (4), Quite happy (3), Not very happy (2), Not at all happy (1)

Income source: The World Bank, WDI Online – World Development Indicator – 2009

Source: Veenhoven, R. World Database of Happiness Findings in Nations, People's Republic of China Erasmus University, Rotterdam – Last revision: 1–10–2009.

The per capita income (PCI) of Chinese between 1981 and 2010 ranged from $220 to $4,260 (World Bank, 2009). The increase in PCI has occurred as China's economy has risen strongly. However, rising PCI has not meant increasing happiness (Table 2). In 1995, when the PCI was at a low of $530, the mean happiness was as high as 3.05 (on a four-point scale). In 2007, when the PCI was the highest, $2,490, the mean happiness was 2.94. These results confirm what Easterlin found in 1974 that studies across countries and over time find very little, if any, relationship between increases in per capita income and average happiness.

The fact that the China is able to stage successful international events suggests that in urban areas the Chinese population has access to a panorama of activities. They include: sport activity; enjoying music or movies; watching sport games; card/board games, travel/tourism, Internet/PC com/games, watching TV, reading, arts/crafts/hobbies, socialising with friends and others. The extent of access to the leisure opportunity structure can explain in part why Chinese are on the whole a happy people. But according to Mauro Motoryn, the director of the Brazilian Happier Movement, a non-governmental organisation backing the happiness legislation, the bill has a serious purpose in a country (Brazil) still marked by a gaping divide between rich and poor. Motoryn is quoted as saying:

> Happiness isn't a game, people confuse it with something superfluous and it isn't. We need quality health care, which we don't have. We need quality education, which we don't have. (Yapp, 2011: 1)

Thus far, happiness has been examined from collective perspective. It may now be relevant to view the concept in an individual sense.

An Artist's View

My daughter bought a painting entitled: Me ... My World – Peace of Mind. It was painted by an artist in Singapore. I was intrigued by the work (Figure 1) and got in touch with the artist – Sarbani Bhattacharya. I asked her to interpret the story that the painting conveyed. Her response was:

> The main frame in the middle shows me (soul of human being), one's own Single World. The small four pieces represent the 'Natural World' outside one's individual World. The whole set of painting shows the Peace you feel when you realize the inter-dependency ... the fishes from the outside world happily swim to your World, the birds from Nature love to fly to your world and one sits to talk with You as it considers You are not an Outsider. Trees shower You with flowers ... natural breeze brings that fragrance to you ... the Red colour background shows the Warmth ... so it the feeling of Oneness with Nature and realizing the inter-dependency with Nature ... which gives You the Peace and Eternal Happiness.
>
> (Personal communication with Sarbani Bhattacharya, 15 May 2011)

I discussed the painting with the artist and said to her that I could understand achieving happiness in unison with nature. But the reality of life was that we have to deal with human beings and that was not easy. I asked her to sketch the problems a modern day wife had with her family. She sketched one and called it 'An Unhappy Relationship' (Figure 2). The main frame showed an intensely troubled wife saddled with problems of the car, job, school, parents, friends, money and drugs. But her foremost problem was her husband represented in the four pieces that were influenced by employment. He was the breadwinner but led a harried existence as the pace of life accelerated. He felt he was on a treadmill that could not stop. There was pressure at work with deadlines to meet from demands of a dominating boss. When he wanted to balance his life by spending more time with his family, he was told that his loyalty was needed in the office that considered him family. Finally, when he got home in the early hours of the morning, the wife questioned him angrily on the lack of time spent with the children and queried further whether he knew how many children they had! The moral of the story is that happiness is not easy to achieve in the modern world especially when the quest for increased income (more than what is needed) penetrates family relationships. The happiness concept

Figure 1

Me ... My World – Peace of Mind

Painting: Sarbani Bhattacharya

Figure 2
An Unhappy Relationship

Sketch: Sarbani Bhattacharya

influenced by several variables is taken seriously in many parts of the world and China is no exception. The concept is examined through activities, time and experience – the major dimensions of leisure.

Comparing Happiness and Leisure

The dimensions of leisure are time, activity and experience (Jackson, 2006). Layard (2005) reported on research done by Kahneman et al. (2006) on 900 working women in Texas. They investigated average happiness derived from involvement in activities, the fluctuations of happiness at different times of the day, and happiness derived from interacting with people. The study highlighted three aspects of happiness that parallel the dimensions of leisure. It is, therefore, tempting to equate happiness to leisure, but they are not the same as argued earlier. But the authors' motives were different. They attempted to show the fluctuations of happiness with different activities, times of day and with interaction with people.

Fifteen activities were selected and measured for average happiness (AH) and average hours a day (AHD). Average happiness was measured on a five-point scale. The top eight activities for average happiness were: sex (AH 4.7, AHD 0.2); socialising (AH 4.0, AHD 2.3), relaxing (AH 3.9, AHD 2.2), praying/worshipping meditating (AH 3.8, AHD 0.4), eating (AH 3.8, AHD 2.2), exercising (AH 3.8, AHD 0.4), watching TV (AH 3.6, AHD 2.2) and shopping (AH 3.2, AHD 0.4). The least happy from the bottom were: commuting (AH 2.6, AHD 1.6), working (AH 2.7, AHD 6.9), housework (AH 3.0, AHD 1.1), computer/email/Internet (AH 3.0, AHD 1.9), taking care of my children (AH 3.0, AHD 1.1), talking on the phone (AH 3.1, AHD 2.5), and preparing food (AH 3.2, AHD 2.5). The measurement of average happiness on watching TV was interesting as nearly all individuals around the world spend time viewing the screen. Robinson and Martin (2008) commented that television was a predictor of unhappiness. It led them to state two interpretations. First, television viewing was a pleasurable enough activity with no lasting benefit. It pushed aside time spent on other activities. The other activities might be less immediately pleasurable, but would provide long-term benefits in a person's condition. Consequently, television did cause people to be less happy. Second, television was a comfort for people who were already unhappy. People with few social skills or resources for other activities could engage in it. Despite chronic unhappiness and personal debilitation, the unhappiest people could click the remote and be passively entertained.

Layard (2005) stated that happiness is a feeling and feelings fluctuate at different times during the day. Citing Kahneman et al. (2006), he showed how people felt better as the day progressed with a dip over the lunchtime period. People felt happiest in the evenings and before bedtime.

Experiencing happiness when interacting with others was best with friends (AH 3.7, AHD 2.6) and least with bosses (AH 2.4, AHD 2.4). In between were: relatives (AH 3.4, AHD 1.0), spouse/partner (AH 3.3, AHD 2.7), my children (AH 3.3, AHD 2.3), clients/customers (AH 2.8, 4.5 AHD), co-workers (AH 2.8, AHD 3.4) and alone (AH 2.7, AHD 3.4). These results show that experiences with others fluctuate from person to person. Associating with friends, relatives and family result in high average happiness. The terms 'feeling' and 'experiences' have been used interchangeably in this paper. However, dimensions of feeling and experience from two different sources will be examined in the following section.

Dimensions of Feeling and Experience

Two continuums of feeling were identified along two intersecting axes. The unhappy – happy continuum ran left to right on a horizontal axis. The unaroused – aroused continuum was vertical and intersecting with the horizontal at a right angle with the horizontal axis. The two intersecting continuums resulted in four quadrants: top left, agitation; top right, joy; bottom right, contentment; and bottom left, depression (Figure 3).

Joy is linked to casual leisure that is immediately intrinsically rewarding, relatively short-lived pleasurable activity requiring little or no special training (Stebbins, 1997). Activities such as playing with the children, walking in the park, watching television and many, many others can be joyous.

Contentment may be experienced in serious leisure. Stebbins (1992) coined the term. It has the following characteristics: the systematic pursuit of amateur, hobbyist or volunteer activity; participants find the activities substantial, interesting and fulfilling; and typically they launch themselves in a career centred on acquiring and expressing its special skills, knowledge and experiences. The most enjoyable leisure experiences are when persons are so engrossed in the activity that they are oblivious to the passage of time. These persons are said to experience 'flow' (Csikszentmihalyi, 1990).

Layard (2005) placed depression in the unhappy and unaroused quadrant. Depression brought about by computer addiction is rampant in several countries

Figure 3

Two Dimensions of Feeling

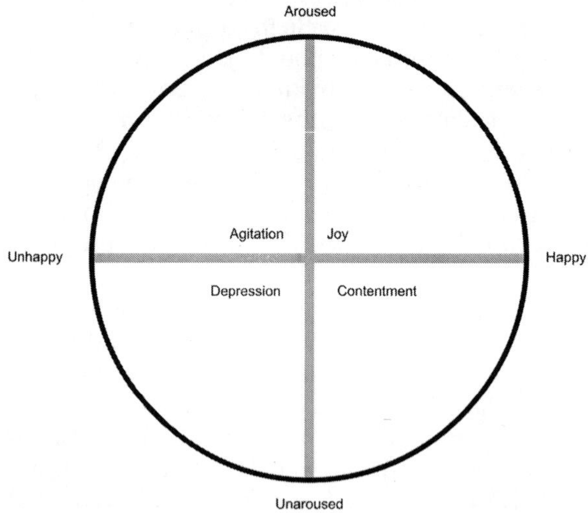

Source: Layard (2005) p. 21

in Asia, including China, South Korea and Taiwan (Fitzpatrick, 2008). The disorder has caused individuals to experience fear, anxiety, avoidance of social interaction, withdrawal from family, personal relationships and deviant behaviour (Orzack, cited in Fitzpatrick, 2008). Interventions are available through medication, individual therapy and community support programmes (Sane Australia, 2011). Community support programmes provide 'leisure' activity solutions for depressive disorders. South Korea has used boot camps as an intervention tool to combat individuals who are afflicted with computer addiction (Fitzpatrick, 2008). Boot camps use discipline, military exercises and physical training to break defiant adolescents to improve behaviour. Although therapists may disagree with such a tactic, the programme affirms that it has restorative value (Boot Camps Australia, 2011).

Agitation is placed in the unhappy and aroused quadrant. Children who are caught up in computers, television and electronic games spend most of their playing time indoors resulting in problems such as obesity, attention-deficit disorder and isolation. Louv (2005) suggested that the motivation to play outdoors and in the natural environment was decreasing alarmingly. Isolation in closed and built environments led to the problem known as Nature Deficit Disorder (NDD). Reducing the deficit between young people and nature was in our self-interest, 'not only because aesthetics and justice demands it, but also because our mental, physical and spiritual health depends on it.' (p. 3). Louv referred to the attention-restoration-theory developed by Kaplan and Kaplan (1989) which asserted that people can concentrate better after spending time in nature or even looking at scenes of nature.

Feelings can be negative or positive. A range of experiences is positive. These have been differentiated and shown to have distinct characteristics.

Pine and Gilmore (1999) distinguished between four types of happiness: entertainment; educational; escapist; and aesthetic (Figure 4). An audience through the senses passively absorbs entertainment experiences. Watching a group of Hawaiin dancers and listening to the accompanying music would be entertaining. With educational experiences, an individual actively participates with a view of increasing knowledge and skills. Taking a guided trek through a wooded area could aid one's knowledge and respect of the environment. The mind and body are actively engaged. People in an escapist environment are engaged and are immersed in the activity when they manouvre a canoe through the rapids. One may be passively immersed in an aesthetic environment appreciating its beauty and tranquillity. Tourists travel distances to experience the majesty of mountains and the tranquillity of their surrounds. Thus, happiness in leisure environments may be experienced in different ways – entertainment, educational, escape and aesthetically.

Caron Midgley (2008), writing for *The Times*, said that study after study showed that money fails to buy happiness. She questioned whether celebrity wives buying expensive vintage and sports cars made their celebrity husbands any happier. The answer was 'no'. Once people are wealthy, they become habituated to being rich. They want to know what the next big thing is. Consequently, they are constantly striving for better things. They desire to acquire better material goods and diverts from the path of being happy. They are on the 'hedonic treadmill'. Midgley cites James Montier, a global equity strategist, who said that once a person is earning UKP25,000 and upwards, basic needs for food, shelter and healthcare are covered. Money becomes increasingly irrelevant to genuine happiness. He suggested that if one wants to raise happiness, then money should be spent on experiences such as safaris, trekking and concerts.

Figure 4

The Experience Realms

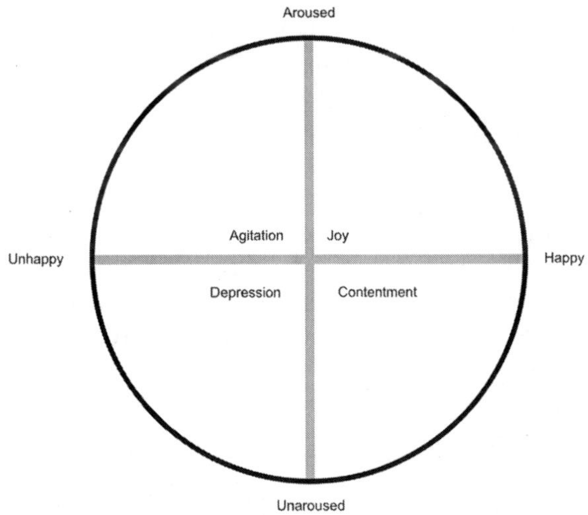

Source: Pine and Gilmore (1999).

Note: 'Esthetic' is the authors' spelling.

These are activities that provide experiences that Pine and Gilmore (1999) referred to earlier.

In a survey of a random sample of staff in *The Times* office, the responses to the question of what made people happy were: 'Watching *Desperate Housewives* with a bottle of wine and a large pizza', 'Going for a walk by the Thames on a sunny day with my three-year old daughter', 'Sex'. 'My football team winning in the 90th minute', 'Looking at my little house when it was clean and tidy and counting my blessings', 'Tea, crumpets and a good book in front of the fire in winter', 'My faith' (Midley, 2008).

Studies tell us that the pursuit of happiness does not rely on money (given that one has enough for basic needs). Spending time on fulfilling experiences will result in happiness. This may explain why the poor in the slums of Mumbai and in different regions of the world are happy despite their meagre resources for survival.

Summary and Conclusions

This paper examined happiness from a global perspective. Despite nations, becoming richer, happiness levels were more or less constant. It was found that generally wealthier nations were happier than poorer ones. Within nations richer people tended to be happier than the poor, although there were small proportions of unhappy well-to-do people. Likewise, there were few among the poor that were happy. It was shown that subjective well-being is heritable and one's genes could charter one's ongoing disposition. The social comparison theory is alive and well with the thought of 'keeping up with the Joneses' in prominence. Countries of Latin America were happier and countered the trend of developed countries with rising incomes. Although per capita incomes were less in some Latin American countries, their happiness levels compared favourably with advanced economies. Occupations influenced general happiness, with those in helping others, people with technical, scientific and creative expertise being most happy. The least happy were workers in unskilled and service positions. China as a case study showed that it is a happy country with a leisure opportunity structure that could promote the goal of enshrining happiness in its policy.

At an individual level, it was shown that happiness was influenced by the Big Seven Factors: family relationships; financial situation; work; community and friends; health; personal freedom; and personal values. In modern society life balance was difficult to achieve as time encroached on family and leisure. Happiness was analysed by activity, time and experience and the question was raised as to whether it equated to leisure. Finally, dimensions of feeling and happiness were explored. Interventions were suggested for negative disorders of agitation and depression. They were chosen as 'leisure' solutions. The happiness realm of experience identified as: entertainment; educational; escapist and aesthetic was described. They were cited as avenues to promote personal happiness.

It could be concluded that leisure has a close relationship to happiness. Development as in gaining extra income, does not necessarily lead to more happiness. Genes play a part in determining the set points in which happiness operates for individuals. Moving out of the rising tide of social comparison may aid in improving individual happiness. Negative feelings can be restored to positive ones, by appropriate interventions. Finally, investing in experiences can go a long way in stepping off the 'hedonic treadmill'.

References

Boot Camps Australia. (2011). Welcome to Boot Camps Australia. Retrieved from the Internet, Boot Camps, Australia, 15 May 2011.

Brickman, P. and Campbell, D.T. (1981). Hedonic Relativism and Planning the Good Society, in M. Appley (Ed.), *Adaptation-level Theory*: A Symposium (pp. 287–305) New York: Academic Press.

Bryner, J. (2007). Survey reveals most satisfying jobs 17 April 2007 in *Live Science* retrieved on 28 March 2011 at http://www.livescience.com/1431-survey-reveals-satisfying-jobs.html

Csikszentmihalyi, M. (1990). *Flow: The Psychology of Optimal Experience.* New York: Harper and Row.

Davis, J.A., Smith, T.W. and Marsden, P.V. (2007). *General Social Surveys, 1972–2006: Cumulative Codebook.* Chicago: National Opinion Research Center.

Diener, E. Suh, E., Lucas, E. and Smith, H. (1999). Subjective Well Being: Three Decades of Progress. *Psychological Bulletin,* 125, pp. 276–302.

Easterlin, R.A. (1974). Does Economic Growth Improve the Human Lot? in P.A. David and M. Reder (Eds.), *Nations, Households in Economic Growth.* New York: Academic Press, pp. 98–125.

Ebstein, R.B., Novick, O., Umansky, R., Priel, B., and Osher, Y. (1996). Dopamine D4 receptor (D4DR) exon III polymorphism associated with the human personality trait of novelty seeking. *Nature Genetics,* 12, pp. 78–80.

Erickson, T. (2009). Generations in China, *Harvard Business Review* 28 March 2009 retrieved from http://blogs.hbr.org/erickson/2009/03/generations_in_china_.html

Firebaugh, G. and Tach, L. (in press). Income, Age and Happiness in America. In Peter V. Marsden (Ed.) *Trends in the United States.* Princeton: Princeton University Press.

Fitzpatrick, J. (2008). Internet addiction: Recognition interventions. *Archives of Psychiatric Nursing,* 22 (3) April, pp. 59–60.

Goffman, E. (1971). *The Presentation of Self in Everyday Life.* Middlesex, England: Pelican Books. (First published in the USA in 1959).

Graham, C. (2009). *Happiness Around the World: The Paradox of Happy Peasants and Miserable Millionaires.* London: Oxford University Press.

Hamer, D.H. (1996). The heritability of happiness. *Nature Genetics,* 14, pp. 125–26.

Headey, B. and Wearing, A. (1989). Personality, Life Events and Subjective Wellbeing. *Journal of Personality and Social Psychology,* 57. pp. 731–739.

Helliwell, J. (2006). Implications for wellbeing in Holly M. Donohue and Li Wen Jie (eds.), *Leisure in context: Implications for Human Development and Wellbeing. Selected presentations 9th World Leisure Congress Hangzhou, China, October, 2006,* Hangzhou: Zhejiang University Press, pp. 28–31.

Indexmundi (2011). China demographic profile 2011. Retrieved from http://www.indexmundi.com/china/demographics_profile.html on 31 October 2011.

Inglehart, R. (1990). *Culture Shift in Advanced Industrial Society.* Princeton: Princeton University Press.

Inglehart, R. (1997). *Modernization and Postmodernization: Cultural, Economic and Political Change in 43 Societies.* Princeton: Princeton University Press.

Inglehart, R.F., Foa, R., Peterson C., and Welzel, C. (2008). Development, Freedom, and Rising Happiness: A Global Perspective (1981–2007). *Perspectives on Psychological Science*, 3(4): 264–285.

Jackson E.L. (2006). Setting the Stage: Introduction to the World Leisure Consensus: Symposium on leisure and the quality of life. In Jackson E.L. (ed.) *Leisure and the Quality of Life: Impacts on Social, Economic and Cultural Development.* Hangzhou: Zhejiang University Press.

Kahneman, D., Krueger, A.B., Schkade, D.A., Schwarz, N., and Stone, A.A. (2006). A survey method for characterizing daily life experience: The Day Reconstruction Method. *Science* 3, 1776–1780. *Psychological Bulletin 125,* pp. 276–302.

Kaplan, R. and Kaplan, S. (1989). *The experience of nature: A psychological perspective.* New York: Cambridge University Press.

Kenny, C. (2004). Does development make you happy? Subjective Wellbeing and Economic Growth in Developing Countries. *Social Indicators Research*, 65, pp. 1–22.

Larsen, R.J. (2000). Towards a Science of Mood Regulation. *Psychological Inquiry,* 11, pp. 129 – 141.

Layard, R. (2005). *Happiness: Lessons from A New Science.* London: Penguin Books.

Louv, R. (2005). *Last Child in the Woods: Saving our Children from Nature-Deficit Disorder*. London: Atlantic Books.

Lykken, D., and Tellegen, A. (1996). Happiness is a Stochastic Phenomenon. *Psychological Science*, 7, pp. 186–189.

Lyubomirsky, S., Sheldon, K., and Schkade, D. (2005). Pursuing Happiness: The Architecture of Sustainable Change. *Review of General Psychology*, 9, pp. 111–131.

Midgley, C. (31 January 2008). Unhappy? That's rich ... *The Times,* Archive article retrieved 30 June 2011 from http://www.timesonline.co.uk/tol/life_and_style/article723047.ece

Pine, J.B. and Gilmore, J.H. (1999). *The Experience Economy.* Boston, Mass.: Harvard Business School Press.

Robinson, J.P. and Martin, S. (2008). What Do Happy People Do? Published online: 31 July 2008, Springer + Business B.V.

Sane Australia (2011). Depression. *Sane Factsheet.* Retrieved from the Internet 25 July 2011.

Seligman, M.E.P. (2002). *Authentic Happiness: Using the New Positive Psychology to Realize Your Potential for Lasting Fulfillment.* Milsons Point, New South Wales: Random House Australia.

Stebbins, R.A. (2011). Leisure and Happiness. *Leisure Studies Association Newsletter,* 90 (November), (in press) (also available at www.soci.ucalgary.ca/seriousleisure – Digital Library, 'Leisure Reflections No. 28').

Stebbins, R.A. (1997). Casual leisure: A conceptual statement. *Leisure Studies, 16,* pp. 17–25.

Stebbins, R.A. (1992). *Amateurs, Professionals, and Serious Leisure*. Montreal, McGill-Queen's University Press.

The Economist (17 March 2011). Don't worry, be happy: The government introduces the country's new mantra. *The Economist,* retrieved from http://www.economist.com/node/18388884

Thinley, J.Y. (2006). Gross National Happiness: An Alternative to GDP? In *Leisure in context: Implications for Human Development and Wellbeing. Selected presentations 9th World Leisure Congress Hangzhou, China, October, 2006,* Hangzhou: Zhejiang University Press, pp. 47–53.

Veenhoven, R. (2009). Happiness in the People's Republic of China, World Database of Happiness Findings in Nations, Erasmus University, Rotterdam/Last revision: 1–10–2009.

White, A. (2007). A Global Perspective of Subjective Well-being: A Challenge for Positive Psychology? *Psychtalk, 56,* pp. 17–20.

Williams, D.E. and Thompson, J.K. (1993). Biology and Behaviour: A set-point hypothesis of psychology functioning. *Behaviour Modification,* 17, pp. 43 – 57.

World Bank (2009). WDI Online – World Development Indicator – 2009.

Yapp, R. (2 February 2011). Brazil considers 'happiness bill' as carnival approaches. *The Telegraph,* retrieved from http://www.tclcgraph.co.uk/journalists/robin- yapp/, Sao Paulo on 1 May 2011.

8

Getting the Big Picture of Leisure

ROBERT A. STEBBINS

There is plenty of talk these days about getting the 'big picture' of some event, trend, problem or situation. And, typically, that talk is also about the lack of a big picture on such matters. In fact, this kind of discussion is now so common that one major dictionary – *Webster's Collegiate Dictionary* (11th ed.) – considers it an established idea (not colloquial) defining it as the 'entire perspective on a situation or issue'.

The need for big-picture thinking in intellectual circles is well recognised, at least as suggested by the lengthy list of articles and books on the subject found in Google Scholar (search term: 'big picture thinking'). These offerings are there for good reason. For, as historians Cunningham and Williams (1993: 407) have pointed out:

> big pictures are, of course, thoroughly out of fashion at the moment; those committed to specialist research find them simplistic and insufficiently complex and nuanced, while postmodernists regard them as simply impossible. But however specialist we may be in our research, however scornful of the immaturity of grand narratives, it is not so easy to escape from dependence – acknowledged or not – on a big picture. When we define our research as part of the history of science, we implicitly invoke a big picture of that history to give identity and meaning to our specialism.

Naomi Ellemers (2013: 1) describes this same (lamentable) orientation in contemporary social psychology.

> During the past 20 years, practices in social psychology have drifted toward the publication of brief research reports as the main outlet for empirical findings, resulting in an exponential increase of the number of publications in our field. Recent developments questioning the reliability of these findings have increased the focus on (methodological) details and have prompted efforts to establish the robustness of isolated phenomena. Both types of developments carry the danger of impeding rather than promoting progress in the field. We can only build a cumulative knowledge base when we succeed in connecting these dots. Developing and examining broader theories about psychological processes and their implications can help connect different insights and

elucidate their further implications in a way that can be used and understood within and beyond the boundaries of our discipline.

And Richard Rosenfeld (2011: 1) holds that 'microanalysis holds sway over macroanalysis in contemporary criminology. All of criminology would be better off if greater attention were devoted to the big picture – the relationship between crime and the interplay of institutions in the social systems of whole societies'.

The preceding paragraph suggests that a lack of big-picture thinking is a critical problem in modern research, even while a big-picture kind of debate rages on a far more general level about the primacy of micro versus macro and agency versus structure as preferred analytic stances in the social sciences. Jonathan Turner (2005) reviews the many attempts to resolve this debate. But all are very general, he maintains, leaving out of consideration important specifics that could explain how these two poles are interrelated.

Context and the Big Picture

So big picture thinking is, it seems, a sort of necessary evil in the social sciences in an age of rampant narrow specialisation, where the latter proclivity seriously limits our full understanding of the subject being considered. Note that small-picture analysis is not, in contextual terms, necessarily micro or macro, agency or structural – it may fall at any point on the scale. Rather its distinctive feature is its narrow focus.

The word *context* is my preferred summary term for the micro-macro/agency-structure levels of phenomena. It includes a variety of collective formations, many of which unfortunately are commonly given short shrift in the diversity of abstract arguments about context. These formations include the social worlds, formal organisations, social institutions, spatial arrangements, social movements, and global postmodern tribes that characterise modern social life (discussed in Stebbins, 2016).

Context can be fruitfully studied on three levels: micro, meso and macro. The term 'meso structure' was coined by David Maines (1982) to identify the intermediate field of interaction lying between the micro sphere of agency, emotions, beliefs, immediate social interaction and so on and the macro sphere of such all-encompassing, broad-ranging abstractions as community, society, culture, social-class, social trends and the large-scale organisations. On the meso-structural level, human (micro-level) interaction continues to be discernible in interpersonal relationships, small groups, social networks, social worlds and lifestyles.

Context in Leisure Studies

Turner's own answers to the micro-macro/agency-structure question come close to the aims of this edition of Leisure Reflections: to understand leisure we must recognise that the domain of leisure also consists of these three levels. Over the years *homo otiosus* has created a wide variety of arrangements (e.g. organisations, social worlds, subcultures) to meet his leisure needs and interests. Furthermore, there is considerable 'embeddedness' (Turner's term) in these arrangements. For example, leisure participants fit into their surrounding social worlds, they form organisations some of which may spawn national or international federations, and they go in for activities that reflect certain values of the day (e.g. the modern interest in adventure, physical fitness, individuality).

By contrast, certain other meso and macro level phenomena have been much more fully examined. In leisure studies they include statements about leisure trends (e.g. Rojek, Blackshaw), historical changes in leisure (e.g. Spracklen, Cross, Gelber), and cultural practices as leisure (e.g. Chick, Rojek, Roberts). Some of the social problems generated from time to time by the search for leisure can be conceived of in contextual terms, among them inequality of leisure opportunity, deviant leisure, unhealthy leisure practices and annoying leisure activities.

Moreover, Turner (2005) mentions that human action 'can be constrained'. Thus, intrapersonal, interpersonal, and structural leisure constraints fit in this contextual analysis in distinctive ways. Leisure constraints inhibit choice of or participation in particular leisure activities. Structural constraints are associated with, for example, race, gender, religion, social class and the availability of financial resources. Interpersonal constraints spring up in, for instance, dyadic, interactive and small-group situations. The intrapersonal variety is evident in, among others, belief, attitude and psychological conflict.

The first two categories of constraints – intrapersonal and interpersonal – would not commonly stir much interest among the scholars caught up in the micro-macro/agency-structure debate, whereas the third category – structural constraints – most certainly would. The intrapersonal constraints are bodily conditions and psychological states such as attitudes and personality that discourage taking up particular leisure activities. At the interpersonal level constraints emerge in social interaction, typically that occurring within family and friendship circles. Such processes as coach's favouritism, scheduling of rehearsals and screening of group members are included under this heading.

Facilitators as Context

According to Raymore (2002) facilitators to leisure are 'factors that are assumed by researchers and perceived or experienced by individuals to enable or promote the formation of leisure preferences and to encourage or enhance participation' (p. 39). This definition is an adaptation of Jackson's (1997) definition of constraint, where facilitator is seen (by Raymore) as its antonym. Nevertheless, the two are not polar opposites, since facilitation is not necessarily achieved by overcoming one or more constraints or even achieved because of their absence. Writing on the relationship of facilitators and constraints to leisure motivation, Raymore argued that 'the facilitator is the condition itself, not the process through which that condition energises or motivates behaviour leading to (i.e. facilitating) or limiting (i.e. constraining) participation' (pp. 43–44). Raymore wrote on facilitation, because he believed that the popularity of constraints as an object of research was creating an imbalance relative to their importance in a full explanation of leisure participation.

In this conceptualisation, facilitators may be regarded as resources for leisure activities. Furthermore, as with constraints, facilitators may be intrapersonal, interpersonal and structural. Raymore theorised that intrapersonal facilitators are individual characteristics, traits, and beliefs that enable or promote the development of leisure preferences and that encourage or enhance leisure participation. The interpersonal facilitators, which originate in other people or groups of people, have similar effects. It is likewise with structural facilitators; they are found in social and physical institutions, organisations, and belief systems.

Inherited characteristics constitute an important class of intrapersonal facilitators. For example, being endowed with exceptional muscular strength, vocal clarity or facial beauty enhances success in rugby, operatic singing or fashion modelling, respectively. Knowing the coach, being a member of an outstanding musical group or working in an electronics shop may facilitate on an interpersonal basis getting invited to join a football team, experiencing top honours in a chamber music context, or having access at discounted prices to computer equipment. Structurally, an individual's participation in a leisure activity may be facilitated by membership in an amateur science society or fishing club with exclusive use of a private pond or by adherence to a religion that allows the faithful access to a retreat.

Be that as it may, I am arguing here that both are types of context. Furthermore, this distinction can be fuzzy, especially when constraint and context refer to the same condition or situation. And speaking of conceptual fuzziness we also find leisure facilitators, where it can happen that one person's facilitator is another's constraint (e.g. favouritism by a team's coach, bias in a jury at an art show).

Contextual analysis of the kind set out in this article is therefore, in light of its relative absence, unavoidable. Someone must connect the dots. Yet, the vagueness of the theoretic work carried out in the name of micro-macro/agency-structure analysis has not, I suspect, endeared itself to small-picture, mainstream social scientists. Leisure studies has its share of small-picture specialists and scholars who confine their theory and research to either the macro or the micro pole.

Nevertheless, small picture, specialised research can do its part. Authors here should contextualise the subjects they are writing about or, if this has already been done, refer their readers to the appropriate sources. For example, I have routinely asked my students writing about a serious pursuit to provide a chapter or section of a chapter bearing on its history. Since much of social life has its meso and macro background, we should in our specialised studies of it point out how and where our work fits in this context. That would enlarge the small picture while still retaining its detail. It would also give an aperçu of the bigger picture forming its background. Interestingly, the amateur, hobbyist and volunteer participants in my ethnographic research and that of others have shown a reasonably sophisticated understanding of the micro, meso and macro contexts of their passion. We should pay attention to this understanding, even in our more specialised research projects.

Conclusion: Contextual Study in the Lay and Scientific Communities

The previously-mentioned list of entries on the big picture found in Google Scholar suggests that the lay public also finds this point of view to be foreign. An equally long list exists in Google Chrome, albeit one aimed predominantly at organisational and managerial efficiency and somewhat more infrequently, at creativity. So might we ask the question: is big picture thinking an uncommon orientation, whether in the social sciences or in the wider lay community?

To the extent that the version of contextual study presented here is seen by the lay community as esoteric and consequently unimportant, or at least incomprehensible, money and time devoted to it could well be difficult to justify. In parallel, it might be argued by granting agencies and university administrators that such an interest is merely intellectual fun and games, and that these two scarce resources should therefore be channeled elsewhere. Some lay and scientific people may remember the days of opacity (approximately 1945 to1975) that grew from functionalist thought, and see contextualisation as more of the same. In any case, widespread unfamiliarity with and unfathomability of the contextual approach inside and outside the social sciences is bound to hinder its adoption as a legitimate and needed extension of social theory, research and policy. In all three spheres many will still say to the suggestion that we theorise and conduct research with contextualisation in mind: 'why bother'?

In fact, leisure studies has benefitted substantially from this supposedly offbeat interest, for by studying the constraints to leisure, we have brought scrutiny of its pursuit to the wider world of micro-to-macro context. An important contribution here has been to introduce to the agency/structure debate a conceptual avenue along which to examine some of the missing details of contextualisation. These are needed to understand the seemingly arcane workings of context and thereby grasp a deeper than heretofore understanding of human social life. This is no small achievement. But, if we are to have a more complete explanation of leisure activities, we also need recognition of certain specifics like constraints and facilitators as they operate on the different levels of context. Otherwise the approach is too vague:

There is nothing inherently contradictory about these two positions, since human action can be constrained without being determined, while structures can be reconstituted by acts of individuals. But, simply saying this does not explain anything; and when the agency-structure question is conflated with the micro-macro issues, theories are typically rather vague (Turner, 2005: 406).

References

Cunningham, A. and Williams, P. (1993). De-centring the 'Big Picture': The Origins of Modern Science and the Modern Origins of Science. *The British Journal for the History of Science* 26: pp. 407–432. DOI, 10.1017/S0007087400031447.

Ellemers, N. (2013). Connecting the Dots: Mobilizing Theory to Reveal the Big Picture in Social Psychology (and why we should do this). *European Journal of Social Psychology*, 43(1), pp. 1–8.

Jackson, E.L. (1997). In the Eye of the Beholder: A Comment in Samdahl and Jekubovich (1997), A Critique of Leisure Constraints: Comparative Analyses and Understandings, *Journal of Leisure Research*, 29(4), pp. 458–468.

Maines, D.R. (1982). In Search of Mesostructure: Studies in the Negotiated Order. *Urban Life*, 11(3), pp. 267–279.

Raymore, L.A. (2002). Facilitators to Leisure. *Journal of Leisure Research*, 34, pp. 37–51.

Rosenfeld, R. (2011). The Big Picture: 2010 Presidential Address to the American Society of Criminology. *Criminology*, 49(1), pp. 1–26.

Stebbins, R.A. (2016). *Leisure Activities in Context: A Micro-Macro/Agency-Structure Interpretation of Leisure*, New Brunswick, NJ: Transaction Publishers.

Turner, J.H. (2005). A New Approach for Theoretically Integrating Micro and Macro Analysis, in C. Calhoun, Rojek, C. and Turner, B. (eds.) *The SAGE Handbook of Sociology*. London: Sage, pp. 405–423.

9

Leisure, Sports and Social Change

VISHESH KUMAR GUPTA

The author, at the outset, may assume that the present paper is thematic in nature and concerns examining and analysing the phenomenon of leisure, increase in its amount and the question of filling that meaningfully. Equally important is the focus on the phenomenon of sport, growing increase in its importance as leisure time activity. Further, our main emphasis has been on the increasing importance of leisure value in terms of corresponding increase in the sport value. And in final analysis, the principal thread running through discussion is how a sport as leisure time activity serves as a force or instrument of social change.

As a prelude to it, however, the author may see merit in devoting some space to first discussing the origin, and growth of both 'leisure' and 'sports' and to explaining the meaning these terms have come to assume in popular usage. To deal with leisure, it may broadly be said that the leisure as a topic in its own right, has hardly seized the imagination of sociologists. This may be the reason that until recently the sociology of leisure has been considered a byproduct of the Sociology of Work (Haralambos 1980: 262). However, due to the chronological variations and historical development, the social scene is under-going a steady change brought about by the increasing importance of leisure values in an advanced industrial society. And it may serve to explain why leisure has certain traits symptomatic of the civilisation emanated from the industrial revolution.

Origin and Growth

Leisure, with its existence in some form or the other in different periods of human civilisation, came to be treated as venerable an institution as work itself (*The International Encyclopedia of Social Sciences* 1972: 248). Now tracing back to its origin in the primordial societies, work and play figure together forming part of the ritual essential for the life and the community. Conflict between them was of no consequence since play became part of the work. Nevertheless it will be stretching out of the point if we place the shamans or witch doctors, free from ordinary labour, as a primitive form of 'leisure class' in Veblen's sense (ibid.) Hence, it can easily be deducted that 'leisure is not a term applicable to societies of the too ancient period'. Similarly leisure, in the modern parlance, was somewhat non-existent in the recorded agrarian societies with the working year following a time-table. Of course as a natural rhythm of the slackening off of work, relaxation, rest, songs, games and ceremonies went with the daily round, and in certain terms it lacked the characteristics of leisure as we look upon it today. De Grazia attributes the early beginnings of leisure to the aristocratic and courtly way of life in the western societies. Nevertheless, leisure should not and does not fit in with the activities of the idle elites because it presupposes work in the modern sense (De Grazia, 1962).

Now to come to the 'modern leisure', there are two governing conditions. First, it should become the unfettered responsibility of the individual allowing for the individual's choice to be determined by more impersonal social necessities. Secondly, the work should be set apart from other activities separating it from free time. These preconditions are existent only in the industrial and post-industrial civilisation (*The International Encyclopedia of Social Sciences* 1972: 249).

Now to deal with the growth of leisure, it tends to become visible in the rural life of the modern society, as the agricultural labour and rural life is getting influenced by the industrial mode of organisation and urban values of industrialisation, respectively. Hence it may be inferred that leisure emerges having a separate entity from the growth of industrialism, while it was either missing or vague in a tribal or agrarian society. Moray attributes increase in leisure to the effect of cybernetic society emphasising automation and thereby giving more and more free time to the worker (Moray 1963: 11) Similarly, Anderson puts it, leisure is an 'unintended creature of technological efficiency', a 'child not planned for' (Anderson 1964: 90 and Ritzer 1979: 425).

Having outlined the origin, growth, nature of leisure, now let the attention shift to the meaning of leisure. The term 'leisure' has received various interpretations in different communities as the cultures and subcultures varied. It may imply that it has more than one meaning subject to the contextual setting. Classical Greek interpretations of leisure emphasise peace, quiet, and contemplation. The Greek thought of leisure refers to it as a pure form of being 'in which activity is performed for its own end' (De Grazia 1962: 15; Smith and Preston 1977: 425). In later Christian thought, leisure was contemplation of God. This concept dominated Western thought until the Renaissance, when the perception of leisure became more contemporary (Smith and Preston,1977: 425–26).

Today, we perceive leisure as free time. Hence, Tom Burns argues that leisure provides considerable freedom for the individual to exercise choice and design and to create and find meaning in life (Haralambos op. cit., 261). Leisure is a product and a form of realisation of surplus time (labour and values) in society. Its expanded reproduction requires an increase not a decrease of surplus labour (Zachary, 1986: 141).

For our purpose, we have taken it to mean simply time-free from work. To add, it is a time-free not only from regular employment but also from overtime spent in travel to and from the work place. Free time includes leisure as well as all the other activities that take place outside the gainful employment. To add further, leisure also includes free-choice as well as freedom from the fundamental obligations prescribed by other forms of social organisation' (*The International Encyclopedia of Social Sciences*, op. cit., 250)

Now let us deal with the aspect of growing increase in the amount of leisure and how fulfilling is that? Due to the advances in automation, mechanical equipment and computer applications leisure hours have increased tremendously. These new devices with their modes and forms of uses have made leisure abundant rather that redundant replacing instead of displacing it. In the cybernetic society of today this increase in leisure undoubtedly may assume such proportions as leisure may become problem no. 1 of the society of future (Gisbert, 1979 and 1987: 339–43 and 409 respectively).

From the preceding discussion now a pertinent question emerges: what people will do with their increased leisure resulting from the part-time employment and longer holidays? To put it slightly differently there is a possibility of the cybernetic society, having two kinds of men: 'Alphamen' using their leisure in activities productive of the stability and progress of the society at large, and 'Beta men' using their leisure for their own comforts and conveniences. The future shape of the society shall be what the moral convictions of members will make of it (Gisbert, 1979: 344). Dubey holds leisure as a necessity but emphasises the need of promoting channels for its creative and productive utilisation (Dubey, 1988: 58)

Dealing with various popular leisure activities, 'Leisure Future', a published report of an independent group of Britain, states that, family outings are going to become more popular. People may love more going to the seaside, up and down mountains, and visiting relations and friends. The report further admits that the most popular leisure activities will be home-based such as, viewing TV, playing video cassettes, games and rather indoor games. Actually choice of leisure activity or recreation depends on personal tastes and liking with one person going to cinema another to exhibition, still social activity and the like (Bharathan, 1987).

Having outlined the origin, growth, nature, definition of leisure in the first part of the paper, now we may devote the second part to discussing briefly the meaning and importance of sports and the issues involved in this social phenomenon.

Though the impact of sports today is reflected in almost every facet of the modern life, nature and role of the sport has provoked less serious sociological interest. It is in the past decade only that sociologists have placed value on it recognising its crucial role in modern society.

Meaning and Nature of Sport

When we try to define 'sport', we must consider its relationship to 'play' and 'games' (Ritzer et al., 1979: 511–12). Play is free spontaneous activity engaged in voluntarily. And thus it is not for any objective or ends, such as, financial reward, the adulation of one's peers or social status. 'Games' may be defined as 'any form of playful competition whose outcome is determined by physical skill, strategy or chance employed singly or in combination. 'Sports' primarily involving physical activity can be distinguished from games by the degree of organisation involved in establishing and conducting the activity. The degree of organisation and institutionalisation may, however, register a great range of differences within the category of sport. To sum up, play, games and sports can be considered along a continuum of organised activity. And lastly, we may conclude that sport is something that is defined as such by a culture.

To come to deal with sociological aspects involved in sport it has, in the first place, essentially the properties of a social phenomenon with its nature of activity socially defined, and the goals, objective, and the rules agreed upon by the teams thereby developing a distinct subculture. At the same time it reflects social organisation among team members, officials, and even fans and participation herein is amenable to variables of race, social class and sex. Secondly, it provides an excellent and convenient laboratory to examine a variety of sociological issues or phenomena such as, social positions, roles, values, social stratification, social change and social control. Thirdly and lastly, apart from serving as a microcosm to analyse general processes, it also reflects the dominant norms and values of a specific society similar to those that the Max Weber identified, with the 'Protestant Ethic', as success, achievement, hard work, perseverance and competition. Another set of sport values concerning order, discipline, team work, and sublimation of self render sports a conservative force strengthening traditional values, beliefs and practices.

Now to discuss the relation between leisure and sports they should not be divorced from each other. No leisure time activity can arouse the interest that sports can. Both are dovetailed and interwoven. Hence, we can not analyse leisure in a logico-meaningful way keeping the sport in isolation. The growing popularity of sports during leisure time may be attributable to various arguments and explanations which the following paragraphs may clarify.

Leisure Time Sports and Social Change

To shift attention to the global view of 'leisure and social change', it can easily be inferred from the foregoing discussions that leisure time sports play the most vital and rather crucial role in bringing social change. We may in this context draw mainly upon the psychological and functional perspective of the leisure time sports. First to make brief mention of psychological perspective about sports, Ogilvie and Tutko, on the basis of their research, pointed out that participants and their coaches in sports showed certain specific personality traits with a strong need for achievement. And as a dominant personality possesses 'great psychological endurance, self control, low resting levels of anxiety and slightly greater ability to express aggression' (Ogilvie and Tutko, 1971: 50).

In the second place, taking functional perspective, prominent among several other functions of leisure time sports is that of validating society's values. These values reflecting society's normative structure, once internalised in an athlete's personality, become instrumental as a part of an athlete's total personality as well as entire social situations. To amplify, participation in sports 'builds character' that socialises individuals to confirm to existing cultural ideals of the society and to promote the spirit of individual sacrifice for the good of group, humility, ability to accept defeat graciously and good citizenship helping an individual in developing socially desired personality. Supporting the view, Kamphorst holds the leisure time activities whether physical, social, economic, religious or recreational are grounded in the personality or character of individual formed in early childhood in the process of socialisation. It helps individuals internalise personality traits considered desirable by the society (Kamphorst, 1986: 79).

Needless to say sports has long been intimately related to the social, political, economic and religious institutions. In the context of the relationship between social structure and leisure time activities, it may be said that leisure time sport activities have flourished comparatively in a dense population having occupational specialisation with substantial leisure time. It means that complex urban societies marked by organic solidarity in Durkheim's concept are more productive for leisure time sport activities particularly, the organised sports, as compared to primarily natural and agrarian societies having mechanical solidarity. Similarly, varying social, structural, cultural and economic influences among the rural fashion the leisure time sports activities generating new forms of social interaction (Modi, 1985: and *Contributions to Indian Sociology,* 1986: 162). Thus our relatively informal, unorganised and participant-oriented rural pastimes tended to become organised, commercialised and highly specialised forms of mass communication. The institution of family has been affected by the sports events in more than one way. It is a common observation that politicians are found eager to identify with sport celebrities and successes of sports teams. The economy is also activated by the large amount of money spent on various items of sports. Many religious organisations may be seen drawing up various athletic programmes. Leisure time activities are sometime closely interwoven with our ritual observances and scared festivals.

Urbanisation and industrialisation proved of paramount importance in changing the nature, extent and forms of sports. Urbanisation serving the goals of modernisation brought new structural changes and innovations in the sphere of leisure and mode and pattern of social interaction (Singh, 1986: 158). Further it affected greater physical proximity with more opportunities for competitive sport activities. And thus generated organisation of teams and leagues along with a mass of spectators. Migrants in large numbers from rural to urban turned to sports as the most suitable means of occupying their leisure time. Thus, time sport activities came to be reckoned with as a major integrating force bringing together people from different ethic and economic backgrounds.

Leisure time sport activities have had a close relationship with social class similar to that as Thorstein Veblen described in his classic 'Theory of Leisure Class' (Veblen, 1934). He argued that the availability of leisure time was one of the most prominent indices of social status and aspect of 'conspicuous leisure' in late 19th century. As for the bearing of social class on the leisure time sport activities, it is a common observation that some sports, such as, horse, racing, hunting, polo, baseball, golf and tennis are reserved still for leisured social elites. In this context it should not be a revelation that, on occasions, selection of a player in a team gets influenced by consideration of the ascribed status of a particular player.

Industrialisation, with improved transportation and communication facilities, proved instrumental in bringing technological revolution that transformed the nature and extent of sport from regional to national and international phenomenon. As a corollary to growing industrialisation, modern technology and culture equipment now forming part of the little tradition in India, make people particularly in the urban areas adopt new schedules of work, personal habits and leisure (Singh, 119). Communication makes possible wide publicity and immediate reporting and revolutionaries printing process with mass publication generating collective interest in the sports during leisure; thus, unleashing the forces of social change.

To conclude, leisure time sport activity by its properties of an inherent social phenomenon unleashes the forces of social change of a varied description. And thus it sounds logical that the sociological understanding of human society embraces understanding of sports.

References

Anderson, Nels (1961). Work and Leisure. London: Routledge and Kegan Paul.

Anderson, Nels (1964). *Dimensions of Work: The Sociology of a Work Culture*, New York: David Mckay.

Bharathan, D. (1987). 'Leisure Increase Productivity', *Social Welfare*, Vol. XXXIV, No. 4.

De Grazia, Sebastian. (1962). *Of Time Work and Leisure*, New York: Twentieth Century Fund.

Dubey, S.C. (1988). *Modernization and Development: The Search for Alternative Paradigms*. New Delhi: Vistaar.

Gisbert, P. (1979). *Fundamentals of Industrial Sociology*. New Delhi: Tata McGraw Hill.

Gisbert, P. (1987). *Fundamentals of Sociology*, New Delhi: Orient Longmans.

Haralambos, M. (1980). *Sociology: Themes and Perspectives*, New Delhi: Oxford University Press.

Kamphorst, Tues, J. (1986). 'The Deeper Layers of Leisure Activities', *Sociological Abstracts*, Aug 34/3 Suppl. 141.

Modi, Ishwar (1985). *Leisure, Mass Media and Social Structure*, Jaipur: Rawat.

Moray, N. (1963). *Cybernetics: Machines with Intelligence*, London: Burns and Oales.

Ogilvie, Bruce C. and Tutko, Thomas A. 'Sport: If You Want to Build Character, Try Something Else', *Psychology Today*, October 1971, 5.

Ritzer, George et al. (1979). *Sociology: Experiencing a Changing Society*, London: Allyn and Bacon.

Singh, Yogendra, (1986). *Modernization of Indian Tradition: A Systemic Study of Social Change*, Jaipur: Rawat.

Smith, Ronald W. and Preston, Frederick. W. (1977). *Sociology: An Introduction*, New York: Martin's Press.

The International Encyclopedia of Social Sciences. (1972). Vol. 9–10, New York: MacMillian.

Veblen, Thorstein. (1934). *The Theory of Leisure Class*, New York: Modern Library.

Zachary, Staikav. 'Reproduction of Leisure', *Sociological Abstracts*. Aug 1986. Suppl. 141.

10

Role of Leisure in the Reproduction of Inequalities

Puerto Rico Case Study

ANAYRA O. SANTORY JORGE, LAURA L. ORTIZ-NEGRON, EDUARDO BURGOS-SUAZO AND ANGELLYN SANTON GONZALEZ

Puerto Rico's Contemporary Economic Context

Puerto Rico has remained a colony of the United of States of America (USA) since the American invasion in 1898 during the Spanish-American War. Its economy relies heavily on manufacture, which in 2014 represented 48 per cent of the \$103,675,700 gross domestic product, followed by the service sector, in particular real state and rental, which contributes a 41 per cent (Planning Board, 2014). However, in terms of personal income, federal transfers to individuals are very significant, specially to the poorest. Last year, nutritional assistance programmes benefitted more than 670,000 families who received \$1,868,700 (Planning Board, 2014; Gómez, 2015). A very hard to estimate group of workers participates in Puerto Rico informal economy in order to keep, among other reasons, their necessary federal and local government subsidies (Benson-Arias, 1996; Muñiz-Varela, 1986, 1996, 2014). The New York Federal Reserve Bank calculates that Puerto Rico informal economy amounts to 23 per cent of the country gross national product which it estimated to be \$70,000,000 for the year 2013. It is important to notice that federal transfers benefit both individuals and local government at all levels, including the Puerto Rico Commonwealth, public state size agencies and small town municipalities. In 2014, the Commonwealth government received \$2,326 million, public enterprises \$179 million and municipalities \$420 millions (Planning Board, 2014).

Despite these subsidies, Puerto Rico's economy started a downward spiral in 2006, two years earlier than the onset of the global recession marked by the bankruptcy of Lehman's Brothers. An economic recovery is not yet in sight. In April 2014, Puerto Rico's labour participation rate reached its lowest point in recent history (40.0%) when Puerto Rico employed labour force dropped below the one million mark (Government Development Bank for Puerto Rico, 2014). The unemployment rate for the previous year, i.e. 2013, was 14.1 per cent, even when the island population has been undergoing the second largest emigration process in its contemporary history (Bureau of Labor Statistics, Department of Labor, 2013).

The United States Census Bureau, estimated the island population at 3.6 million, down from 3.808 million in the 2000 count (Mead, 2013). The poverty rate for 2012 was 45.4 per cent, which amounted to 1.6 million people living below the poverty threshold established at $11,720 per person (United States Census Bureau, 2013). Puerto Rico poverty rate was three times as high as the USA 2012 national average: 44.9 per cent versus 15.9 per cent. Not only poverty is more widespread, but also Puerto Rico has become a more unequal society than the United States. While the GINI coefficient for Puerto Rico in 2013 was 0.547, the USA national coefficient was 0.481 (United States Census Bureau, Data Integration Bureau, 2013; Noss, 2011). In 2010, in Puerto Rico, the average family income in the top 20 per cent was 33 times higher than the average income of those at the lowest 20 per cent. For the same year, the average family income of the top quintile in the USA was only 15 times higher than the average family income of the lowest quintile (Marxuach, 2012).

Besides the many daunting and present social problems related to income inequalities, one of Puerto Rico's leading think-tanks, the Centre for the New Economy, has warned the country about the contracting effects that inequality has on aggregate demand. If inequality increases, the middle-classes tend to rely more on credit to maintain its consuming habits. This short-term solution further reduces the available income for savings and investments, postponing the resurgence of economic growth (Marxuach, 2012). Personal consumption expenditures have risen steadily for the last nine years, between 2005 and 2013. Last year they suffered their first contraction (Planning Board, 2014). This could be explained either by the increments in immigration or by consumers' increasing difficulties with keeping up consumption through credit. However, consumer culture is still the hegemonic regime in Puerto Rico where shopping centres, cars, highways, credit cards, and cell phones proliferate and shape many of the practices of people's everyday life (Guilbe, 2000).[1] The deepening fiscal crisis of the Commonwealth of Puerto Rico, whose bonds have been devalued to their lowest ratings in contemporary history, and the broader economic crisis signaled by nine years of economic contraction, is an important aspect of the context in which our pilot study on free time and leisure activities was carried out. We postulate that given the current context of socioeconomic crisis free-time and leisure shall tend to be ever more precarious.

Study Method

Our main research objective was to produce basic data on patterns of free-time and leisure activities and to document their multiple meanings among the participants. Free-time is defined in this study as consisting of time spent outside of working hours, including both paid and unpaid work, and daily life obligations. In the same register, we defined leisure as a temporal domain, wherein activities that bring enjoyment and autonomy are valued in themselves and differentiated from the world of work and everyday obligations. From a sociological and cultural approach we conducted a two-phase pilot research on free time and leisure activities among Puerto Rican adults.

The first phase was conducted employing a quantitative survey. The second phase includes qualitative data gathered in the course of in-depth interviews. In this first phase, a quantitative survey makes available basic descriptive statistics on sociodemographic data, free time and leisure topics. Some of the survey questions asked participants about how much free time they thought they have and do they usually do with it. Others inquire about their definition of leisure and explore the realm of leisure activities participants engage in. Our quantitative research instrument was a questionnaire consisting of 20 closed questions on the topics of free-time and leisure activities, including the sociodemographic variables. For the administration of this questionnaire, we used a sample of people living in Puerto Rico who were 21 years of age or older. The data collection consisted in the administration of this questionnaire both face-to-face and online, through the platform SurveyMonkey. All participants completed a consent form. A total of 346 participants completed the survey from December 2013 to March 2014. The data processing, analysis, and depuration was carried out through the SPSS programme. We produced frequency analysis and crosstabs for the variables under study. In order to determine the significant relations between independent and dependent variables, we worked with the statistical test chi-square using the values between 0.000 and 0.100, the free degrees, and evaluating the significant grade p =.05. Also, submit with the assumption that the expected frequency for the cells should be 5 or more. This quantitative data collection and analysis also served to generate a first picture within the research topic and to prepare for the second phase.

In this article, we discuss the statistically significant differences we found between the answers given by groups at each end of the economic, social, and cultural capital gradient. The differences to be discussed highlight issues like the quantity of their free time, its use and the leisure activities they choose. Pierre Bourdieu (1986) categories of capital allow us to acknowledge that inequalities are not only to be understood or measured in financial terms and that different forms of inequalities can have different impacts on our study subject.

We use some of the data collected in the demographic questions as indicators of a participant's economic, cultural and social capital. Personal income has been interpreted as an indicator of economic capital and the amount of years of formal education as an indicator of cultural capital. Social capital is harder to be identified. Following Small (2009) work, we relied on formal institutional ties as an indicator of social capital. In our interpretation of the participants' demographic data, institutional ties are those provided by an employer, a higher education institution or acquired by having retired from a salaried job. We are aware that in a jobless economy with entrenched unemployment and pervasive informal and precarious occupations, formal institutional ties might not be the most reliable indicator of social capital.[2] Other indicators of social capital, like being related to the military as a war veteran or a national guard member will be identified in the second stage of our research through the planned in-depth interviews.

Socio-Economic Characteristics of Participants

The data gathered on personal income revealed that 46 per cent of the participants earned less than $15,000 annually, making our sample slightly wealthier than of the general population in Puerto Rico where 41.2 per cent of the households earn less than $15,000 (United States Census Bureau, Data Integration Bureau, 2013). Among our survey 21 per cent participants earned more than $15,000 but less than $35,000; 22 per cent earned more than $35,000 but less than $75,000 and 6 per cent stated that they earned $75,000 or more. There was a 5 per cent that did not offer information about their individual earnings. As for occupation, 42 per cent have full-time jobs while 25 per cent worked part-time jobs. Earning low incomes while holding full and part-time jobs, characterised the majority of our sample. However, according to the US Census Bureau (2013) these percentages are higher than those for Puerto Rico's work force. The US Census Bureau indicates that 35.6 per cent people between 16 to 64 years work full time (35 hours or more), 13.8 per cent worked part-time (34 hours or less) and 50.6 per cent did not work in the last 12 months.

In our sample, slightly younger that the Puerto Rican population, 44 per cent of the participants were younger than 35 years; 31 per cent were less than 55 years; 24 per cent were less than 85 years and 1 per cent were 85 years or more. According to the US Census Bureau (2013), in Puerto Rico 50 per cent of the population is older than 37.7 years. In our survey, as for gender, 65 per cent of the respondents were females, 29 per cent males, 4 per cent chose being identified as members of the LGBTT community and 2 per cent chose not to identify themselves with any of the gender options. In Puerto Rico's population, 52.2 per cent are females (United States Census Bureau, Data Integration Bureau, 2013).

While 9 per cent of the participants had a high school diploma or less, 42 per cent had a bachelor degree or some educational experience after high school. This makes our sample a group with more formal education than the general population in Puerto Rico in which only 33 per cent completed some years of studying after high school (United States Census Bureau, Data Integration Bureau, 2013). As for further academic studies, 34 per cent of our sample had graduate degrees and 15 per cent had some post-bachelor studies.

How Much Free-time Participants Have?

Our operational definition of free time is time spent away from any kind of work: wage, informal and domestic labour, and from taking care of others. We considered that a participant had free time if in any single day of the week he or she could spare a block of 12 hours without engaging in salaried, informal, domestic work or taking care of others. This might seem as a pretty high threshold for determining if someone has free time or not, but we find it consistent with the participants' cultural understanding that in order to have free-time one should have the equivalent of at least one day every week without any labour engagements. This is in fact a lenient interpretation of the International Labour Organisation, Covenant 106 (1957) that established a 24 hours resting period in a seven days period of work for every worker in the service sector.

Using these criteria of free time we found statistically significant differences in the perception of free time during Friday and Saturday between those with the lowest income (less than \$15,000 a year) and for those with higher incomes (75,000 or more). The results shows for Friday X^2 (2) = 18.34, *p* =.000. For Saturday, the result was X^2 (2) = 8.32, *p* =.016. None (0%) of those with more economic capital have the perception of having a 12 hours block of free time on Fridays and only 17 per cent reported having a similar amount of free time on Saturdays. Of those with less economic capital 36 per cent reported having a 12 hours block of free time on Fridays and 36 per cent on Saturdays. Only 23 per cent of those with higher incomes reported having more than 12 hours of free-time on Sundays, the day most likely to be declared as free among all participants. However, a free Sunday is no longer a generalised experience among participants. Among the factors that could explain the reported time crunch are: (i) the increasing flexibility of labour, (ii) the precariousness of many job positions, (iii) the domestic production of items or services that would have been obtained through the market before the prolonged economic crisis, and (iv) a heightened awareness, especially among females, that being away from a salaried work or staying at home are not equivalent to having free time.

In terms of cultural capital, the results show a statistically significant difference between people with lower formal education (high school diploma or less) and people with graduate degrees (MA or Ph.D) with regard to their amount of free time on Sundays. The results indicated X^2 (2) = 9.62, *p* =.008. Only 28 per cent of participants with a graduate degree reported a 12 hours block of free time on Sundays versus 52 per cent of those with a high school diploma or less. The distribution of free time between those with less cultural capital and those with more greatly resembles that which was obtained for differences with regard to economic capital. There were no statistically significant differences in the reported amounts of free time for any other day of the week even when the group with less cultural capital consistently reported having more free time than their richer counterparts.

These results suggest that the everyday routine of those with more cultural capital make it more difficult to keep different forms of work related activities from seeping into the weekend, traditionally expected to allow for more free time. The relatively low percentage of participants who reported having a free 12 hours period during the weekend (the highest percentage was 52 per cent for those with lower formal education) suggests that the modern patterns of free time are eroding for all the participants irrespective of income or formal education. It could also be the case that a different, and higher standard, of what participants consider free time to might be emerging.

Another possible interpretation of these findings is that participants with higher economic or cultural capital income are engaged in economic activities that either demand or have allowed for different and still uncharted patterns of free time.[3] We did not find any new allocation pattern of free time periods. What we did find was that seven out of ten participants with higher cultural capital reported having two hours or less of free time during workdays, from Monday to Thursday. This suggests a dramatic free time and consistent time crunch for those in this group. Such findings would be congruent with those of Aguiar and Hurst (2009).

It could be the case that jobs that require graduate studies – liberal arts professionals and academics, for example – demand a constant renewal of skills and information in order to perform well at them. Nonetheless, those who hold these jobs have not escaped the precarious conditions of workers in other economic activities and are forced to devote more time 'to work before work' than other precarious workers. It is also important to notice that people with graduate degrees need to engage in work related activities that demand levels of concentration that can be achieved better in 'quiet time environments', alien to most corporate or institutional work places. Some of the most important demands of the jobs that require or benefit from a graduate degree need to be undertaken in a different ambiance away from the turmoil of most offices. Preparing for teaching a class or engaging in academic writing, for example, are not usually done during 'normal' office hours; neither is completing the researching for a case if one is a lawyer or fiddling with a new design project if one is an architect. We will need to explore further if time devoted to work might be expanding for the most educated because it cannot be completed in the spaces assigned to regular working hours. In a jobless economy as Puerto Rico seems to be, having less free time could be interpreted as a blessing in disguise if it is indeed a potential indicator of an intellectually demanding or highly creative job however precarious. These interpretations will be fine-tuned with the results of the interviews to be realised during the second stage of our research.

The most interesting results that we obtained from comparing the free time patterns of the participants are related to levels of social capital (Bourdieu, 1986; Small, 2009). As an indicator of social capital we explored the institutional ties of participants as per their occupational status: employed, studying, enjoying retirement benefits or combining any of this occupational status. By making these distinctions we were assuming that institutional affiliations carry with them a series of responsibilities that have an effect on how participants structure their time, which determined, among other factors, how much free time they enjoyed. We also considered that institutional participation could have a potential effect on leisure opportunities and activities. Going to work or to school or having spent a considerable amount of one's time doing so, as is the case with retired participants, offers greater opportunities for getting to know and spending time with people with similar interests or backgrounds, which can lead to friendships. Apart from this fairly non-controversial assumption, we took into consideration the fact that employers and educational institutions, as well as retired personnel associations, provide access and promote leisure activities. These activities might include becoming a member of a coworkers sport team, meeting regularly for drinks afterhours or midafternoon coffee, or participating in formal institutional initiatives, like visiting the company's gym during lunch time or participating at the university stress-management programme.

We compared the amount of free time of those in any of the previous groups with those who were house-makers, were unemployed, self-employed in the informal sector or not working because of some disability. We expected that the group with evident institutional affiliations would have both (i) less free time and (ii) more leisure opportunities than the ones with less institutional ties. The findings showed that this assumption was wrong. There were no statistically significant differences with regard to free time between participants with more obvious institutional ties and the ones with less on any day of the week. Institutional ties did not have impact on the amount of free time during the weekend while income or educational level did.

This means, for example, that one of our participants can be both working and studying and has as little free time during the weekend that another participant that is a homemaker, does not hold a salaried job or receives a disability pension. Whatever their weekend routine might be, participants at both extremes of the social capital gradient report that the weekend does not signal being away from their job related responsibilities, domestic chores or family obligations. This finding could be interpreted as buttressing the impression that our study's participants are keenly aware of how different everyday tasks amount to 'being at work' like anyone in a salaried job. It also suggest that a series of necessary activities, like cleaning or going to the supermarket, or culturally important rituals, like visiting relatives have been assigned to time slots during the weekend, modifying the traditional shared perception that the weekend is free. Which are these activities that consume the time expected to be 'free' is something to be explored in the second qualitative stage of our research.. However, we are ready to suggest that even when institutional ties do not have an impact on the amount of free time an individual has during the weekend, they do have an effect in the kind of activities he or she chooses during what he or she considers free time. It also has an effect on the kind of activities he or she chooses as leisure. We will be discussing these results in the next two sections.

We found statistically significant difference between some of the activities chosen during their free time by participants with the lowest economic capital versus those selected by participants with the higher economic capital. Among the answers that reflect a statistically significant difference was shopping X^2 (2) = 7.46, p =.024; leisure X^2 (2) = 7.45, p =.024; educational (e.g. study, teach, take courses, seminars or conferences) X^2 (2) = 8.54, p =.014; and social activities X^2 (2) = 6.84, p =.033; tasks and errands related to family care X^2 (2) = 9.92, p =.007; and cleaning and up keeping the house X^2 (2) = 7.05, p =.029. Less than half the participants – 45 per cent – with higher incomes chose cleaning up and keeping their homes as an activity they perform in their free time, versus 71 per cent with the lowest income. Community service showed no statistical significant difference between low income (15,000 or less) and high income (75,000 or more) X^2 (2) = 5.95, p =.051. However, the fact that no one in the higher income rank chose community work as an activity they perform on their free-time, while 20 per cent in the lowest income rank reported engaging in it seems to us a clear difference between the two groups.

Consistent with our previous findings, a higher percentage of those with less social capital – 34 per cent – report engaging in community service versus 13 per cent with more. The result shows statistically significant difference X^2 (2) = 19.69, p =.000. A 66 per cent of participants with less social capital reported visiting the doctor or seeking other medical services in their free time versus 28 per cent of those with more. This finding shows statistical significant difference

X^2 (2) = 36.46, p =.000. For religious activities, the result shows statistical significant difference X^2 (2) = 26.85, p =.000. Almost half – 49 per cent – of those with less social capital spends part of their free time engaging in religious activities versus 25 per cent of those with more. When it comes to everyday errands, like making payments or requesting services on behalf of family members, our data shows statistical significant difference X^2 (2) = 9.25, p =.010. Among participants with more social capital, 60 per cent committed free time to the obligations and tasks related to family care while only 43 per cent of those with less social capital did the same.

What we find most relevant of these findings is that a distinct pattern appears to emerge in the reported uses of free time among those with less economic, cultural, and social capital. An increasing percentage of those with less income and less institutional ties devoted time to community services. When someone does not have the financial resources and the institutional scenarios that could facilitate meeting other people and establishing connections, community service is a way of increasing social capital (Bourdieu, 1986). It is also an alternative strategy for solving common problems in the face of fewer financial resources and fewer institutional affiliations. The percentage of those with less cultural capital that devote free time to religious activities (48%) is practically the same than the percentage of those with less social capital (49%). This could suggest that participants that lack institutional scenarios for meeting and networking are more inclined to search for other forms of institutional support and rapport, as could be found in community service and religious activities, than those with more formal education and more institutional affiliations. Among the participants, the risk of social isolation is compensated by the frequency of choice of these free-time activities. It is as if participants invest their free time knitting other forms of social networks when lacking the paradigmatic modern forms of institutional rapport that represent having a job or going to school. Hence, little wonder that those with less formal institutional ties reported being equally busy as those that have access to one or more of these institutions.[4]

What Do Participants do for Leisure?

We selected the ten most common leisure activities mentioned by all the participants and then checked if there were statistically significant differences with regard to these activities among those with lower versus higher incomes, high school diploma versus university degrees and, among the group with less institutional ties versus those with more.

As Table 1 shows, the second most common leisure activity among participants was taking a nap or lying down for a while. Participants with less economic capital and with lower cultural capital – 78 per cent and 77 per cent respectively – chose lying down or taking a nap as a leisure activity. We found that there is a statistically significant difference among those at the lower gradient of cultural capital (X^2 (2) = 11.45, p =.003) and economic capital (X^2 (2) =17.22, p =.000) versus their higher counterparts with regard to this activity. No statistically significant difference with regard to differences of social capital (X^2 (2) = 5.59, p =.061) was found in relation to this leisure activity. However, those with the highest income also take naps – 59 per cent – as well as those with higher educational levels – 55 per cent – which suggests that enjoying short periods of sleep is part of all the participants' cultural options as leisure goes. The only other leisure activity that proved to be dependent on personal income was watching TV. The data shows that those with the higher income are those who watch more TV – 73 per cent – versus 48 per cent of those with lower incomes: (X^2 (2) = 13.67, p =.001). For the last half century, television was the canonical symbol of American leisure society where family recreation and interaction were centred upon it. Among our participants with lower income it seems that is loosing its grip.[5]

Table 1

Most Frequent Leisure Activities among Participants

Leisure Activities	*F*	%
Share with family or significant other	234	67.6
Lying down, take a nap	232	67.1
TV	203	58.7
Watching movies at home	201	58.1
Listening to music	188	54.3
Using the internet	187	54.0
Reading books	184	53.2
Going to the movies	181	52.3
Going out with friends	169	48.8
Going out to restaurants or coffee shops	162	46.8

Note. The numerical base of this table is the 346 persons interviewed. The sum of the percentages could be greater than 100 per cent as the persons could indicate more than one response, reason for which there is a multiple count for each of the responses given.

If we compare the choice of leisure activities of those with less cultural capital and those with more, we discover the expected result that reading books is an activity chosen by those with more cultural capital. For instance, 59 per cent of those with graduate degrees read books for leisure versus 32 per cent of those with lower formal education. The result for this activity shows statistical significant difference X^2 (2) = 6.83, p =.033. Also noticeable is that 51 per cent of those with higher cultural capital use the internet for leisure versus 38 per cent of those with less cultural capital. With regard to the internet the results indicated statistical significant difference X^2 (2) = 4.85, p =.088. We also found statistical significant difference in the leisure activity of eating out between groups with more cultural capital and those with less: X^2 (2) = 6.33, p =.042. Eating one meal out of the home was a leisure activity selected by 51 per cent of those with more cultural capital versus only 26 per cent of those with less. The results also showed significant statistical difference between the group with less cultural capital and those with more in relation to spending time with their family as a leisure activity X^2 (2) = 5.76, p =.056. Another leisure activity were we found statistical significance among those with higher cultural capital and those with lower cultural capital is watching TV: X^2 (2) = 6.90, p =.032. Of those with higher cultural capital, 58 per cent selected TV as a leisure activity versus 81 per cent of those with less.

When the results are analysed in terms of the gradient of social capital, we found that among those with less institutional ties 77 per cent chose spending time with their family as a leisure activity versus 65 per cent of those with more social ties. The use of internet for leisure shows significant statistical difference X^2 (2) = 8.38, p =.015. It is an activity chosen by only 33 per cent of those with less social capital versus 58 per cent of those with higher social capital.

If we examine the 10 most frequent leisure activities reported by the participants the first seven listed occur usually within the domestic sphere: sharing with family, lying down, reading books, surfing the web, watching movies or TV. Most of these activities are also usually done alone. Our study reveals a solipsistic leisure that does not offer opportunities for social interaction except among those with whom participants are quite intimate. Only sharing with the family requires at least someone else, although going to the movies is usually done in company. Among the leisure activities most frequently chosen, going to the movies is the only leisure activity that requires leaving the house for a public space that, in Puerto Rico, as in many other places, is privately owned.

The material culture required for this selection of leisure activities is very basic. It consists of a bed, a couch or a hammock, some books, TV, an Internet connection that can be established through a cell phone, the increasingly common tablet or a computer. Participants spend their leisure time with what is easily at hand, and for most of them is their family, a significant other, or a place to take a nap. There could be many reasons for lying down for a while, but the most obvious ones are not getting enough sleep or being overworked, physically or emotionally tired. Our participants have little free-time, and when they spend it in leisure, they're most likely either sharing with those closest to them or at rest.[6]

The domesticity of the most popular leisure activities and its concomitant privacy do have implications for the reproduction of inequalities. We will point out at least two possible implications. First, leisure that is predominantly domestic does not contribute to the exposition to cultural experiences that can destabilise entrenched beliefs established as common sense and every day practices. The domestic sphere, and the social relations that it nurtures, is a very stable cultural space were the intrusion of different perspectives that might challenge what is taken to be common sense and established *habitus* is not to be expected or welcome. We do not invite people over who do not share most elements of our worldview; neither do we raise our children in a wildly different way to how we ourselves live, at the street. This domestic world does not only share and reproduce practices and beliefs, but also constitutes a series of relations in which power is distributed according to age, gender, and rank, among others. The privacy of the domestic sphere shelters all these elements – practices, beliefs and power relations – protecting their stability and therefore contributing to its reproduction.

Second, we should expect that only cultural products that are akin to socially hegemonic relations and its current distributions of capitals will have access to the privacy of the domestic sphere mainly through movies, TV, newspapers, and radio broadcasting. In this respect, the domestic sphere could be playing the cultural and political role of a resonance box rather than a shelter from current media-products, its symbols, and common interpretations. Even when these cultural products could be semantically and symbolically ambiguous it's hard to imagine a sheltered domestic sphere as a place for developing counter cultural appropriations unless this becomes a personal goal.

Final Remarks

We would like to highlight two preliminary conclusions: one with regard to the uses of free time, the other with relation to leisure activities. One of our preliminary conclusions is that among our participants free time is not 'functionally free'. It morphs according to their position in the scales of economic, cultural and social capital. Our data suggest that free time is the time we use either (i) to increase some form of capital, (ii) to compensate for a form of capital we might be lacking in relation to other forms, or (iii) to distribute some of our capital in personal rewarding non-delegable ways. As we discussed earlier, if someone has little income, then it is more likely that some of her free time will go to finding community solutions to common problems. If one has less institutional support because one lacks institutional affiliations, then it is more likely that one's free time is devoted to community services, religious, and social activities, or spending time with one's family. It is also more probable that one's free time is devoted to going to the doctor, as it is also the case when one has less cultural capital. On the other hand, if one has a higher amount of cultural capital then it is more likely that one would spend one's free time engaging in activities that will cultivate and add to it.

Our data also suggests that free time is used among those with higher economic capital for some form of distribution that is not monetary. Those with higher economic capital were more likely to use their free-time attending to the well-being of family members or making home and community improvements. Free time seems to allow for different balancing acts between different forms of capital. Those that depend on cultural capital for obtaining economic capital use their free time for maintaining or increasing it. Those with lower social capital spend their free time investing in social networks. Even when they are financially in a better position to delegate these tasks, those with higher economic capital employ their time in the often personally rewarding experience of taking care of others, which commonly elicits gratitude. After all, the most gratifying use of time is simply engaging in activities that are non-delegable from the perspective of the agent.

Our second preliminary conclusion is highly contextualised and it depends on the very local practice of lying-down or takes a nap as a common form of leisure. According to our findings, when our participants finally get some leisure, and not just some free time, it seems that the body desperately imposes its demands and orders rest. Leisure time seems to be devoted to labour recovery. The less economic and social capital participants have, the more obvious this pattern becomes. The mental, physical, and emotional overload of subjects faced with insecure employment, lack of free time, unemployment, pollution, violence, crime, and the intensification of crisis discourse is the social context that may explain, among other factors, this common activity. Social overload and overwork shapes our contemporary society where work is disappearing as we have come to know it in modernity (Aronowitz and DiFazio, 1994). This is worsened by the exhaustion of the economic strategies deployed by Puerto Rico's governments in the last 20 years and the fact that full employment has never been a goal or a fact of our colonial history. Leisure, as an autonomous practice for the subject, appears as an elusive dimension, as different ways of working saturates every pore of daily life. We are keenly aware that today's concept of leisure is one whose frontiers are blurred. We will have to search for leisure in unexpected places as it might appear imbricated in working hours, consumer culture, and sport activities (Munné, 1992; Stebbins, 2001; Junius, Tedrick and Boyd, 1996). However, the idea of free time that guided our research, and that has also fueled the imagination of all those that have fought for shorter work days and weeks, and that makes us long for the next vacation, that is, the idea of a time unpolluted by all our multiple responsibilities; that free time seems to be a mirage with diminishing legitimacy. The State and media discourse is insistent and recurrent in its exhortation to find work, to work longer hours, and to increase productivity. However, as our study suggest, most people could use a little extra time to get just a little more sleep.

Notes

1. Thus, Puerto Rico's colonial status and its uninterrupted coloniality (Quijano, 1992; Mignolo, 2010) is not the sole determinant of this regime. It is a context, but consumer culture in Puerto Rico has to be assessed on its own terms. However, the intersection of both dimensions reveals interesting peculiarities of Puerto Rican consumer culture. For example, 62 per cent of all Puerto Rican families have a banking account. Among those, only 28 per cent have a credit card and of those who have such a credit line, 82 per cent carry a standing balance (García, 2013).
2. Institutional ties are those that link a student to its academic centre, an employee to his or her employer, a retired person to its former employer and its association for retired workers. Following Small (2009), we expect social capital to be a result of individual initiatives to reach out to others and, perhaps more significantly, the amount of institutional ties any subject could have. For one, being institutionally affiliated increases the opportunities for developing social capital by promoting a structured context for interactions. However, Small remarks that this is not the most important effect of institutional participations on someone's social capital. Institutions are related to others forming networks and someone who participates in one institution can benefit from this institution's own network. A university employee, for instance, can choose to deposit his or her money in the bank that manages the university accounts and which has arranged with it to open a branch on its premises. The employee can also improve the access to credit at the cooperative formed by people affiliated to the university without knowing anyone at these places but by just having one institutional tie: to its employer. On the other hand, someone who is

unemployed, a house-maker or is at home because of some disability, could be more at risk of social isolation because it lacks institutional ties.

3. They are different from those that became standardised in Puerto Rico during the second half of last century, that is, a work/study week of five days from Monday to Friday, with two days away from school or wage-labour.
4. Participants with apparently no institutional ties could have other kind of 'ties': community, cultural, religious, political and informal groups ties. We have to wonder if in a particularly 'jobless economy', as Puerto Rico's seems to be, formal work and wage labour are to be considered pivotal to institutional ties.
5. The access to TV in Puerto Rico during the first three decades of broadcasting, 1950s until the mid-1980s, depended only on having a TV set and electric power. Since the late 1980s, in order to watch TV, people need to pay high prices for cable or satellite antennas. Therefore, not all people have access to these services and the more varied TV offers is available only to those with relatively higher incomes.
6. The State is surprisingly absent in the choice of leisure activities among participants. Movie theatres are privately owned in Puerto Rico, public libraries are almost nonexistent, book stores are very scarce and internet service does not have any subsidy for the poorest. Also, in the context of a prolonged economic crisis, people tend to stay at home.

References

Aguiar, M., and Hurst, E. (2009). *The Increase in Leisure Inequality, 1965–2005*. Washington, D.C.: AEI Press.

Aronowitz, S., and DiFazio, W. (1994). *The Jobless Future: Sci-Tech and the Dogma of Work*. Minneapolis-London: University of Minnesota Press.

Benson-Arias, J. (1996). Posfordismo Puerto Rico–USA, *Bordes, 3*, pp. 29–40.

Bourdieu, P. (1986). The Forms of Capital. In Richardson, J.G. (Ed). *Handbook of Theory and Research for the Sociology of Education*. New York: Greenwood Press.

Bureau of Labor Statistics, Department of Labor (2013). Empleo y desempleo en Puerto Rico 2013. Retrieved from http://www.trabajo.pr.gov/pdf/Estadisticas/2014/GT/EMPLEO%20Y%20DESEMPLEO%20EN%20PUERTO%20RICO%20PROMEDIO%20A%C3%91O%20NATURAL%202013%20(REV.%20CENSO%202010).pdf

Federal Reserve Bank of New York. (2014). *Actualización del informe sobre la competitividad de la economía de Puerto Rico 2014*. Retrieved from http://www.newyorkfed.org/outreach-and-education/puerto-rico/2014/Spanish-Puerto-Rico-Report-2014.pdf

García, L. (2013). Dos de cada cinco hogares no tienen una cuenta bancaria. *Sin comillas*. Retrieved from http://sincomillas.com/dos-de-cada-cinco-hogares-no-tienen-una-cuenta-bancaria/

Gómez, A.R. (2015). Casi la mitad del país recibe el Pan. *Primera Hora Digital*.

http://www.primerahora.com/noticias/gobierno-politica/notacasilamitaddelpaisrecibeelpan-1086454/

Government Development Bank for Purto Rico (2014). Labor Force Seasonaly Adjusted. Retrieved from http://www.gdbpr.com/economy/documents/01LABOR-2014-05-28.xls

Guilbe, C.J. (2000). *Historia y desarrollo de los centros comerciales en Puerto Rico.* San Juan: Administración de Fomento Comercial.

International Labour Organization. (1957). Convenant 106 Weekly Rest (Commerce and Offices). Retrieved from http://www.ilo.org/dyn/normlex/en/f?p= NORMLEXPUB: 12100: 0:: NO:: P12100_INSTRUMENT_ID: 312251

Junius, S., Tedrick, T., and Boyd, R. (1996). Leisure or Work?: Amateur and Professional Musicians' Perception of Rehearsal and Performance. *Journal of Leisure Research, 28*(1), pp. 44–56.

Marxuach, S. (February 2012). La desigualdad y el crecimiento económico sustentable. Retrieved from http://grupocne.org/wp-content/uploads/2013/05/AEC2012-Event-Proceedings.pdf

Mead, K. (20 September 2013). PR population under 3.7M; income, poverty hold. *Caribbean Business.* Retrieved from http://www.caribbeanbusinesspr.com/news/census-data-pr-population-falls-below-3.7-million-income-poverty-rates-hold-89054.html

Mignolo, W. (2010). *Desobediencia epistémica: Retórica de la modernidad, lógica de la colonialidad y gramática de la decolonialidad.* Buenos Aires: Ediciones del Signo.

Munné, F. (1992). *Psicosociología del tiempo libre: Un enfoque crítico.* México, D.F.: Editorial Trillas.

Muñiz-Varela, M. (1986). *Crisis económica y transformaciones sociales en Puerto Rico 1973–1983.* Río Piedras: Centro de Investigaciones Sociales, UPR.

Muñiz-Varela, M. (1996). De Levittown a La Encantada: 'Más acá' de las 936. *Bordes, 3*, pp. 41–50.

Muñiz-Varela, M. (2014). *Adiós a la economía.* San Juan, PR: Ediciones Callejón.

Noss, A. (2011, September). Household Income for States Counties: 2009–2010. Retrieved from http://www.census.gov/prod/2011pubs/acsbr10-02.pdf.

Ortiz-Negrón, L., and Santory-Jorge, A. (2014). El ocio: Apuntes sociohistóricos y desacatos teóricos para su estudio en Puerto Rico, *Revista de Ciencias Sociales, 28*, pp. 88–101.

Ortiz-Negrón, L. and Román, M. (2012). From Live Long and Prosper to Die Well: ¿Réquiem para el trabajo?. In Tania García Ramos, et al. (Eds.), *La crisis del trabajo en el siglo XXI: Perspectivas desde las ciencias sociales.* (p. 10–22). Río Piedras: Centro de Investigaciones Sociales, UPR.

Quijano, A. (1992). Colonialidad y modernidad-Racionalidad. *Perú Indígena, 13*(29), pp. 11–20.

Planning Board of Puerto Rico. (2014). Economic Report to the Governor. Retrieved from http://gis.jp.pr.gov/Externo_Econ/Ap%C3%A9ndices%20Estad%C3%\ADsticos/Ap%C3%A9ndice%20Estad%C3%ADstico%202014.pdf

Small, M. (2009). *Unexpected Gains: Origins in Network Inequality.* Oxford: Oxford University Press.

Stebbins, R. (2001). Serious Leisure. *Society, 38*(4), pp. 53–57.

United States Census Bureau, Data Integration Bureau (2013). Population Estimates. Retrived from http://www.census.gov/popest/data/puerto_rico/totals/2012/index.html

11

Leisure and Mental Health

Sociological Study of Women Experiencing Leisure during their Mental Illness

MADHU NAGLA

Globally, mental disorders are prevalent across all cultures – more than 450 million people suffer from mental disorders worldwide (Hyman et al., 2006). The World Health Organization (WHO, 2001) estimated that mental disorders would account for 15 per cent of the total burden of disease in the year 2020, and showed that mental disorders would be the principal cause of years lived with disability internationally. Despite advances in pharmacological and psychological treatments, the quality and adequacy of healthcare for persons with mental illness remain fragmented, disconnected and often inadequate, frustrating the opportunity for recovery (WHO, 2003).

The World Mental Health Atlas 2011 (WHO, 2011) reports that only 59 per cent people worldwide living in a country where there is dedicated Mental Health Legislation. A recent article in *The Week*[1] magazine reported that in India, we have over 10 crore people suffering from a mental illness. There are just 43 mental hospitals, about 4000 psychiatrists.[2] Budget allocation to mental health is about as low as 1 per cent whereas experts put it close to 10 per cent.[3] Much stress is laid on hospital admission and treatment. This again increases the cost of healthcare. No provisions are made for home treatment, recreational and leisure facilities.

Gender is a crucial determinant of health including mental health. It influences that power and control men and women have over the determinants of their mental health, including their socio-economic position, roles and social status, access to leisure activities access to resources and treatment in the society. According to MANAS Foundation (2008) Indian women have more psychiatric morbidity as compared to their male counterparts because of lack of opportunities, suppression, violence/abuse, patriarchal attitude, etc. As such gender is important in defining susceptibility and exposure to a number of health risks. Mental health of women is a serious sociological concern particularly in the Indian context. It is embedded in social and economic structure of the society. The Indian women face gender-based discrimination at every stage of life and in turn their psychological health becomes a cause of concern. The gender discrimination in all spheres of life also discriminate women in terms of accessibilities and opportunities of leisure available to her. Women have restricted entry into the leisure activities as it is regarded as the domain of men folk. Constant denial of leisure activities in the form of outdoor activities, watching of films, listening of music and many more other activities results into the deprivation state and in turn results into some forms of mental illnesses. It is accepted that both men and women have a fundamental right to health, thus, it becomes necessary to examine the impact of absence of leisure activities on women on her mental health.

People of all ages and abilities can experience emotions, engagement, relationships, meaning and accomplishment – all elements of positive mental health and well-being – from involvement in personally meaningful and enjoyable physical activity, recreation, leisure, sport or play. Moreover, it is clear that mental health and well-being is a family and community affair. Positive mental health is influenced by relationships formed with significant others, including family, friends and adult leaders (e.g. recreation leaders and coaches). At the community level such relationships contribute to social cohesion and sense of belonging, both of which are important components of mental health and well-being. Leisure and recreation pursuits can also be outlets for coping with stressful life circumstances and can provide opportunities to receive and give support, and to experience a sense of competence, and assisting people to develop skills and knowledge to overcome barriers to participation, to develop skills and self-confidence, and to experience success, positive emotions and sense of belonging are important to incorporating leisure and recreation as part of a continuum of mental health promotion, prevention, and treatment services.

Recreation and leisure activities are essential for mental health and physical well-being across life course. They are critical components of efforts to recover from and stay well when living with a chronic physical or mental health condition. Making these opportunities available to more people more often has the potential to make a significant difference to the mental health and well-being of citizens, families and communities.

The benefits for mental health are equally important. Several studies have demonstrated links between regular physical activity and a reduction in the symptoms of mild or moderate depression, stress and anxiety. Passive leisure also has benefits for mental health by providing an outlet for the mind. It may provide physical rest, tension release and opportunities to enjoy nature and escape from the daily routine.

Participation in leisure and recreation activities can also have social benefits. It creates opportunities for socialisation and contributes to social cohesion by allowing people to connect and network with others. It can also contribute to family bonding when families do things together in their leisure time.

India is the home to one of the largest number of people suffering from various mental health problems ranging from simple anxiety disorders to schizophrenia. Although about 10 per cent of disease burden is caused by poor mental health, it has not received a fraction of the attention it deserves. Poor mental healthcare facilities, particularly in rural areas; lack of social awareness and efforts to mitigate the impact of chronic conditions; and poor commitment and capacity have made the lives of millions of Indians with some mental health issue utterly miserable.

Leisure as a Context for Active Living

Leisure is defined as a relatively freely chosen humanistic activity and its accompanying experiences and emotions (e.g. enjoyment and happiness) that can potentially make one's life more enriched and meaningful. The meaning-seeking or meaning-making functions of leisure have a long tradition in the leisure research field (Shaw, 1985; Samdahl, 1988; Henderson et al., 1996; Kelly and Freysinger, 2000). Recently, Iwasaki (2008) identified key pathways to meaning-making through leisure-like pursuits in global contexts. He showed that in people's quest for a meaningful life, these leisure-generated pathways seem to simultaneously involve both 'remedying the bad' (e.g. coping with/healing from stressful or traumatic experiences, reducing suffering) and 'enhancing the good' (e.g. promoting life satisfaction and life quality) through facilitating, for example, positive emotions, identities, spirituality, connections and a harmony, human strengths and resilience, and learning and human development across the lifespan. Overall these notions of leisure emphasise: (a) meaning oriented emotional, spiritual, social and cultural properties of leisure that reflect a broader and humanistic perspective than physical activity alone, and (b) the role of meaning-making through leisure in promoting active living, health and life quality for people, including individuals with mental illness. Leisure is a key context for active living and an important pathway toward recovery, health promotion and life-quality enhancement. Leisure represents broad aspects of human functioning including emotional, spiritual, social, cultural and physical elements. The forms that leisure expressions take (e.g. sport, exercise, art, crafts, visits with friends) are secondary to the meanings derived from and associated with the leisure experiences, and it is the outcomes/meanings derived that present the potential contributions to these pathways (Iwasaki et al., 2010).

Theoretical Paradigm

Leisure is a way of life reflecting more clearly our basic needs and higher potential as human being. More meaningful leisure activities and a wider acceptance of a right to recreation could reduce the significance to us of work and of affluence for its own sake (Hookway, 1978).

Miller and Robinson (1963) believe that leisure and recreation are cultural universals, being found as common elements in the behaviour of individuals in all societies; however Kaplan's (1960) approach explains the functions of leisure. Nakhooda (1961) puts leisure and recreation in the category which involves freedom of choice and voluntary participation in any activity, leisure can be harmful if the right kind of activity is not chosen. In her opinion, to make a judicious use of leisure, recreation becomes necessary. In the opinion of Finlay (1967), recreation includes many activities that are usually not thought of as play-music, drama, the crafts, every free activity and especially creative activity for the enrichment of life. Roberts (1983) states that since in industrial revolution a general process of structural differentiation within society has taken place with special institutions emerging to centre to the needs such as education and social welfare which previously catered to multipurpose groups and organisations. Leisure is just one amongst man's activity which has been subjected to a process of structural differentiations.

Leisure as a social phenomenon can be understood and explained only in the context of a social organisation. Social structure influences the nature and form of leisure and its activities. In a given society at a particular time, it allows, dictates, or is conducive to, a particular mode of leisure. It is not only determines the form and nature of leisure but also determines the extent and limit of participation whether any person would be allowed to participate or not would depend on the social status, gender in a given society (Modi, 1985). On the other hand, leisure itself helps in generating new structures and social norms. History abounds in instances which support the contention that social structure influences the nature and form of social norms and are generated by leisure.

Foucault argues that social reality is created in various ways through the activities of people. The resulting social reality provides a discourse, which is a way of conceptualising an issue and provides a framework for discussion and action. Mental illness is no longer considered an illness but a reversible disease, this does not mean that disorder is not severe enough to require that sufferer receive government assistance, more resources and more help in general. This assistance, however, must be geared toward improvement, not perpetual inadequacy and exclusion. In fact, the idea that mental disorders are reversible would tend to call for more financial and structural interventions, such as psychotherapy, better work opportunities, adequate leisure and all the features of a healthy society. An important thing to consider is that the narrative of mental illness has not been successful in helping sufferers and, indeed, research and evidence show that cases of mental illness are increasing annually, adding substantially to society's burden, which indicates that mental illness is largely constructed by dominant Western ideology. Concept of madness is a social construction that is regulated, reproduced, maintained and elaborated on by social structures that perpetuate the myths and ideology of mental illness. The paradigm of mental illness as disease has been endured over centuries. Rationality, the opposite of madness, which is based on scientific method has reduced over emotional and spiritual drives (Foucault, 1973).

Review of Literature

Leisure's potential has increasingly been shown in a series of empirical research. For example, Lloyd (Lloyd et al., 2007) study with 44 Australian clubhouse members with mental illness found a significant association between leisure motivation and recovery. Lloyd's findings are consistent with Hodgson and Lloyd's (2002) qualitative study showing that the involvement in leisure activities play a vital role in relapse prevention for individuals with dual diagnosis of mental illness and substance misuse, and with Moloney (2002) and Ryan (2002) who emphasised that the engagement in leisure is instrumental in a journey for recovery from a consumer perspective. Trauer et al. (1998) in their study with 55 clients who had serious mental illness reported positive effects of leisure on intellectual stimulation, relaxation and enjoyable relationships with others. Frances's (2006) evidence-based review highlighted the role of outdoor recreation as a vital therapeutic means of people with mental illness, particularly its role in facilitating positive identity and life quality. Babiss' ethnographic study of women with mental illness provided evidence that expressive activities such as art, music, writing and dance promote the process toward recovery, specifically as a vehicle for learning about self and for identifying feelings one cannot express verbally. Babiss indicated that 'expression just for the sake of expression has value' while emphasising 'the stunning importance of the human interaction and the human touch' (2002: 118). In fact, self-expressions and meaningful interpersonal interactions are two key benefits of leisure and recreation (Driver and Bruns, 1999).

Yanos and Moos' (2007) integrated model of the determinants of functioning and well-being among individuals with schizophrenia identified leisure activities as a key dimensions of social functioning. Minato and Zemke's study (2004) with 89 community residents with schizophrenia in Sapporo, Japan showed that leisure can act as a stress-reliever. Davidson et al. (2005) found that going out and engaging in normal activities, having meaningful social roles and maintaining positive interpersonal relationships outside of the formal mental health systems were found as salient themes of recovery processes. Carruthers and Hood (2004) stressed the role of therapeutic recreation services for individuals with mental illness in facilitating resilience, thriving and life satisfaction. Pedlar et al. (2008) pointed out the importance of informal recreation opportunities (e.g. informal get-together during which women inmates with mental challenges living in a prison system spent a leisurely evening together with people from the community) rather than a conventional formalised intervention to facilitate friendship and community reintegration. The notion of leisure as an antidote to depressive symptomotology was shown in Fullagar's study (2008) with 48 Australian women with depression. This study drew on post-structural feminist theories of emotion to explore the significance of leisure within women's narratives of recovery from depression.

Harvey et al. (2010) study shows that people who engage in regular leisure-time activity of higher intensity are less likely to have symptoms of depression. The study also found that the context in which activity takes place is vital and that the social benefits associated with exercise, like increased number of friends and social support, are more important in understanding how exercise may be linked to improved mental health than any biological markers of fitness. This may explain why leisure activity appears to have benefits not seen with physical activity undertaken as part of a working day.

Gautam et al. (2007) try to explore whether participation in leisure social and religious activities are related to depression and satisfaction with life in older adults of Nepal. They found that specific activity participation was a significant correlate of lower levels of depression and higher levels of satisfaction with life among older adults in Nepal. The findings explore the need for further research on activity participation in developing countries so that it can be useful for healthcare practitioners and those involved with the activities of aged populations in developing countries.

No studies have been identified that examine the pattern of involvement of women in various activities, and the association of activity involvement with mental health, notably depression and satisfaction with life. In India, very few opportunities are found for women to actively and openly participate in changing leisure activities because of the rigid patriarchal system.

Women and Leisure

Leisure is a basic need of human life. It provides physical and mental relaxation to person. It is equally important for both man and woman. But the Indian society being male dominated, there is a big difference between leisure of man and woman. Traditionally, women have always been treated as subordinated to men in the every aspect of life. Their place of work is confined to do household chores. They move only within the narrow sphere of kitchen cooking, child bearing and rearing and catering to the relatives, in-laws and husband. They have practically no idea of the busy world outside. On the other hand, the man is attached with the outside world. He is the one who is related with the economic activities of the family by doing job. It is considered that he has a right to spare time for physical and mental health, while woman has no need for it. Various norms and values of society have also limited the leisure activities of women whereas not so in the case of men.

Leisure researchers have often acted as a prophet of good fortune or doom. Some have predicted a new age of leisure, a society of wealth, and a drastic reduction in working time. Kenneth Roberts (1981) distinguishes an 'optimistic' scenario (increase in wealth, more gratification at work, extended leisure) from a 'pessimistic' scenario (limited growth, ecological constraints). He opts for a moderate scenario: an irrefutable growth in leisure as it occupies a larger space than before. But he reminds us of the danger of generalisation. We are not moving towards a society of leisure but towards a society in which leisure is an undeniable and larger component.

Leisure activities for women have changed immeasurably in the last 50 years. While men's and children's activities largely involve play and competition, women have seemed to spend whatever leisure time they have had in the productive arts. Grandmother used to say that idle hands were the devil's workshop. Girls were encouraged to knit, sew, embroider or weave. While these activities were necessary tasks for our female ancestors, they took away leisure time as an arena of choice, if indeed any leisure time remained after families had been fed, children bathed and put to bed, and the pile of ironing and mending whittled down. Today women may choose quilting and other crafts as their favourite leisure time activities. But equally, they can go shopping, to the cinema or participate in kitty parties. And they can choose gardening as much for the love of digging into the rich earth as for the pleasure of cooking new varieties of meals.

The evolution of work activities into leisure time hobbies will keep social anthropologists filling books for years to come. So will the social revolutions that lead to profound changes in the very definition of what constitutes leisure time. If mom cooks something extra as a special dish after work, most families recognise that as dinner. If dad spends half of Sunday cooking special lunch of fried rice and curry *chole* (chick peas), we are more likely to identify this as his gourmet-cooking hobby. But the reverse can also be true if mom has taken up chainsaw sculpture and dad is happily knitting an Afghan.

Women's lifestyles and leisure choices are no longer predictable, nor are they static. The passion and interests that are put on hold while women pursue careers, education and family responsibilities may suddenly take root when the nest is empty and time is available. Many women have chosen to include yoga and fitness routines among their lifestyle choices, recognising the physical and mental health benefits of exercise (Nagla, 2006). The value of recreation and social participation is generally acknowledged, but for no group are these of greater health value than for women.

Women and Mental Illness

Standard histories saw the 19th-century medical treatment of madness (developed from the reforms of Pinel in France and Take Brothers in England) as an enlightened liberation of the mad from the ignorance and brutality of preceding ages. But, according to Foucault (1988), the new idea that mad were merely sick ('mentally' ill) and in need of medical treatment was not at all a clear improvement on earlier conceptions (e.g. the Renaissance idea that the mad were in contact with the mysterious forces of cosmic tragedy or the 17th – 18th century view of madness as renouncing of reason). Moreover, he argued that the alleged scientific neutrality of modern medical treatment of insanity is in fact covers for controlling challenges to a conventional bourgeois morality. In short, Foucault argued that what was presented as an objective, incontrovertible scientific discovery (that madness is mental illness) was in fact the product of eminently questionable social and ethical commitments.

Fullagar (2008) found evidence that leisure: (a) helped one up positive experiences of self beyond the experiences with the medical/clinical treatment, (b) had transformative effects on gender identity (learning really 'who I am'), (c) generated 'hope' that there is life beyond depression and (d) enabled the women to exercise a sense of entitlement to play and enjoy life. Importantly, recovery-oriented leisure practices involved setting new boundaries for self (e.g. personal space) and others, and elicited emotions (e.g. joy, pleasure, courage) that facilitated transformation in ways that biomedical treatments could not. Fullgar stated, 'The recovery practices adopted by women were significant not because of the 'activities' themselves but in terms of the meanings that attributed to their merging identities (e.g. alone or with others)' through creative (e.g. art/craft, gardening, writing, reading, music, community, bowls, dance, Yoga, Tai Chi, swimming, mediation) and social activities (e.g. cafes, dance courses, support groups, pets, church, helping others).

Mental Health Care Act

The Lunacy Regulation Act, 1853, Indian Lunacy Act, 1912 and the Lunatic Asylum Amendment Act, 1853, were some of the archaic legislations that dealt with mental illness. Insane were referred to as lunatics or idiots thereby treating them as persons who were extremely dangerous for the mainstream society. It was in 1920, that the name mental hospital was substituted for Lunatic Asylums.

The Mental Health Act, 1987, was a positive step in ameliorating the conditions of persons with mental illness in India. The enactment of the Mental Health Act brought along with it a lot of positive changes from the erstwhile draconian legislations, yet has left a lot to be done.

The National Health Policy, 2002, also dealt with mental health, recognising that mental health disorders have much more to them than what meets the age having serious bearing on the quality of life of the person affected by it. The plan had envisaged a network of decentralised mental health services.

India is a signatory to the convention on Rights of Persons with Disabilities, 2006, and ratified the said instrument in October 2007. The convention inter alia provides that every person with disabilities has a right to respect for his or her physical and mental integrity on an equal basis with other (Article 17).

The experience with Mental Health Act, 1987, has been far from satisfying. In order to devise a strong mechanism to address the concern of persons suffering with mental illness and to ensure compliance with International instruments, the Draft Bill on Mental Health and Family Welfare known as Mental Health Care Bill, 2012 was put in place. The Bill seeks to protect, promote and fulfil the rights of persons with mental illness and to provide treatment care and rehabilitation to improve the capacity of the person to develop his or her potential and to facilitate his or her integration into community life.

The present study focuses on experience of women in leisure activities and its relation to the mental health of women in India. The following issues are raised for the exploratory study:

- Does engaging in leisure activities correlate with depression and satisfaction of women?
- Do women get less opportunity to actively participate in leisure activities?
- At what level the doctor suggests mentally ill women to engage/participate in leisure activities?

Methods

District Mental Health Programme (DMHP) started in Haryana in 1999 and district Kurukshetra was selected under the supervision of psychiatric department of Post Graduate Medical College of Rohtak. After the successful start of DMHP, Kurukshetra, two more districts covered in 2008 which are Hissar and Gurgaon. This study was carried out in the outpatient department of psychiatry, district hospital, Gurgaon. This is a secondary care health institution. Gurgaon district is situated in National Capital Region of Delhi, the capital of India. Gurgaon is about 32 km away from New Delhi, the National capital of India. Gurgaon has 12 primary health centres and 75 sub-centres at rural level. Training programmes for medical officers and paramedical staff is a regular feature at psychiatric department of Gurgaon hospital. It is a part of district Mental Health Programme guidelines.

All new first 194 female patients of psychiatric disorders who reported to the department formed the study population for the present study. Patients' data is generated from psychiatric diagnostic disorders consisting of 242 female patients who had been diagnosed and treated in the psychiatric unit of DMHP, Gurgaon. Intensive interview is carried out with the patients and also with their relatives. Some narration given by the patients about their life sequences episodes are also presented in the form of case histories. Data is collected between May–June 2010. Since we do not have tools to measure the chronicity of mental illness, neither we are specialised in doing so, therefore, we thoroughly interacted with them and ascertained certain information in the form of episodes or certain other levels of information. Although doctors call them the precipitating factors in causing the mental illness. We have taken 194 women who are mentally ill.

Description of Sample

The mental distress of women grouped according to age shows that prevalence is high in women in reproductive years. Most of the studies break off at the age of 50 years or so. Among the studies that do include old age, some showed a decrease in distress among women. However, it is also seen that widowhood brings in heightened mental distress.

Table 1 depicts that in the age-group of 20–30 years, there are 35 (18.04%) mentally ill patients, and in another age group of 31–40 years, there are 92 (47.42%) cases. Thus, the majority of the cases are in the age group of 20–40 years which is the most active and productive period in life. However, in the age group of 41 years and above, there are 67 (34.52%) cases.

Table 1 shows the prevalence of mental distress and several other socio-economic variables. It is seen that symptom rate is linked more with being married than being single. Being widowed, separated or divorced is also linked with a higher symptom rate. The studies show greater distress in married women as compared to married men and greater stress in single women as compared to single men. Several studies have been cited showing that marriage is a stressful occupation for women. Widowhood brings heightened mental distress. A study by Sandhya (1994) studies the forced changes in life after widowhood. Our study also shows that there are as many as 128 (65.97%) patients who are married as compared to 61 (31.44%) who are unmarried. There are only 5 (2.55%) women who are widows.

Table 1 depicts that there are 64 (32.98%) patients who are illiterate; 107 (55.15%) at the education level between primary and senior secondary level; only 22 (11.34%) patients are either graduate or postgraduate, whereas only one patient is having a professional qualification.

Correlating mental illness with the structure of the family, it was noted by many of the studies that mental distress was much greater in nuclear families than joint families. Chakraborty (1990) found that joint families are perceived as fostering greater emotional bonding between members, as having more care givers to take care of the vulnerable and the weak, especially women and the elderly, and as being based upon mutuality and cooperation amongst its members. These studies led to an unabated hysteria among professionals after the 1970s, that the greater fragmentation of Indian society into nuclear families will increase conflicts, stress and strains, particularly among the women folk. Sethi and Manchanda (1978) explain the greater stress among the female members in completely joint families as the result of the conflict emanating from

Table 1

Socio-Economic Profile of the Mentally Ill Women Respondents

Age-groups	20–30yrs 35(18.04)	31–40yrs 92 (47.42)	41–50yrs 53(27.31)	51–60 yrs 14 (7.21)	Total 194 (100)
Marital status	Married 128 (65.97)	Unmarried 61 (31.44)	Widowed 5 (2.55)	—	194 (100)
Education	Illiterate 64 (32.98)	Primary – 12th Class 107(55.15)	Graduation-Postgraduation 22 (11.34)	Professional 1 (0.51)	194 (100)
Family	Nuclear 149 (76.80)	Joint 45 (23.19)	—	—	194 (100)
Nativity	Rural 85 (43.81)	Urban 109 (56.18)	—	—	194 (100)
Monthly income	Below ₹ 5,000 96 (49.48)	Rs 5,001–10,000 65 (33.50)	Rs 10,001–20,000 17 (8.76)	More than ₹ 20,000 16 (8.24)	194 (100)
Occupation	Housewife 124 (63.91)	Labourer/class IV work 60 (30.92)	Professionals (teachers etc.) 4 (2.06)	Shop/small business 6 (3.09)	194 (100)

the desire to loosen the traditional family ties. Chakraborty (1990) argues against romanticising the joint family as these families engage in a process of positive selection thus excluding economically dependent or other vulnerable people. Since nuclear family is the trend of the urban society and Gurgaon is also regarded as hi-tech city, therefore, 146 (76.80%) of the our respondents are living in a nuclear family and only 23.19 per cent are part of joint family system.

As in the case of family structure, the urban background is also reflected in the data gathered from the hospital. Little more than 50 per cent of mentally ill patient women are from urban background, and less then 45 per cent are from rural background. Most of our mentally ill patients are not working or in some cases even if they are working, they are engaged either as labourers or in lower class occupations. The income of almost 50 per cent respondents is below ₹ 5,000 per month. It may also be due to the fact that because of their poor economic background, they are in the government hospital for the treatment.

The illiterate, poor refuges, unemployed and women in low paying work or sex-workers, household maids and beggars are most vulnerable to mental distress. Studies in India have shown that even though fewer women get admitted to mental hospitals for care, once they are admitted there they stay for a longer period of time. The reason for this longer stay, range from economic reason to the attitudes of hospital towards appropriate feminine behaviour. Lobbying for easy discharge may be seen as aggressive and assertive behaviour, which is an indication that the woman has not recovered fully. The ideal woman patient is expected to be compliant, patient, passive, dependent and submissive. The data on occupations structure presented in Table 1 shows that majority of patients, i.e. 124 (63.91%) are housewives, another 60 (30.92%) are working as labourers or engaged in lower income paid occupation. The data clearly depicts that only four women are professionals who are school teachers and clerks and another six are doing very small business, like running shop, etc.

The majority of females (75.25%) in the sample reported that they spoke to their neighbours occasionally, visited friends on occasional basis (77.7%), and were occasionally involved in religious activities (77.31%). The majority of women in the sample reported singing prayers and *bhajans* (87.11%), listened to the radio and watched television daily (65.46%). Women who never participated in any physical activities were 68.55 per cent.

Overall, less than one-fourth of women participated in talking with neighbours, visited friends, socialised with others, did physical exercise and participated in festival activities on daily basis except watching television/radio listening and reciting prayers and *bhajans*.

The answers came in multiple response form. Although, we do not claim that on the onset of mental illness, the non-experience of leisure is a cause of mental illness. However, we separately asked women about their overall experience of leisure during mental illness in their life. The data reveals that the experience of majority of respondents (53.09%) regarding leisure gives physical and mental alertness. They found that leisure keeps people physically and mentally healthy which in turn affect their roles in the family. Fifty-two or 26.80 per cent said that by experiencing leisure one could find social time for themselves, and 79 (40.72%) reported that it provides an experience of pleasure in true sense. Forty-five (23.19%) viewed leisure as a form of individual liberation.

Table 2

Leisure Activities among Mentally Ill Women

Leisure Activity	*Occurrence of leisure activity*	*n=194*	*Percentage*
Talk with neighbours	Never	8	4.12
	Sometimes	146	75.25
	Daily	40	20.61
Visit friends	Never	10	5.15
	Sometimes	150	77.31
	Daily	34	17.52
Socialise with others	Never	29	14.94
	Sometimes	158	81.44
	Daily	7	3.60
Watch TV, listen radio	Never	4	2.06
	Sometimes	63	32.47
	Daily	127	65.46
Do physical exercise	Never	133	68.55
	Sometimes	52	26.80
	Daily	9	4.63
Recite prayers and *bhajans*	Never	4	2.06
	Sometimes	21	21.10.82
	Daily	169	87.11
Festival activities	Never	5	2.57
	Sometimes	170	87.62
	Daily	19	9.79

Table 3

Overall Experience of Leisure Among the Mentally Ill Women

Overall experience	*Number of respondents**	*Percentage*
Feeling physically healthy	103	53.09
Feeling mentally healthy	81	41.75
Feeling physically and mentally healthy	133	68.55
Social time for self	52	26.80
Experience of pleasure	79	40.72
Individual liberty	45	23.19

*Multiple responses permitted

Table 4

Advice of Doctors for Leisure Activities Reported by Mentally Ill Women

Doctor's Advice for Leisure Activities	*No of Respondents*	*Percentage*
Participation in leisure activity should be a part of life	16	8.24
Doctor only casually advices for participation in leisure activities	34	17.52
Doctor never advised for participation in any sort of leisure activity	144	74.22
Total	194	100.00

Since the women we interviewed were seeking treatment from the hospital for their illness, therefore we asked them about the prescription of the doctor for their illness. Regarding the medication for their illness, the doctor prescribed some or other form of medicines for their treatment, however, we also curiously asked about their treatment process in the form of some extra non-medication prescription. It is quite surprising to note that majority of our respondents, i.e. 144 (74.22%), reported that they did not get any advice from the doctors regarding participation in leisure activities. Only 34 (17.52%) doctors casually advised or recommended to participate in leisure activities for overcoming mental illness. Very few, i.e. 16 (8.24%), doctors thought that leisure should be a part of the treatment process and leisure should be an activity in the daily routine.

It is found from the interviews of the mentally ill women that majority of them, i.e. 95 per cent do not completely adhere to any particular system in the course of their treatment from mental illness. People's consultation with one faith healer to another and doctors from the private to the government hospitals may not be a matter of exercising choice but a pragmatic adaptation to the poor quality of treatment in different course of treatment and patients try hard to get the best out of what is available.

On the basis of patients' narratives regarding the treatment they received from the doctors or from the faith healers in terms of leisure activities.

The middle aged woman (30 years, in patient) migrated from western Uttar Pradesh belongs to poor economic background. She said that an allopathic doctor is giving medci8ine and faith healer is giving some type of water and powder. She was given advice for not eating certain things, but at no point of time she was advised for engaging herself in recreation and leisure activities.

A 40 year old woman from Bihar had been suffering from acute depression. The doctor admitted her in the hospital. Doctor asked her history of illness and other related episodic events in her life. She accepted that after getting admitted to the hospital she felt better may be because of the strong medicine given by doctor. However, doctor was not able to treatment her illness from the root of it. It may be that doctors are not finding the root cause of the illness and simply concentrating on the medicine part. She thinks that she wants to forget her bad past by engaging herself in leisure and social activities but unable to do it.

Another patient was a 35 years old woman from Gurgaon itself and suffering from schizophrenia. During diagnosis, she explained to the doctor about her victimisation of domestic violence. Doctor prescribed medicines and asked her to take them regularly. According to her, when she takes medicines her condition is better as most of the time she feel sleepy. As and when she ignores medicines, she suffers from the illness. According to her at no point of time doctor suggest her to engage herself in recreation and leisure activities.

A 37 year old woman from nearby village in Gurgaon is suffering from depression. The doctor prescribed medicines to her for 10 days and then asked her to come again after 10 days. The woman said that she spent 3400 rupees in one month and she did not get a single medicine from the hospital. She said that if she would have spent the same money for recreation or leisure activities, she would have been cured from her illness. She asserted that her family members too are ready to spend money for her treatment but not for leisure.

From above all the interviews of women, it is clear that mentally ill women feel that leisure and recreation are important for keeping oneself mentally and physically healthy. However, neither doctors feel it necessary to prescribe or suggest leisure participation as essential for treatment nor the family members of the mentally ill find its importance in the treatment process. It may be due to the financial hardship or may be the women are kept outside the purview of the leisure activities.

Conclusions

The study of mental illness among women and leisure activity can contribute to our understanding of a number of fundamental dynamics underlying male dominant societies. Our study reveals the inseparability between the values of a society and the changing perceptions of women in visualising the importance of leisure for mental health. The study helps to document the importance of leisure activities among women particularly in Indian society which challenges conventional gender division in leisure. Leisure alerts, it individualises, and allows freedom of expression. The stereotypical medical prescription of doctors based on medicine also smacks of not allowing space to leisure activities for sound mental health.

Notes

1. http://week.manorameonline.com/cgi-
2. http://www.firstpist.com/living/suicide-nation-can-the-mental-health-bill-change-anything-in-India-503557.html.
3. Article1, http://www un.org/en/documents/udhr/index.Shtml#a18.

References

Babiss, F. (2002). An Ethnographic Study of Mental Health Treatment and Outcomes: Doing What Works, *Occupational Therapy in Mental Health*, 18: pp. 1–146.

Carruthers, C. and C.D. Hood (2004), 'The Power of the Positive: Leisure and Well-being', *Therapeutic Recreation Journal*, 38: pp. 225–245.

Chakraborty, Ajitia (1990), *Social Stress and Mental Health: A Social-Psychiatric Field study of Calcutta,* New Delhi: Sage Publications.

Davidson, L. et al. (2005). Processes of Recovery in Serious Mental Illness: Findings from a Multinational Study, *American Journal of Psychiatric Rehabilitation,* 8: pp. 177–201.

Driver, B.L. and D.H. Burns (1999). Concepts and Uses of the Benefits Approach to Leisure, in E.I. Jackson and T.L. Burton (eds.), *Leisure Studies: Prospects for the Twenty-First Century,* State College, Pa.: Venture Publishing, pp. 349–369.

Finlay, John H., *cit* Butler, George D. (1967). *Introduction to Community Recreation,* New York: McGraw-Hill Book Co., p. 3.

Foucault, Michael (1988). *Madness and Civilization: A History of Insanity in the Age of Reason,* New York: Vintage.

Frances, K. (2006). Outdoor Recreation as an Occupation to Improve Quality of Life for People with Enduring Mental Health Problems, *British Journal of Occupational Therapy,* 69: pp. 182–186.

Fullagar, S. (2008). Leisure Practices as Counter-Depressants: Emotion-Work and Emotion-play within Women's recovery from Depression, *Leisure Sciences,* 30: pp. 35–52.

Gautam, Ramraj, Tami Saito and Ichiro and Kai (2007). Leisure and Religious Activity Participation and Mental Health: Gender Analysis of Older Adults in Nepal, *Bio Medical Central Public Health,* 7: p. 299.

Harvey, Samuel B. et al. (2010). Physical activity and Common Mental Disorders, *British Journal of Psychiatry,* 197, pp. 357–364.

Henderson, K.A. et al. (1996). *Both Gains and Gaps: Feminist Perspectives on Women's Leisure,* State College, PA: Venture Publishing, Inc.

Hodgson, S. and C. Lloyd (2002). Leisure as a Relapse Prevention Strategy, *British Journal of Therapy and Rehabilitation,* 9: pp. 86–91.

Hookway, R. (1978), *Issues in Recreation,* England: Penguin Books.

Hyman, S. et al. (2006) (eds.). *Disease Control Priorities in Developing Countries,* New York: Oxford University Press. pp. 605–626.

Iwasaki, Y. (2008). Pathways to Meaning-Making through Leisure in Global Contexts, *Journal of Leisure Research,* 40: pp. 231–249.

Iwasaki, Y. et al. (2010). Leisure as a Context for Active Living, Recovery, Health and Life Quality for Persons with Mental Illness in a Global Context, *Health Promotion International,* 25, 4: pp. 483–494.

Kaplan, Max (1960). *Leisure in American: A Social Inquiry,* New York: John Wiley & Sons, Inc.

Kelly, D.A. and V.J. Freysinger (2000). *21st Century Leisure: Current Issues,* Boston, Mass.: Allyn and Bacon.

Lloyd, C. et al. (2007). The Association Between Leisure Motivation and Recovery: A Pilot Study, *Australian Occupational Therapy Journal,* 54: pp. 33–41.

MANAS Foundation (2008). *State of Mental Health in Delhi: Prevalence of Psychiatric Morbidity, Subjective Well Being and Patterns of Help-seeking Behaviour,* New Delhi: Planning Commission.

Mental Health Atlas-2011 Country Profiles (2011). www.who.int/mental_health/evidence/atlas/profiles/en/

Miller, Norman and Dunae P. Robinson (1963), *The Leisure Age: Its Challenge to Recreation,* California: Wadsworth Publishing Company, Inc.

Minato, Mand R. Zemke (2004), 'Time Use of People with Schizophrenia Living with the Community', *Occupational Therapy International,* 11: pp. 177–191.

Modi, Ishwar (1985). *Leisure, Mass Media and Social Structure,* Jaipur: Rawat Publications.

Moloney, T.(2002). My Journey of Recovery, *New Paradigm,* 5th December.

Nagla, Madhu (2006). Yoga, Health and Leisure: Attitudes of Women in Haryana, *World Leisure Journal,* 2, 48, pp. 23–34.

Nakhooda, Zulie (1961). *Leisure and Recreation in Society,* Allahabad: Kitab Mahal.

Pedlar, A. et al. (2008). Incarcerated Women and Leisure: Making Good Girls out of bad?, *Therapeutic Recreation Journal,* 42: pp. 24–37.

Roberts, Kenneth (1981). *Leisure,* London: Longman.

Roberts, Kenneth (1983). *Youth and Leisure,* London: Allen and Unwin.

Ryan, K. (2002). Road to Recovery. *New Paradigm,* 4th December.

Samdahl, D.M. (1988). A Symbolic Interactionist Model of Leisure: Theory and Empirical Support, *Leisure Sciences,* 10: pp. 27–39.

Sandhya (1994). *Widowhood: A Socio-psychiatric Study,* Delhi: Mohit Publications.

Sethi, B.B. and R. Manchanda (1978). Family Structure and Psychiatric Disorders, *Indian Journal of Psychiatry,* 20(3), pp. 283–288.

Shaw, S.M. (1985). The Meaning of Leisure in Everyday Life, *Leisure Sciences,* 7: pp. 1–24.

Trauer, T. et al. (1998). A Study of the Quality of Life of the Severely Mentally Ill, *International Journal of Social Psychiatry,* 44: pp. 79–91.

World Health Organization (2003). *Investing in Mental Health,* http;//www.who.int/mental-health/media/investing-mnh.pdf.

World Health Organization (WHO) (2001). *The World Health Report 2001- Mental Health: New Understanding,* New Hope.

Yanos, P.T. and R.H. Moos (2007) Determinants of Functioning and Well-Being among Individuals with Schizophrenia: An Integrated Model, *Clinical Psychology Review,* 27: pp. 58–77.

12

Leisure, Tourism Development and Environment Interface

Reflections from Uttarakhand Tourism

BHAGWAN S. BISHT

Uttarakhand, with an area of 53,483 sq km, is the ninth Himalayan state of Indian republic. Laying in between 28°53' 24' to 31°27' 50' north latitude, and 77°34' 37' to 81°02' 22' east longitude, this Himalayan state is referred to as a miniature of India due to its diversified geo-climatic conditions, socio-cultural complexes and ethnic compositions. Located on the fringe of two international boundaries of Nepal in east, and Tibet in north, the state of Uttarakhand is internationally known for its innumerable tourist destinations, including various hill stations, wild life sanctuaries, national parks, water, land and aerial adventure sports and above all for pilgrimage tourism centres located in its various river valleys, mountain peaks and dense forests. During last decade a tremendous growth recorded in tourism sector particularly in terms of influx of tourists (domestic and foreigner) in the state. According to tourist statistics of Uttarakhand, year 2000–2010, total 311.08 lakh tourist (309.7 lakh domestic and 1.36 lakh foreigners) visited in the state in the year 2010 in comparison to 111.36 lakh tourist (110.79 lakh domestic and 0.57 lakh foreigners) visited in the year 2000. This estimates approximately 2.8 times increase than that of the base year 2000. But falls down respectively to 268.09 lakh in 2011, 284.33 lakh in 2012 and 209.99 lakh in 2013 due to some natural calamities occurred in and around tourist destinations of Uttarakhand. Correspondingly to cater the growing need of the increasing number of the tourists in the state the infrastructural facilities related to tourism have also been created in and around the tourist destinations and also in its route. The mission of the state government is to develop Uttarakhand as a tourist hub, and the tourism as the core-sector of employment and revenue generation.

In this backdrop the main objective of the paper is to analyse scientifically the 'leisure, tourism–development and environment interface' and its pervasive environmental, socio-cultural and economic impacts respectively on the places in and around of the tourist destinations, the host communities and the stakeholders of the tourism industry in the state of Uttarakhand.

The study goes with the hypothetical proposition that 'sustainable-tourism–development-strategy can only serve the goal of tourism–development with its triple principles (the environmental, social and economic) and would also satiate the needs, motives and purposes of the respective stakeholders of tourism industry.'

The findings of this paper are based on the primary field information collected through quasi-participant observation and participatory group appraisal method. The stakeholders of the tourism industry in general and the tourists, service providers, the host community, i.e. the indigenous communities living in and around the tourist destinations were used as the source of primary information. The relevant secondary sources like public documents, research findings of the earlier researches, and the relevant published literature have also been used to substantiate the analysis and the findings of the study.

Conceptual Premise

Leisure, tourism–development and environment overtly appear to be the different concepts but covertly all the three are closely interrelated and interwoven phenomena and can be understood on the basis of cause-effect relationships.

Leisure

Conceptually, 'leisure' is a complex and a broad concept with various time-space oriented implications. According to *Concise Oxford English Dictionary* (2011), 'leisure' means 'free time': time at one's disposal; and also 'enjoyment of free time'. The literal meaning of 'leisure' as *Concise Oxford English Dictionary* spelled out sounds about the 'time period which remains at the disposal of the person concerned and is supposed to be spent for enjoyment and merry making'. *Wikipedia* explains leisure in terms of 'free time', 'relaxing' and 'time-passes'. It explains that 'leisure, or free time, is time spent away from business, work, domestic chores and education, it also excludes time spend on activities such as sleeping.' But so far as the genesis of the English term 'leisure' is concerned, its first known use earmarked in 14th century in middle English as 'leiser', from Anglo-French 'leisir', from 'leisir' to be permitted, from latin 'licere' which is meant by the, 'time free from work or duties'. In the course of time, the implications and the notions implied with the 'leisure' changed with the change of time and space. As Dumazedier (1967) mentions, 'leisure' as the product of the civilisation born from the industrial revolution. Sebastian de Grazias (1964) opines that 'leisure' existed in truest sense only in ancient Greece during the time of great philosophers Plato and Aristotle. Contrary to such notions and the narratives, Modi (2010: 13) asserts leisure as universal phenomena and opines that, 'leisure exists universally and that it has a dynamic character, while it is structural in nature, and cultural in orientation and operation.' The leisure, as such, is a multidimensional phenomenon can be understood in the context of the psychology, culture, economy and society which ascertained the leisure seeking behaviour of a person concerned. It is, perhaps, the only reason that Josef Pieper (Modi et al., 2010: 2) has stated that 'leisure is a receptive attitude of mind, a contemplative attitude, and it is not only the occasion but also the capacity for stepping oneself in the whole of creation'. But today leisure, as Cheng Siwei (2010: 5) opines, has become a new social and cultural phenomena which satisfies the need of free development. Not only it helps in adjusting the economic structure of the society but also in altering the traditional form of industry. Narrating the importance of leisure in men's life, Modi (2010: 12) further states that 'leisure has been acclaimed as one of the greatest saviour of the mankind. World would not have been a happy place if there was no leisure'. Cheng Siwei (2010: 6), stating the functional form of leisure, opines '... enjoying leisure time in the present means to work better in future. Especially those who are involved in highly creative jobs often need inspiration and that comes from the enjoyment of leisure'.

Joffre Domazedier (Parker, 1975: 91–101) distinguished from distinct definitions of leisure which begin broadly and gradually narrow in scope. The first and broadest one defines leisure as a style of behaviour that may occur even at work, the second defines it as any non-work activity, the third further excludes family and household obligations, and finally the narrowest defines leisure as activities dedicated to self-fulfillment. Domazedier's four definitions are not exhaustive. Even leisure is deeply concerned with the culture of a given community. The culture reflects in the pattern of leisure the community have and also the way it spends its leisure. Perhaps Modi (2010: 12) has therefore referred Sebastin De Grazia (1964) who pronounced in his masterpiece *Of Time, Work and Leisure*, 'you tell me your leisure, I shall tell your culture'.

Thus, the existing views and notions attributed to leisure reveal its multi-dimensional as well as multifunctional nature. But, in the present context, 'leisure' has been taken as a motivating factor with its inherent multifarious socio-psychological and economic implications which leads a person for tourism of various kinds in general.

Tourism Development and Sustainability Concerns in Question: Retrospection

Apart from the literal meaning implications, the leisure tourism, since its inception, traversing through the ages has transformed under the principle of immanent and induced change into 'leisure-tourism-industry' and the 'leisure-society' as its consequential impact. But the emergence of 'leisure-tourism-industry' and the 'leisure-society', due to their diversified positive and also of the negative impacts on environment, society, culture and economy have ever been in question and therefore a concern of discourse for the scientists and also for the policy makers. The concerns in question have always remained how to ensure and develop 'sustainable tourism' so that the benefits of tourism can be maximised and the negative impacts can be removed or minimised to its lowest and ineffective level. To my mind its answer and therefore a solution lies only in the spirit and philosophy of 'sustainability' and 'sustainable development' as have been employed as early as 1970 (Stiver, 1976) for describing an economy in equilibrium with basic ecological support system, and in United Nations World Commission on Environment and Development (UNWCED) also called the Brundtland Commission 1987 report 'Our Common Future', as the form of development that meets the need of the present without compromising the ability of future generations to meet their needs (*Wikipedia*). In 1988, the United Nations World Tourism Organization (UNWTO) defined the sustainable tourism as, 'leading to management of all resources in such a way that economic, social and aesthetic needs can be fulfilled while maintaining cultural integrity, essential ecological processes, biological diversity and life support system; later on in 1992 the Earth Summit at Rio established the triple principles of sustainable tourism; environmental, economic and social sustainability and have since been adopted worldwide' (Tolia, 2012: 60). Besides this, in the writing of Agyeman, et al., (2002: 5), the 'sustainable development' and 'sustainability' have been used in terms of the better quality of life for all, now and into the future in a just and equitable manner. While Needham (2011) did it in terms of need satisfaction of the present generation contributing for the need satisfaction of the future generation.

Thus, basing on the spirit and philosophy of 'sustainability' and 'sustainable development' the sustainable tourism has the potential as a powerful source of employment generation and also a source of income. It (the sustainable tourism), as Capetown Declaration on responsible tourism has characterised, 'minimises negative economic, environmental and social impacts, generates a greater economic benefits for local people and enhances the well-being of host communities, improves working conditions and access to the industry, involves local people in decision-making, makes positive contributions to the conservation of natural and cultural heritage, provides more enjoyable experiences for tourists through more meaningful connections with local people, and a greater understanding to local cultural, social and environmental issues, provides access for people with disabilities and is culturally sensitive, engenders respect between tourists and hosts and build local pride and confidence.' (www.responsibletourismpartnership.org/capetown.html).

It is the reason that the United Nations Environmental Programme (UNEP) and UNWTO in a publication, 'Making Tourism more Sustainable', listed the aims of sustainable tourism and also suggested some development guidelines and the management practices for all forms of sustainable tourism in all types of tourist destinations. The sub-committee chaired by the joint secretary (tourism), Government of India, 2010, has also defined Sustainable Tourism Criteria (STCI) and the indicators of accommodation and tour operator sector for India (www.incridibleindia.org), so that the aims and objectives of the sustainable tourism can be achieved according to the UNEP, UNWTO and STCI, 2010. But the multipronged inevitable impacts, which can broadly be categorised as the positive and negative impacts of the fast growing world's largest industry of tourism, are viewed, felt, and also reflected upon their consequential effects on the overall environment and therefore cannot be ignored in a casual manner. Because, in spite of the various induced efforts, the major concern pertaining to the development of 'sustainable tourism' for the sustainability of the world's largest tourism industry and also its benefits equitable for the present and future generations still stands and therefore needs to be addressed meaningfully and in a very objective manner.

It is self evident by nature that the 'leisure' irrespective of any society, may be that a primitive, semi-primitive, agricultural, industrial or the post-industrial, has a place in men's life. Bisht (2010: 11) has aptly stated that, 'there is a provision of leisure in every walk of human life. Somewhere it is planned and managed institutionally by the respective organisations and institutions and somewhere the nature itself offer a period of time to the people to use it as leisure'. This is also true in the present era of globalisation and liberalisation, and the information technology revolution has made it more effective, motivating and accessible to all the people of every social category in the universe. The expanding consumer culture corresponding to the increasing economic standard of the people and the hectic lifestyle of this competitive world has accelerated the leisure activities and also the need of leisure in human life. A person belonging to any social category and also of any socio-economic background wishes to have some leisure in his/her life. Thus, people indulge in leisure activities sometimes for merry making and keeping oneself free from one's prolonged monotonous routine set of activities, sometime for change by changing the place and the stereotyped scheduled agenda, sometime to relax oneself by spending some moments with their near and dear in some eco-friendly places away from home, sometime by performing the task and activities corresponding to their own hobbies and sometime by visiting far off places within or outside the country. Thus, every person has leisure and a particular type of inherent notions about leisure. But the difference lies in its utilisation pattern. Cheng Siwei (2010: 6) has rightly stated that 'indeed we all have leisure time no matter rich or poor. It is only the content and manner to utilise it that differentiates us.'

If we turn the pages of the history of human development we envisage the different forms and patterns of leisure and also the utilisation system of leisure time. Right from primitive to the 21st century knowledge-society, we have evidences of the leisure the people had and also the way of spending the leisure time. For instance, the primitives after having stomachful food used to have some leisure time which they would spend, sometime by resting or sleeping beneath the trees or elsewhere in the sun shade during summer, and sometime by lying or sleeping in the sun in winter. In agricultural societies, the seasonal leisure or the free time between the harvest time used to be utilised and synchronised with seasonal activities or ritual celebration and chatting or playing cards, hunting and similar other activities. But in modern societies, the people under the impact of consumerism make provision for leisure and also schedule for utilisation pattern of leisure time as per one's day-to-day, weekly, monthly and annual needs. These emerging trends of leisure and leisure psychology have multifarious reflections in society; somewhere in the form of leisure industry, somewhere in the form of leisure society, somewhere as leisure tourism, somewhere as leisure trips and somewhere in all the forms altogether. As a matter of fact the changing leisure psychology has evolved multi-dimensions of worldwide leisure society – and tourism is one of its various dimensions. In other words, it can be stated that the prevailing psychology after leisure is manifested in the form of tourism that motivates people towards various type of touristic activities. It promotes tourism development at tourist destinations and is viewed in the form of infrastructural development, community-based services, government initiatives and people's participation. The development of road and railway communications, air services, hotels, motels, restaurants, roadside country inns, *dhabas*, tea-stalls, and facilities of drinking water, health services, safety and security measures, development of side-scene, job opportunities for skilled and non-skilled work-force throughout the tourist destinations grow as a by-product of leisure. This sort of development takes place overtly to cater to the essential needs of the tourists but covertly for earning maximum benefits from the tourists. Almost the same trend has been viewed even in the case of Uttarakhand tourism.

Since the availability of infrastructural facilities has a decisive role in pulling the tourists, hence the stakeholders; particularly the government and the local bodies looking after tourism activities strive to ensure suitable infrastructure facilities like road communication, transportation, drinking water, electricity, medical facilities and boarding and loading facilities for the tourists. On the other hand, private players like hoteliers, restaurant-owners, skilled and non-skilled human resources, tour operators, guides and others, etc. engaged in tourism industry also offer their services in their respective manner. They constantly strive to extend the facilities in their respective areas by abiding or not-abiding the norms set by administrative and governing agencies of the government. But in all respect, the environmental impacts of tourism activities are inevitably viewed in and around the tourist destinations which sometime resulted in the form of environmental hazards as well as of environmental pollution. Even the impact of tourism and touristic activities are also viewed in human psychology and human relations. It is apparently reflected in the behaviour patterns of the people involved directly or indirectly in tourism activities and finally ascertains their socio-cultural and economic status and also the scope of the network of social relations of the stakeholders. But the viability and also the sustainability of the socio-cultural and economic status and the environmental conditions emerged out of the tourism activities depend on the approach and the technology followed by the stakeholders for tourism development. Thus, the type of leisure psychology emerging in the society more rapidly and being followed by some as their basic need and natural opportunity, and by some only by nodding acquaintance, but altogether, is leading tourism and the touristic activities and finally impacting the overall environment of the tourism destination. This process explains the interface between leisure, tourism–development and the environment.

With this backdrop, this paper tends to analyse the interface between leisure, tourism development and environment with special reference of Uttarakhand tourism in India through case study method.

Tourism Scenario in Uttarakhand

The state of Uttarakhand consists of two main regions administratively known as two commissionaires, namely the Kumaun Commissionaire – the eastern part of the state forming international boundaries with Nepal and Tibet in east and north and the Garhwal Commissionaire – the western part of the state forming state boundaries with Himachal Pradesh, Haryana in north-west and Uttar Pradesh (mother state) in west and south. Geographically, Uttarakhand state is divided into five physical zones – the sub-mountain zone, made up of Tarai and Bhabar plains; the Shivalik zone, made up of Sivalik hills and Dun valleys which lies to, the north of sub-mountain region of Uttarakhand; the lower Himalayan zone also known as lesser Himalaya and situated in between 1,000 mtrs. to 2,500 mtrs. elevation; the higher Himalayan zone; and the trans-Himalayan zone.

The varieties of tourist destinations endowed with rich bio-diversity are scattered all over Uttarakhand State right from its sub-mountain region, i.e. tarai-bhabar plains to the trans Himalayan ranges.

The pilgrimage related to different religious communities is one of the major attractions for religious tourists in Uttarakhand. For Hindus, the religious destinations are in the form of Char Dham Yatra[1], Panch Kedar[2], Panch Prayag[3], Sapt Badries[4], Pancha Shila[5], various Shakti Peeths[6], and many others. For Islam followers, Piran Kaliyar[7] (a tomb of a sufi-saint) and many other historical mosques located in different localities in Uttarakhand are the pulling centres of Islamic faith. For Sikh followers, Shri Hemkund Sahib[8], Ritha Sahib[9], Nanakmata[10] are some of the attractions for those who believe in Sikh religion and also for those who wish to visit to have blessings and the fruit of pilgrimage. For Christians, the Methodist Churches located in Mussoorie, Nainital, Almora and Pithoragarh show way to the followers of Christianity and others to visit those shrines every year.

For the people loving adventure sports like mountaineering[11], trekking[12], camping on Bugyals[13], skiing[14], rafting[15], angling[16], mountain biking[17], parasailing and paragliding[18], Uttarakhand is one of the best destinations in India. It has developed adventure holiday offers for all types of adventure activities.

Uttarakhand is also regarded as one of the best region for eco-tourism. The snow covered mountain peaks, the tranquilling meadows, sky blue high altitude lakes, dense forests and wetland best suited for varieties of flora and fauna altogether invite the tourist for eco-tourism.

For nature lovers, national parks[19], wild life sanctuaries[20], alpine meadows (Bugyals), lakes[21], hot springs[22], glaciers[23], pilgrimage namely Chardham yatra, Nanda Devi Raj-Jat Yatra[24], Kailash Mansarovar Yatra[25], etc. and the enchanting landscapes, forests, views of Himalayan ranges and snow-clad mountain peaks are the panoramic spots which lure them willy-nilly towards Uttarakhand to visit for the heart's contentment.

Besides this the prevailing social harmony free from all sorts of pathogenic social evils like terrorism, insurgence and criminal acts, and all sorts of accessibility tempt even more the tourists of all classes and categories to visit Uttarakhand on priority basis (Bisht, 2010: 195).

The year-wise increasing number of tourists (domestic and foreign) visited since the creation of Uttarakhand embodies and reflects the growing trend of tourism. Also, increase of tourists in Uttarakhand in the period from 2000 to 2010 and then its gradual decline since 2011 onwards is evident from Table 1.

Table 1

Tourist Statistics of Uttarakhand, 2000–2013

(Year-wise tourists visited in Uttarakhand w.e.f. 2000 to 2013 in lakh)

Year	*Domestic*	*Foreign*	*Total*
2000	110.79	0.57	111.36
2001	105.49	0.55	106.04
2002	116.52	0.56	117.08
2003	129.30	0.64	129.94
2004	138.30	0.75	139.05
2005	162.81	0.93	163.74
2006	193.58	0.96	194.54
2007	221.54	1.06	222.60
2008	230.64	1.12	231.76
2009	231.54	1.18	232.72
2010	309.72	1.36	311.08
2011	266.66	1.43	268.09
2012	282.92	1.41	284.33
2013	208.65	1.34	209.99

Tourists' Profile Visiting Uttarakhand

The inferences drawn from group interviews and group appraisal methods exhibit that there are many types of tourists who visit Uttarakhand every year. They can be grouped into five major categories: (i) the holiday birds or the vacationer tourists may be grouped together as the leisure tourists. The majority of tourists falls in this category and they like to visit tourist destinations of Uttarakhand like Mussoorie, Dakpatthar, Nainital, Bhimtal, Ranikhet, etc. because these places are comparatively nearer and easily accessible in all respects, and comparatively safer from the security point of view and attractive in terms of natural beauties, views, landscapes, and lakes and springs to enjoy and to make their leisure tour memorable. The tourist of this category belongs to lower middle to middle-class families who just fly to enjoy and celebrate their week-end holidays or the short duration vacations for leisure. The tourists from the nearby places who can travel to the tourist destinations overnight or by eight-hour journey belong to this category. (ii) The tourists having ardent desire, nourished for years, in their hearts to visit places of religious importance for salvation and therefore make the scheduled pilgrimage may be categorised as the religious tourists. This category of tourists belongs from the lower class to upper class people of all religions imbued with spiritual feelings. To satisfy their years long marshal day dreams the aged or the aging people in general go for pilgrimage particularly for 'Char Dham Yatra' consisting of the destinations starting from Haridwar onwards to the Yamunotri, Gangotri, Kedarnath and Badrinath, etc. and sometime to Hemkund Sahib. But presently due to availability of road communication and other transport facilities up to pilgrimage centres, the aging people along with their family members, including the minors having no spiritual concern visit the religious destinations so that every person of the family belonging to different age groups, likings, and ideology may enjoy the trip as per his/her motive and aspirations. But this changing trend has reduced the religious sanctity of the religious destinations and also of the spiritual feelings of the pilgrims and of pilgrimage. (iii) There are people attracted towards Uttarakhand for some adventurous involvements and may be categorised as adventure tourists. Besides this, (iv) there are people who simply attracted towards the natural beauty of Uttarakhand, its landscapes, snow covered mountain peaks, views, dense forests, sunrise and sunset views, flower valleys, cascading rivers, sky blue water lakes, springs, wildlife centuries, etc. and may be categorised as the nature lovers. (v) One more category of the tourist refers to the people of different and special likings, i.e. yoga, meditation, spiritual practices, pranayam, stress management, acupressure, etc. and come to find the inner self by the healing power of the Himalaya to ensure healthy balance of mind, body and spirit to lead a stress free, peaceful, longing free and socially a healthy life. This category of the people may be termed as yogic and spiritual tourists.

In the real sense, it is Uttarakhand tourism that offers the most favourable, suitable and accessible conditions corresponding to the people of different classes and categories, faith and ideology, likings and aspirations, etc. And, therefore, the influx of the tourists has tremendously increased beyond its carrying capacity particularly after the creation of Uttarakhand state. It is so because the Uttarakhand government has made every possible effort to develop infrastructural facilities to cater the needs of increasing number of tourists to ensure tourism development in the state. Even to regularise the tourism, the tourist routes are channelised in the form of tourist circuits (Bisht, 2010: 192–198) and have classified the tourism potentials and offers as something for everyone as per one's choice.

Facts, Figures and Findings

The study reveals that Uttarakhand tourism has attracted more and more tourists to its various tourist destinations in a subsequent manner since its creation and also used it as the source of revenue and job generating industry in the state. But the ground realities show that the tourism industry in the state could not be developed according to the guidelines and criteria as suggested respectively by UNWTO and STCI corresponding to the increasing number of tourists in the state. Even the study conducted by the Ministry of Tourism of Government of India (www.incredibleindia.org) at important tourist destinations aptly concluded that 'lack of hygiene and sanitation is a major irritant for foreign and domestic tourists', and also suggested that, 'therefore creation of awareness as well as making the requisite facilities available will be given high importance during 12th Five Year Plan 2012–17'.

However, as is observed during intensive fieldwork there is heavy infrastructural development in and around tourist destinations and also in their routes in the form of restaurants, hotels, guest houses, lodges, resorts, tea stalls, and transport related facilities, etc. Alone in Char Dham Yatra routes there is tremendous infrastructural development noticed. A number of restaurants, hotels, tea-stalls and the transport facilities other than air services and government road transportation have abundantly been available to cater to the need of the tourists. Even, the two major corporations of Uttarakhand government namely the Garhwal Mandal Vikas Nigam (GMVN) and the Kumaun Mandal Vikas Nigam (KMVN), offer boarding and lodging facilities and have launched package tours for tourists to various tourist destinations. So far the GMVN and KMVN have a wide range of neat and clean hotels, tourist guest houses, tent colonies, low priced dormitories and also fleet of transport including a variety of luxury coaches, vans, cars, etc. As per available data, both GMVN and KMVN have respectively 96 and 46 lodging facilities available across various tourist destinations. Besides this, there are many more private players like accommodation operators who have erected lodges, hotels, resorts, tourist guest houses, etc. with smart linkages with the tour operators. Correspondingly the developing tourism industry has created a number of jobs for the local peoples and even for the unskilled workers in hospitality sector and also in other tourism activities. According to a study (Bisht, 2013) conducted by the author on unorganised sector workers engaged in tourism industry in the state, there were 2,07,950 unorganised sector workers comprising chefs/cooks, steward, waiter, kitchen steward, housekeepers, receptionists, security personnel and head load workers, porters, pony porters, coolies, *dandiwalas*[26] and *kandiwalas*[27], rickshaw pullers, hotel guides, tour guides, hand rickshaw pullers, boat sellers, etc. Besides this, there is a considerable number of workers engaged in road transportation and other tourist operational activities consisting of the accommodation and operator sectors. During the study, the tourism industry under reference, particularly the accommodation and operator sector were assessed in the context of the potential indicators evolved by STCI principles of long term sustainability/management systems considering environmental, socio-cultural, quality health and safety issues, etc. (www.incredibleindia.org)

It is observed throughout the tourist circuits that the needy and greedy people including the locals and outsiders (the people from outside Uttarakhand state) have established small scale to large scale tourism related business and earning centres ranging from tea-stall, restaurants to the motels to multi-storey hotels and lodges abiding and not-abiding the prevailing rules, regulations and the norms and criteria. Even the roadside commercial and residential constructions which are sometime used even for commercial purposes, along with the cascading river banks, are very common and commonly used to make possible the stay of year-wise increasing number of tourists. Even the tourists prefer to stay in such type of accommodations located in the vicinity of the cascading rivers to have the pleasure of proximity of nature and nature gifted elegances. Besides this, the motorable roads have also been constructed up to the tourist destinations by cutting the fragile hill slopes, the rocks and forests on the path.

The assessment of the Uttarakhand tourism reflects a distorted picture of the environmental conditions in and around the tourist destinations. The negative impacts on the socio-economic and cultural complexes of the host communities, the service providers and also on the tourists are apparent. Resultantly the ages old religious as well as the leisure and adventure tourism in some major tourist circuits like of Kedarnath Dham – the Mandakani, Pindar, Kali, Dholi and Gori river Valleys of Uttarakhand transformed into dark tourism in

2014 due to the negative rather devastating impacts of natural disaster taken place since 2010 in general and in the year 2013 in particular.

In fact, the natural disasters in the disaster prone fragile ranges of Uttarakhand Himalaya are very common. The historical records demonstrate that there have been a long history of earthquakes as well as of floods having occurred in Uttarakhand. It is a scientifically proven fact that, The state of Uttarakhand is among the most seismically active parts of India. Many events of magnitude 5.5 or more have struck the region since the time immemorial. The largest instrument recorded earthquake in Uttarakhand occurred on 19 October 1991. The past history record exhibits about the earthquakes occurred chronologically on 1 September 1803 in Kumaun Garhwal area, 26 May 1816 in Gangotri area of Uttarakhand, 16 June 1902 in Pokhara-Kinnaur area of Uttarakhand, in 1906 in Gangotri area Uttarakhand, on 27 July 1926 near Changabang peak, Uttarakhand, 4 June 1945 near Nanda Devi Peak Uttarakhand, 28 December 1958 in Ramaeshwar – Devi Dhura area, Uttarakhand, 27 June 1966 in Athpali, Dunga area, Uttarakhand, 19 October 1991 in Pilang – Bhatwari area, Uttarakhand, 5 January 1997 in Dharchula area, Uttarakhand, 28 March 1999 in Chamoli – Pipalkoti area of Uttarakhand, 27 May 2003 in Bangina region, Uttarakhand, 14 December 2005 in Pokhari – Gopeshwar region, Uttarakhand, 5 August 2006 in Thal area, eastern Uttarakhand, and on 22 July 2007 in Surka ridge, Uttarakhand.

Moreover, there is also a long history of flood disaster in Uttarakhand. Eminent geologist K.S. Valdiya (2013: 5) asserts that 'cloud bursts or excessive rainfall over shorter spells has been a regular, a recurrent happening, particularly on the forbidding slopes of the great Himalaya comprising Kedarnath, Chaukhamba (Badrinath), Trisul, Nandadevi, and Panchachuli. The tragic events of 2009 (Munsiari – Tejam area in eastern Uttarakhand and 2010 and 2012 disaster in Uttarkashi, Chamoli and Rudraprayag districts in Garhwal bear testimony of this fact'. Valdiya (2013: 9) further states, 'in mid-June 2013 the rivers in spate flowed all through the full width of their floodways including the lower and middle terraces. The people occupying the floodways had to pay the price and they did with extremely tragic consequences'. It was estimated that out of the causalities occurred all over the flood disaster areas, 95 per cent were from Uttarakhand alone. Destruction of bridges and roads left about 1,00,000 pilgrims and tourists trapped in the valleys leading to three of the four Hindu Chota Chardham pilgrimage sites. The Indian Air Force, the Army and paramilitary troops evacuated more than 1,10,000 people from flood ravaged area (source: http://en.wikipedia.org/wiki/2013_North_India_floods).

The available data reveals that the losses caused due to Uttarakhand flood disaster of 2013 were many times more than that of the losses a single earthquake or flood caused in the past. The maximum parts of the infrastructural facilities created to cater the need of the tourists were not as per STCI and the UNWTO guidclincs. Most of the lodges, hotels and restaurants built illegally and unwisely on the river sites were already in the danger zone and under the limit of the river flow, and some were built on the floodway though imperceptible but prone to disaster in an unscientific manner. These were the shelters where majority of the tourists and also the service providers stayed and were swept away with the rampaging flood caused due to cloud burst on 16–17 June 2013. Veteran geologist Valdiya (2013: 09) aptly maintained that 'depending on discharge, velocity, obstacles, etc. the river changes its course. Looking at the picture of the Kedarnath area it will be quite apparent that until recently there were two prominent channels and a couple of very shallow, small imperceptible ones – now abandoned, and encroached upon by shops, residential houses, hotels, *dharamshalas,* etc. And this time (6–17 June 2013), the Mandakini (a river) in spate returned to its long abandoned very shallow middle channel, wiping away all the obstacles that were unwisely constructed. A river in fury could not but have destroyed the impediments in its natural way'. Even the losses could not be assessed accurately. The service providers consisting of the hotel and restaurant staff, hotel and tour guides, transport service providers, the shop keepers, even the priests working in religious centres like Kedarnath temple, had no registration. Even the biometric records entry, health check-up, police verification and also registration of the tourists at the entry point was not in function. That's why the influx of the tourists could not be managed as per carrying capacity of the tourist destinations. No disaster management system was functional throughout the tourist destinations. Safety and medical measures were almost ineffective in the disaster affected tourist destinations, no quick relief supply chain was operative, no safe and alternative route were there for exit of the stranded tourists. All the bridal and pedestrian were washed out. The lodges, hotels, restaurants, halting platforms on the route to tourist circuits, even the residential houses were all swept away by the flood. As per estimation, there was a loss of commercial establishments worth ₹ 46,85,50,000 in the Kerdarnath valley only. Lakhs of pilgrims stranded at various places of the tourist destinations, thousands of tourists and service providers were missing, while 1,08,653 tourists were rescued to safer places in rescue operations. (http://www.ndmindia.nic.in)

Thousands of service providers engaged with tourism sector lost their lives and are listed as missing persons. A village namely Badula in Ukhimath block (Rudraprayag) has lost almost all its male members particularly the youths engaged in tourism pursuits as the service providers and were the only earning member of various households who left their widows and family helpless forever. Thousands of people lost their source of livelihood. Even the earnings of the state government was adversely affected. The interim assessment report indicates loss/damage worth ₹ 800 to ₹ 900 crore (equivalent to GBP 8 to 9 million). The state government is dependent on leisure and religious tourism for the revenue so this had been a setback by three years' (Uttarakhand Floods, Joint Shelter Assessment, 22 August 2013, *Sphere India*).

In the current tourist season, i.e. May–June 2014, the number of tourists visiting the disaster affected Kedarnath valley and also other tourist destinations like Munshyari and Dharchula in Pithoragarh District, Uttarakhand, has reduced beyond imagination. It is due to flood disaster in the state since 2011 onwards that the number of tourists reduced to 209.99 lakh in 2013 than 311.08 lakh in 2010. In the year 2014, the number of tourists, as the tourist flow towards disaster affected destinations has assessed by the author itself in the peak summer session w.e.f. May to June 2014, has been meagre and therefore disappointing. The study units, including hoteliers, restaurant owners, shop keepers, the GMVN and KMVN personnel and officials operating accommodation and the tours, and the officials and employees of revenue department shouldering the responsibility operate and monitor the tourist activity in disaster affected areas, even the service providers engaged in different tourist activities in their respective capacities, the priests, the saints, etc. the private tour operators, hotel and tour guides, consensually asserted that the arrival of tourists in disaster affected tourist destinations has drastically reduced to 5 to 10 per cent in comparison to the base year tourists arrival in 2000. The latest report of the market research division of the Ministry of Tourism, Government of India, also substantiates that the Himalayan state of Uttarakhand has been eliminated from the list of the top 10 states of India having the maximum arrival of tourists in 2013. (www.tourism.gov.in). This has adversely affected the livelihood and also the socio-cultural system of the host communities. Even the recent government policy of free boarding and lodging for the tourists visiting Kadarnath valley – the worst disaster hit destination, could not restore the trust of the tourists. It is for the reason that the income of Badri–Kedarnath Temple Committee drastically reduced to ₹ 34,26, 000 in the pilgrimage season of 2014, in comparison to the Temple Committee's income of ₹ 4,50,66,135 earned within a month in the year 2013 prior to the natural disaster. The fall is evident from Table 2.

Table 2

Income of the Badri-Kedarnath Temple Committee (2010–2014)

Years	*Income (₹)*	*Duration*
2014	34,26,000	1 Month 22 Days
2013	4,50,66,135	1 Month
2012	5,92,29,827	6 Months
2011	5,14,71,912	6 Months
2010	3,66,99,097	6 Months

Source: www.jagran.com dated 26 June 2014

Presently the kind of tourist visiting the disaster affected destinations in the aftermath of 2013 disaster predominantly consists of (i) the tourist visiting only to have a look and assess the disaster affected areas and the tourist destinations (ii) people who have lost their near and dear ones in the flood devastation and hope to discover the dead bodies or the skeleton whatsoever for their cremation and to console for their heavenly peace (iii) people who were there during the disaster of 2013 but narrowly escaped from the devastation and now wish to express their gratitude to Lord Shiva by worshipping the almighty, with their physical presence (iv) people interested to assess the revival and reconstruction work of the disaster area particular the temple premises of Lord Kedarnath which all alone could be saved by the 'charismatic rock' rolling down with the flush flood but suddenly stopped horizontally stretching to its ends some 10 to 15 mtrs away from the back side of the temple and dividing the current of the speedily flowing flood into two parts and thus saving the holy shrine from destruction, (v) researchers like the author, and also the media persons who were interested to unveil the hidden facts and the hard truth of the disaster affected tourist destinations, and (vi) the groups of pilgrims on the way to all India pilgrimage package tour were also seen occasionally there.

Thus, the aforesaid analysis concludes that the dominantly emerging leisure psychology has a motivational impact on the people irrespective of their age, gender, region and class category towards tourism of different kind. The growing figures of tourist in general and in particular case of Uttarakhand is its living example. This leisure motivated tourism is giving the way, space, scope and opportunity for tourism development and concurrently leading its consequential impacts viewed in the form of (i) the growing infrastructural facilities in and around the tourist destinations. As Valdiya (2013: 9) also stated that '... now in places like Rishikesh, Srinagar, Rudraprayag and tens of others, not only houses and *dhabas* but also multi-storied hotels, resorts, and other complexes have been built some precariously along the banks of the channels' (ii) the creation of job opportunities for both the skilled and non-skilled workforce (iii) the changing economic status of the stakeholders, (iv) the structural and cultural changes of the host community and (v) the environmental changes with its unprecedented and unpredictable effects directly on the host community but entirely on the nature as a whole.

It is, therefore, asserted that the leisure, tourism–development and environment are interrelated phenomena and can be comprehended scientifically through cause-effect relationship. But at the same time, as the primary information reflect in the case of Uttarakhand tourism it is also asserted that the sustainable-tourism-strategy, developed in accordance with the ecological conditions of the tourist destination concerned, can only serve the goal of tourism along with its triple principles: (i) the environmental (ii) socio-cultural and (iii) economic, and not only this, it would also satiate the need and purpose of tourists visiting different tourist destinations with their respective motives. And the non-observance of sustainable tourism criteria would minimise the positive impacts and maximise the negative impacts of tourism and finally would be resulted in the form of environmental degradation, socio-cultural disintegration and economic deprivation. As is evident in the case of Uttarakhand where the non-observance of the sustainable tourism-criteria led tourism–development caused man-made losses resulted due to Uttarakhand disaster 2013 aftermath, and transformed the trend of the world famous religious tourism of Kedarnath valley, in particular into a type of tourism very much resembling to the dark tourism in the year 2014.

Suggestions for Sustainable Tourism Development

An objective assessment of Uttarakhand tourism reveal that no specific and viable criteria and guidelines have so far been followed for the tourism development particularly in the state like Uttarakhand which is located in the fragile mountain zone and has naturally been disaster prone. Hence, for sustainable tourism development in the state my humble opinion is as under:

(i) The region specific sustainable tourism development criteria (RSSTDC) are urgently needed to be evolved and followed for tourism development in the state.

(ii) The carrying capacity of every tourist destination must be ensured through standardised parameters established for accommodation and tour operators. Correspondingly the entry of the tourists be made as per carrying capacity of the tourist destinations, and the exit record of every tourist should be ensured and kept intact.
(iii) The infrastructural development should be ensured scientifically with the due consultation of the group of scientists and the rules and regulations should be adhered to by the stakeholders and be monitored institutionally by the government through any independent competent agency.
(iv) The manpower engaged in any capacity with the tourism industry should be registered and be issued an identity card for this purpose.
(v) Disaster Management System (DMS) should be developed meaningfully in the state along with a functional relief supply chain throughout the tourist circuits in general and the disaster prone areas in particular.
(vi) The concept of responsible tourism should be brought about at ground level and the responsibility of every stakeholder should be fixed and be monitored from time to time by the government and its related agencies.
(vii) The tourism code of ethics should be established and be observed by all the stakeholders. For example, in the context of the Indian/Uttarakhand tourism, the feelings implied with the captions mentioned with the tourism emblem like *Athiti Devo Bhava* (guests/tourists are just like the gods), Incredible India (incomparable the Indian Tourism) and Uttarakhand ... simply heaven! need to be vindicated and it is possible only through the observance of tourism ethics.

Notes

1. Char-Dham Yatra – Literally 'Char-Dham' means 'four abodes' and yatra means 'pilgrimage'. In the context under reference *Char-Dham Yatra* refers to the pilgrimage to the four heavenly abodes: (i) *Yamunotri* – the place of origin of the scared river the Yamuna. The temple of goddess is situated there. (ii) *Kedarnath* – the place where Lord Shiva (the god of destruction of all evil) resides permanently. This is one of the 12 *Jyotirlingas* (twelve abodes where Lord Shiva is supposed to have lived in India). The Kedarnath temple named after *Kedar*, another name of Lord Shiva, is believed to have been built in 8th century AD by Adi Shankaracharya himself. (iii) *Gangotri* – the origin of the river Ganga, the holiest of all rivers in India. (iv) *Badrinath* – the shrine dedicated to Lord Vishnu (the god of protection of all living beings). According to a legend, goddess Lakshmi, the wife of Lord Vishnu took the form of *Badri* – a local berry tree to protect Vishnu from the direct heat of Sun and also of rain while he was in penance. Pleased, Vishnu pronounced that his temple would be after the form of the goddess Lakshami, i.e. *Badri*, hence the temple is named as *Badrinath*.
2. Panch Kedar – Refers to five Hindu temples dedicated to Lord Shiva – the god of destruction of all evils and evil deeds. The five temples for visited worship are: (i) *Kedarnath* – located at an altitude of 3,583 mt (11,755 ft.). (ii) *Tungnath* – located at an altitude of 3,680 mt (12,070 ft.). (iii) *Rudranath* – located at an altitude of 2,286 mt (7,500 ft.). (iv) *Madmaheshwar* – located at an altitude of 3,490 mt (11,450 ft.). (v) *Kalpeshwar* – located at an altitude of 2,200 mt (7,200 ft.).

3. Panch Prayag – Literally it means the 'five sacred river-confluences' in Uttarakhand Himalaya: (i) *Vishnuprayag* – the confluence of river Alaknanda which originate from the glacier field of Chaukhamba joined by the Saraswati river near Mana and then meets the Dhauli Ganga river, whose origin is from the Niti pass. After travelling 25 km from its source, it forms the '*Vishnu Prayag*'. It is said sage Narad offered worship to Lord Vishnu at this confluence. An octagonal shaped temple located near the confluence dated to 1889 is credited to Maharani of Indore, Ahalyabai. (ii) *Nand Prayag* – it is the confluence where Mandakini river joins the main Alaknanda river. According to a legend, a noble king Nand performed yagnya (the fire sacrifice) and sought blessings of the gods. Hence, the confluence is named after Nand king. (iii) *Karan Prayag* – a location where Alaknanda river is joined by Pindar river that originates from the Pindar glacier below the Nanda Devi hill range. As per *Mahabharat,* Karna (a great warrior) did penance here and earned the protective gear of armor (*Kawach)* and earrings (*Kundal*) from his father, the Sun god. The name of the confluence is thus derived from the name of Karna. (iv) *Rudra Prayag* – it is the confluence of river Alaknanda and Mandakini. It is named after Lord Shiva who is also known as 'Rudra'. This was the place according to a legend where Lord Shiva performed the *Tandava* (a vigorous dance), the source of the cycle of creation, preservation and dissolution. He played his favourite musical instrument, '*Rudra Vina'*, here and enticed Lord Vishnu to his presence and converted him to water. (v) *Dev Prayag* – it is the confluence of two holy rivers, the Bhagirathi and the Alaknanda. Beyond this confluence, the river is known as Ganges. The holiness of this place is considered equal to the famous '*Triveni Sangam'* – the confluence of three sacred rivers – Ganges, Yamuna and Saraswati at Allahabad in UP, India.
4. Sapt Badri – Consists of seven Hindu temples dedicated to Lord Vishnu and located in the Indian state of Uttarakhand. The abode of Vishnu in the Alaknanda river valley starting from Satapanth, about 24 km above Badrinath and extending up to Nand Prayag in the south, is known as Badrikshetra (the area of Vishnu) in which all the Badri temples are located. Badrinath Temple, called *Badri-Vishal* (altitude 10,279 ft.), is the primary temple followed by six others, namely Adibadri, Vridha Badri, Dhyan Badri, Ardha Badri, Bhavishya Badri and Yogdhyan Badri.
5. Panch Shila – This means five large stones symbolising great Hindu mythological authorities and are located around the *Taptkund* – Narad Shila, Narsimha Shila, Barah Shila, Garur Shila and Markandeya Shila. These five stones are of great mythological importance and visited by thousands of pilgrims every year.
6. Shakti Peeths – Chair of powers named respectively after the goddess of Wisdom (*Saraswati*), Power (*Durga/Kali*) and Wealth (*Laxmi*). Some of them are: Kalimath, Rajrajeshwari (Deval Garh, Pauri), Jwalpa (Pauri), Hariyali devi (Chamoli), Hatt-Kalika (Gangolihat – Pithoragarh), Dronagiri (Dwarahat – Almora), Punyagiri (Tanakpur – Champawat), etc.
7. Piran Kaliyar Sharif – It is the Dargah of 13th century Sufi saint of Chishti Order, Alauddin Ali Ahamad Sabir Kaliyari, also known as Sarkar Sabir Pak and Sabir Kaliyari. It is located in Uttarakhand near Rookee and Haridwar. At a distance of 20 km from Haridwar at the bank of river Ganga. A symbol of humanity and unity, also known a Kaliyar Sharif, it is the burial place of 'Sufi Saint named Aliuddin Ali Ahmad Sabir'.
8. Sri Hemkund Sahib – This is a popular Sikh pilgrimage situated at the elevation of 15,000 fit from the sea level in the Himalayan region of Northern Uttarakhand – Himalaya in India. According to Bachitra Natak, the autobiographical account of

the tenth Guru Govind Singh, it was at Hemkund 'Adorned with Seven Snow Peaks' where he mediated in his previous birth

9. Shri Reetha Sahib Gurudwara – Named after *Reetha*, the soap nut tree, the Sikh shrine 'Gurudwara Shri Ritha Sahib' is one of the religious destinations for Sikh pilgrims. It is located at Reetha Sahib village district Champawat, Uttarakhand. It is said due to the spiritual power of Shri Guru Nanak Dev Ji, who visited this place and had discussion with Gorakhspanties Jogis who lived there, the bitter soap nut turned sweet, and Bhai Mardana Ji could eat it to satiate his hunger. (www.sikhiwiki.org)
10. Gurudwara Nanakmatta Sahib – It is a historical Sikh shrine, located in the town Nanakmatta in Udham Singh Nagar District, Uttarakhand. Guru Nanak Dev Ji visited this place during 1514 AD. This was the place where the devotees of Guru Gorakhnath used to live and this place was called Gorakhmata. Guru Nanak Dev Ji taught the devotees the path of true meditation and salvation. Since then the place came to be known as Nanakmatta where the Gurudwara Nanak Mata is situated (www.nanakmattasahib.com).
11. Mountaineering – The main areas preferred by the mountaineers are located around Gangotri glacier and Nanda Devi sanctuary in Uttarakhand.
12. Trekking – Uttarakhand offers 25 main treks grouped as (i) easy, (ii) moderate and (iii) strenuous. The easy treks include Almora-Jageshwar-Binsar Trek, Devariya Tal-Chandrashila Trek, Rajpur-Mussoorie Trek, Nainital-Betalghat Trek, Almora-Dunagiri-Kausani Trek. The moderate treks include Nag-Tibba Trek, Govind Ghat-Ghangariya-Valley of Flowers – Hemkund Trek, Joshimath-Auli-Kwari Pass Trek, Joshimath-Tapovan-Khulara-Kwari pass Trek, Yamunotri pass-Ruinsara – Har ki Doon Trek, Pindari Glacier Trek. The strenuous treks include Panch Kedar Trek, Gangotri-Gaumukh-Nandanvan – Tapowan Trek, Gangotri-Kalindi Khal Trek, Dodital-Yamunotri Trek, Milam Glacier Trek, Om Parvat-Adi Kailash Trek, Nanda Devi base camp Trek, Khatling Trek, Roopkund Trek, Gangotri-Bhojkharak – Kedar Tal Trek, Chhiplakot Trek.
13. Bugyals – The Uttarakhand Himalaya is blessed with some beautiful alpine grasslands called 'Bugyal' in local parlance. Bedini Bugyal, Auli Bugyal, Dayara Bugyal are some important alpine grasslands (Bugyals) for camping in summers, from March to June every year.
14. Skiing – In Uttarakhand, Auli is one of the highest winter sports resorts in the world. It offers a 180E panoramic view of Himalayan peaks like Nanda Devi, Kamet and Mana Parbat. The other main sites of skiing are Dayara Bugyal, Mundali and Munshyari (www.gmvn.com).
15. Rafting – It is the most popular adventure sport in Uttarakhand. Bhagirathi, Yamuna, Alaknanda, Dhauli Ganga, Tones, Kali and Sharda River offer a thrilling experience for white water rafting. During the year, September–November, and March–May are the best months for rafting in Uttarakhand.
16. Angling – There are some spots on river Ramganga that flows through Corbett National Park, the torrential river Kosi, the Yamuna Bridge near Kempty Fall in Mussoorie, the Beas Ghat on the Ganges and Pancheshwar on the Mahakali River where the 'Mahasheer', a shy, slippery fish is found in abundance and thus offer for angling the Mahasheer. The months of October–November and April–June are ideal for angling.
17. Mountain Biking – Every year from March to May and October to mid-November, Uttarakhand offers good trails for mountain bikers. One can ride around the Tarai forest along the foothills of Nainital close to Corbett National Park. Ranikhet and Dehradun to Mussoorie is another interesting biking trail.

18. Parasailing and Paragliding – Uttarakhand has the best-liked paragliding locations in the world. It includes locations like Naukuchiyatal in Nainital, Pithoragarh, Rishikesh, Mussoorie, Pratapnagar, Dayara Bugyal, Dhanaulty Ridge and Bedni Bygyal for parasailing and paragliding and attract the enthusiastic tourists from all corners of the world.
19. National Parks – An enchanting attraction for nature lovers are the various National Parks like Corbett National Park, Rajaji National Park, Valley of Flowers and Nanda Devi National Park, etc. with a wide variety of rare and endangered species of flora and fauna.
20. Wildlife Sanctuaries – Wildlife sanctuaries located in Uttarakhand include the Gobind wildlife sanctuary, Kedarnath wildlife sanctuary, Askot wildlife sanctuary, Sonanadi wildlife sanctuary, Binsar wildlife sanctuary and Mussoorie wildlife sanctuary, etc. visited by thousands of tourists every year.
21. The Lakes – Known as the paradise of Uttarakhand mountain, lakes include, the Nainital, Bhimtal, Naukutiyatal, Sattal, Khurpatal, Naldamiyanti Tal, Vasuki Tal, etc.
22. Hot water springs – Suryakund, Gangnani, on the way to Gangotri, Gaurikund on the way to Kedarnath, Garamkund, Tapovan, Taptkund, Naradkund, Surajkund, Sahastradhara are some hot water springs.
23. Glaciers – The glaciers of Uttarakhand include Athasi – Balati Glacier, Chorabari Glacier, Gangotri Glacier, Gomukh Glacier, Kafani Glacier, Kalabaland Glacier, Kedarnath Glacier, Meolo Glacier, Bandarpoonch Glacier, Khatling Glacier, Doonagiri Glacier, Milam Glacier, Namik Glacier, Panchachuli Glacier, Pindari Glacier, Ralam Glacier, Satopanth Glacier and Sona Glacier, Sundardhunga Glacier (Uttarakhandtourism.net/glaciers).
24. Nanda Raj – Jat Yatra – This is a grand religious festival celebrated once in every 12 years after the name of Goddess Nanda, the wife of Lord Shiva. Thousands of devotees carry the deity on this 280 km trek that ends in about 20–22 days at Homkund to give her a ceremonial send off to the icy abode of her husband, Lord Shiva at the Gaungti Peak.
25. Kailash Mansarovar Yatra – 'Kailash' is a mount, and 'Mansarovar' is the lake located in the mount Kailash hence named as 'Kailash Mansarovar'. Both, the lake Mansarovar and mount Kailash are considered holy by Hindus, Jains, Buddhists and Bons. In the ancient religious text of these sects, mount 'Kailash' is referred to the centre of the world as it is located at the heart of six mountain ranges that symbolise a lotus. The rivers Indus, Brahamputra, Karnali or Ghager and Sutlej originated around this area. Kailash Mansarovar is the most important pilgrimage of the Himalayan region (www.kmvn.gov.in).
26. Dandiwalas – The porters carrying a person/tourist on 'sedan chair'/palanquin for wage earning.
27. Kandiwalas – The porters carrying a person/tourist on the 'Cane Basket' made up of strips of local bamboos, tiding it with their back for earning their living.

References

Agyeman, J. Bullard, R.D. and Evans, B. (ed.) (2003). *Just Sustainabilities: Development in an Unequal World*, Cambridge, Mass., USA:MIT Press, (referred from http://sdt.unwto.org/content/about-US-5), Town.html.capetown declaration on responsible tourism.

Bisht, Bhagwan S., (2010). Religious Tourism in Uttarakhand, India: A Source of Eternal Peace, Spiritual Happiness and Social Solidarity, in *Leisure and Civilization: Interdisciplinary and International Perspective* (ed) Ishwar Modi, Ma Huidi and Ning Zequn, China Travel and Tourism Press.

Bisht, Bhagwan S. (2013). The Unorganized Sector Workers in Uttarakhand: A Need for Policy Interaction, in *Population, Health and Development: Perspectives on Uttarakhand (ed), T.V. Sekhar* et al. New Delhi: Academic Foundation.

De Grazia, Sebastian, (1964). *Of Time, Work, and Leisure*. New York: Anchor Books

Dumazedier, Joffre, (1967). *Toward a Society of Leisure*, New York: The Free Press

Modi, Ishwar, (2010). Leisure: A Pathway to Human Happiness and Social Harmony, in *Leisure and Civilization: Interdisciplinary and International Perspective* (ed) Ishwar Modi, Ma Huidi and Ning Zequn, China Travel and Tourism Press.

Needham, M.T., (2011). A Psychological Approach to a Thriving Resilient Community, *International Journal of Business, Humanities and Technology*, Vol. 1 no. 3, New York, USA: CPI.

Parker, Stanley, (1975). The Sociology of Leisure: Progress and Problems, *The British Journal of Sociology*, Vol. 26, No. 1, USA.

Pieper, Josef, (2010). 'Leisure, The Basis of Culture', quoted by Ishwar Modi in *Leisure and Civilization: Interdisciplinary and International Perspective* (ed); Ishwar Modi, Ma Huidi and Ning Zequn, China Travel and Tourism Press.

Stevenson, Angus and Maurice Waite, (2011). *Oxford English Dictionary,* (ed.) Oxford: Oxford University Press.

Sewei, Chang, (2010). 'On the Significance of Leisure and Foreground for Leisure Industry', in *Leisure and Civilization: Interdisciplinary and International Perspective* (ed); Ishwar Modi, Ma Huidi and Ning Zequn, China Travel and Tourism Press.

Stiver, R., (1976). *The Sustainable Society: Ethics and Economic Growth*, Philadelphia: Westminster Press.

Tolia, R.S., (2012). *A Planning Framework for the Mountain States of India*, Uttarakhand: Centre for Public Policy, Doon University.

Valdiya, K.S., (2013). Excessive Rains and Landslides in the Main Central Thrust Zone and the Wrath of Rivers, in O.P. Varma (ed). *Geology and Geoheritage Sites of Uttarakhand with Special Reference to Geoscientific Development of the Region.*

Uttarakhand Floods, Joint Shelter Assessment, 22 August 2013, Sphere India.

www.responsibletourismpartnership.org/capetown.html

www.incridibleindia.org

http://en.wikipedia.org/wiki/2013_North_India_floods

http://www.ndmindia.nic.in

www.tourism.gov.in

www.jagran.com

13

Impact of Leisure on Quality of Life and Social Development

Reflection on Urban India

SUKANT K. CHAUDHURY

It is a great pleasure in writing a piece for the festschrift volume for Professor Ishwar Prasad Modi who specialised in leisure studies for a long period of time. He virtually built up the Research Committee 13 of International Sociological Association. He has been the President of the Research Committee since 2006. Further, Professor Modi has been truly an institution builder who as Secretary and President of the Indian Sociological Society took many steps including starting a Hindi journal *Samajshashtriya Sameeksha*, and *e-journal* and an *e-newsletter*. He has been a guiding force for many of us in several ways. I feel honoured writing something for him. This paper has been presented in the Yokohama World Sociology Congress held from 12–19 July 2014.

Quality of life has been vital for social development of a community. Earlier it was economic development, now it is a social development with better quality of life. Today, quality of life includes safe existence, healthy life, non exploitative, free thinking and good education with awareness and of course good and quality leisure. The creative utilisation of leisure has been crucial to social development. Urban India has been accustomed with leisure in various manners. Traditionally people took pleasure in performing rituals, meeting kin and relatives or going for a pilgrimage. Of late things have changed. People have started combining leisure with pilgrimage, kinship with pilgrimage and so on. The present paper analyses a few cases taken in this regard in the city of Lucknow. It is clearly pointing out to the fact that in urban India and affluent section have more opportunity for creative utilisation of leisure but in practice they do not avail it, whereas, the lower strata neither have avenues nor have financial support for creative utilisation of leisure because they lack an average quality of life.

Leisure and its creative utilisation have been crucial to social development (Chaudhury, 2013b). In the development scenario despite criticisms social development holds the key towards the human development. The economists would emphasise upon increasing of per capita income and better distribution system. Sociologists have been emphasising the fact that culture has been supreme for the holistic development of human beings, which has overall influence on the economic activities of the individual. We have had many theories concerning capitalism, alienation, sane society, lonely crowd, and so on. However, the leisure theory is hardly paid attention. In every stages of society, like simple and complex; traditional, transitional and modern; under developed, developing and developed, we have different patterns of leisure.

Leisure is referred to a quality of life, i.e. leisure as a mark of a 'gentleman' (Stanely, 1975). It is a time which is free from work and other necessary activities such as eating and sleeping; play activities which are outside normal routines; and experiences which are intrinsically rewarding. Leisure can be distinguished from paid employment but it is difficult to separate it from other forms of work such as house work or voluntary work. It is differently experienced; people with jobs, especially men, have more clearly demarcated leisure time and activities than those with domestic responsibilities, such as housewives, whose work is never done (Parry and Coalter, 1982).

Leisure has been crucial to the existence of human beings today. Social development requires both work and leisure in a balanced manner. Leisure is cultural in nature hence; different societies have different concepts and types of leisure. In this manner leisure has been structural to every society. Spirituality is an integral part of many societies (Chaudhury, 2013a). Spirituality comes under essentials of living conditions for human beings. Spirituality is linked with ethics and both are philosophical issues concerning sociologist. On the one hand, we can correlate both – because spirituality culminates into high ethical standards, a strong personal guidance of social control measure and morality taking cognizance of culture – on the other hand, ethics and spirituality are different concerns in the sense ethics is the guidance to public conduct and spirituality deals with personal well-being.

Keeping in mind the above issues on leisure, let us delve into urban India. I will begin with some of the constructions of sociologist and anthropologist about urban society in India. Urban society includes towns, cities and metros with a specific way of life. An urban society can be defined as an area having higher density of population, people engaging mostly in occupations other than agriculture and domestication of animals, having a distinct ecology and a culture different from that of the large society's culture.

Quality of Life

Dube (1988) says that conceptual models of 'quality of life' are a relatively recent phenomenon mostly associated with new thinking about the goals of development; but what constitutes a good or satisfying life has been the subject of thought ever since humanity developed cultures, and, within their framework, began functioning according to a scale of values. Anthropological studies of small-scale and relatively undifferentiated communities – commonly known as a primitive tribe – present a wide diversity of ways in which human groups learn to relate to nature, society and the supernatural. They seek to understand and explain the reality surrounding them, even though a part of their understanding may be based on myth and legend, magic and supernaturalism. Despite the inadequacy of knowledge and the non-scientific character these cultures have proved durable. Mighty civilisations have flowered and perished; but tribal cultures have endured. The notions of god, satisfying and desirable lifestyles are implicit in their normative structures, scheme of values and cultural emphases. Societies of larger scale and civilisations – small and large – have been more explicit in this regard. Their normative structure defines more clearly what is desirable and good, although each one of them has set tolerance limits and permits variations in goal definition and goal attainment. Many civilisations have succeeded in establishing a balance and harmony between people, nature, and society; some in their pursuit of a high quality of life have created conditions that ultimately led to their decay and disintegration. There has always been a certain gap between the desired and the desirable and it has been the endeavour of all social systems to bridge it; some have succeeded, others have failed (Dube, 1988).

Further, Dube (1988) provides a list of human needs and quality of life requirements: (a) *Survival: at individual level:* adequate nutrition, including ready access to uncontaminated water supply, adequate housing, adequate clothing, access to preventive and curative medicine, security of life and property, and gainful employment; *at societal level:* Organisation of food security/production and distribution systems; supply of clean water, housing schemes for low income groups, organisation of production/distribution systems for clothing, organisation of network of medical facilities, security and police, employment schemes, mass education; covering areas of nutrition, water use, child care and healthcare, management of the environment, (b) *Societal: at individual level*: sustenance from infancy to adolescence, socialisation mechanisms, control mechanisms, sense of participation, opportunities for receiving positive response – reward and recognition, harmonising individual and social needs; *at societal level:* access by all to at least minimum sustenance needs, adequacy and consistency of socialisation process, un ambivalent norms and their universalistic enforcement, growth of participative institutional structure, multilevel reward/recognition system for individual achievement and contribution to society, promotion of egalitarian ethos and recognition of primacy of social needs, (c) *Cultural and Psychic: at individual level:* personal freedom, consistent with social needs, leisure and opportunities to use it productively, access to enjoyment of the products/achievement of culture, opportunities to make an individual contribution to above point, sense of personal worth, opportunities for personal advancement; *at societal level:* promotion of an ethos of tolerance of cultural and religious differences, and upholding of legitimate personal freedom, organisation of useful leisure time activities, a policy for the promotion and dissemination of culture and the arts, promotion/recognition of excellence and multilevel and multifaceted opportunities of lifelong education, (d) *Welfare: at individual level:* being able to overcome man-made deprivations and discriminations, being able to lead useful life despite natural or accidental handicap; *at societal level:* abolition of discriminatory practices based on gender, race, religion, with special attention to degraded and culturally deprived groups, special schemes for the mentally and physically handicapped and affirmative action for above two points. (e) *adaptive: at individual level:* sense of history, awareness of forces shaping the modern world, predisposition to adjust quickly and smoothly to changes in the physical and socio-cultural environment, and constructive social criticism; *at societal level:* education for raising consciousness, effective communication strategies for adaptive change, developing social indicators and conduct of regular social audit, advance warning systems regarding impending crises and continuous modification of institutional structures, and (f) *progressive: at individual level:* urge to explore, arrive at new understanding, and disseminate the implications of this knowledge; *at societal level:* exploration of new frontiers of knowledge in science and technology, humanities and social sciences, with accent on application of findings for progress. In this manner quality of life essentially requires some creative leisure activities (Chaudhury, 1993).

Urban societies have the following characteristics: (i) the cities and towns have a higher density of population than the rural areas. (ii) cultural heterogeneity is found in the urban areas because people from various areas having different cultures migrate to the towns in search of employment, education, medical and health care. Cities have a distinct environment that is not natural but a man-made environment.

The occupation of the urban areas is mainly non-agricultural, i.e. based on manufacturing, trade and commerce, professional and governance, etc. In urban areas more social mobility is found in the sense people gradually adapt to class structure (lower, middle or upper class based on economic criteria). Formal social control is found in the urban areas in the form of courts, police and other administrative bodies. In urban areas, interaction among people is based on secondary contact and not primary contact. It means face-to-face and individual-to-individual interaction between people is not possible in the urban areas.

People in the cities have an urban way of life which means they have formal interaction, impersonal behaviour, non-kinship relationships, cultural exhibitionism, passing leisure time in clubs, parks, restaurants, cinema halls or markets.

The urban economic organisation is based on market and monetary economy. Civil facilities like road, electricity, water, communication, park, hotels, cinemas, etc. are found in urban areas. Anonymity is a feature of urban societies. It means people do not know each other in the city as in the village.

In India the urban area has the following characteristics: (1) An area having some urban administrative unit like a Municipality, Metropolitan Council, Notified Area Council or Cantonment Board, etc. (2) An area having more than 5,000 populations. (3) 75 per cent of population engaging in non-agricultural occupation. (4) Should have a density of 400 persons per sq mile. (5) Having some urban amenities like an industrial area, a large housing, settlement, having tourist importance or having centres of entertainment and some civic amenities. On the basis of population, India has seven types of cities (Atal, 2006) as shown in Table 1:

Table 1

Nomen Culture of Cities and Town in India

Nomenclature	*Population*	*No. of towns in 1991*
Metro	10,00,000+	23
Class I City	1,00,000+	296
Class II Town	50,000+	341
Class III Town	20,000+	927
Class IV Town	10,000+	1,135
Class V Town	5,000+	725
Class VI Town	less 5,000	185
Total		3,609

Urban society has several social problems such as congestion of population, slums, crime and acute shortage of resources and facilities (such as water, electricity). Certain problems emerge from anonymity in cities, where personal relation and primary group have broken down. It causes tremendous mental pressure and tension. That is why psychological ailments are numerous in cities. Because of large migration to cities, unemployment is found in large number in the urban areas causes a lot of frustration among the people happens due to push and pull factor.

Push factor means that lack of employment in the villages pushes the villagers to the towns in search of jobs. Pull factor means the relatives in the town invite their close people and try to give them jobs. Besides the entertainment aspect of urban life attracts or pulls the people to the towns.

The migrants in the cities do not have a respectable place to stay. They generally settle down as clusters on the outskirts of the cities. These clusters grow into slums. Their conditions deteriorate from bad to worse with the passage of time. There is a high incidence of crime in the cities. It is mainly found because of unemployment, and frustration among the youth and also due to the large density of population.

Having said this, let us examine the urban leisure situations. It can be classified under class, caste, religion, elite, etc. In the class situation we will follow Lloyd Warner's typology: upper-upper, lower-upper, upper-middle, lower-middle, upper-lower, and lower-lower. The upper-upper class is at the top of the world, today they are thinking of having leisure activities in some space station. Practically, most of them spend time abroad, visiting some pilgrim centre and having leisure activities in their mansion. Their residences are well equipped with swimming pools, theatres, bars, or for that matter, dance floors. They have a great destination, i.e. they are own bungalows or hotels in hills stations or forest areas. However, the problem with them is that of combining leisure with work, hence not having a true leisure, therefore probably they are not becoming creative. Almost all of them are having lifestyle diseases like hypertension, thyroid, diabetes, obesity, cardiac problem, arthritis and so on. The requirement of them is the rational aspect of modernity, i.e. being goal oriented in their mindset.

The lower upper-class is not much different from the upper-upper in the sense; their mindset is similar but resources may be less. It may include all three types of elite: corporate elite, political elite and military elite. They may not have their own airplanes or own swimming pools but they hire them. Today most of them engaged planning of leisure activities in the leisure centres like any tourist spot in India or abroad. They combined leisure pilgrimage and leisure with kinship.

The upper middle-class also includes all three types of elite: corporate elite, political elite and military elite. It also has the intellectual elite which includes journalists, professionals like engineers, doctors, teachers of colleges and universities. For them tourist packages offered by various tour operators have become very attractive and successful. Before going most of them collect information about the place including shopping, food and beverages, tourist's spots, etc. from the internet. They are very much computer savvy and tech-savvy. Most of them have successfully utilised their leisure activities by inculcating creative attitudes. They would go to tourist place which is preferably less crowded, have their morning and evening walks, and resting the whole day and not covering too many places in a day.

The lower middle-class mostly is involved in combining pilgrimage with leisure and kinship with leisure. For example Ramesh, 42-year-old, lives with his wife and two sons in Mumbai, working in a corporate sector as an assistant. He regularly visits his old parents living in Lucknow at the time of some rituals like Karva Chauth, Holi, and Deepawali. Besides this, he also visits them during any lifecycle rituals of any close kin particularly to attend wedding and death rituals. He does not find time to visit tourist places for leisure activities. However, he is very satisfied whenever he is with parents at Lucknow. But staying with relatives may sometimes bring in lot of mental tension? Ramesh agrees but he defends his situation. However, these days, the lower middle-class also has started going to tourist destinations with packages. They have full information of historical places, tourist places and pilgrim centres, which was not the position earlier.

The upper lower-class is a combination of neo middle-class and lower-class. They have just gained money and other material goods. They have come across information regarding leisure, tour operators, tourist agencies, tourist destinations in various states of India, hill stations in India, pilgrim centres in India, etc. They are watchful about the holidays schedule in the offices they are working and in the schools their children are studying. Girish Pal says that they could visit Nainital for two days, i.e. 30 April and 1 May 2014 as they were holidays. But 30 April was the voting for Lok Sabha elections in Lucknow. Girish Pal ignored it and was not much concerned about the elections.

The lower-class on the surface shows that they are very happy with whatever they earned, which is far from the truth. They have no time and money for leisure. Unless they work everyday they cannot have a bellyful meal. For them leisure means participate in some religious ritual or family ritual. Most of the males enjoy consuming country liquor with lot of non-vegetarian food, smoking *bidi* and chewing tobacco.

Globalisation has ushered in a new era in leisure activities (Agarwal, 2012). Widespread development in communication system, transportation system, and knowledge system has brought in true social development in different classes of people. Gone are those days when people would buy eagerly foreign goods but today everything is available within the country. Gone are the days when people could not think of flying and today they often visit abroad for shopping or holidaying.

In this manner leisure for urbanites has a variety of meanings; it is different for different classes. Leisure is directly linked with time and space. People normally follow the latest pattern of leisure and urban Lucknow is no exception.

References

Agarwal, Arvind Kumar. (2012). 'Globalization, Leisure and Tourism: A Critical Analysis from Third World Perspective', *The Eastern Anthropologist*, Vol. 65, No. 3 and 4.

Atal, Yogesh. (2006). *Changing Indian Society*. Jaipur: Rawat.

Chaudhury, Sukant K. (1993). *Myopic Development and Cultural Lens*. New Delhi: Inter-India.

—. (2013a). Ethics and Spirituality among Indian Tribes: Some Issues, *The Eastern Anthropologist*, Vol. 66 No. 2–3.

—. (2013b). Spirituality and Leisure: Reflections on Tribals in India, paper presented in the International Conference On Leisure, Health And Well-Being (Holistic Leisure and Health), Mid-term Conference of ISA, RC13 Sociology of Leisure, 18.-20. September, 2013, Szeged, Hungary

Dube, S.C. (1988). *Modernization and Development: The Search for Alternative Paradigms*. New Delhi: Vistaar Publication.

Parry, N. and F. Coalter (1982). 'Sociology and Leisure', *Sociology*, 16(2): 220-231.

Stanely, Parker (1975). The Sociology of Leisure: Progress and Problem, *The British Journal of Sociology*, Vol. 26, No. 1.

14

Family and Value in Contemporary Chinese Culture

From a Globalisation Perspective

MA HUIDI

The practice of 'family instructions'1 (家 训) started in Zhou Dynasty, about 3,000 years ago in China. They are part of the important components that make up the moral and ethical instruction in 'benevolence and virtue'. Regarded as the guidelines for moral cultivation and behaviour for the ancient Chinese people to live a life in social harmony, they are a vehicle to pass on the Confucian ideological tradition and inheritance.

As the cherished familial heritage passing down in the family from generation to generation, different schools of 'family instructions' all focus on ethical and moral cultivation as the core of their teachings. When one's personal life is cultivated, one's family will be regulated and then one's state will be well governed; and when all the states are well governed, there will be peace and harmony throughout the world. One of the distinguishing features of the Chinese cultural tradition is the trinity of self, family and state. 'Self-cultivation is subordinate to family regulation which in turn becomes the basis for good state governance and peace and harmony in the world.' Family is both the place where we get our backing and where we belong and the basis of the state.

Together with state-run schools and private schools, the home schooling of 'family instructions' constitutes the education system in the ancient China, instilling in the younger generation the ideals of self-cultivation as the basis for regulating the family and running the state in order to obtain peace and harmony all over the world. In the Western world, we also discover the education systems that put producing 'good citizens' and 'good person' as their core values. There is a similar conviction that individuals are closely linked with the rise and fall of their countries. 'Family instructions' emphasises character cultivation and pays particular attention to the unity and harmony of a person's innermost being and the external world. Their values can serve as a powerful wakening call to the people living in the age of globalisation and provide new dimensions of thinking in designing mechanisms for globalised cultural system planning and communication.

Traditional Chinese Culture: Two Characteristics

The traditional Chinese culture goes back thousands of years. The sages in ancient times, through their philosophical wisdom, educational theories and practices, moral teachings, rules of conduct, and refined aesthetic tastes, gave birth to this 'land of courtesies and decorum' and the fine tradition of 'respecting our teachers and attaching great importance to education.' Among many others, two Chinese characteristics have played a large role in forming the particular Chinese wisdoms and ways of being.

The first one is the phenomenon of trinity of self, family and state. 'Self-cultivation is subordinate to family regulation which in turn becomes the basis for good state governance and peace and harmony in the world.' Family is both the place where we get our backing and where we belong and the basis of the state. The renowned modern Chinese sociologist Fei Xiaotong once commented on this with a vivid metaphor, 'Once a stone is thrown into the water, ripples upon ripples will spread outwards; a man is the centre generating his waves of social influence.'[2] An individual is therefore that piece of stone and the family, the state, and the world are those spreading ripples. This particular relationship between the individual, the family, and the state has made 'family instructions' extremely important in the ancient society.

The earliest comments on this logical relationship between the individual, the family, and the state are found in The Great Learning of *The Book of Rites*: 'The ancients who wished to illustrate illustrious virtue throughout the kingdom, first governed their own states well. Wishing to govern well their states, they first regulated their families. Wishing to regulate their families, they first cultivated their persons. Wishing to cultivate their persons, they first rectified their hearts. Wishing to rectify their hearts, they first sought to be sincere in their thoughts. Wishing to be sincere in their thoughts, they first extended to the utmost their knowledge. Such extension of knowledge lay in the investigation of things. Things being investigated, knowledge became complete. Their knowledge being complete, their thoughts were sincere. Their thoughts being sincere, their hearts were then rectified. Their hearts being rectified, their persons were cultivated. Their persons being cultivated, their families were regulated. Their families being regulated, their states were rightly governed. Their states being rightly governed, the whole kingdom was made tranquil and happy.' Here, self-cultivation refers not only to cultivate one's moral character, broaden one's knowledge, be kind and gentle in disposition and refined in manner, but also to be a cut above ordinary people in one's state of mind and norms of conduct. Regulation of family means winning the respect in the familial clan, not just one's own family. State governance entails ability to manage regional and state affairs outside one's patriarchal clan. Peace and harmony in the world means the ability to bring security, prosperity, and felicity to the masses and friendship and peace between people and states.

According to (尚书) *Shang Shu: The Book of Historical Records*, an ancient Chinese classic, Shun praised Yu by saying: You are 'industrious in state affairs, frugal in private life, and hardly ever complacent and pretentious. You are truly a wise man.' The original Chinese word 'bang' is not exactly a state as we know it today, but the meaning is clear: Yu is a great man because he has devoted his life to the public good at the expense of his own and family life. And he never goes about bragging about his achievements.

Mencius, as a great master in the Confucian cultural tradition, said in *Li Lou, Part One, of Mencius,* 'I want to develop and nourish the vast *qi* in myself. The world harmony lies in the state; the good governance of the state lies in the family; the prosperity of the family lies in self-cultivation.' According to him, the state governance, the good household management, and the self-cultivation are all based on benevolence and virtue. It is the foundation on which social harmony and human relationships are built.

This cognitive principle of getting to know the outside world through thoroughly understanding ourselves and gaining the abstract knowledge through the intimate daily living has influenced emperors and common people alike through ages. Confucian masters expect to see the shared common fate and mutual dependency of the state and the family via self-cultivation. As a result, each and every individual will play an important role in the universal society.[3]

The second characteristic is the ideas of benevolence and virtue. 'Benevolence is humanity' (Chapter 20, *The Doctrine of the Mean*). It emphasises the virtue in human relations. Benevolence is the element connecting 'filial piety' and 'rites' in human relations and between humanity and nature in universe. It also expounds the ultimate human value in both the natural world and the human society and develops into a unique concept in the traditional Chinese philosophy.

There is a close relationship between benevolence and rites. 'Unless you study the rites you will be ill equipped to take your stand.' (Book XVI of *The Analects*) Without proper training in 'rites,' one does not have solid grounding in being a functioning member in a human society. 'Rites' is truly a fundamental part of Confucianism and occupies the first place in the 'six arts'.[4]

'If for a single day a man could return to the observance of the rites through overcoming himself, then the whole Empire would consider benevolence to be his' (Book XII of *The Analects*). Rites and benevolence are considered equally important and this constitutes the core of the whole concept of benevolence and virtue.

'Rites' also contains much of the humanistic spirit and embodies the moral values that are later expressed by Mencius' 'four senses': the sense of concern for others, the sense of shame and disgust, the sense of humility and deference, and the sense of right and wrong. They are the starting points of benevolence, fairness, propriety, and wisdom, or otherwise known as the 'four virtues.'

'Family instructions' have inherited the tradition and the spirit of self-cultivation and benevolence and virtue. These concepts become the basis of all future family instructions.

Family Instructions: Personal Bible for Living One's Life

Together with state-run schools and private schools, the home schooling of 'family instructions' constitutes the education system in the ancient China, instilling in the younger generation the ideals of self-cultivation as the basis for regulating the family and running the state in order to obtain peace and harmony all over the world. Moral and ethical self-cultivation is the core of all different schools of family instructions. They all focus on instilling in the young the Confucian norms of conduct: being benevolent, fair, reasonable, wise, loyal, cordial, good, respectful, frugal, and deferential in everything. We often find the following teachings in most of family instructions: (1) respect for family rules and state laws; (2) peace and harmony among patriarchal clan and home village; (3) expression of filial piety for parents and respect for the elders; (4) observance of rites and norms of conduct; (5) observance of ceremonies in honouring ancestors. Funerals of parents must be conducted with meticulous care and sacrifices to remote ancestors must not be forgotten; and (6), lifetime pursuit of self-cultivation and learning. All these instructions have had profound influence upon generations of the Chinese people.

For thousands of years, 'family instructions' have been the go-to source for bringing up the young morally and the basic venue to spread the fundamentals of family regulation, state governance, and norms of conduct and behaviour. According to research, the earliest 'family instructions' are those given by King Wen of Zhou state to his son. In *Injunctions to Boqin*, he says that those who are morally superior yet conduct themselves with courtesy will be honoured; those who possess vast land and resources yet behave frugally will enjoy peace and security; those who occupy high social and government positions and yet restrain themselves with discipline will have greater fame; those who have a strong army and yet defend the land with caution will be victorious; those who are intelligent and wise and yet regard themselves as slow will enjoy greater benefits; and those who are erudite and yet consider themselves in need of more learning will have vaster knowledge. Go now and take office in the state of Lu, but don't be foolishly conceited and belittle others because of your new position.[5]

During the Period of the Three Kingdoms in China, there is Zhuge Liang, a well-known statesman who is a symbol of wisdom in the Chinese folklore. In his family instructions to his sons he has this to say: In order to perfect his ethics and manners, a gentleman needs solitude to cultivate himself; he needs to live a simple lifestyle to elevate his moral standards. Without living an austere life, he can not really know his ambition; without solitude, he can not travel far in his goals. When studying, he must be single-minded. Talents come from learning. Without learning, he can't possibly broaden his scope of knowledge. Without ambition, he lacks motivation to pursue learning. Zhuge Liang seems to have condensed his life experience and knowledge into these instructions on self-cultivation, learning, and pursuit of goals. His family instructions are among the most well-known that have passed down through the ages and are still influential today.

From the above two family instructions, we can see that the ancient sages put the 'cultivation of virtue' at the top of the 'three immortal achievements'[6] and its core is loyalty and filial piety. Filial sons are loyal to their country. Children are expected to respect their parents, have a strong sense of gratitude, and requite their parents for their care and upbringing; public servants are expected to work hard and be fair and square in carrying out their official tasks. 'Never slight a good deed because it is trivial; never yield to evil temptation no matter how small.'[7] These are conscientious actions expected of everybody.

'Family instructions' also carry admonitions about how to navigate the complex social relations. 'One who nears vermilion becomes red and one who nears ink becomes black,' meaning that we must choose the company we keep carefully, mingling with good friends and staying away from bad ones. We must aim high, learning from those we'd like to emulate so that we become as good as them. We must forgive others like we'd like to forgive ourselves; we must be critical of ourselves in the same way we are critical of others. Do not ask for perfection in other people and never abandon old friends because of their trivial flaws. Learn to live with the weaknesses in those whom we love; try to find the best in those we loathe. 'Maintaining harmony' is the fundamental criterion in friendship. That does not mean going along in misdemeanours in order to win friends, but it does mean helping and encouraging each other to go for common ideals.

'Family instructions' also have practical advice on matters such as how to read and what to read. For instance, reading is always a matter that is closely related to how to conduct oneself. One must choose what one reads carefully, never be fooled by bad books. When reading, one must be fully focused, both mentally and physically. Reading should be done from the easy to the difficult, from being widely read to being thoroughly familiar with one's classics. Always reflect on what one has read.

The family instructions such as Zhuge Liang's *Instructions to My Sons*, Zhuxi's *Aphorisms on Running a Household*, *Three-Character Classic*, and *The Thousand-Word Injunctions* become very popular because they are easy to understand and recite, easy to remember and memorise, and not hard to apply, for they are closely connected to ordinary people's daily lives. Consequently, they become textbooks people use for ages to establish proper family tradition and rectify undesirable propensities in the young.

The original 16 character aphorism from Zhuge Liang's *Instructions to My Sons* '静以修身，俭以养德；淡泊明志，宁静致远' (One needs solitude to cultivate oneself; one needs a simple lifestyle to elevate one's moral standards. Without living an austere life, one can't really know ones ambitions; without solitude, one can't travel far in his goals) has impacted Chinese people's values for almost two thousand years. Teachings from other family instructions have similarly influenced and shaped people's ways of livings and patterns of behaviour from generation to generation. For example, 'When eating, don't forget that it's not easy to obtain such a simple meal; when dealing with pieces of cloth and ends of thread, always remember that resources are scarce.'[8] (*Zhuxi's Aphorisms on Running a Household*.) *Three-Character Classic* starts with 'In the beginning, people are born kind. They have similar temperaments; what they learn make them different. Without proper teaching, they will go astray … . Respect your teachers and practice your rites … . First come benevolence and fairness, and rites, wisdom, and loyalty. These five fundamentals, what genealogies have to tell and you will know the beginning and the end of things.'[9] For a more one should never mess up … . After you learn your classic, go and read histories. Study detailed discussion on the impact that these instructions have had on the Chinese ways of living and norms of conduct, readers may read another article co-written by this author for reference.[10]

This author's own family instructions have borrowed and incorporated from *Zhuxi's Aphorisms on Running a Household* and put special emphasis on how to teach children to be upright and honest person. Though the author's father was a merchant in the old society, he has inherited and believed in the old tenets such as 'Even though the business doesn't go through, the kind feelings remain', 'losses are a blessing', and 'do your work earnestly and be an honest person'. I still remember how bad things were in the early 1960s when China was suffering from 'three years of natural disasters'. We could see some one begging in the streets. Whenever beggars knocked on the door, father would answer it by bringing them a bowl of hot soup or some warm food. He did leave such a deep impression on all the siblings and provided us with the best food for thought. This is the best legacy he's left us.

Fan Zeng is a famous contemporary Chinese artist. He comes from a family that has produced poets after poets for 450 years. It can be truly said that the torch of art and scholarship has been passed on in the patriarchal clan uninterrupted from generation to generation and the family fame has spread far and wide. What is more important is that the long line of poets and artists from this refined family has been men of high moral calibre as well. They stick to their ethical principles, strive to be role models in what they do and are patriots, showing to the world that they are both men of courage and gallantry as well as of artistic talents and refined taste. In 2010, when the China government was promoting and protecting non-tangible cultural inheritance, the Ministry of Culture commended and honoured this family of 13 generations of poets as a fine example to encourage renaissance of the 'family instructions' tradition.

Having existed for thousands of years in China, 'family instructions' have played a significant role in regulating social structures, promoting healthy folklores, encouraging frugal habits, and straightening out social and family relationships. They have also contributed to self-cultivation, pursuit of knowledge, refinement of taste, and betterment of life in general.

German philosopher Oswald Spengler said that the Chinese philosophy is that of ethics, for morality is the core and the strength of the Chinese cultural tradition.[11]

Contemporary Chinese historian Liu Yizhi says, 'The state in the West is built on religion; it is built on traditional human relations in the East.' China has always been a country without a 'national religion', but definitely a country with 'national morality.' That is to say the Chinese have never followed a single religious faith as a national religion, but they all respect and obey the same set of ethical and moral principles. Morality is our spiritual home.[12]

The formation of this 'national morality' has benefitted greatly from the tradition of 'family instructions'.

'A Good Citizen' and 'A Good Person' in the West

In ancient Greece, the cradle of the western civilisation, we can find similar cultural underpinnings and tradition. *The Republic* raises the issue of how to educate a good citizen. The aim is for each citizen to cultivate ethical senses of 'justice' and 'common good'.

To realise this goal, *The Republic* proposes an educational system and focuses on the concept of education as formation. Formation originates from historical accumulations and constant repetitions and efforts from individuals and the end results come about without learners consciously willing them. The basis for formation is habit that determines rules, customs, and patterns of behaviour we follow and moulds our lifestyles and norms of conduct. According to this education system, children of ages 4–6 years are mainly engaged in playing, listening to fairy tales, songs, fables, and music. When they are between 6 and 13 years, they start to learn to read, write, calculate, sing, and doing gymnastics, horse riding, and archery. They are expected to rein in their wild and anti-social behaviour through training in music, games, manners, dancing, and religious activities. At this stage, the educational focus should be on emotional refinement and moral cultivation. Upon graduation at 16, most of the young people enter the workforce. Those between ages 17 and 20 years can receive a higher form of education to further their will power and courage. For them, academic courses of arithmetic, geometry, astronomy, and music are compulsory. People aged between 20 and 30 years must study philosophy, mainly dialectics, for it is the leading subject among all branches of knowledge. The ultimate aim of education is to produce a man of courage, felicity, wisdom, morality: a unity of four virtues.[13]

In parallel to the educational system is the establishment of 'the best regime', which covers all modes of living: moral and religious practices, customs, folklores, and the refinement of emotions. These are the things that make a nation as it is. Later, Aristotle raises the distinction between the 'good person' and 'good citizen'. He believes that a 'good citizen' requires not much more than patriotism. A citizen is good so long as he supports and defends the laws of his country. The reason is simple: they are yours to defend. However, a good citizen is not equal to a good man, because a good citizen is relative to the regime in his country. A 'good person', on the other hand, is good wherever he is. Good people love the good, not because they own them, but because the good are intrinsically the best. The essence of Aristotle's Agathon is inseparable from the values that an individual contributes to his city state. A city state and its norms are above the family and genetic relationships. It can even be viewed as a big, extended family and will bestow honour only on those who esteem it. Consequently, a city state displays the masculine qualities such as reason, order, autonomy, and independence. A family, on the other hand, has more feminine qualities such as devotion, conformity, conservatism, and ancestor worship. And disharmony within a city state and discord in soul are regarded as the worst forms of evil. The ancient Greeks search for the ideal regime and have a beautiful name for it: *eros*.[14]

Not many books have influenced the western culture as much as *The Republic*. According to the research done by Steven B. Smith, city state and soul are essentially very similar. This view is the core metaphor contained within *The Republic*. All originates from this: city state and soul in essence are similar and vice versa. As individuals, we live within a society and are moulded by it; and in return we help mould the society in which we live. A comparison of city state to soul helps understand how a society rebuilds itself and moulds its citizens and how its citizens in turn help the society function better. What are the benefits of a perfect city state? What are the goals that it strives to serve? The philosopher-kings (highly ethical and philosophical rulers) may be the ideal kings that we hope to find. The ultimate aim is for us to comprehend the education of the soul.[15]

Although *The Republic* contains many elements of utopia, the value of its social theory has endured and it is still tempting to put many of its tenets into practice.

We have also noticed that our next-door neighbour Japan has drawn on the achievements of 'family instructions' in China during the long course of cultural exchanges and turned them into similar familial instructions with the Japanese characteristics and stylistic features. The earliest example is the *Collections of Private Teachings* by Kibino Makibi (695–775). It appeared about 1,500 years ago. In the eyes of the Japanese, a state is an assembly of family clans and a family clan is a miniature of a state, with the Emperor as its head. Therefore, being filial to one's parents in a family is similar in nature to being loyal to the Emperor of the country. The only difference is that of size and scale. Loyalty is applied onto the national scale; piety to parents is limited to a single family. It can be said that children's filial feelings towards parents can be transformed into loyalty to the Emperor in later years. This is one of the characteristics in regard of moral teachings in modern Japan.[16]

Another virtue espoused by the Japanese is practice of frugality and fight against extravagance. The famous Hosokawa Shigekata once said, 'Be very frugal in everything. Don't waste even the gurgling water in a well, let alone the precious metals and rice money.' The antiquarian Ise Teijo said in his *Teijo's Familial Injunctions,* 'Food is the sustenance of life. Plain food and water is all we need to avoid starvation and continue our life. Indulgence in delicious food by wasting money to satisfy such desire is nothing less than extravagance. Housing is shelter against natural elements. So long as we are protected from wind and rain, a small and narrow dwelling is adequate. One's housing depends on one's financial means. Building a luxury house beyond one's means is extravagance.' Finally, Asakura Soteki has this to say, 'Be thrifty every day and save all the odds and ends; be prodigal with money in times of war, even if one has to spend a fortune.'[17] (Words from Asakura Soteki.)

The Japanese familial injunctions focus on social functions and openness and still play an important role today. The multinational Japanese enterprises all have inherited different aspects of this cultural tradition. Panasonic follows sincerity as their motto; Toshiba upholds the idea of making contributions to the society; Toyota sticks to the exuberant management style of constant learning and innovation. Their successes undoubtedly benefit a great deal from their cultural heritage.[18]

Today, Japan is still widely known for its politeness, for its social order, and for the excellent quality of its products. According to a report in the British daily *The Independent,* 30 January 2015 issue, based on factors such as safety, living costs, and livability, Tokyo is considered the safest city to live in the world, despite the fact that it has a population of 30 million people and is one of the biggest metropolitan centres. It has few crimes and little violence. Osaka, another Japanese city, is rated as the third safest city in the world.[19] This phenomenon does not happen by chance. It must have a close connection with the continuity of its cultural tradition, including that of familial injunctions.

What Do 'Family Instructions' Tell Us?

We have discussed some forms of family cultural traditions both in the East and in the West, both in China and in Japan. I am sure that similar familial instructions in other parts of the world exist in their own unique ways. Apparently, all of them are communal and national cultural assets and provide us with profound and enduring considerations.

Consideration number one: the individual, the family, and the state are united as one. For the Chinese, 'self-cultivation is subordinate to family regulation which in turn becomes the basis for good state governance and peace and harmony in the world.' Family is both the place where we get our backing and where we belong and the foundation of the state. Because of this special relationship among individual, family, and state, family instructions play a very important role in regulating human relations and social harmony. In the West, people believe that 'city state and soul in essence are similar and vice versa. As individuals, we live within a society and are moulded by it; and in return we help mould the society in which we live. A comparison of city state to soul helps understand how a society rebuilds itself and moulds its citizens and how its citizens in turn help the society function better.'

Though vastly different, the eastern and western cultures converge onto the same path regarding the familial instructions. Family constitutes the basic cell of the society and is the foundation of the state. Therefore, social design without considering the all-important family factor is impossible, for it will result in both family and state having very shaky foundations.

Consideration number two: the regimes in the early human societies and states all emphasise the importance of fostering and establishing human talents; and the first task in such an educational endeavour is to cultivate virtue. Confucius says, 'Of the things brought about by the rites, harmony is the most valuable,' and 'virtue never stands alone. It is bound to have neighbours.' (The Analects) These words applied appropriately become the art of the ancient Chinese in internal governance and external diplomacy with neighbouring states. In the West, 'philosopher-kings'[20] head 'the political regimes'. People who want to ameliorate others must ameliorate themselves first. They must create a city state within themselves, free themselves from chaos, unruliness, radicalism, and stubbornness, and be cured of irritable disposition and profound agitation. Philosophy is the medication for human prejudice and the effective control mechanism for wanton desires.[21] This consideration reveals to us unmistakably that our age is in need of ethical, erudite, and noble statesmen, not run-of-the-mill politicians, and certainly not fraudulent and dishonest political quacks.

Consideration number three: all the individuals are members of the globalised world. In other words, we are the basis upon which the globalisation is built. The modern communication technology, especially the internet, is so pervious and pervasive that a localised and individual incident can turn into a global event, with unforeseen and fortuitous consequences. In recent years, we have been saddened by the fact that so many terrorist acts and attacks are committed by very young participants and perpetrators. We can't help asking if the family education and discipline has been declining in nations the world over. Can the world enjoy peace when 'family instructions' are gone? Politicians all claim to be looking out for the 'interests of people', but have neglected to protect the justice and development of individuals and their families.

Consideration number four: right questions have not been raised about the meaning and significance of globalisation because politicians control the 'right of speech.' They have never seriously dealt with issues such as these: Why do we need globalisation? What are the best ways to go about it? Where is the conscience and what are the duties of the politicians involved in the endeavour? During the 2014 international sociology conference, the main topic that participants discussed and debated heatedly is 'global inequality.' Unfairness and injustice are rife in the world and regional wars, killings, incidences of violence and poverty, acts of hegemony occur daily on this globe we call home. The prospect to realise the 'New Millennium Development Goals' remains daunting. How do we deal with issues such as youth problems, racial problems, migrant worker problems, racial discriminations, and problems of regional inequality? What can we learn from our reflections on our past efforts?

Consideration number five: globalisation is the inevitable result of evolution of human civilisation. Judging from the present situations, globalisation has been concentrated on constructing mechanisms and systems to unify the global economy and markets. Eventually, political and cultural cooperation and integration will be brought along and spurred up. Under these circumstances, it is important to gradually transform and update very narrow nationalistic and ethnically-confined concepts and fulfil the goals of inclusiveness and integration while sparing no efforts in maintaining multiculturalism and integrity of ethnic cultures. I believe all human cultural heritages contain elements of truth, loving-kindness, and beauty as well as universal human values of equality and justice. Contemporary politicians and state administrators can all obtain useful lessons from wisdom of traditional family instructions and apply them in their efforts to improve state governance and political skills.

Conclusion

From the above considerations we feel entitled to ask that adequate care and attention be given to individual families in designing and planning for the future society. Obviously, families are constituent cells that make up a society and also a sanctuary where members find solace and feel safe. They also serve as the school where people learn their first life lessons. Family instructions, family schooling and family traditions help cultivate self-discipline and are not within legal confines. In a globalised social environment, efforts should be made to maintain and protect the integrity of family while we choose social design and policy options.

Globalisation has made this world smaller and shortened the distance between peoples as well as strengthened cultural inclusiveness through different cultures complementing each other. To make this world a better place, the fundamental requirement is more useful and beneficial for exchanges and dialogues. While researching on the topic of family instructions, this author suddenly realises that all our cultural heritages, enlightened concepts and ideas, and value systems converge. It probably implies that cultures and civilisations tend to merge in the same directions and share universal characteristics. On the other hand, 'harmony, not uniformity' should remain the motto. We should acknowledge, endorse, and respect differences and encourage inclusiveness and mutual understanding of different cultures.

We live in a world that abounds in myriad belief systems and varied national customs and folklores. It would be naive and simple-minded to expect that globalisation can be accomplished according to one standard model. We must draw experiences and learn lessons from history of human civilisations. Globalisation needs support from indigenous cultures.

Although as scholars we are usually unable to be directly involved in policy making and implementation process, what we can do is to study and spread the quintessence of our indigenous cultural traditions. The Chinese scholars can carry on the literati tradition of 'conveying the truth through literature' and the practice of 'the unity of knowing and doing' and influence by their own fine examples the politicians and other people around them. If we all contribute our bit, the accumulated efforts will surely help assuage sorrows, eliminate barriers, prevent conflicts, and diminish hatred. They can also help narrow the gap between the East and the West, between the rich and the poor, between Christians and Muslims, and between the left and the right.

Notes

1. 家训, literally means 'family instructions or admonitions.' However, China has been a patriarchal society for thousands of years and almost all the family instructions were written by fathers or a patriarch in a family clan and then passed on from generation to generation.
2. 费孝通, (乡土中国), 三联出版社, 1948
3. 参阅叶匡正文, "家与国", 载 (河北青年报) 2009–05–18
4. They include rites, music, archery, charioteering, reading and writing, and arithmetic. Starting around 1,046 BC during Zhou dynasty, aristocratic education system required students to master these basic skills.
5. 翟博主编, (中国家训大典), 海南出版社, 2004 年, 第 1 页。
6. They are achievements in virtue, public cause, and ideas. It is a proposition in the Chinese ethical thinking, put forward by Shusun Bao, a prominent politician in Lu State during the Spring and Autumn Period, around 530 BC Achievement in virtue means cultivation of very high moral standards; achievement in public cause means concrete accomplishments for the benefit of the state and the people; and achievement in ideas means establishing original insights and ideas.
7. From the testamentary edict left by the founding king Liu Bei of Shu state during the Period of the Three Kingdoms to his son Liu Shan.
8. Composed by Zhu Bailu during mid-17 century. His high moral standards and his writings are revered. His *Aphorisms on Running a Household* are widespread and profoundly influential.

9. Composed by Wang Yinglin during Southern Song Dynasty, around mid-13th century. It has been used as a primer for very young kids for centuries. In the 1980s, UNESCO designated it as a worldwide classical primer. Because of its rich moral teachings, the book has often been used a standard supplementary reading to 'paternal instruction' in China.
10. MaHudi and Liu Er, 'House Codes' in the Benevolence-Centred Culture of China, *Leisure and Civilization: Interdisciplinary and International Perspectives,* China Travel and Tourism Press, p. 94.
11. (德)斯宾格勒著, 张兰平译, (西方的没落), 陕西师范大学出版社, 2008 年
12. 转引自李汉秋文, "中华传统节日皆以人伦为灵魂", 安徽大学文典大讲坛, 2013年11月10日。
13. 参见郑晓沧编译, 《柏拉图论教育》
14. 参引斯蒂芬 B. 斯密斯著, 贺晴川译, (耶鲁大学公开课: 政治哲学), 北京联合出版社, 2015 年第 9–11 页。
15. 斯蒂芬 B. 斯密斯著, 贺晴川译, (耶鲁大学公开课: 政治哲学), 北京联合出版社, 2015 年第 57–58 页。
16. 玄璇文, "日本人的家训", (世界博览) 2006年11月 第11期
17. 同上
18. 同上
19. 世界上最安全城调查", 见 2015 年 2 月 3 日, 参考消息报, 八版
20. Platon put forward the idea, the purpose is to repose in the true philosopher grasp the supreme power of the state.
21. 参见斯蒂芬 B. 斯密斯著, 贺晴川译, (耶鲁大学公开课: 政治哲学), 北京联合出版社, 2015 年第 75–76 页。

15

Leisure Tools, Children and Globalisation

RASHMI JAIN

Children are vital part of society and are fundamental to its future. They are society's future parents, workers, citizens, providers and consumers. The way, in which the society treats children, provides for their childhood and the extent to which it listens to children are core social values. These values keep on changing with change in time. Scant attention has been paid to understand the historical dimensions of childhood. Most of the philosophers of ancient times conceptualised children as a Lockian tabula rasa, a passive recipient or object of the adult community's efforts to rear and educate. In almost all ancient cultures, the child was seen as a being that was helpless, not capable of directing his own affairs, who had to be legally represented in the community by an adult, usually the father. The children's distinctive qualities of helplessness and the need for love and play were widely accepted in all the ancient civilisations. The medieval period all over was witness to upheavals, invasions, warfare and survival dominated all thought. In the 18th century, the writings of philosophers and educators picked up themes from Plato and Aristotle, placing children and early development at high levels of importance. By early 19th century, three broad viewpoints on childhood rearing emerged corresponding to 'break the will' school, the 'hardening' school developed from Rousseau's doctrine and the 'gentle treatment' school based on the work of educators. All through this childhood was seen as reflection of the imprint of society. The studies conducted during these times concentrated on child-rearing practices, impact of socialisation on children, child development and the like.

The child as a subject of study came into existence in the beginning of 20th century. Children were seen as objects of purely humanitarian concern – as 'children in distress' or as 'children in poverty' (UNICEF, 1996). Much child research in Latin America, Africa and Asia continues to remain strongly focused on children in exceptionally difficult circumstances or especially disadvantaged children, such as child prostitutes, child soldiers, street children, child labourers and child slaves (for example, Connolly and Ennew,1996; Ennew, 1994; Hecht, 1998; Miljeteig, 1999). The middle of 20th century saw children as not another cause but part of every cause and stressed on the need to create services to help children directly such as maternal and child healthcare, early childhood care, primary education and the like. It is only recently that sociologists have started focusing their attention on children and childhood other than from an adult-centric perspective. Within the traditional socialisation paradigm children were thought of as incomplete adults whose experiences were not worth investigating in their own right, but only insofar as they constituted learning for adulthood (Thorne, 1987).

The notion of treating children as possession of their parents crosses the boundaries of all nations. The children are usually understood as 'incomplete vulnerable beings progressing with adult help through stages needed to turn them into mature adults' (Mayall, 1994). The process of globalisation has transformed the organisation, functioning and structure of traditional social institutions of marriage, family, kinship, caste and community. This has in turn transformed the social status, roles, inter and intra-personal relationships which need a closer enquiry. The world is today compressing into a global village. The boundaries of nation–state and its protected environment are withering away. Globalisation is a process that opens nation–states and societies to many influences that originate beyond their borders. According to Robertson (1992), globalisation refers to both the compression of the world and an intensification of consciousness of the world as a whole. Giddens (1990) describes it as an irresistible force, transforming all aspects of contemporary society, politics and economy. These changes are likely to decrease the primacy of national economic, political and social institutions thereby affecting the everyday context in which children grow up and interact with the rest of society. Children's culture is closely related to the surrounding environment, which dictates the spaces where they play, the materials which they use and their access to recreational resources (Punch, 2003).

The impact of globalisation can be as varied as its constituent characteristics. Deregulation, opening of markets, promotion of international trade have caused a rise in the living standard for many or few on one side and marginalised some sections of society on the other. The universalisation of experience, an integral part of globalisation, has had a dramatic impact on our sense of time and space. The societies are increasingly being governed by fast emerging global market economy. The development of consumer society is transforming not only the economy but also the way individuals are looked at. The market forces look at profits as their benchmark of success and are ready to redefine the age-old practices of locating their products in the traditional milieu. The changing role patterns in the family system have allowed for greater participation by children in day-to-day affairs. This has been facilitated by the increasing exposure of the children to fast growing global media, acceptance of global way of living and development of consumption culture. The children of today live in a world dominated by the market economy of which they have become an integral part. The process of globalisation means that many of the cultural and leisure options available to, for example, Indian children, have become similar to those of their western counterparts.

Globalisation has broken down cultural boundaries through the wide availability of air travel, accessibility of telecommunications and the promotion of mass tourism. The culture of globalisation is playfully hybrid as the elites consume a mish-mash of the local and the global, oscillating between such things as reviving traditional wedding rituals and global travel. The opening of opportunities for foreign travel, higher disposable incomes, a corporate culture, irresistible offers by travel companies and easy payment plans have resulted in an increase in family travel involving children. The penetration of multinational capitalism into Indian society brings with it popular TV serials, fast food chains, shopping malls, theme parks and sports entertainment.

The booming toy industry, the emergence of exclusive kids' stores, brand imaging, and innovative promotional schemes are responsible for creating Little Adults. Early decision-making, peer pressure, me-too and me-alone syndromes, the portrayal of the child as an adult, double incomes, greater affordability of children over leisure goods, and democratic values, are some of the reasons which make a case for the emergence of 'Little Adults with a mind of their own'.

Objectives of the Study

This study was conducted with the following objectives:

- Examine the impact of globalisation on Indian children.
- Observe change in leisure patterns among Indian children.
- Analyse their changing patterns of social interaction.
- Look at the new leisure tools available to children and observe their impact on children.
- Analyse the impact of media narratives on children.

Methodology

Four public schools of Jaipur were chosen for the study. A group of 30 students (15 girls and 15 boys) in the age group of 12–14 years were randomly drawn from each school taking the total number of respondents to 120. The school selection was done keeping in mind the need to ensure homogeneity amongst the chosen respondents. All the respondents chosen belonged to upper middle-class background and had access to Cable/Dish/Tata Sky, Internet connection. A structured schedule was administered to them and some case studies were taken up to enable greater sociological insights. Cross checking was also done from some parents to see the validity of the responses.

Results and Discussion

Children and Global World

The revolution in information and communication technology, the shrinking of time and space and the creation of what Marshall McLuhan (1964) called 'the global village' have transformed the way the children of today are experiencing childhood. The children of the developing countries today have become a part of the global generation of children who, though living in different parts of the world, know and consume the same international brands, listen to the same music and share the same role models. The main factor responsible for this transformation has been the enormous increase in leisure tools and their easy access to the children.

The current generation of children is growing up in what Beck (1992) and Giddens call the risk society. The evolution from late modern industrial society to a late modern society is causing the scholars to reflect and study change in the traditional institutions like class, family, state and democracy. Qvortrup (1990) believes that childhood and living conditions of childhood are fundamentally influenced by the same economic, political and social powers that constitute the context of adult's lives.

The children today are experiencing a hi-tech fast paced world quite different from the world that today's older adults experienced in their childhood. The culture of globalisation is playfully hybrid as the elites consume a mish mash of the local and the global oscillating between reviving traditional wedding rituals to global travel. The opening of opportunities of foreign travel, higher disposable incomes, corporate culture, irresistible offers by travel companies, easy payment plans have resulted into an increase in family travel involving the children. The children of today are globetrotting with or without their parents and consuming global culture. They are as at home in Paris, London or New York as in Mumbai or Jaipur. The looming presence of global brands in India also is partly responsible for this phenomenon.

Global companies like Mc Donald's, Nike, Disney, Mattel in collaboration with their Indian counterparts, the advertising agencies and the marketers are selling the idea that Indian children can now shed their histories as postcolonial subjects and become a part of a global generation (Global generation is a marketing term that refers to a generation of young people who although living in different parts of the world, know and consume the same international brands and media narratives). The children of today are influenced more by global happenings than by local ones. The increased use of Internet as leisure tool has also added to the development of children as little adults.

Children as Consumers

Children in the West are encouraged to be the author of their own lives (Beck, 1997). They seem to utilise these possibilities and to present themselves as social actors with their own interests and rights. Children grasp every opportunity to show themselves as individuals and that too as an adult. The market recognises children and youngsters as consumers with their own desires and means. On the basis of specific consumption patterns, children develop their own (sub) cultures. Zinnecker (2001) states that lifestyles and life histories were once exclusively attributed to adults, while recently children's cultures and children's lifestyles have become popular research domains.

The children today are being turned into consumers at a very early age through the desires and encouragement of parents, who want to relive their childhood through their children. They provide them the necessary financial support. The result of all this is that the children become a market segment for such items such as sweets, snacks, soft drinks, toys as they pursue gratification and self sufficiency (McNeal, 1987).

Children are effectively fitting into the consumer role owing to time pressure and income effects in dual career families. Sharad Vadhera (2004) argues that moreover, exposure to mass media and discussions with parents ensure that children are not only aware of new brands available but also know how to evaluate them on various parameters. While younger children clearly affect parental behaviour and purchases, adolescents have full cognitive development and an understanding of the economic concepts required for processing information and selection.

Children not only want things but have acquired the socially sanctioned right to want – a right which the parents loath to violate, layered into direct child enticement and the supported autonomy of the child. The cultural market place is now a key arena for the formation of the sense of self and of peer relationship, so much so that parents are often stuck between giving into kid's purchase demands or risking their child becoming an outcast on the playground (Cook, 2001).

Children wield enormous purchasing power both directly and indirectly. Marketers see them as current as well as future market and hence brand loyalty at a young age helps in the quest of continued sales later. The dictum of consumerism and corporate capitalism dictates that social good comes through subtle greed and meeting the demands of the people. Putting candy at the eye level of the children or at the entrance of the newly opened malls creates a demand that otherwise may not have been there or at least not in as much intensity.

Children and Changing Patterns of Social Interaction

Children have both voice and agency. They construct their own social networks and social reality, sort out their own values, assess and cope with the perplexing around them in their own way. The children today are experiencing hi-tech fast paced world quite different from the world their parents experienced in their own childhood. The changing family lifestyles, income effects in dual career families, exposure to mass media have resulted in more segregation and less frequent interaction between the younger community members and older individuals. Grandparents often live far away limiting opportunities for interaction with them to special occasions or holidays. Many activities that traditionally took place at home, tasks like caring for frail elders, minding young children and teaching them cultural and social skills are now being performed by people outside the family. Moreover, the children are moving away from traditional games that involved them as a group and taught them the necessary social skills.

The children today are being more involved in solitary forms of gaming like computer games, mobile games, video games like play station, gameboy, etc. They like to spend most of their free time either in front of TV or sitting at the computer chatting with their friends. The use of mobile is also increasing in the children. According to a study conducted by the Australian Institute in 2007, the use of mobile phones for children was aimed at parents as a security measures for the children but most kids who own mobiles are motivated by status and aesthetics in their purchasing decision. Now with the launch of new mobile phones with the popular children's character 'Hello Kitty' in July, phones worth $ 600 are being targeted at tweens as fashion accessory. With global presence of companies, products being launched elsewhere are brought immediately in India as well and the children are aware of the same. This type of high-pressure consumerism clearly risks the commercialisation of their childhood and could negatively impact their development by having to take an adult financial responsibility at a young age. In the study conducted it was found that 95 per cent of the respondents had phones loaded with latest technology and accessories. The children could not even imagine themselves having a phone without colour screen, camera and bluetooth. The financial background of the respondents varied from upper middle-class to elite. Children have started exhibiting signs of 'competitive consumption' as they try to keep up with their peers.

Table 1

Member of Interaction Sites

	St. Xaviers N=30	*S.M.S N=30*	*Step by Step N=30*	*Vidyashram N=30*	*Total N=120*
Boys	14	15	15	14	58
Girls	13	15	15	12	55
Total	27	30	30	26	113

In the study conducted, it was found that nearly 94.17 per cent of the children interviewed were members of a social interaction site and regularly chatted (sent scraps) to their net friends. They were worldly wise in not disclosing their identity in their profiles posted on net. They were also hiding their real age since the sites are meant for persons above 18 years of age. All the parents were aware of this fact and did not object to it. Most of the respondents used Orkut as a means of communicating with their friends. No sex-wise difference was noticed on this issue.

Children are turning towards the Internet today not only for information but also for comfort, interaction and company. Table 2 shows that the Internet is more used for visiting networking sites (96.67%) than for taking help for homework (20.83%) or increasing their knowledge (28.33%); 19.17 per cent of the respondents admitted to using Internet for visiting porn sites. During in-depth interviews conducted, it was found that the children who had admitted to visiting porn sites were those who had no parental control over them. Both their parents were very busy in their professional and social lives, which made these children lonely. They had no grandparents living with them and thus had no one to check on them during the day.

Table 2

Purpose of Using Internet

Purpose	*Boys N=60*	*Girls N=60*	*Total N=120*
Homework	10 (16.67)	15 (25)	25(20.83)
Sending e-mails	48 (80)	44 (73.33)	92(76.67)
Chatting with friends	36 (60)	45 (75)	81(67.5)
Social network sites	57 (95)	59 (98.3)	116(96.67)
Downloading games/music	54 (90)	40 (66.67)	94(78.33)
Surfing for fun	54(90)	49 (81.67)	103(85.83)
Knowledge enhancing	16 (26.67)	18 (30)	34(28.33)
Others(adult sites)	12 (20)	11 (18.33)	23(19.17)

Figures in parentheses are in percentage

The growing popularity of social interaction sites like Orkut, Facebook, MySpace, Hi5, Friendster, Fropper, etc. is testimony to the trend. The growing urbanisation has resulted into space crunch in the cities forcing the children to move away from outdoor activity. The shrinking size of family is responsible for the loneliness of the children, which prompts them to visit social interaction sites. The children especially the girls are vulnerable at this age and are prone to be involved emotionally (During the interviews, girls showed signs of being more easily influenced on the Internet than boys and accepted 'friend' requests without even knowing who the requesters were).

Leisure Tools in the Globalised World

Leisure as a social phenomenon can be understood and explained only in the context of a social organisation. Social structure influences the nature and form of leisure and its activities. It not only determines the form and nature of leisure but also determines the extent and limit of participation (Modi, 1985). Attitudes towards leisure are closely related to culture (Kaplan, 1960). Dumazedier (1974) identified relaxation, entertainment and personal development as the three main functions of leisure. According to him, any programme for the realisation of human potentialities must be based on the satisfaction of needs, but the concept of need may be interpreted in various ways. Jain (2007) addresses the issue of access to leisure among the disadvantaged in India. According to her the cable revolution in India has been successful in directing the free time of women and children towards the constant churning-out of family drama serials. Most of the day-to-day leisure of the masses is spent in front of TV sets in homes in developing societies. What is available on this medium leads to mental malnutrition and poor emotional and spiritual health. This mental, emotional and spiritual degradation is not good for the values cherished by Indian society.

The importance of leisure time activities in the psychological, cognitive and physical development of children is recognised in all societies. Technological advancement paved the way for not only a reduction in manual labour but also in community time. Leisure tools like radio, television, 'Game boy'; PSPs, mobiles, and gaming stations have been targeted to provide leisure for the lonely. They work as vehicles for the segregation of human beings.

The proliferation of Internet and the easy access of it on cell phones has changed the way leisure activities are performed. The cell phones have now come in the hands of the children. Information communication technologies have affected leisure time habits of children as larger portion of socialising now takes place through text messaging and online meetings. It was found that 76.67 per cent of the respondents were regularly using the Internet to e-mail friends or relatives while 75 per cent used it to for instant messaging. The children prior to the development of globalised world were restricted in terms of the choice of leisure tools. Sports, outdoor play with other children figured very strongly in their lives. Sports improved not only physical fitness but also contributed to the development, self-concept, social skills and values of teamwork and tolerance.

Games, an activity designed to develop mental and social skills of the children is losing to the tech savvy games of the global age. Today games can be played on computers without any need of a playmate. The virtual reality of games on the computer provides a real life like situation. They also give power to the child and initiate them towards violence. Popular games like Counterstrike, Contra, Need for Speed, GTA, FIFA World Cup, Halo3 and the like have a large following. These games inculcate a fighting spirit tilted towards violence. It was found that boys played these games more often and longer than girls. Girls were found to be playing games on sites hosted by Disney and Barbie. The children today prefer playing games sitting in gaming parlours and not in the sports ground. Today's society has seen the emergence of new forms of leisure tools like Internet, television, play stations, gameboy, computer games, gaming stations, ipod, mobile phones. These tools have led to the displacement of traditional activities like sports. All these leisure tools have one thing in common which is that they are all ways of providing leisure to the solitary. The habits developed by using modern technology may create a culture of 'individualised leisure time' as children are increasingly devoting their free time to computer screens and mobile keypads. It is very common to find two children of the same age group sitting in one room and playing with their own gameboy/PSP/iPod and not feeling the natural desire to communicate with each other. The parents are too happy to provide the children with such gadgets since they liberate them as well from the chore of babysitting.

On being asked about the number of hours spent on these leisure tools it was found to have a mean of 4.5 hours as opposed to 2.1 hours spent on studying. A look at the daily schedule of children shows that they have only an average of 7 hours left with them after they reach home from school out of which they are spending 4.5 hours on leisure tools and 2.1 on studies which leaves only 40 minutes for any other activity. Most of the respondents (90%) reported eating food while watching television.

Children and Television

Another by-product of globalisation is the global reach of television in homes. The television has created a universe of what can be termed 'hyper reality'. (Umberto,1986; Baudrillard, 1988). It fosters a consumerist society and creates a society of people detached from their own real world. The reality of television seems to be more real to viewers than actual reality. Viewers are fooled into living mentally and emotionally in a world with no place limits and no time limits.

The media reports of children imitating the acts of popular serials like 'Shaktimaan'. 'Superman' raises a question on moral level. Contemporary morality is mediated through media forms, and children's views on human relationships may be formed not in relation to family or even proximal role models but rather in terms of stereotypes set within TV programmes (Editorial, *Childhood*, 1996).

The popularity of serials, like Shin Chan, Hathodi, Perman, and channels like Disney channel, Cartoon network, Nickedeon, has glued the children to their television sets. From the child's point of view, images from television and toys are literally everywhere. When the respondents were asked as to how many hours they watched television all admitted to watching television for 3 hours a day as against 1 hour of outside play. Most respondents complained that they didn't have any playing companion or space because of which they didn't play.

The children have extended excess to television due to its availability in all homes. Three quarters of the respondents had two television sets in their homes that allowed them exclusive watching rights; 98 per cent were subscribers to cable network or had their own dish network. The programmes aired on television do not discriminate between adult and child viewing. The reality shows on the television like Voice of India, Boogie Woogie, Sa Re Ga Ma Pa, Chak de Bacche have fanned the embers of ambitions amongst the children. Children as young as 6–7 years are seen performing and emoting on songs not meant for their age. The parents not only allow their children to participate in these shows but also encourage them. Parents want their children to participate in these shows, judging by the fact that the auditions held for some of these shows in Jaipur draw huge turnouts of children and their parents These shows not only engage the children as viewers but also allow them access to power over the judges' decisions through the system of voting through SMS.

Table 3

Do You Wish to Participate in Reality Shows?

	Boys	*Girls*	*Total*
Yes	55	51	106(88.33)
No	05	09	14(11.67)
Total	60	60	120

On being asked if they would like to participate in any reality show (Table 3), 88.33 per cent wanted to participate in reality shows and enjoyed watching them. These shows not only engage the children as viewers but also allow them access to power over the judge's decision through the system of voting through SMS. The contestants in the reality shows seek votes from the viewers on the basis of caste, region, and sex. This whole exercise encourages the child to assume adult behaviour.

Table 4

Use of SMS Voting for Reality Shows

SMS Voting	*Boys*	*Girls*	*Total*
Yes	48(80)	53(88.33)	101(84.17)
No	12(20)	07(11.67)	19(15.83)
	60	60	120

As shown in Table 4, it was found that 84.17 per cent of the respondents used SMS voting to lend their support to the contestant of their choice. Regional identity figured prominently as their reason for doing so.

Children and Advertising

Children are major targets for TV advertising whose impact is greater than usual because there is an apparent lessening of influence by parents and others in the younger generation (Bagdikian, 2000). Advertising campaigns are increasingly targeting children to be consumers and overly conscious of materialistic things, perhaps even at the expense of human qualities. One of the main reasons for such a fascination in children in this way is because of the potential purchasing power that they have. According to a recent survey carried out by Cartoon Network in association with Synovate India, children exercise a major influencing power or alternatively termed as 'pester power' on parents in buying even big items like cars. They spend nearly ₹ 291 crore as pocket money (The survey was conducted in 14 Indian cities covering 4,043 children). Advertising apart, giving a fillip to this manic consumption is the 'me-too' syndrome. The peer pressure is so strong that they buy similar brands or products simply to be 'in-group'. Hence, this generation dons the same look, hairstyle, accessories and gizmos to get that extra surge of confidence leading to homogenisation of culture, a by-product of globalisation.

Table 5

Influence of Advertisement on Children

	Boys	*Girls*	*Total*
Influenced by advertisements	52	56	108(90)
Not influenced by advertisements	08	04	12(10)
Total	60	60	120

Researches have shown in detail how television helps children to form the attitude and skills of consumerism starting from the children's ability to recognise and understand advertising and link it to their requests and purchases. When asked the question as to how many children bought things because of the advertisement shown on television, 90 per cent of the respondents admitted to be influenced by the TV advertisements. The media has made the children conscious of their appearances and responsive to advertising, particularly that with celebrity endorsements. For children, consumption has become more than simply acquisition of goods and services; it serves as an important vehicle for self-expression and identification (Zollo, 1995; Cook, 2000).

Table 6

Type of Advertisements that Influence them the Most

Type of Advertisement	*Boys*	*Girls*	*Total*
Humorous	57	49	106
Action Packed	58	34	92
Family Oriented	23	52	75
Involving Celebrities	55	58	113

It was found that children were influenced more by advertisements being endorsed by celebrities. The reasons for this influence could be attributed to their easily influential age. The children in the tweens are not mature enough to distinguish between fantasy and reality. They believe that the products being endorsed are being used by the celebrities themselves and hence good. The above table reveals that girls were more influenced by family oriented advertisements than boys. Girls in Indian society are indoctrinated in family values at a very early age.

Brand Equity and Children

The children today are highly brand conscious. It was found in the study that almost 99 per cent of the respondents reported using only branded items. Brands like Nike, Adidas, Reebok, Barbie, and Disney are popular amongst them. The typical child today sees a friend in Action man, Barbie doll and the like. The images of these characters are found everywhere from clothing, furniture, lunch boxes, bags, water bottles, nowadays extending even on the walls of the children's rooms. The birthday parties are also organised as theme parties sparking off competition among the children and their parents to out-do one another. They do not wish to buy any item other than branded products. Most of them had to fight, cajole, plead or bully their parents into providing them brands. They are highly conscious of their image, which is linked with the global presence of brands. Exposure of mass media and discussion with parents ensure that children are not only aware of new brands available but also know how to evaluate them on various parameters. While the younger children clearly affected parental behaviour and purchases, adolescents have full cognitive development and an understanding of the economic concepts required for processing information and selection.

Children and Decision-Making

Not only do the children today have more disposable income at younger ages but they also have significant influence over family purchases. Marketing experts call it pester power or the 'nag factor' – the ability to get kids to nag their parents to buy a specific product or take them to a specific restaurant. Potentially children constitute the most lucrative market because they are actually three markets in one (McNeal, 1987)

1. Current market – children are viewed as having needs, money to spend on items that satisfy their needs and have a willingness to spend money.
2. Future market – for most goods and services.
3. Market of influential – The children are turned into consumers at a very early age in our society through the desires and encouragement of parents who also provide the youngsters with the necessary financial support. The Indian parents also try to live their aspirations through the children.

Table 7

Influence of Children over Family Purchases

	St. Xaviers	*SMS*	*Step by Step*	*Vidyashram*	*Total N=120*
Electronics	27	29	28	24	108
Vehicles	20	25	28	22	95
Grocery	24	21	23	25	93
Gifts	21	23	22	19	85
Furnishings	16	18	22	21	77
Home products	18	22	25	24	89

N=30 each for all schools

Parents Prepare Children for Adulthood

The child rearing practices in the urban upper middle-class families have changed drastically. Following the self-sufficiency model developed in the West, parents in India too nurture a strong desire to prepare their children for adulthood as soon as possible. The decreasing number of children per family, increasing number of women entering the job market, availability of larger disposable incomes, desire of the parents to please their children, unburdening of the guilt of parents for not being there for the child, all result in pampering the child with material gifts purchased from the marketplace. The children are being initiated into money awareness at an early age (4–5 years) by way of monthly allowances (which they are often free to spend as they like). The parents desire to provide necessary money skills to the children so that they can cope without assistance.

Emergence of Little Adults

As Punch (2003) says, 'it should not be assumed that certain children in particular situations can only be perceived as either similar to or different from adults, since such boundaries are fluid as children's lives move between adult and child roles. They may use different identities to suit different situations in their lives (see also James and Prout, 1996), and they may also switch between their distinct roles according to particular activities or the arena in which they find themselves. It is worth remembering that children not only take on different child or adult roles in different contexts or with different people, but can also negotiate both roles at the same time, changing almost simultaneously.'

The 'end of childhood' seems to constitute an important debate globally (Buckingham, 2000; Kenway and Bullen, 2001). Postman (1983) declares that the mass media are the main causes of the 'disappearance of childhood'. Parents have a hard time providing guidance and influence over their children when there are so many conflicting influences from outside.

Postman describes the present society as one in which children and adults watch the same movies and tele-romances, listen to the same pop music and play the same computer games. The adults in such a society become more childish as they try to pursue youth culture, whereas the children to whom all secrets of adulthood are revealed, especially those concerning violence and sex, become seemingly mature. As the differentiation between childhood and adulthood becomes blurred, concepts which distinguish the adult from the child, such as independence and responsibility, become unclear too. The children of today have mastered the knowledge needed by adults, leading to a role reversal. They no longer turn to parents for counselling, guidance, information or even comfort. Parents have a hard time providing guidance and influence on their children when there are so many conflicting influences from outside. The children today are skeptical of authority that is not based on an ethic of reciprocal respect. This represents a challenge to the social institutions that have been in the forefront of childhood change. The diversification of children's lives for example in terms of their family situation, the rise of consumerism with its heightened expectation of choice, the proliferation of sources of ideas and knowledge, the diffusion of democratic norms – all these are creating new kinds of childhood and new varieties of children. The effect is the creation of a generention of children who seem to have a greater sense of personhood, distinct from their parents at an early age. The children are being transformed into Little Adults without having acquired the necessary maturity and knowledge which underpin adulthood.

Note

This paper presents analysis of the data collected in the year 2010 as part of UGC SAP DRS project. A part of it has been published in the *World Leisure Journal*, Vol. 52, No. 1, 2010

References

Baudrillard, J. (1988). 'Simulacra and Simulations,' in Poster, M. (Ed.), *Selected Writings*, Stanford: Stanford University Press, pp. 166–184.

Bagdikian, Ben H. (2000). Media Monopoly, 6th ed., Boston: Beacon Press.

Beck, U. (1992). *Risk Society: Towards a New Modernity*. London: Sage.

Beck, U. (1997). 'Democratization of Family', *Childhood* 4(2): pp. 151–168.

Buckingham, D. (2000). *After the Death of Childhood: Growing up in the Age of Electronic Media*, Cambridge: Polity.

Christian, Downie and Kate Glazebook (2007). 'Mobile Phones and the Consumer Kids' Australian Institute, Research Paper No. 41, February.

Cook, Daniel. (2000). 'The Other Child' Study: Figuring Children as Consumers in Market Research, 1919–1990s, *The Sociological Quarterly*, Vol. 41, No. 3, pp. 487–507.

Cook, Dan (2001). 'Lunchbox Hegemony; Kids and the Market Place, Then and Now', LiP magazine, August.

Connolly, M. and J. Ennew (1996) 'Introduction: Children Out of Place', *Childhood* 3(2): 131–45 (Special Issue on Working and Street Children).

Dumazedier, J. (1974). *Sociology of Leisure*, Amsterdam: Elsevier.

Editorial (1996). The Globalization of Childhood or Childhood as a Global Issue, *Childhood*, 3, Sage Publications, pp. 307–311.

Ennew, J. (1994) *Street and Working Children: A Guide to Planning*. Development Manual 4. London: Save the Children.

Giddens, A. (1990). *The Consequences of Modernity*, Cambridge: Polity Press.

Jain, Rashmi (2007). 'Access to Leisure: Impact of Forces of Liberalization, Privatization and Globalization on Socially Disadvantaged Groups in India', *World Leisure Journal*, Vol. 49, No.1.

Hecht, T. (1998) *At Home in the Street: Street Children of Northeast Brazil*. Cambridge: Cambridge University Press.

Kaplan, Max. (1960). *Leisure in America: A Social Inquiry*, New York: John Wiley, p. 14.

Kenway, J., and Bullen, E. (2001). *Consuming Children*, Buckingham: Open University Press.

Mayall, B. (1994). *Children's Childhoods: Observed and Experienced*, London: The Palmer Press.

McLuhan Marshall. (1964). *The Global Village: Understanding Media,* New York: Mentor.

McNeal, James U. (1987). *Children as Consumers: Insights and Implications*, Laxington, Ma.: Lexington Books.

Miljeteig, P. (1999) 'Introduction: Understanding Child Labour', *Childhood* 6(1):5–12 (Special Issue on Child Labour).

Modi, Ishwar. (1985). *Leisure, Mass Media and Social Structure,* Jaipur: Rawat Publications.

Postman, N. (1983). *The Disappearance of Childhood,* London: W.H. Allen.

Punch, Samantha, 2003, Childhoods in the Majority World: Miniature Adults or Tribal Children?, 37; 277. Accessed at: http://soc.sagepub.com/cgi/content/abstract/37/2/277

Qvortrup, J. (1990). *Childhood as a Social Phenomenon: An Introduction to a Series of National Reports*, Wenen: European Centre.

Rizzini, Irene and Malcolm Bush (2002). 'Globalization and Children', *Childhood,* Sage Publications.

Robertson, R. (1992). *Globalization,* London: Pine Forge Press.

Smith, R. (2000). 'Order and Disorder: The Contradictions of Childhood', *Children and Society,* 14(1): pp. 3–10.

Thorne, B. (1987). 'Revisioning Women and Social Change: Where Are the Children?' *Gender and Society,* 1(1).

Umberto, Eco (1986). *Travels in Hyper-reality,* New York: Harcourt Brace Jovanovich.

UNICEF. (1996). *The State of World's Children,* Oxford University Press.

Vadhera, Sharad. (2004). 'Advertising to Children in India', *Young Consumers*, Vol. 6, pp. 75–78.

Zinnecker, J. (2001). 'Pre-Adolescent Children: An Essay' in M. DuBois-Raymond, H. Siincker and H.H. Kriiger (ed.) (2001). *Childhood in Europe*, New York: Peter Lang, pp. 43–61.

Zollo, P. (1995). 'Talking to Teens', *American Demographic*, Vol. 17, No. 11, pp. 22–28.

16

Sociological Perspectives of Education for Lifestyle Counselling

Case of Szeged, Hungary

KLÁRA TARKÓ AND HABIL ZSUZSANNA BENKÕ

The health of a nation is defined primarily by lifestyle and quality of life: education, working and living conditions, civilisation and cultural level, community norms. People living under less favourable conditions generally have worse health status. The starting point of our paper is to show the reader the dimensions and factors influencing our lifestyle and give some Hungarian examples to underline the actual influences these factors perform. Then we will focus on one factor, namely education and describe the training of lifestyle counsellor health promoters.

Let us first start with the definition of lifestyle. There were several definitions born from international and national professionals. Ágnes Losonci (1977) conceptualised lifestyle very poetically, as follows: 'From all those abilities and aptitudes that are provided and bounded by the society, from all those abilities that are allowed by the society to be unfolded from people's personality or that are unfolded, from all those constraints that people do on behalf of the upkeep and reproduction of their own being, from all those needs that are evoked and strengthened by social and individual being how do people live, organise, think about society, their close and distant relations, for the sake of their real and extendable aims, manage themselves, their power, time, all these together and form their life in all these, can people make use of everything that is given.'

For operationalisation we have chosen one definition developed by a Hungarian Sociologist, Rudolf Andorka: 'Lifestyle is the system of everyday activities, that is, the *forms of activities* members of the society perform in their everyday life, the *average time* spent on these activities, *where* they do, *with whom*, *why* and *what do these activities mean* for them' (Andorka, 2002: 463).

The elements of lifestyle, that is the activities performed, are: work, education, social relationships, consumption, nutrition, clothing, interior design and leisure. Average time spent on different activities can be studied for example with the method of time budget survey, which is a method in social statistics studying and analysing lifestyle as a hierarchical system of activities. Subjects of this survey keep a log on what, where and with whom people do during the 24 hours of a day. The system of daily activities can then be organised into three major categories.

1. Physiologically bound time containing sleeping, eating, personal hygiene, dressing, passive rest.
2. Socially bound time containing work, housework, shopping, child-rearing, learning and connected transport.
3. Leisure activities containing cultural activities, social life and physical training among others.

'Where' can be indoor and outdoor, with whom can mean alone, with friends, family, in small groups, etc. The 'why' of doing certain activities can be for example to earn money, to recreate our ability to work, or to preserve our health. The meaning of an activity for us can be either a pleasure or a pressure, might be a source of segregation or on the contrary, social integration.

Max Weber's lifestyle model emphasises the role of life opportunities, life chances and choices (Benkõ, 2000). Life opportunities provide the conditions for choosing one's lifestyle. Life chances are the chances of actually realising the given values. For realisation it is the social environment that ensures the structural prerequisites. Opportunities, chances and choices in everyday life mean that people have a free choice within the wider or tighter boundaries provided by their social environment and related social pressure. At the same time, lifestyle is not only a dependent of one's social position, but it also plays a considerable role in designating one's position in the social structure, that is social stratification is also regularised according to lifestyle and related reputation.

Based on the lifestyle model of Max Weber, Zsuzsanna Benkõ (2000) was the one who organised the factors influencing our life opportunities and life choices into the model shown in Figure 1.

Figure 1

The Model of Healthy Lifestyle

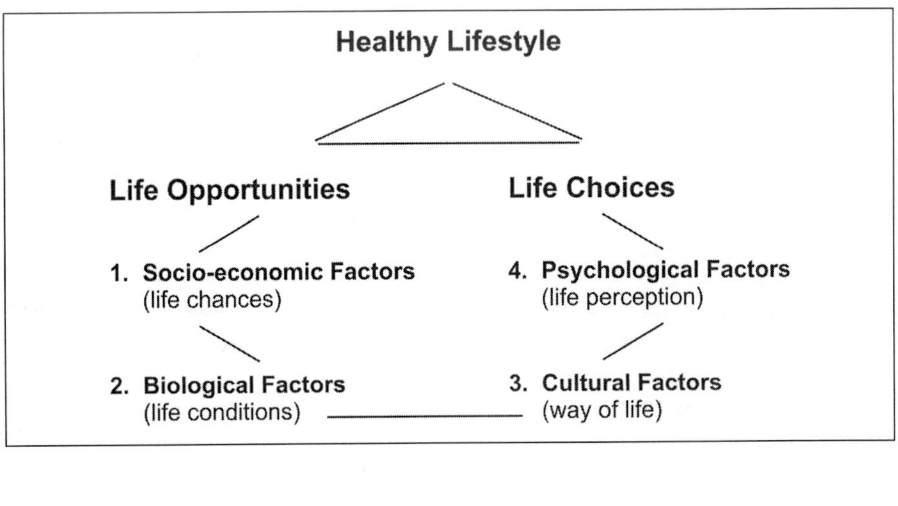

Our choices are influenced by our life conditions like gender, race or the physical health one values. Our lifestyle choices are not always inevitably rational considering the given life opportunities and chances; rationality is often overridden by our traditions, beliefs, customs and self sacrifice (Benkõ, 2000). Cultural factors, like nationality, ethnicity, value orientation or religion are also important. And last but not least psychological factors like internal-external sense of control or stress-coping mechanisms are also decisive (Benkõ, 2009).

Education is highlighted here, as that will be the focus of the last part of our paper, but first let us show some Hungarian examples on how the above factors influence the health – and the leisure within – opportunities of people.

Unequal Life (health/leisure) Opportunities (Hungary)

Let us start with one element from the biological factors: *gender*. There is a well-known difference between the life expectancy at birth of women and men. Hungarian data from 2014 indicates that for men it is 72,13 years, while for women it is 78,91 years. There are *regional differences,* where the lower years appear at the socio-economically more disadvantaged Northern Hungary (men: 70, 52, women: 77, 97), and the highest years are observable in the capital, Budapest (men: 74, 14, women: 80, 04). (https://www.ksh.hu/docs/hun/xstadat/xstadat_eves/i_wdsd008.html). Related we can mention an other factor – *ethnicity*, as in Northern Hungary are those areas where the Romany population is the most condensed in Hungary, and the average life expectancy at birth for the Romany is 10 years less than it is for Hungarians (Benkõ, 2010; Tarkó, 2010). The *level of education* is also decisive. We can definitely see a huge gap between the life opportunities of men with the lowest and with the highest level of education (Kovács and Hablicsek, 2006).

Time budget national surveys make it evident, that women have more responsibilities as socially bound time, while men have more time in general for leisure activities. Studying the time spent for leisure, people living in villages had the lowest amount of minutes spent on leisure. In sociological sense villages are socio-economically lower status settlements. In terms of leisure, the relationship with education level is an inverse one. People of lower education level has more leisure time, though it does not mean, that they spend it for useful leisure.

Staying with the question of education, let us examine what can education mean in terms of our lifestyle. It is too easy to say, that only professionals can help us in staying and becoming healthy. The truth is, that not only professionals, but the individuals themselves are also liable for their health. Individuals try to form their health state according to the abilities and motivations they have. Healthy lifestyle choices are made not only for the sake of health itself, but health is a mean of achieving something that is more palpable for people: better work performance, longer life, physical fitness or better looks. Healthy lifestyle in this sense is an accomplishment achieved by the individual him/herself. Education, among others, helps the individual in communicating and possessing the wide scale of possibilities to choose from, the ability to decide what is scientifically proven, and choose the best fit for his/her needs and conditions.

On the other hand, no matter what level of education the client has, there are trained professionals whose task is to help individuals and groups of people to utilise their opportunities and make the best out of them. Different social classes follow different track in terms of the quality, extent and characteristics of a healthy lifestyle. Let us now talk about the training of the above professionals.

Education for Lifestyle Counselling

Aims, competencies, knowledge and skills

The Recreation organisation and health promotion bachelor was brought to life in 2006, following the Bologna Process, when the three cycle higher education model was adapted. This bachelor education is three years long (six semesters) and 180 credits altogether. Following the first two years of founding and core studies, students can specialise to become health promoters, minority health coordinators or recreation organisers (Tarkó and Benkõ, 2013). Here we would like to focus on the health promoter specialisation.

The health promoter – Lifestyle counsellor specialisation aims to train professionals, who are able to:

- Fulfil counselling, mediating and promoting roles in the area of healthy lifestyle.
- Shape, form and influence the lifestyle habits of individuals, families, communities and the society, for the sake of preserving and promoting health.
- Contribute to the development of mental health promotion culture and to education for a health- and environment-conscious life.

The health promoter – Lifestyle counsellor professional is competent in:

- Creating a 'health map' for individuals – in the family, in the workplace – including physical and mental status and lifestyle elements (leisure, nutrition, time management, environment).
- Build personalised (individual and community level) counselling activity, health promoting actions, campaigns and projects on identified needs.

With his/her knowledge in the socio-demographic determinants of unequal opportunities and the means and 'language' of addressing and approaching different social groups this professional can bring the best out of life opportunities and life chances to promote healthy choices.

First let us see those subjects within the education of lifestyle counsellors that provide the foundations of being able to 'navigate' in the social environment, then we introduce the readers into the practice oriented field work students undergo.

Social determinants of health and leisure, and so the issue of unequal opportunities are addressed during the following courses:

- Introduction to health promotion
- Sociology: general, family, lifestyle, deviance, health, minority
- Communication (theory and skills development)
- Social skills development
- Education of special needs pupils
- Lifestyle camp

- Social policy, health rights
- Health promoting organisation development, project management
- Health promotion of minorities
- Workplace health promotion, prevention
- Field practice

One can be a good professional only if he/she knows his/her clients: their position in the social stratification system, what does it mean in terms of their lifestyle, possibilities, opportunities and chances, what means do they have to break out of unfavourable conditions and make their lives better. We can not talk about people in general, there are several groups of people with different needs, conditions and means. Lifestyle counsellors should be well aware of these differences and plan their counselling activity accordingly. Figure 2 depicts that there is no special social sub-system for health.

Figure 2

Health and Social Sub-systems

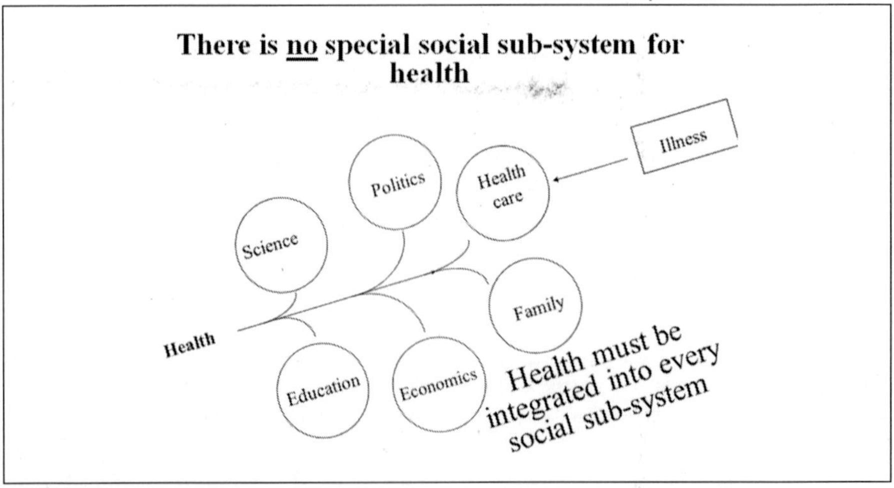

Based on Luhmann, 1996

If we consider the social sub-systems, while illness belongs definitely to healthcare, health does not have one special subsystem, but it can be and must be integrated into every social subsystem. This means, that health promoting lifestyle counsellors have a wide range of possibilities to act, and also have to be skilled in addressing these different kinds of settings. Places for field practice can vary also accordingly.

How and Where Do Students Practice Their Future Profession?

Within the recreation organisation and health promotion bachelor practical competencies are developed on multi-level and in several forms. The aim is to be able to apply the competencies, skills and methods obtained during lectures and seminars on the most frequent settings of health promotion and recreation.

First stage of this field practice is the lifestyle camp (2 credits) in the 1st semester. In the camp students can gather experience about lifestyle elements with the help of playful tasks, physical exercises and social skills development activities. This is not only a community experience, but also a foundation for their studies. An important element of this professional socialisation is the participation of higher grade students also, who are assisting the teachers' work.

The next important stages of practical training are three short term field practices in the upcoming three semesters (2+2+5 credits). Within these 3 field practices students try out the most important methods of surveying the important settings of health promoting activities. Then students perform in small groups community level state and needs assessment, followed by the fulfilment of a small scale intervention called action. Teachers in the meantime supervise students' work.

Students specialised in health promotion follow their practical training during two terms of professional field practice (6+17 credits). Students are trained in organisations that are consistent with their future plans. Regarding that health promotion interventions are needed in every social sub-system, our students can be successfully trained in health, fitness and wellness centres, NGOs, educational and health services as well as in other kinds of public or private, profit oriented or non-profit oriented sectors.

In the first semester of the professional field work students become involved in the work of the chosen organisation, health promotion setting. After making personal contact they survey and analyse the individual and organisational background of a potential health promotion activity, the professional relationships of the given setting and the regular work activity they perform. Students – according to their level of competence – join the everyday activities of the setting. Part of students' task is also to collect background information among the clients or the employees of the setting to prepare a possible individual lifestyle counselling, of course keeping to the ethical regulations needed. Students keep a log on their work, and their work is aided by teachers and field coordinators as supervisors.

In the second part of the professional field practice students perform individual lifestyle counselling based on the experiences of the previous semester, as well as they plan and fulfil a health promotion project. This process is aided by teachers through skills development courses and seminars.

In this 6th semester students use all practical and theoretical knowledge and competencies they obtained during their studies. They spend 36 hours in the field practice setting in the 5th semester and 100 hours in the 6th semester.

Conclusions

Bachelor level education is often accused of not being able to create professionals who can stand on their own. We are proud to declare, that according to the feedback of the labour market and from higher education professionals also, this is a well balanced and professionally organised training, where we successfully educate lifestyle counsellors for real life.

The above bachelor level professional mobilises his/her skills in the general inequality system, while there are also more special inequalities, like the unequal opportunities of national and ethnic groups, which come more and more into the foreground. To address these special conditions a more specialised professional is required, who acquires additional skills through postgraduate education. The institute trains Health Promoting Minority Coordinators also, whose focus is on revealing and addressing the unequal (health) opportunities the national and ethnic groups are exposed to.

References

Andorka, R. (2002). *Bevezetés a Szociológiába.* (Introduction to Sociology), Budapest: Osiris Publishers.

Benkõ, Zs. (2000). A családok életmódját meghatározó társadalmi tényezõk. (Social Determinants Determining the Lifestyle of families) *Szenvedélybetegségek, Addictologia Hungarica* 2000\1, pp. 54–58.

Benkõ, Zs. (2009). Különbözõ kulturális és vallási értékek befolyása. (The Influence of Various Cultural and Religious Values) in. Benkõ Zsuzsanna (2009): *Egészségfejlesztés*. Módszertani kézikönyv. Szeged: Mozaik Publishers, pp. 45–48.

Benkõ, Zs. (2010). Minorities in Hungary: The Romany. in Marjaana Soininen, Tuula Merisuo-Storm (eds.), *Looking at diversity in different ways.* Turku: Uniprint, 2010. pp. 77–92.

Losonci, Á. (1977): *Az életmód az idõben, a tárgyakban és az értékekben* (Lifestyle in Time, in Objects and in Values), Budapest: Gondolat Publishers.

Kovács, K. and Hablicsek, L. (2006). *Iskolázottság és halandóság* (Education and mortality). Demographic Research Institute, Budapest.

Tarkó, K. (2010). Prejudice and How Minorities are Viewed in the Hungarian Society and in the Visegrad Countries, in Marjaana Soininen, Tuula Merisuo-Storm (eds.), *Looking at Diversity in Different Ways*. Turku: Uniprint, pp. 63–73.

Tarkó, K. and Benkõ, Zs. (2013): Evidence-Based Leisure Studies in Higher Education: Using the Results of a Transnational Lifestyle Research, in Fabio Massimo Lo Verde, Ishwar Modi, Gianna Cappello (eds.): *Mapping Leisure across Borders.* Cambridge: Cambridge Scholars Publishing, pp. 364–37

Luhmann, N. (1996). *Social Systems* (Writing Science). Stanford: Calif. Stanford University Press. p. 684.

https://www.ksh.hu/docs/hun/xstadat/xstadat_eves/i_wdsd008.html

17

Post-Retirement Leisure in Japan

SCOTT NORTH

Rapid economic development made Japan the first non-western example of modernity. Now the world's most rapidly aging society, it is the leading example of post-modern socio-demographic change (Coulmas et al., 2010). The concern of this paper is leisure in later life: What possibilities for leisure does Japan offer its elderly? I approach this philosophical and practical question by analysing the general context of post-retirement leisure in Japan to identify its dominant characteristics.

Retirement is generally understood as the absence of employment. What leisure is possible without work to contrast with it? A recent study of elderly female learners of Noh drama described their leisure practice as 'a social space that allows for modes of being different from those of the everyday constraints of human life' (Moore, 2014: 104). Thus, there is a realm of Japanese leisure apart from recovery from work.

Some scholars of Japanese leisure characterise retirement activities of the elderly in terms of the Serious Leisure Perspective, a heuristic scheme of categories elaborated by Robert Stebbins (Stebbins, 1982 and 2012). The basic definition of serious leisure is *non-coercion*, nevertheless, activities in this category 'require perseverance, significant personal effort, a control of the body, and a quest for self-actualization' (Moore and Campbell, 2009: 226).

Consideration of Japan's post-retirement leisure raises questions: Will older Japanese people's vision of the good life after employment push society in a new direction? Will their later life leisure practices move the 'fulcrum for balancing work and life' (Stebbins, 2012: 64–65) for future Japanese generations? To find out this paper first introduces antecedents for contemporary Japan's leisure strategies. It then discusses the leisure practices of nominally retired elderly Japanese. The focus is on the leisure culture of the *dankai sedai*, the baby boomer generation, born immediately after World War II (1947–1951), who reached age 60 and began retiring in 2007.

The *Dankai Sedai*, Demography and Leisure Practices

In 1860 the average Japanese lifespan was about 42 years. By 1991 it had reached 75 (Leitner and Leitner, 2012: 4). Today, the average is 82.7 years overall and 87 years for women (OECD, 2014: 5). The longer lives and post-retirement leisure of the *dankai sedai* are of interest because of cohort effects: as the largest generation, their leisure patterns will set the stage for generations to follow (Clammer, 2010: 609). Those born in the period 1947–1951 comprise 10 per cent of Japan's population. Combining the even older generations, the elders come to more than 20 per cent of the total (Soumucho, 2010).[1] As the protagonists of a period of strong economic expansion, these older Japanese have arguably the best opportunity for post-retirement leisure that any generation has had. Their careers took place during the heyday of so-called lifetime employment, but even those who did not win corporate competitions for careers were able to dream of retiring in some comfort. They also were the first generation of Japanese to be able to embrace foreign travel during and after their working lives (Funck, 2010: 583). The leisure of these retirees is a window on the world of the most affluent and privileged generation in Japanese history. Their needs and consumption habits are reshaping the pace and content of daily life.

The Leisure Heritage of the *Dankai Sedai:* A Conceptual Map of Japanese Leisure History

Relative paucity of individual free time and top-down leisure promotion are characteristic of modern Japan. Employment structured time use and constrains leisure. Moreover, industrial development and global competitiveness are dominant national goals. Quality of domestic life in Japan, including leisure, has been a secondary consideration. Tracing the language of leisure through modern Japanese history, we find little room for individual autonomy or leisure (Linhart, 1998). Edo period (1603–1868) leisure was characterised by moral uses of time, such as temple and shrine pilgrimages and organised study groups devoted to traditional arts, such as flower arranging, tea ceremony, poetry, dance, and calligraphy (Nishiyama, 1997).

Raku inkyo, 'relaxed retirement', symbolised the changing role of leisure as Japan developed into a modern nation. In 18th century Japan, *raku inkyo* denoted a time of life when Japanese male elites withdrew from household and financial concerns, turning such affairs over to the next generation and spending their remaining days in 'disengaged and leisurely retirement' (Formanek, 2010: 333). This image was lampooned as dilettantism during the Meiji period (1868–1912) when the emperor's subjects were to exhibit lifelong commitment to the development of the state and its rise in the world order (Formanek, 2010: 336–337). *Inkyo* notions spread to the common classes after 1800. As society became less poor, various forms of commercial nightlife sprang up (Frustuck, 1998). But even so, leisure took place within a normative framework of hierarchical social relations. Individual leisure was rare because, 'Time was not a personal possession' but belonged to families, villages, companies, or the state (Smith, 1986: 167). Purveyors of leisure activities were compelled to market them as philosophies or 'ways' to self-improvement or enlightenment (Cox, 2002).

The 20th century Japanese leisure continued to be constrained by work obligations and moral concerns. Workers preferred income to leisure; seeking 'free time' was seen as betrayal of obligations to employers and co-workers (Smith, 1986: 185–186). Leisure travel to Japan's colonies was promoted as patriotic duty. Pre and post-World War II quotidian leisure forms (*asobi, tanoshimi, yoka*) were regarded as low-class diversions from serious pursuits. Western scholars were warned away from investigating them by image-conscious Japanese, who said they were not suitable for academic study (Linhart, 1998: 2). In the wake of defeat and amid the need to rebuild Japan, *yoka* (spare time) activities again acquired a moral tone (Cox, 2002: 180). Cooking, archery, martial arts, baseball, and seasonal activities were branded as contributions to culture or civilisation.

Postwar, the Japanese state's increasing interest in leisure was manifest in its prescription of activities, such as foreign travel, that would demonstrate Japan's standing as an 'advanced industrial nation.' (Leheny, 2003) Although Japanese leaders called for *yutori* (a less constrained society, in which one has time and space to follow one's muse), realisation was thwarted by economic stasis and subsequent re-emphasis on employment as all-encompassing (McCormack, 2001). A late 1980s rush of ski resort and golf course construction was the result of political influence buying, and the expensive leisure facilities thus created benefitted the upper classes (McCormack, 2001). For most male wage earners, work remained the central life interest and leisure, too, was company centered (Allison, 1994). The swelling numbers of professional housewives found meaningful pursuits to occupy their *yoka* (unassigned time) in local and national government sponsored culture industries (Ochiai, 1996). Turn-of-the-millennium declines in annual work time were statistical illusions caused by the rapid increase in part-time employment (Morioka, 2006). Full-time male work hours probably increased (Mouer and Kawanishi, 2005: 74–75) even though the number of holidays grew.

Japanese workers take less than half of their paid leave, a situation attributed to high living costs, heavy work loads, concern for reputation at work, and pressure (tacit or otherwise) from management not to take holidays (Cole, 1992; *Japan Times*, 2014). An ethic of self-sacrifice with feudal roots (*messhi houkou*) remains the corporate membership ideal. Moreover Japanese are not socialised for leisure (McCallum, 1998). Instead, life bounded by organisational and institutional deadlines produces workers who respect schedules as transcendent truths. Schools and employers promote time-use habits and life course expectations that are seen to reflect national values.

Japan hit the 'takeoff stage' of leisure development in the mid-1980s, as westernised leisure practices proliferated (Russell, 1996: 149). But just as empire building, war, and reconstruction had thwarted leisure development before, economic stagnation after 1990, and global financial turmoil since 2008, have constrained Japanese leisure development. This then is the background for the *dankai sedai* and their post-retirement leisure. Norma Field (2001: xi) summed it up thus: 'The potential for a society providing general well-being was hijacked by the mad desire for ever accelerating growth.' The *dankai sedai* experienced increasing hopes of leisure amid the drama of development. A Frivolity Stigma attached itself to those who did take things seriously enough. Stereotypically the boomer generation of men venerated *ganbarism*: being tough, holding out to the bitter end. Self-sacrifice was useful for postwar recovery and subsequent economic growth, and it has important implications for the post-retirement leisure of that generation.

The Current Context of Post-Retirement Leisure

Idealised postwar life course norms permit retirement at the end of devotion to work (for men) and family (for women). In a classic analysis of Japanese life course (Rohlen, 1978), elders gradually shed cares and responsibilities, returning to a child-like state, a picture of aging that agrees with centuries-old pattern of pre-industrial later life (Formanek, 2010). But industrial production drew young people into the cities, leaving rural elders to fend for themselves, while simultaneously enduring diminished social status in comparison with the high incomes of their city-dwelling children (Ogawa, 2010: 149). A perverse ageism took root, in which 'older people, even if they want to be active, are of no use and have to face discrimination...' (Ogawa, Takeo, 2010: 150). The negative connotation of aging increased as the number of the elderly grew.

Concern for welfare costs is generating a push for active ageing, in which 'golden' elders care for one another. With new legislation and good health among a large majority of the elderly, Japan is reinterpreting age (Clammer, 2010: 599). In place of the negative stigma, old age is positively 'characterized by independence, participation, self-realization, care, and dignity' (Ogawa, Takeo, 2010: 154–155). Older Japanese citizens are, of demographic necessity, drafted as labour resources, and their leisure, too, is being used to reduce welfare costs and promote lifelong active service to the needs of the state. Whether the *dankai sedai* welcome this top-down imposition is questionable. One astute commentator notes the desire of the young olds (60s) for an autonomous 'second life' of hobbies and educational activities is 'markedly different from the elderly of previous generations' (Shiraishi, 2010: 530).

Later Life Gender Convergence?

There are no 'asexual Japanese' so discussion of leisure must consider gender differences (Taira, 1986: 2). Men seldom make post-retirement plans (Clammer, 2010: 599–600) and *dankai sedai* men largely failed to build social ties or develop leisure interests outside their firms (Iwao, 2010). Both genders report being healthy and satisfied: at age 75 years, 70 per cent of elders are healthy and 80 per cent report being satisfied with their lives (Funck, 2010: 582), but women's better health and longer life spans will make them the majority of the active elderly. With longevity has come a reappraisal of age, as well as convergence in formerly gendered leisure practices. Because of postwar democratic education, spouses increasingly share post-retirement pastimes (Iwao, 2010). Couples take advantage of weekday discounts offered by theatres, museums, and culture classes, such as photography, pottery making, and dance (Clammer, 2010: 600). As *dankai sedai* men retire, women's drive to be independently active has interacted with men's need to restore relations with their life partners, giving rise to diverse activities that provide 'individual gratification' (Iwao, 2010: 545). Retired men are taking up practical skills (cooking) and hobbies they can share with their spouses. That said, leisure activities can also be ways to avoid post-retirement intimacy – by practicing gender specific leisure, both men and women may maintain separate schedules. This limits interaction and prevents confrontation, a strategy for coping with tensions caused by being together again after so many years of work-induced separation.

Supporting Post-retirement Life and Leisure

The general insufficiency of Japanese old age pensions (half of senior households say their finances are 'tight or very tight' (Funck, 2010: 582)), means that retirement leisure, particularly stereotypical western-style activities like golf, will only be available to those boomers who were fortunate enough to amass large nest eggs. Moreover, most workers must bridge a five-year gap between retirement and the start of pension payments (Ogawa, Takeo, 2010: 158). Japan's shrinking labour force means that the expanding population of elders is supported by an OECD-lowest ratio of 2.4 workers under 65 for each retiree. (OECD, 2014).

Income gaps associated with household types outline the contours of elder leisure. In 1975, 55 per cent of elders lived with supportive adult children, but by 2005 only 22 per cent did. The 30 per cent of elderly who lived with only a spouse and the 22 per cent who resided alone were most likely to experience poverty (Shirahase, 2010: 221). Worst off are the more than 50 per cent of elder women who live alone (Iwao, 2010: 531). Japanese household savings fell as the population aged and will continue to fall (Horioka, 2010). More than 60 per cent of elderly households live on less than 3 million yen per year: a minimal stipend in one of the world's most expensive countries. Reductions in public assistance and decreasing support from children mean worsening poverty among the elderly (Fukawa, 2010: 924–925).

Regional Variation

Parallel with class-based differences, there is an urban-rural divide in leisure practices (Clammer, 2010: 599). Government support for traditional regional leisure, the craft and cultural activities popular with the elderly, has declined due to administrative mergers. Preservation of semi-sacred local rituals may thus become more difficult in smaller rural settlements (Thompson, 2010). Exceptions will persist, though, as long as there are participants. Much depends on the vigour of local elder communities. Anthropologist Klein (2011) notes that while some elderly exhibit withdrawal and loneliness, in other places mutual support activities, volunteer work, or hobbies give people strong reasons to participate, such as the rural men she studied whose maintenance of the local tradition of raising fighting bulls gave coherence to families and the local community, as well as providing a basis for manly camaraderie.

Post-Retirement Employment among Older Japanese

When pensions, investments, retirement savings, and family support fall short, the elderly substitute wage labour for post-retirement leisure. Comprising 10 per cent of the labour force, six million Japanese pensioners work (Matsuyama, 2012), more than in any other industrialised country (Meyer-Ohle, 2010: 951). Some are rehired by their former firms to do their old jobs at much lower salaries, which they accept in order to bridge the gap between retirement at age 60 and pension receipt at age 65. For others, self-employment, contract labour, and piecework at home provide income. A few may engage in semi-romantic rural adventures like 'retirement farming', but elders are especially prominent in non-profit or low-profit enterprises that provide public benefits (Ogawa T., 2010: 159–160; Rix, 1996). Work gives older workers' lives meaning. Even above age 65, 31 per cent of men and 13 per cent of women continue to work. More than half of men want to work to age 69 'to stay healthy' (Funck, 2010: 582). Older workers in good health, who have maintained continuous employment, have low unemployment rates and employment for older Japanese has remained steady since the late 1980s (Asao, 2014: 58).

Employing the elderly reduces Japan's welfare burden: welfare related to elder care (including pensions) currently consumes 30 per cent of public expenditures (OECD, 2014: 4). Taking these jobs, Japanese aged 60 and above learn how to live successfully on reduced salaries and 'ease into retirement' (Meyer-Ohle, 2010: 959).

Future pension and employment reforms are likely to keep more elderly Japanese in the work force. The government may even abolish retirement age altogether (Meyer-Ohle, 2010: 954). That would effectively abolish even the pretense of retirement for a lot of people. Through continued work, the government hopes the elderly can contribute to economic growth (Ogawa, N., 2010).

In sum, even the later life of the *dankai seidai* emphasises economic activity more than individual leisure. Government's schemes to keep people employed may have as much influence on the leisure choices of many older Japanese as constraints imposed by pension and savings shortfalls. The bulk of leisure may be as it was during working life: woven into the fabric of the everyday, either incorporated into productive activity, or appropriated during less constrained moments.

Quotidian Leisure Practices of Retired Japanese

Sedentary television watching and listening to music occupy the elderly the most, but active pursuits, such as gardening, reading, walking, caring for pets, and various forms of community participation and socialising, including karaoke and travelling with friends, are also common ways of passing the golden years. Many elderly seek activities that give them opportunities to be outside with friends and to connect with nature. Physical therapy also functions as an inexpensive form of therapeutic leisure for some elders who enjoy the chance to talk with others in crowded treatment rooms. Heated and air-conditioned public spaces, such as libraries and shopping centres, attract elders. Visiting electronic stores to take advantage of massage chair displays is a surprisingly common pastime of older men. The weekday use of facilities by retired Japanese has been described as 'colonization of leisure spaces' (Clammer, 2010: 609), a trend that will grow as the *dankai sedai* become a larger percentage of daytime travellers. Their shaping of the daily discourses and practices of leisure will have potent effects on the expectations of younger generations about age appropriate activities and identity.

Shopping and Consumption

Post-retirement will likely be part-time, so expanded leisure is predicted even for those who continue to work. Increased free time may be dominated by consumption: playing in the marketplace. Three types of aging influence elders' consumption patterns. First, values change due to *cultural ageing*. For example, women spend more than men as they age and buy more on impulse (Sekizawa, 2010: 1002–1003). Food consumption is a primary pleasure, and the diet becomes traditional: more vegetables and less meat – boiled rice and pickled plums, sautéed vegetables and copious amounts of tofu. Such nutrition enables longevity. Material desires are for simple things, such as newspapers. Second, *social ageing* guides the pursuit of age appropriate leisure within the limits imposed by available free time and disposable funds. Hot spring visits, historical hiking tours of foreign countries, and consumption of live music and art exhibits are forms of leisure that many *dankai sedai* Japanese embrace with utmost seriousness. Except in the households of the very poor, data indicates that wives' leisure interests benefit more than those of husbands from accumulated financial resources. Sports cars attract *dankai sedai* men (Sekizawa, 2010: 1009), but so do welfare vehicles that accommodate wheelchairs (Moerke, 2010). Women prefer to spend on home renovations and they are more enthusiastic than men about acquiring new skills and arts through lessons in dancing, music, or crafts (Sekizawa, 2010: 1009), Third, *physiological ageing* may require consumption of diapers, dentures, and drugs, as well as a ever-expanding range of products designed to help elders do things they once did without aid: bathing, brushing their remaining teeth, eating, going to the toilet, remembering where they put things, getting into or out of beds, baths, vehicles, or up and down stairs. Robots to push wheelchairs or keep a remaining spouse company are likely to become common in the near future.

Is all this consumption leisure? Stebbins (2012: 111–112) suggests that consumption can initiate or facilitate leisure, but many forms of leisure require little or no consumption. The elderly's zeal for educational consumption and late-life self-improvement learning make them 'a huge untapped market' (Clammer, 2010: 603) that can fill empty classroom seats that will grow more numerous as the young population shrinks.

Media Use

Retired Japanese are more likely to watch TV than listen to university lectures. Those over age 60 watch TV more than five hours a day. Because elders are also readers (Shiraishi, 2010), print journalism may hold on longer in Japan than in the West, providing an informative and inexpensive pastime.

The early urban-rural digital divide in Internet use has been offset by rapid diffusion of web access (Clammer, 2010: 602). Increase in web time does not correlate with a decline in TV time (Shiraishi, 2010), meaning that the elders log many hours of screen time. Internet growth brought with it the possibility of 'virtually unlimited and effectively free' entertainment, news, and sports, as well as opportunities for social networking that might even include political activism (Clammer, 2010: 608). The social effect of web-enabled politics as a serious vocation for older men deserves scholarly attention. Organisational skills honed in corporate environments are easily adapted for use in social media in various useful ways, including political activism and welfare activities.

Sex and Intimacy

There is little literature on sex as leisure in later Japanese life, but what does exist shows sex, especially extra-marital sexual exploits, as a double-edged form of self-expression that also varies with class. On the one hand, engaging in clandestine sexual relations is an accepted sort of leisure activity for men of a certain social position and income. Such sex, or at least the desire for it, is proof of continuing virility and zest for living, a 'barometer of wellbeing' (Moore, 2010: 153). For women, however, it is sexual restraint that validates the wifely sense of self in later life. Marital relations in later life increasing resemble sibling ties, as sexual relations assume a diminished role in marital satisfaction (Moore, 2010).

Sports

An overview of sport and the elderly (Manzenreiter, 2010) notes the tendency for behaviour to spread copycat-style. The more sedentary one's neighbours are, the more sedentary one becomes. This tendency has been exacerbated by the failure to meet targets for building sports facilities that the elderly can use. Healthy aging requires investment, but Japan's government is handicapped by high debt, and demand from elders for such facilities is probably undermined by the dominance of passive leisure among older age cohorts.

And yet, there is a significant boom in mountaineering that is supported by elderly women and their love of mountain wildflowers. Mountain huts take care to cater to their tastes. Gateball (croquet) and ground golf remain popular. And golf, once the expensive preserve of wealthy businessmen, seems to becoming more affordable as green fees fall on weekdays in an effort to attract players to Japan's overbuilt golf infrastructure. The elderly are also the main consumers of traditional sports, such as sumo. Various board games also satisfy retired elder's competitive urges.

Tourism, Travel, and Lifestyle Migration

Thanks to good health and the spread of ideas about active aging, *dankai sedai* Japanese whose family situations permit it are likely to spend retirement as enthusiastic travellers (Funck, 2010). The purposes and destinations of their travel are reportedly gendered, with men opting for golf and fishing, while women favour shopping for souvenirs, flowing viewing, and hiking. Local surveys of tourists show that both genders enjoy hot springs and other natural attractions, as well as eating local delicacies and visiting historical and cultural sites, all with aim of gaining 'a sense of fulfillment' (Funck, 2010: 588). Both Japanese tourists and their destinations are aging so resorts are being reconstructed to accommodate frail elders. Foreign package tours offer excursions within the physical capabilities of older travellers. Their preference for cultural and nature sightseeing is growing stronger and tastes are becoming more fixed (ibid., 580, 587), suggesting that the practices of this generation will drive investment in a few specific types of leisure infrastructure and facilities at the expense of others.

Leaving Japan or long-stay tourism are also options. Retirement yen go farther in less expensive foreign locations (often a short flight from Japan). Whether in Australia or South-East Asia, life in retirement communities provides an enhanced lifestyle featuring cultural activities, crafts, affordable golf, and acceptable medical care, as well as a later life that is possibly more interesting and meaningful. Escape from Japan, and its sometime burdensome family and neighbourhood obligations, can be a ticket to a more relaxed retirement. Migrants speak of 'slow and healthy life' rich in exercise and hobbies. Some of these so-called pension refugees who do not have money worries take up residence in hotels, there by avoiding the need to do housework (Ono, 2010).

Elder Care Centres and Clubs and Intergenerational Leisure Activities

Less affluent and less mobile retirees find meaning leisure activities closer to home. Described as, 'A bulwark that mitigates enfeeblement and loneliness,' (Pekkanen and Tsujinaka, 2010: 718) elder clubs and neighbourhood associations tied to local governments are sites for social activities like festivals, sports events, and study groups. *Kouminkan*, small public facilities that host occasional residents' meetings, are also used for karaoke, *igo* and *shogi*, ping pong competitions, and study circles.

Government led promotion of intergenerational leisure tried to reduce costs by mobilising local resources. Volunteering engineered from the top down (*houshi*) is sometimes criticised as creating a 'volunteer subjectivity' that involves 'subjugation of the individual to a norm by means of internalization.' (Ogawa A., 2010: 723) In such cases, the activity could not be leisure in Stebbins' scheme. On the other hand, authorities' promotion of active social participation is not coercion for Japanese. A study of a non-profit, community-supported centre or 'coffee shop' providing daycare services to elders in Osaka revealed these clubs as imaginative and low-cost forms of leisure that inspired hope among the aging participants by getting them out of the house. Some city financial support helped this form of communal elder daycare make ends meet (Kavedjiza, 2013).

Leisure activities at old age clubs often mobilise volunteer groups and make use of intergenerational differences to boost *ikigai* (reason for living) and stimulate 'active social participation.' (Thang, 2010) In some cases, elders give instruction to young students about local history, regional traditions, foods, or crafts. They teach poetry (haiku) and calligraphy, as well as providing afterschool care. 'Narrative as an intergenerational activity' (Thang, 2010: 182), makes the experiences of the elderly valuable to the community and gives meaning to the lives of the elders, while reducing the burden of care on the state. Even more common, however, is a pattern in which young people reach out to the elderly. Through music and other performances, sports days, buddy systems, pen pal activities, and visits to elders' homes, student volunteer activity provides 'education of the heart' for students and leisure in later life for elders as long as there is support from governmental funds (Thang, 2010: 184). These intergenerational programmes are now part of the new notion of public assistance programmes that help poor elderly become engaged and included via mutual support and integration in local services (Fukawa, 2010: 930–931).

Traditional Acts and Traditional Arts as Leisure

Japan's traditional arts, including drawing and painting, calligraphy, haiku poetry, flower arranging, tea ceremony, noh chanting, *hogaku* (koto and shakuhachi music) and others have sometimes been treated as manifestations of a higher realm, which can only be accessed through diligent practice guided by a master. These arts are contrasted with other traditional activities, such as *enka* folk songs, festival dancing, puppetry, photography, bonsai plant cultivation, and pottery making (Clammer, 2010: 605), which, though often pursued with great seriousness, are generally undertaken without hopes of enlightenment.

Practice and high-level mastery of traditional arts provides both a reason for living and a way of earning respect in old age (Moore and Campbell, 2009). Studying at the feet of a master, elderly participants in traditional arts connect with the timeless essence of the ancient practitioners of the same arts, enabling the possibility of unlimited personal growth and maturity. Progress is measured and legitimated through examinations and ranks, the familiar structures that order Japanese life. Like employment, an art and its practice become a *'ba,'* a social location that anchors identity. This is serious leisure, and serious living. The student submits to and merges with the discipline.

Exploration of traditional arts reveals an ostensibly austere, spiritual possibility for post-retirement leisure. It is the area of traditional arts where Stebbins's notion of serious leisure finds perhaps its best fit with Japanese leisure practices. Long experience is an asset that positions elders to learn the deepest lessons. The traditional arts venerate age and honour the beginner mind. This is ancient Japanese philosophy in action, embodied, ephemeral, infinitely perfectible. Despite the divide between traditional arts and modern leisure pursuits, shared cultural strategies of leisure make both into venues for polishing the spirit. This is a notion worth exploring further: the idea that no matter what the object of devotion, whether it is calligraphy or noh, ballroom dance, or gateball, festival planning or karaoke, the similarity of leisure's social organisation permits similar possibilities for growth.

Conclusion: A Japanese Philosophy of Post-Retirement Leisure

As sketched above, there is variety and richness to post-retirement leisure in Japan. The majority of Japan's elder citizens report being healthy – those without financial constraints are fewer, but that is the situation elsewhere, too. The observer is impressed with the attention to detail, and the strategies of organising elder leisure being of a piece with other aspects of the society. Leisure is not separate from other cultural practices.

We should thus be guardedly hopeful about prospects for post-retirement leisure. The durability of Japanese strategies for taking leisure in later life seriously is a source of optimism. Another is the potential for leisure to transform other aspects of Japanese life as it has done in the past (Ikegami, 2005). More elders engaging in serious leisure practices means more potential for leisure to become social capital with switchman capability to reinvigorate

Japanese thinking about definitions of progress and the good life (Stebbins, 2012: 99).

The Japanese expression for doing things right is *chanto suru*. It means doing things just so, devoting proper attention so that each action becomes worthy in its own right. Although it is a daily folk philosophy, it probably has roots in Zen practices, wherein being one with the activity, no matter how humble (sweeping leaves, pulling weeds) ennobles the performer. Elders in the Osaka daycare mentioned above used the word to describe exercising agency to control the pace of activity so that familiar sorts of human relations could be maintained. Their philosophy of living amounts to doing things right, not in relation to absolute standards, but rather in line with one's own conditions, in time with the natural rhythms of one's current self. That means not going faster than you can breathe comfortably, breaking work down into bits that can be accomplished easily, keeping the focus suitably narrow, finding leisure in every moment. This way of leisure permits harmony between self and situation regardless of one's condition. It holds out the possibility that even the less fortunate Japanese classes may achieve a measure of leisure mastery in the post-production portion of their lives.

Note

1. Post-retirement leisure refers to the activities of people aged 60–65 and above. Japan's official retirement age is creeping up to 65 and may soon be abolished altogether.

References

Allison, A. (1994). *Nightwork: Sexuality, Pleasure, and Corporate Masculinity in a Tokyo Hostess Club*. Chicago: University of Chicago Press.

Asao, Y. (2014). Employment of older persons, in Japan Institute for Labor Policy and Training (ed.) *Labour Situation in Japan and Its Analysis: General Overview 2013–2014*. Tokyo: Japan Institute of Labour, pp. 55–58.

Clammer, J. (2010). Pastimes, in: Coulmas F. et al. (eds.) *The Demographic Challenge: A Handbook about Japan*. London: Brill, pp. 599–611.

Cole, R.E. (1992). Work and Leisure in Japan. *California Management Review*, 34(3), pp. 52–63.

Cox, R. (2002). Is there a Japanese way of playing? in Hendry J. and Raveri M. (eds.) *Japan at Play: The Ludic and the Logic of Power*. London: Routledge, pp. 169–185.

Coulmas, F., Conrad, H., Schad-Seifert, A. and Vogt, G. (eds.) (2008). *The Demographic Challenge: A Handbook about Japan*. London: Brill.

Conrad, H. (2010). Human Resource Management Practices and the Aging Workforce. in Coulmas F. et al. (eds.) *The Demographic Challenge: A Handbook about Japan*. London: Brill, pp. 979–997.

Field, N. (2001). Forward to the revised edition, in McCormack G. *The Emptiness of Japanese Affluence* (Revised Edition). Armonk, New York: M.E. Sharpe.

Formanek, S. (2010). Traditional Concepts and Images of Old Age in Japan, in Coulmas F. et al. (eds.) *The Demographic Challenge: A Handbook about Japan.* London: Brill, pp. 321–343.

Frühstück, S. (1998). Then Science Took Over: Sex Leisure, and Medicine at the Beginning of the Twentieth Century, In Linhart S and Frühstück S (eds.) *The Culture of Japan as Seen through Its Leisure.* Albany: State University of New York Press, pp. 59–79.

Fukawa, H. (2010). Poverty Among the Elderly, in Coulmas F. et al. (eds.) *The Demographic Challenge: A Handbook about Japan.* London: Brill, pp. 921–931.

Funck, C. (2010). Ageing Tourists, Ageing Destinations, in Coulmas F. et al. (eds.) *The Demographic Challenge: A Handbook about Japan.* London: Brill, pp. 579–598.

Horioka, C.Y. (2010). Survey of Household Saving Behavior, in Coulmas F. et al. (eds.) *The Demographic Challenge: A Handbook about Japan.* London: Brill, pp. 879–897.

Iwao, S. (2010). Gendered Age, in Coulmas F. et al. (eds.) *The Demographic Challenge: A Handbook about Japan.* London: Brill, pp. 531–545.

Japan Times. (2014). More workers taking vacation. 18 January. Available at: http://www.japantimes.co.jp/opinion/2014/01/18/editorials/more-workers-taking-vacation/#.UtsKxByu62w

Kavedzija, I. (2013). An Attitude of Hope: Crafting Networks of Support in an Aging Community. Ethnographies of Hope in Contemporary Japan. Graduate School of Human Sciences, Osaka University, 19 October.

Klein, S. (2011). Bullfighting and Meaning in Life in Oki, Japan. *Asian Anthropology.* 10(1), pp. 101–120.

Leitner, M.J., and Leitner S.F. (2012). *Leisure in Later Life,* 4th ed. Urbana, Il: Sagamore Publishing.

Leheny, D. (2003). *The Rules of Play: National Identity and the Shaping of Japanese Leisure.* Ithaca: Cornell University Press.

Linhart, S. (1998). The Japanese at play: A Little Known Dimension of Japan, in Linhart S. and Frühstück S. (eds.) *The Culture of Japan as Seen Through Its Leisure.* Albany: State University of New York Press, pp. 1–21.

McCormack, G. (2001). *The Emptiness of Japanese Affluence* (Revised Edition). Armonk, New York: M.E. Sharpe.

Manzenreiter, W. (2010). Sports and Demographic Change in Japan, in Coulmas F. et al. (eds.) *The Demographic Challenge: A Handbook about Japan.* London: Brill, pp. 614–632.

Matsuyama, K. (2012). In Japan, Retirees Go On Working. Global Economics, *Bloomberg Businessweek*, . 30 August. Available at: http://www.businessweek.com/articles/2012-08-30/in-japan-retirees-go-on-working/

McCallum, J. (1988). Japanese Teinen Taishoku: How Cultural Values Affect Retirement. *Ageing and Society*, 8(1), pp. 23–41.

Meyer-Ohle, H. (2010). Labour Market and Labour Market Policies for the Aging Society, in Coulmas F. et al. (eds.) *The Demographic Challenge: A Handbook about Japan.* London: Brill, pp. 947–962.

Ministry of Health, Labour and Welfare, Government of Japan. (2004). Change in spread of two-day weekends. (In Japanese) Available at: http://www.mhlw.go.jp/shingi/2004/09/s0928-7/c07.html

Moerke, A. (2010). The Ageing Society and Reactions of the Automobile Industry: A Case Study, in Coulmas F. et al. (eds.) *The Demographic Challenge: A Handbook about Japan.* London: Brill, pp. 1017–1032.

Moore, K.L. and Campbell R. (2009). Mastery with Age: The Appeal of the Traditional Arts to Senior Citizens in Contemporary Japan. *Japanstudien* 21, pp. 223–251.

Moore, K.L. (2014). *The Joy of Noh: Embodied Learning and Discipline in Urban Japan.* Albany: State University of New York Press.

Moore, K.L. (2010). Sexuality and Sense of Self in Later Life: Japanese men's and Women's Reflections on Sex and Aging. *Journal of Cross Cultural Gerontology* 25, pp. 149–163.

Morioka, K. (2006). *Structure of Social Inequality: Faultlines of Globalization.* (In Japanese) Tokyo: Sakurai Shoten.

Mouer, R. and Kawanishi H. (2005). *A Sociology of Work in Japan.* London: Cambridge University Press.

Ochiai, E. (1996). *The Japanese Family System in Transition: A Sociological Analysis of Family Change in Postwar Japan.* Tokyo: LBTC International Library Foundation.

OECD. (2014). *Society at a glance 2014. OECD Social Indicators: OECD Publishing.* Available at: http://www.oecd.org/japan/OECD-SocietyAtaGlance2014-Highlights-Japan.pdf

Ogawa, A. (2010). 'Induced' Voluntarism: A New Role for Schools? in Coulmas F. et al. (eds.) *The Demographic Challenge: A Handbook about Japan.* London: Brill, pp. 721–732.

Ogawa, N. (2010). Population Aging and Economic Growth: The Role of Two Demographic Dividends in Japan, in Coulmas F. et al. (eds.) *The Demographic Challenge: A Handbook about Japan.* London: Brill, pp. 821–839.

Ogawa, T. (2010). Changing Social Concepts of Age: Towards the Active Senior Citizen, in Coulmas F. et al. (eds.) *The Demographic Challenge: A Handbook about Japan.* London: Brill, pp. 145–162.

Ono, M. (2010). Long-stay tourism: Elderly Japanese Tourists in the Cameron Highlands, Malaysia. *Senri Ethnological Studies*, 76, pp. 95–110.

Pekkanen, R. and Tsujinaka, Y. (2010). Neighbourhood Associations and the Demographic Challenge, in Coulmas F. et al. (eds) *The Demographic Challenge: A Handbook about Japan.* London: Brill, pp. 707–720.

Rix, S.E. (1996). The Challenge of an Aging Work Force: Keeping Older Workers Employed and Employable, in Bass, S. Morris, R.A. and Oka, M. (eds.) *Public Policy and the Old Age Revolution in Japan.* New York: The Haworth Press, pp. 79–96.

Rohlen, T.P. (1978). The Promise of Adulthood in Japanese Spiritualism, in Erikson E. (ed.) *Adulthood.* New York: Norton, pp. 129–147.

Russell, R.V. (1996). *Pastimes: The Context of Contemporary Leisure.* New York: Brown and Benchmark Publishers.

Sekizawa, H. (2010). The Impact of the Ageing of Society on Consumer Behavior and Consumer Markets, in Coulmas F. et al. (eds.) *The Demographic Challenge: A Handbook about Japan.* London: Brill, pp. 999–1016.

Shirahase, S. (2010). Income Inequality in the Aging Society, in Coulmas F. et al. (eds.) *The Demographic Challenge: A Handbook about Japan.* London: Brill, pp. 217–234.

Shiraishi, N. (2010). Media Use in the Aging Society, in Coulmas F. et al. (eds.) *The Demographic Challenge: A Handbook about Japan.* London: Brill, pp. 513–530.

Smith, T. (1986). Peasant Time and Factory Time in Japan. *Past and Present*, 111(1), pp. 165–197.

Soumucho, Tokei Kyoku. (2010). Will the 2012 Problem affect the Dankai Seidai? (In Japanese) Available at: www.stat.go.jp/info/today/032.htm

Stebbins, R.A. (1982). Serious Leisure: A Conceptual Statement. *Pacific Sociological Review*, 25(2), pp. 251–272.

Stebbins, R.A. (2012). *The Idea of Leisure: First Principles.* New Brunswick: Transaction Publishers.

Steger, B. (1996). Hurried work, Hurried Leisure and Time to Sleep: The Case of Japan. Conference on New Strategies for Everyday Life, Tilburg, The Netherlands.

Taira, K. (1986). Delight of Plight of Old Age in Japan? Problems of Work, Leisure, and Equality. Faculty Working Paper Number 1227, College of Commerce and Business Administration, University of Illinois at Urbana-Champaign.

Thang, L.L. (2010). Engaging the Generations: Age-integrated Facilities, in Coulmas F. et al. (eds.) *The Demographic Challenge: A Handbook about Japan.* London: Brill, pp. 179–200.

Thompson, C.S. (2010). Population Decline, Municipal Amalgamation, and the Politics of Folk Performance Preservation in Northeast Japan, in Coulmas F. et al. (eds.) *The Demographic Challenge: A Handbook about Japan.* London: Brill, pp. 361–386.

18

Interrogating Transitions in African Leisure and Labour Cultures as Variables for (Un)Development in Africa

ARETHA OLUWAKEMI ASAKITIKPI

The state of Africa's underdevelopment has been a major issue of concern both for scholars and policy makers mainly because Africa is one of the richest continents in terms of natural and human resources. Though a number of theories and research has been conducted in a bid to understand how and why Africa remains in a state of underdevelopment (especially when compared to other once similarly tagged areas such as Asia and Latin America), this paper intends to consider the concept of underdevelopment through an historical interrogation of labour, leisure and development practices and philosophies. The paper proposes that the poor labour culture of many African nations today is due to the bad leisure culture developed by elites and rulers during and after the colonial reign. The African leisure culture of an addiction to the consumption of western produced luxurious items has meant a drastic reduction of the value of homemade products which unfortunately for many Africans symbolises lack of progress and backwardness. The paper using historical analysis considers social events that lead to such drastic changes and proposes that the seemingly exclusive reserve of the ruling and elite class to relish in a leisure culture of a consumption of western produced luxurious items believed by majority of the citizens to have been as a result of corrupt and autocratic political and economic activities creates negative attitudes in a country's labour force to work; while inciting within such a force an even more determined desire to cultivate similar leisure cultures in order to assume similar identities of power, modernity and sophistication they believe such products command. The paper argues that this interwoven assumption of leisure and labour activities nevertheless is the very bane of Africa's underdevelopment; where a country's labour force works in order to develop a culture of leisure based on the consumption of what their labour cannot produce will lead to a collapse of local economies and ultimately underdevelopment.

Introduction

Labour is considered as an activity that leads to a quantifiable product or output (this can be mental or physical) leading to a capacity for growth. Thus the aim of labour should be a product or output designed to develop or sustain a system or culture (Rodney, 1977). Here, good labour is distinguished from 'bad' or 'painful' labour. Good labour leads to productivity which is beneficial to both the labourer and the society while bad or painful labour is done out of duress (due to slavery or forced labour) which only benefits or develops the enforcer of labour. Painful labour converts the activity of work into a commodity which is essential in sustaining the owners of the labour and the products derived (Hatcher, 1998). Thus, for labour to be an element of sustainability, the product of the labour must benefit both the labourer and the labour owner (which may be an individual or state). The labour activity should also be seen as an activity that goes beyond the acquisition of material or consumable items into a feeling of achievement toward a cause that brings about a general good for the labourer, the owner and the society within which this activity occurs. Such a context is provided through which 'good' labour is the result. Good labour can only happen when there is a just remuneration (both materially and psychologically) for the labour activity done and a positive feeling of achievement for a better good because of the labour done.

For scholars like Aristotle, labour was a means to obtain leisure; but as many more contemporary scholars of labour and economics have discovered, leisure is necessary to maintain a worker's physical capacity to work. Leisure within this context has been associated with variables such as rest, free or spare time (Lloyd and Auld, 2002; Peterson, 1981). Scientifically, leisure can be quantified based on the level of satisfaction, happiness and belief in the future and existing system such an activity stimulates in the individual or individuals involved (Lloyd and Auld, 2002). As with labour, leisure can also be 'good' which not only encourages personal satisfaction in terms of stimulating personal physical and psychological development but also social and corporate advancements (development) (Ehmer, 2014). This is sharply distinguished from 'bad' leisure which encourages idleness of the body and mind resulting in laziness and ultimately unproductiveness of not only the individual but the society as a whole (undevelopment).

The interaction of these three elements (labour, leisure and development) within a country can be summed up simply as follows: a country where a high percentage of the citizens controlling the political and economic sphere have unlimited access to permanent sources of bad leisure induced activities (whether material or immaterial), within a structure that encourages bad labour policies that cannot lead to a quantifiable production or output (whether mental or physical) designed for self-sustaining growth, cannot develop. Thus, in a society where majority of the labour force believe they are working under duress in order to sustain the leisure lifestyle of their labour owners; and thus conceive that they are not being properly remunerated (whether in kind or cash) in a ratio commensurate to their work; will engage in 'bad' labour activities that will harm them and ultimately the system they feel is oppressive. Such 'bad' labour activities may on the surface seem to result in productivity; but within that activity, the labourer engages in risky operations with the aim of destroying the system and may ultimately end up destroying themselves. Such a labourer will also engage in bad leisure activities that incite addiction, violence, and unlawful acts of destruction due to a high level of low self esteem and frustration. If on the other hand, majority of the labour force do not associate their labour activity to the leisure quality of their labour owners; and conceive that their labour is contributing to a good cause which ultimately will be of benefit not only to them (in terms of remuneration) but to the system as a whole, then a more positive leisure culture will be adopted which will sustain the members of the labour force, encourage growth in the system and ultimately lead to development.

The African Philosophy of Work and Leisure

Thomas (1964) believes that in pre-industrial African societies, the distinction between leisure and labour is difficult to establish indicating a fusion of both in everyday life. It can be likened to the state of equilibrium that Adam encountered in the Garden of Eden. The possibility that Adam while in the garden could not distinguish between labour and leisure makes some authors believe that this may have been the philosophy behind the two activities in ancient Africa. Using the Dogon pre-colonial society as an example, he notes that the same words used for cultivation is also used to define the action of dance during religious ceremonies. Within these societies, the element of the collective is especially emphasised as a duty to retain and sustain social relationships while idleness met with disapproval. Play was the preparation for work, reflecting kinship and strengthening social ties. The author suggests that when work was isolated from social ties, then it became labourious and had to be monitored and forced. The need to work within a social setting encouraged the formation of associations and guilds leading to more satisfaction and contentment. Within this context, leisure activities were created thus making labour itself a pleasurable activity.

A number of the pre-colonial African labour systems involved corporate work which revolved around age. A significant aspect of this age that inspired labour system were ritual rites that signified advancement. These rites qualified members of the society who had approached a certain age for limited manual labour and more of mental work. The junior grades had to serve the seniors as part of the requirements for advancement. The philosophy that the strength of the youth should be put into labour activities that will develop the society encouraged the lower age grades to work. Labour in this sense was not an activity done individually but within the corporate action of members of the society of the same gender born in the same season of the year. The bond that kept the age grade members together was encouraged through communal work and communal leisure. The older age grade members of the society served as the guide and advisers keeping the traditions and ensuring the adherence of the cultural norms set down by their ancestors. In some societies, it was a taboo for a member of a certain age grade to lift anything heavy thus work was contracted out to the younger age grade members (Akinwunmi, 1992). The reward of clearing a farm, harvesting crops or building a hut varied from food items to favours in return. Ogbomo (1997) noted that there were cases when an elder would use his or her position to request a youth grade to work but would fail to honour the agreement of a reward by sponsoring a leisure activity of feasting. Such elders may find a deliberate boycott by the youth as a silent form of protest. This traditional system of division of labour meant that the elders did more of mental work through guidance, advice and supervision while the younger ones did the manual labour of farming, building and production. The position of mental labour could only be ascribed as a result of being able to go through years of manual labour. Old age and maturity could thus be likened to rest from labour.

A number of African societies consciously encouraged the philosophy of leisure after labour through stories, songs and proverbs told to the younger generation. African folktales using animals emphasise this relationship insinuating that without adequate labour, harvest cannot be guaranteed. Stories such as the tortoise that dodges work (bad labour) yet expects the social benefits that work attracts were discouraged. The morals attached to these stories encouraged the ideology of work while discouraging idleness and a lack of motivation (bad leisure) labelling it as a vice that could be punished. Chinua Achebe in his novel *Things Fall Apart* describes Okonkwo's father as a reject not only by the society but also by the gods because he was socially seen as lazy, a man that could not produce food for his family because he spent more time engaging in leisure activities that were unproductive. For this pre-colonial society, productive labour and leisure were not only essential for the development of a person but his family and even the society from which existence was defined. It was based on this philosophy that Okonkwo's father faced exclusion not only in life but also in death, banished into the evil forest.

A number of European scholars have tried to prove that the African pre-colonial system was based on a labour-leisure system that was dependent on an oppressive kinship structure which demanded a domination of the elder over the younger; with the elder controlling the means of production (Coquery-Vidrovitch, 1977) and consumption. Power over labour and its products allowed elders of the society to dictate when festivities could occur at the social level; and at individual levels, who and when the younger grades could marry, where and what they could embark upon for economic advancement, and the political positions they could achieve. The age defining concept as a system of oppression in many African pre-colonial systems cannot be underestimated. African scholars such as Ogbomo (1997) noted that a number of small communities were formed when young members of a society had clashes with older members and thus decided to break away from what they termed an oppressive system to form their own. Nevertheless, it must be appreciated that within such systems, the items produced through communal labour were consumed through a communal leisure culture on the one hand; but on the other what was used to pay taxes to more powerful kings or as corporate capital for regional and long distance trade (the profit of which was used in the sponsoring of corporate leisure activities).

Missionaries and later colonial rule altered the structure of many traditional African societies. This occurred in three important ways. First, new methods of labour and leisure were introduced which was drastically different from the traditional ways. Secondly, communal unity and age grades were broken down and individualism was promoted. Thirdly, a new form of remuneration (money) was introduced and it was only through this that western consumable leisure items could be accessed. These structural changes were very significant and they led to a shift in defining and conceptualising labour and leisure in very dramatic ways. Leisure was no longer a communal activity especially when it involved western consumable items because it now served as a signifier of 'sophistication' and 'modernity'. The elders were no longer in charge of mentally directing labour, which was now in the hands of formally educated European youths who worked with the Colonial Administration.

African natives who still engaged in manual labour were ascribed a lower social and mental status by not only the colonial administrators but also other community native members who had been formally trained to work with the colonial administration. This in turn led to a redefinition of wealth, power relations and social status which was no longer based on age grades and a traditional organisation of labour. The reward of labour was also not paid through communal activities of leisure but now to individuals and in European currencies.

According to Abudu (1986), a number of the early manual workers engaged by the colonial administrators were freed slaves and socially rejected individuals. They viewed the colonial form of organised manual labour as another form of slavery which at that time had just been abolished. The colonialists treated the African manual labourer as a child and one that lacked intelligence. The African manual labourer was underpaid and underfed and poorly trained to do anything but manually obey instructions. The motivation to manually work was, thus, very low as the African was aware that his value was based on the conception that he was not a human but a machine of labour. Added to this, a number of the free born natives who took up the option of manual labour, were often depressed at the thought of leaving their familiar atmosphere. Working within the formal labour system also meant sacrificing their agricultural production time which was of more value in relation to traditional social and prestige status. Manual labour was thus not attractive enough for the labourers to be committed resulting in a sense of detachment. The use of forced manual labour to build public facilities thus produced unwilling labour and low productivity (1986: 22). Despite these inhuman conditions, a number of natives took up the opportunities to manually work for the colonial administration. The major attraction to such manual labour was basically to be paid in the European currencies which enabled them to purchase a number of European mass produced goods that had flooded African societies at the time. For a number of the manual labourers, such items were luxurious goods which could be used also for leisure activities such as marriage and of course the compulsory taxes enforced upon every household by the colonial government.

It is interesting to note that a number of the European administrators described the natives as lazy and unwilling to work with a bad attitude to labour for development. The Eurocentric attitude toward the African native as less than human with limited thinking faculty was evident in the conditions of services the natives were forced to work under. The colonial administrator felt justified to provide limited food and welfare packages with the belief that the natives could easily be replaced. The natives on the other hand observed this bad working condition and concluded that it was their labour that was sustaining the colonial culture of leisure. Abudu (1986) notes that if given better working conditions this would not have the case as Africans traditionally observed more positive attitudes to labour. The author buttresses this with an observation that when Africans are engaged in an activity, such as building a hut, or smelting a metal into a weapon or art, they showed a high level of industriousness. The bad labour activities were inspired by context under which the labour occurred.

The philosophy behind the treatment of manual labourers changed slightly with regard to Africans that had some form of western education. Unlike the traditional system which was defined based on age and experience, the new system of labour was based on the ability to understand and acquire European based knowledge. This new knowledge promised protection (and ultimately immunity) and lack of manual labour. Just like the European leaders, being devoid of manual labour means superiority and qualified one to be a leader. Unfortunately it seemed the African elite of the time assumed that the colonial administrators did limited manual work but indulged in a lot of leisure and luxury. This assumption was translated into the public sector work and leisure practices after independence.

The more western formal education the native African had, the less manual labour they were assigned. Such natives were given jobs in offices as administrators and as house helps (cooks, butlers, etc.). They were better paid, had more exposure to western cultures and material items. Indeed the natives that had access to western education and could be 'cultured' attracted more pay and thus more access to luxury goods and western defined leisure activities. Though these labour activities seemed to lead to positive productive growth within the colonial system, they actually encouraged bad leisure activities such as an addiction to the consumption of items the colonial administration associated with 'modernity'. This addiction to a consumption of western produced luxury items became a signifier for the African elitist class leisure. A leisure activity which encouraged the consumption of items they could not produce while devaluing the items they could (Wilk, 2001) was a culture that spread in Africa.

The colonial administrators were very pleased to encourage the elite's constructed form of leisure. They classified leisure into constructive and destructive categories implying that more western oriented leisure activities were associated with cultures of modernity while more traditional forms were evidences of backwardness and lack of growth. To support this, there was a need to introduce leisure forms that eventually proved to be constructive to Europe and its development and destructive to Africa and its development. Akyeampong and Ambler (2002) in their work discuss how certain sports and consumables were deliberately introduced by the colonial administrators with the aim of introducing a more 'civilised form of leisure'. Sporting activities such as soccer was introduced to encourage the natives to develop not only their physical bodies but also their time management as well as team spirits (Akyeampong). Games that were not organised based on European dictates and interests were discouraged and not supported.

Consumables such as alcohol, clothes, food and machineries were imported into Africa in bulk thus crippling local industries. Akyeampong discusses how local brews were discouraged and even banned in order for them to be replaced with imported brands from Europe. The same scenario occurred in relation to cloth production (Renee, 1997; Clarke, 1996). Leisure was to be redefined based not on local communal production but on imported alternatives which could only be obtained through currencies of the colonial government. To obtain these luxuries meant working under the organised labour forms of the administration. This was the foundation of a leisure culture which was developed on a consumer producing economy aimed at satisfying not a need but a social status which developed not the national economy of the consumers but that of the producers. Success as a reward of labour and identity in relation to modernity was now measured based on western acquired goods and not locally produced goods (Friedman, 2005). This was what defined the elite and ruling class of Africa after independence from European colonialism.

Contemporary Africa: Labour and Leisure

Fanon (1963) in an analysis of African countries at independence noted the need of the bourgeois elites to take over the power and material trimmings that seemingly made up the colonial lives of their overthrown rulers. Very little attempt was made to adopt the work attitude of servitude to the mother colony the colonial administrators practiced or the loyalty to the motherland the business tycoons observed. At independence, the masses were expected to portray attitudes of servitude and loyalty to the government that liberated them from the shackles of colonial oppression and primitivism by adopting the work ethics of pre-colonial days where the elders supervised and the younger ones obeyed. The government, being the state, and the elites, representing the elders (due to their western education and riches made from their activities during the colonial era) were to be rewarded with the consumption of western produced luxury goods and hours of leisure.

Ake (2003) discusses the rush for power mainly to loot the national treasury by the public sector which systematically impoverished young African nations. Ayee (2005: iii) in an analysis of the public sector in Africa noted 'excessive politicisation, lack of accountability and representation, inability to promote the public interest and authoritarian tendencies' as variables that limited the performance of African government's ability to perform their tasks of national development and the organisation of the public sector to work for the good of the nation as against personal interests'. The fact that all African countries at independence focused their attention on urban centres represented by established cities that were relics of colonial administration meant that the inhabitants of the cities would be attracted to the consumption of globally branded items and items that would once have been luxurious items became items of necessity (Davis, 2005). This ultimately meant that a large percentage of their income was dedicated to the purchase and consumption of items that were not produced within their countries thus luring the African continent into the global market.

The import of what a nation's citizens consumes and the economic sustenance of the nation was critically reviewed in the book *Culture and Identity* (2005) where:

> ... the act of consumption is considered in relation to capitalism where those who control production control the producer through the market...the consumption of non-necessities in such a view must be understood as a the result of trickery, the psychological manipulation by the market researchers and advertisers that lure producers into the project of increasing production and therefore profits via their own demand. Capitalism must create a system of false needs in order to maintain the never ending need to accumulate capital'. (2005: 2)

With this regard, Larkin (2008) noted the role media played in sustaining the drive initiated by the colonial administrators. Media was used to introduce new forms of 'consumable leisure'. Through visual representations, the consumable leisure culture was formed and labelled as an essential for being 'civilised'. Post-colonial Africa witnessed national development being sacrifice for the procurement of civilisation through consumable leisure.

Rowlands (1996) in the analysis of the Veblen's thesis of conspicuous consumption (competitive feasting and destruction of wealth) discusses what is termed conspicuous consumption. This involves a leisure activity where the actors have a clear and specific goal in mind: to impress others and thus gain their self-esteem or envy. In the process, they believe that they have the ability to demonstrate their own strength by possessing what is denied to others. Within this context are workers of developing and underdeveloped nations working as civil servants, in private companies and as independent entrepreneurs saving a huge amount of their income to purchase foreign produced goods, relishing in the leisure activity of seeing their fellow men envious of such consumption. Consumption of western luxurious goods becomes essential symbols used to define African identities in terms of social class and level of 'civilisation'. The act of consumption is thus associated with leisure whereby the consumption symbolises power and an association with development as defined by the producers through the mass media. Thus the urge to work is not led only by a need to be paid but rather to acquire western produced items as a signifier of a leisure activity of consumption that creates a mass media inspired identity associated with modernity and civilisation.

The push factor for western consumption is made worse when the African worker conceives that the labour activity embarked upon only gives the boss and the rulers access to this much desired leisure culture. The result was an African civil service labour force that lacked commitment and was termed lazy. Abudu (1986: 27) quotes Shehu Shagari, one of Nigeria's past presidents who lamented that the Nigerian citizen's attitude to work was, 'one of the worst in the world ...Nothing works in Nigeria...A little bit if work and plenty of money is the philosophy or work ethic of the Nigerian'. Yet as Abudu notes, this view is very different when the Nigerian worker is self-employed, putting in long hours and dedication to see the growth of a personal organisation. Abudu notes that the problem would likely come from the concept of reward for labour where there is little relationship between the two, factors such as merit, efficiency, and productivity are sacrificed for other factors such as ethnicity, gender and age. These are elements that encourage corruption, favouritism and incompetence (Abudu, 1986; Ahiauzu, 1989; Parboteeah et al., 2014).

The civil service structure of independent African nations was similar to the pre-colonial labour system which consisted of a number of junior workers who did the manual work and were supervised by a few elders who represented the senior cadres. The senior cadres within this context served as supervisors and guides to labour but unlike the traditional system, their position was given to them not because they were once junior workers but because they were either formally trained through the western educational system or they were favoured in one way or the other by the system. Being a senior staff did not only ascribe power over the junior staff but also meant a significant difference in access to financial rewards and wages. Using Nigeria as an example, Abadu gave an historical presentation of the wage differential between junior and senior workers as follows: 1: 54 in 1954; 1: 33 in 1960 and 1: 18, in the 1980s. Within this scenario, the junior workers protested through bad labour activities such as lateness, lack of commitment and productivity and were constantly seeking for higher qualifications to attract better pay. This is especially as official rise within the ranks is almost impossible, thus having higher qualifications was a more secure way of getting a promotion and this is done within the official working hours.

A number of the African senior civil servants had no intentions of mentoring or ensuring that junior workers were guided into taking over their positions. Rather, they relished in the leisure culture of consumption within which an identity of modernity and sophistication was built. Over the years, the African civil service became flooded with junior workers with the governments trying to convince its citizens of their intention to employ and provide jobs. The overstaffing of junior workers resulted in an over concentration of all coordination, planning, supervision and decision-making to only top senior officials who were not equipped to do this because they were not trained to solve local problems due to their western formal training backgrounds. They could not use their knowledge to solve the complex problems that they met in the African public sector. The western knowledge gained only made them aware of the problem but it did not equip them with strategies to solve the problems. They quickly came to realise that attaining an education and using this education to solve issues of development were two different things altogether. With no mental labour being done, there could be no manual labour to be achieved by the overwhelming population of junior workers.

In many African nations, productive labour is not being practiced while bad leisure cultures are being adopted. To ensure access and control over these leisure cultures of western material consumption there was an increase in ethnic divisions, nepotism and corruption in Africa. Foreign imported goods serve not only as functional and status symbols but also an indication of a transition from poverty to civilisation; from suffering to enjoyment. Where traditional signifies manual, exerted labour through toil; foreign signifies a lack of labour (which had obvious physical body advantages such as better health glowing skin brighter eyes, etc.) sophistication and modernity. Most often a comparison is done of a before and after with the before signifying traditional, manual labour, lack, limitation while the after signified foreign items that needed little to no manual labour, abundance and power. The need for the African upper class to be likened to the Medieval European bourgeois who had contempt for manual labour but had access to and had an obsession for leisure signified an identity of progress. Unfortunately this African strive to be identified as modern and sophisticated through their leisure culture of western consumption was the foundation of their nations.

Conclusion: Creating a Global Leisure Labour System for African Development

In today's global context, Africa is seen as a continent of growing importance mainly because of its wealth of natural resources and immense growth opportunities (Parboteech quoting *The Economist,* 2011). Global labour has currently transgressed from manual labour which involved muscles and manual production to mental supported activities. The mind rather than the muscle is the needed ingredient for labour thus making such activities such as administration, social work, legal work, civil rights and advocacy very relevant in global advancement. This means that African governments must redefine their labour tactics which evolved over the years due to social changes in their value of labour and labour cultures. There is a desperate need to involve more sectors designed to think out strategies that will lead to a sustainable system that can be productive and progressive for the benefit of their citizens. There must be the development of policies aimed at enriching Africans in leisure and labour cultures designed for an internal development that can match the global economic sphere. To encourage this, the ruling class and the African elites must adopt a labour culture which encourages its citizens to be a part of the development process by giving them a sense of self-worth in their activities as well as in their wages through personal examples. The senior members must be seen as having the interests of the younger workers at heart and must be trained to mentally think of strategies of local development. As mental leaders, they are not to assume power over leisure through consumption but through constructive leisure that builds and develops not only individuals but also the society as a whole. The African citizens should not feel the need to use their free time to make extra money or improve themselves in order to attract more income which will ultimately be used to consume products not produced from within their local economy. Such free time should be spent on good leisure habits that can help improve the mind and body of not just the individuals but the African continent as a whole.

References

Ambler, C. (2002). 'Mass Media and Leisure in Africa', *The International Journal of African Historical Studies.* Vol. 35 (1), pp. 119–136.

Abudu, F. (1986). 'Work Attitudes of Africans, with Special Reference to Nigeria', *International Studies of Management and Organization.* Vol. 16 (2), pp. 17–36.

Achebe, C. (1986). *Things Fall Apart*. Oxford: Heinemann.

Ahiauzu, A. (1989). 'The "Theory A" System of Work Organization for the Modern African Workplace', *International Studies of Management and Organization*. Vol. 19 (1), pp. 6–27.

Ake, C. (2003). *The Feasibility of Democracy in Africa,* CODESRIA, Dakar Senegal.

Akinwunmi, T. (1992). 'Taboos and Ritual Textiles Among the Owo Yoruba of Nigeria as Instruments for Controlling Social Roles and Textile Quality', *Yabatech Academic Journal*. Vol. 2 (2), pp. 7–12.

Akyeampong, E. (2002). 'Leisure in Africa History: An Introduction', *Journal of African Historical Studies*. Vol. 35(1), pp. 1–16.

Ayee, J. (2005). 'Public Sector Management in Africa', *Economic Research Working Paper Series*. Num. 82, African Development Bank.

Clarke, D. (1996). 'Colonial Intervention and Indigenous Responses: The Introduction of European Broad Loom Weaving in Oyo Town', *Kurio Africana.* Dept. of Fine Arts, OAU, Ife. Vol. 2 (2), pp. 17.

Coquery-Vidrovitch, C. (1977). Research on an African Mode of Production, *African Social Studies: A Radical Reader,* Gutkind, P. and Waterman, P. (ed). London: Heinemann, pp. 77–92.

Davis, D. (2005). 'Urban Consumer Culture', *The China Quarterly No. 183 Culture in the Contemporary (PRC),* pp. 692–709.

Ehmer, J. (2014). 'Attitudes to Work, Class Structure, and Social Change: A Review of Recent Historical Studies', *IRSH* 59, pp. 99–117.

Fanon, F. (1963). *Wretched of the Earth*. London: Penguin Books.

Friedman, Jonathan. (2005). *Consumption and Identity*. Taylor and Francis e-Library.

Hatcher, J. (1998). 'Labour, Leisure and Economic Thought before the Nineteenth Century', *Past and Present*. No. 160, pp. 64–115.

Just, P. (1980). 'Time and Leisure in the Elaboration of Culture', *Journal of Anthropological Research*. Vol. 36 (1) pp. 105–115.

Keith, T. (1964). 'Work and Leisure in Pre-Industrial Society', *Past and Present.* Vol. 29, pp. 50–66.

Kuic, V. (1981). 'Work, Leisure and Culture', *The Review of Politics.* Vol. 43 (3), pp. 436–465.

Larkin, B. (2008). *Signal and Noise: Media Infrastructure and the Urban Culture in Nigeria*. Durham: Duke University Press.

Lloyd, K. and Auld, C. (2002). 'The Role of Leisure in Determining Quality of Life: Issues of Content and Measurement', *Social Indicators Research,* Vol. 57 (1), pp. 43–71.

Mathias, P. (1994). 'Time for Work, Time for Play: Relations Between Work and Leisure in the Early Modern Period'. *VSWG: Vierteljahrschrift Für Sozial-Und Wirtschaftsgeschichte,* 81(3).

Ogbomo, O. (1997). *When Men and Women Mattered: A History of Gender Relations Among the Owan of Nigeria*. Rochester, NY: University of Rochester Press.

Parboteeah, K., Seriki, T. and Hoegl, M. (2014). Ethnic Diversity, Corruption and Ethical Climates in Sub-Saharan Africa: Recognizing the Significance of Human Resource Management, *The International Journal of Human Resource Management* Vol. 25 (7), pp. 979–1001.

Peterson, R. (1981). 'Measuring Culture, Leisure, and Time Use', *The Annals of the American Academy of Political and Social Sciences Vol. 453 (America Enters the Eighties: Some Social Indicators)*, pp. 169–179.

Renee, E. (1997). 'Traditional Modernity and the Economics of Handwoven Cloth Production in Southwestern Nigeria', *Journal of Labor Economics Society of Labor Economist,* University of Chicago, pp. 773–792.

Rodney, W. (1977). 'Technology Stagnation and Economic Distortion in Pre-colonial Times', *African Social Studies: A Radical Reader,* Gutkind, P. and Waterman, P. (eds). London: Heinemann, pp. 107–115.

Rowlands, M. (1996). 'The Material Culture of Success Ideals and Life Cycles in Cameroon', in Friedman KajsaEkholm (ed.) *Catastrophe and Creation: The Transformation of an African Culture.* Barwood Academic Publishers.

19

Social Differentials and Emerging Urban Leisure Trends

A Case Study of City of Dehradun in India

NEHA KALA

The unfolding regime of economic liberalisation, which began in early 1990s in India has led to the emergence of a society which is being described as dynamic and modernising. The new popular image of India as 'shining' and 'rising' is primarily due to the shift towards a new economy which represents the rise of an aspirational middle class in an increasingly globalised work culture. Consequently, new patterns of consumption are evident in an environment of international brands and global economy. Besides the financial and business services, there has been a rapid expansion of leisure services over the last 15 years. It is well-accepted fact that social structure not only influences the nature and form of leisure but also determines the extent and limit of participation. Through a series of brilliant comparative history of some societies both in the West as well as in India, Modi (2010) established a kind of concomitance between the social structure and the structure of leisure in his research. He examined the changes in nature of leisure and recreation along with changes in the structure of Indian society while discussing the leisure patterns of Vedic society, the Imperial society, Monarchial feudal society, Colonial society and Independent India. In the wake of major changes that have transformed the economic and social structure of Indian society, the traditional patterns of leisure have also altered. Modi while characterising the nature and form of traditional leisure in India as 'hierarchical, group institutionalised, group participation oriented, normative and rhythmic', observes that under the influence of social structural changes the nature and form of contemporary leisure, as opposed to the traditional one, is becoming more egalitarian and individualistic. Drawing on his work, a part of my doctoral research which was conducted a decade ago examined the leisure patterns of urban residents of Dehradun. The town of Dehradun then had recently acquired the capital city status of newly carved Uttarakhand state. A comprehensive data collected by means of structured questionnaire-cum-schedule, informal discussions and participant observation of five major occupational categories namely, the unorganised sector; industrial workers; merchants; service class; and elites, brought forth the various aspects pertaining to the leisure lives of urban residents. Since then increased development, more commercial establishments and rapid expansion have transformed this once sleepy town into a busy city. In order to gauge the changes that had occurred over the decade, observations were made during a brief field trip to Dehradun and then telephonic interviews were conducted with few respondents from each category. Besides this, articles in newspapers, journals and social media information served as secondary source. Comparing the earlier and the recent findings, this paper demonstrates how the advent of global market economy has significantly impacted the leisure lives of residents and altered the traditional patterns of leisure.

Phenomenon of Leisure

Leisure is a complex phenomenon pervading every society. Recreation and leisure are the cultural universals, being found as common elements in the behaviour of individuals in all societies (Miller and Robinson). Etymologically, the word leisure comes from the old French *leiser* meaning 'opportunity to do something', which in turn derives from Latin *licere* meaning 'be permitted'. In ancient Greece, leisure meant freedom from the necessity of ponos (work or sorrow) and freedom for engagement with paideia (culture). The origins of the current notions of leisure are found embedded in the traditions and practices of ancient cultures. However, leisure in those days was mostly the privilege of high status groups. It was industrial revolution which set the stage for creation of leisure industry that we know today. The social conditions of industrialisation, urbanisation and modernisation awakened interest in leisure and led to the emergence of theories of recreation and play. The rise of capitalistic monetary economy, since the 19th century, was characterised by reduction of work time and redistribution of time accompanied by typically modern notions of free evenings, the weekends, and paid vacations. Lengthy childhood and retirement were also the outcome of this period. Further, the age-old dichotomy that gave ordained labour for the multitude and leisure for the favoured few was not preserved and parks, libraries, museums and other areas of leisure were gradually made available to public.

Leisure has meant different things to different people and the concept of leisure has changed with the times. It is generally construed as freedom from work or absence of obligations and discretion to use that period of time at one's sweet will. Joblin considers leisure as the experience of freely, actively and responsibly involved in work, play and worship. Leisure is defined as 'burning up of excess energy' by Schiller and Spencer. Leisure as experience of freedom is best described by De Grazia as 'freedom from the necessity of being occupied'. Carr reviews that leisure is the freedom to do what one likes to do if one has means to do it. Josef Pieper conceives of leisure as a mental and spiritual attitude and a condition of the soul. Dahl feels that leisure is not simply a free time but a free spirit. Traditional definitions commonly focus on leisure as a kind of activity, as a specific time-frame or as an attitude or feeling of freedom. Such definitions tend to reflect the western and industrial societies and largely ignore social structures, cultural practices and historical contexts. Recent literature defines leisure as legitimated pleasure, social construction and means of social reproduction (Rojek, 1997). Max Kaplan mentions some essential elements of leisure: an anti-thesis to work as an economic function; a pleasant expectation and recollection; a minimum of involuntary social role obligation; a psychological perception of freedom; a close affinity with cultural values; the inclusion of an entire range from inconsequence and insignificance to weightiness and importance; often, but not necessarily, an activity characterised by the element of play. For Kaplan, leisure is none of these by itself but all of them together with emphasis on one or the other. Broadening its scope further, leisure is seen as a place where individuals may resist, challenge and even transform oppressive and constraining social relations (Henderson et al., 1996).

Though leisure can be categorised as cultural, universal yet particularistic nature of leisure is evident in terms of perception, participation and purpose. It is a well accepted fact that leisure experiences are culturally determined. Perception and connotation of leisure differ from people to people as we move across cultures and habitats. Being situated in Doon Valley, at the foothills of Shivalik ranges, Dehradun is flanked by the holy towns of Rishikesh and Haridwar. The mythological and historical significance of the place makes influence on the urban population here. Influenced by spiritualism and nature, the ideal leisure for many is to be in harmony with own self, with the community and with the nature. Many elderly respondents along with residents belonging to elite class emphasised on the contemplative and esoteric nature of leisure. While maximum respondents from working class and service class see leisure as an opportunity to unwind from stress. However, leisure is not seen as 'residual time', nor do residents identify those activities typically done in leisure time as leisure. There has not been a clear division between work and leisure time in most respondents' lives. In fact, most see leisure intertwined with work as leisure activities are enjoyed either within the domain of work or work-leisure operates simultaneously. Informal groups formed within office, gymnasiums and recreation rooms in office, cafeterias in or around offices serve as leisure space for many respondents. Even office tours are seen as a break from routine and an opportunity to see new place, meet new people or learn new things. Similarly, social functions like weddings, birthdays, house-warming get-togethers liberate individuals from routine on one hand while allowing them to fulfil their social obligations on the other hand at the same time. Words like *'avkash'* (leave), *'sukoon'* (satisfaction), *'aaraam'* (relaxation), *'fursat'* (sparetime) and *'aanand'* (bliss) might not fully represent the meaning of leisure but were frequently used by respondents either as Hindi or Urdu equivalent of leisure or to describe their perception of leisure. Amongst the youth, 'chill out' and 'hang out' are the catch phrases that are indicative of break or respite.

Periodicity of Leisure

Taking leisure as an experience which generally takes place outside working hours so that one has a choice and freedom to select what is to be done during leisure hours, it is important to examine the leisure time trend and the changes in working hours, which are creating new pressures on leisure time. Leisure is shaped by hours of work, public holidays and paid leave entitlements, all of which can vary widely between regions. Each region has its own values and traditions in terms of the importance attached to leisure and the institutional arrangements that shaped it. Therefore, before analysing the common leisure activities, the periodicity of leisure during the weekdays and the weekend was determined. Since the clear cut dichotomy between work and leisure is not prevalent in the Indian society, respondents found it difficult to report the exact time-period of leisure. Moreover, the perception of leisure varied from individual to individual so a vague idea of periodicity was drawn from their approximate responses. The data revealed that the number of leisure hours available to an individual respondent ranged from zero to seven hours. The average leisure time available to the residents in Dehradun on weekdays is 4 hours 36 minutes. An increase of two hours was noticeable in the average leisure time available during the weekends and public holidays. The service class and industrial workers have the maximum average leisure time available to them on weekends which can be attributed to the weekend holiday provided to them as compared to many merchants and wage-earners who engage in work on weekends also. Substantial rise in those working at weekend is evident, thus changing the rhythm of leisure time.

Analysing the periodicity of leisure in terms of occupational category, one finds that the leisure time available to unorganised sector is 5 hours 4 minutes; to industrial workers 3 hours 44 minutes; to merchants 4 hours 36 minutes; to service class 5 hours 18 minutes and to elites 4 hours 12 minutes. Inflexible working hours and long commute distance to work are reasons reported for lowest leisure time available to industrial workers. An upward rise in leisure time is observed amongst industrial workers, merchants and service class, thus strengthening the notion that the more affluent one becomes, the more opportunities for leisure become available. However, an exceptional trend has been observed among the elites and unorganised sector. Probably, due to the nature of their work, the unorganised sector has lesser means but maximum leisure time availability. The reasons that fit most cases is that either their labour depends on the availability of work or they generally work at their own will, as they are not tied by rules of office or market. The data shows decline in the leisure time available to elites. The dichotomy between *money-rich time poor* elite class and *time-rich money poor* unorganised sector is clearly evident.

The periodicity of leisure is relative to age and sex. From the data, it could be safely concluded that younger (21–30 years) and older (61–70) age groups have proportionately more leisure time. The respondents between 21–30 years represent the students or new entrants into jobs, having less familial and social obligations and, therefore, have ample leisure time for them. Similarly, elderly respondents falling in the age bracket of 61–70 years have a lot of time in their hand as their participation in work force declines and have generally completed their familial responsibilities. The respondents belonging to 31–60 age group are most involved in job as well as familial and social responsibilities and obligations and, therefore, have less leisure. Sex-wise distribution of leisure time indicates that on an average males have 2 hours 58 minutes more leisure than females suggesting that women feel more rushed and more responsible for taking care of children and housework. This disparity can be attributed to the dual role of urban women, both as family providers and family care-takers.

Women who do not join the work-force outside their domestic domain feel the pressures of household chores and meeting the needs of children even when they are meant to be enjoying their leisure time.

A decade later, the periodicity of leisure on an average shows decline of two hours on weekdays and weekends. What used to be free time has been hijacked by work, errands, commute and various obligations. Yet the residents felt that they had satisfactory leisure time at their disposal as compared to high-speed lifestyle of metropolitan cities. The affordability and accessibility of various time-saving home appliances and electronic gadgets have reduced the domestic drudgery of middle-class families. However, many respondents working in private sector admitted that most of the time their overbooked schedules hardly left them with any spare second. The women in executive roles, in particular, stated that at times they reach a point when they are too busy to add even a single more task. Between children's scheduled activities and domestic commitments, there is often little time to be present in a meaningful way. New technology like smartphones, tablets, etc. have made work easier but have also rendered the term 'off the clock' almost obsolete. Moreover, the 'rapid pace mentality' and 'multi-tasking' syndrome appears to be an anti-thesis to savouring leisure moments. Being busy as a sign of productivity seems to be taking over urban residents in the recent years which to some extent is robbing them of the desire to linger.

Leisure Activities

It is important to realise that leisure can embrace a whole range of experiences and activities. With more free time available to many members of society and more resources devoted to leisure spending, the growth of urban leisure has been a significant feature of recent social change. On exploring the leisure pursuits of urban residents, wide range of interests were encountered and in order to encompass this diversity similar activities were combined into a category. Irrespective of the various structural characteristics, the three most common leisure activities emerged as:

(i) Audio-visual activities which included cinema-going, listening to radio/tape recorder/CD, playing video-games, net-surfing and most predominantly watching television.

(ii) Intellectual activities like reading newspaper/journals/books, writing, solving cross-word puzzles, etc.

(iii) Group-oriented activities like conversation with friends, going to social-events, making social visits to extended family and friends, etc.

Relaxing, strolling, appreciation of nature, introspection also figured highly in the leisure lives of respondents. Few residents reported active participation in hobby-oriented and association-oriented activities. Involvement in excursionistic activities and in spiritual as well as volunteering activities registered quite a support while selected few showed interest in sports and physical activities. Interestingly, many respondents admitted interest in art and culture related pursuits. Taking the occupation variable, the leisure activities showed slight variation in priority among different sectors. Nevertheless, audio-visual activities predominantly prevail among respondents of all categories reinforcing

Meyersohn's view that mass-media provides a leisure resource appropriate for poor and culturally deprived also. Participation in excursionistic, quietistic, religious, cultural, group-oriented and association-oriented activities was found common in all occupation categories yet the nature of such participation differs among members of these categories. Data also revealed positive correlation between increasing income and inclination of individuals towards art and culture-oriented activities.

There are more similarities than differences between the sexes in terms of most common leisure activities. However, clear difference between the sexes was noticed in terms of preferred activities, participation rate and also the quality of leisure. Females showed much higher participation in family-oriented, group-oriented and socio-cultural activities as compared to males. Concern for providing balance between work and domestic life leaves females with squeezed leisure time for excursionistic and association-oriented activities where males showed higher participation. Similarly, games and sports are dominated by males. The study, thus, reinforces the fact that in a gendered society, the leisure lifestyles of females are generally restricted to collective activities and more within domestic sphere rather than public sphere. Age is also an important variable in determining leisure pursuits. Audio-visual activities are equally popular amongst older respondents though their participation is predominantly confined to television watching. However, it was observed that many respondents from service sector and elite are active in computer-oriented activities and also show keen interest in learning new trends. Quietism, association-oriented and spiritual activities have good participation from the elderly population. They also prefer to enjoy reading, contemplation, strolling and mild exercises.

Changes are evident in the overall leisure profiles of urban residents. The latest developments in information and communication technologies have significantly impacted the work and leisure of residents in recent years. Irrespective of class, age and sex, mobile phones have become tools of constant connectivity with friends and family. Many respondents especially young remain tethered to smart devices that offer unprecedented information as well as fun. Even elite and service class respondents like to be constantly active on social media. i-phones, i-pads and other smart devices are the new leisure providers besides serving various other functions. Interestingly, television viewing remains the most popular leisure activity overall though the viewing time seemed to be compressed as compared to earlier data. There is gradual decrease in the collective pattern of television viewing within the households. Viewing of online videos on individual smartphones and tablets can be cited as one of the reasons for this. Respondents felt that various family-oriented activities consume much of leisure time and therefore, less time remains for quietistic activities like idling, relaxing, introspection and appreciation of nature. Sharp rise was seen in spiritual and excursionistic activities. With the expanding outreach of various religious and spiritual organisations, attending religious discourses and spiritual courses is gaining popularity amongst the urban population. Physical activities like exercises, yoga, sports too showed more participation than before. Orientation of residents towards cultural activities, concerts, exhibitions, fairs and art has increased because of the frequent organisation of such events for the general public in the city.

Leisure Environment

Leisure environment is an important aspect of any study of leisure because the location and the context of the activity are intrinsic part of the experience. Leisure environments can be divided broadly in terms of individual's activity spaces between the intimately and continually encountered domain, like the area of home, and the distant, remote, less known locations. Accordingly, the leisure pursuits can be classified as indoor leisure activities and outdoor leisure activities. Indoor leisure is largely dominated by mass-media which includes broadcast media, print media, audio-visual and electronic media. Home entertainment takes a variety of forms but the majority prefer watching various channels on television. Computer-oriented activities and conversations on mobile also occupy free time of most respondents. With new technological innovations in electronic media, various gadgets especially smartphones which serve all purpose are gradually becoming an integral part of individual's life in general and leisure life in particular. Engaging in gardening, reading, spiritual practices and hobby – oriented activities was also reported by many while playing indoor games was preferred by few.

Beyond the area of home and neighbourhood lies an outside world, which presents a different set of opportunities from our home-based action space. Strolling, shopping, paying social visits and visiting religious places constitute some important preferred outdoor activities of respondents. Eating out has emerged as a major trend in recent times and going to restaurants has become a regular feature of urban lifestyle. The choice of restaurants corresponds to the income status of respondents. After the opening of McDonald's, Pizza Hut, Café Coffee Day, Barista, Domino's, etc, urban respondents have inclined their taste towards them besides the local eateries. Tea-stalls, canteens and cafeteria are the main meeting points of respondents belonging to unorganised sector and industrial workers. These places not only provide meals at low cost but also an avenue for interacting and gossiping. By creating kind of primary group situation where people discuss their daily life, politics, sports and other matters such places bear a cathartic value, thus having refreshing effect on individuals. Going to various clubs for fun, partying, visiting amusement parks and various upcoming attractions in the city are preferred by urban residents. Full spectrum of leisure amenities like multiplex, malls, pubs, various nature-based and amusement parks has made appearance in Dehradun. The frequency of visitation by urban middle class to such attractions shows significant rise. With Dehradun gradually waking up to metro culture, this trend in the growth of visitors to malls and multiplexes is likely to continue. These commercial and recreation hubs have aspects of economy, time and aesthetics intelligently combined which act as magnets for leisure activity. Car travel has added to the range and breadth of catchments of alternative recreational facilities. Mostly, it is the urban environment which dominates leisure of most people yet some respondents like to enjoy the rural retreats around the city. Few adventurous respondents prefer hiking and nature appreciation during their free time. Urban leisure, however, has become increasingly about affluence and mobility and these attributes are selectively distributed among the population.

Short Term Diversions

Today's fast moving life and fast track careers deprive people from enjoying every day leisure. Private sector jobs keep one time pressed on one hand and too stressed on the other. In order to put brakes on such sped-up and filled up lifestyles short term diversions are required to rebound. Such diversions occasionally fill the leisure lives in an environment away from the frequently visited, well-known and intimately and continually encountered domain like the area of home or neighbourhood and in the distant, remote and less-known locations visited infrequently. According to Iso-Ahola's two dimensional theory of leisure motivation, two motivational forces simultaneously influence the individual's leisure behaviour. According to this theory, psychological benefits of recreation emanate from the interplay of two forces, escaping from routine and stressful environment and seeking of recreational opportunities for certain psychological rewards. The two forces are one of seeking and one of escaping. Mannell and Iso-Ahola note that leisure researches have seen tourist activities as 'relatively rare and infrequent leisure episodes', which by implication are not perceived as part of everyday life. However, Moore, Cushman and Simmons feel that it is possible to conceive of tourism alongside other leisure forms, as part of everyday life. Travel itself is also becoming a more everyday occurrence. The popularity of the weekend trip to an overseas or domestic destination as a short 'get away' holiday means that travel is now a far more frequent type of leisure experience than it once was. So, travel and its associated everyday manifestations can be seen as part of continually developing 'travel' and 'tourism' plane that constantly interact with other leisure plane to produce the overall leisure-lives of individuals.

The urge to seek pleasure and to escape from monotonous routine is prevalent among the urban folks here. People resort to short-term diversions either available in their vicinity like visiting shopping centres, gardens, temples, cinema-halls, restaurants, museums, theme-parks or available beyond their local environment like organising picnics or going on a short distance trip, etc. Dehradun has various idyllic locations quite conducive for picnics. Places like Shahastradhara, Gucchu-Pani, Lakshman Sidh temple, Garhi, Kaulagarh, Malsi, Selaqui are popular picnic spots where residents frequently go. However, new developments like malls, multiplexes, resorts have weakened the picnic-going tradition amongst the residents. Besides the routine places like temples, parks and shopping centres within the city, people travel to enjoy the countryside in rural retreat or to a non-urban landscape, or to see touristic sites and monuments in near by region or simply visit tourist resorts, fun and water parks and ethnic restaurants for holiday making. Short distance tours are undertaken by all respondents at various intervals with different motives but such tours are not in the form of weekly episodes as seen in the western world, where weekend trips are a common feature. Various places were reported by respondents which have been clubbed into certain categories according to their motives and characteristics. The data revealed that surrounding towns and areas are the most popular places visited for short distance tours. Mostly, any business or official motive is combined with it. Visiting relatives for some family function like wedding, festival or family get together also provides opportunity to undertake short distance tours. Local residents often feel obligated to take their relatives and friends for sightseeing to nearby places like Mussoorie, Rishikesh, Chakrata, Har-ki-Doon, Haridwar and thus, leisure satisfaction is drawn while simultaneously playing the dual roles of host as well as guest. Propitiatory visits are often taken by respondents to places of religious importance to appease the deity. Similarly, regular visits to surrounding native places are preferred by many urban residents for short-distance tour.

It was found that short distance tours have become a frequent experience for most of the respondents. Most respondents either need a break from monotonous routine or want to escape from loneliness. Short distance tour is preferred as it is less time consuming and economical too. Moreover, people also get to see a new place, which adds to their experience. Earlier visits to native places and propitiatory visits were dominant. Of late, exploring new areas has become a trend. Urban middle-class families are generally nuclear and are less surrounded by kins which allows quick decision-making and less planning. Improved transportation and car ownership have also increased mobility and have made places accessible in less time. Media has also played an important role in increasing awareness of places worth visiting around one's city and thus made many places popular destination for short term diversions.

Conclusion

The study of urban leisure in Dehradun reinforces the view that to great extent, the expanding middle class are the emergent leisure users in contemporary society. The above analysis also revealed the dichotomy between the 'money-rich time-poor' elite class and 'time-rich money-poor' unorganised class. Barring these two classes, an upward rise in leisure time is observed among other occupational categories strengthening the notion that leisure time increases with increasing affluence. Audio-visual activities emerged as the most common leisure activity. While television viewing continues to dominate domestic leisure yet a gradual decline in the viewing time was noticed owing to the presence of other smart screens. Social media and online activities are fast gaining large following. Dominance of market has led to much-diminished role of traditional forms of leisure. The responses suggested that social class limits leisure choice and range of leisure opportunities. The social constraints of gender and age are also reflected in day to day leisure lives of respondents.

The contemporary leisure pursuits in urban areas have been influenced by two countervailing factors. On one hand, the rising standards of housing amenities have increased the focus on the home as the location of increasingly individualised and privatised consumption of leisure time activities. Houses are equipped with video-recorders, satellite receivers, CD players, computers and game machines and, therefore, much time is spent around home base. Television and other electronic media tend to lead to change of behaviour in such way that leisure time is to an increasing extent being consumed by them. Consequently, involvement in physical activities is impacted negatively. Interestingly, visiting and communicating with friends, neighbours and relatives is limited in actuality yet one remains connected virtually. On the other hand, the upper class urban citizen now has access to private car. This permits them great mobility and gives access to a wide variety of local and distant facilities. The data reveals that urban class in India is highly receptive of new leisure amenities and new leisure provisions like multiplexes, fast-food outlets, shopping malls, amusement parks and bowling alleys are gaining popularity in cities. However, access to leisure facilities and opportunities is determined by number of factors: availability, investment, suitability, mobility and awareness yet for most people the crucial influence is that of income. The lower income groups are limited in the amount of spending they devote to recreational activities. Whether this disadvantage is analysed in terms of Marxist sociology through class and life-chances or through Weberian concept of status and lifestyle, the reality is a relatively deprived experience of leisure activities. Low income means that a larger proportion must be spent in necessities like housing, clothing and food with a restricted amount available for pleasure.

Beyond this intimate commonplace domain lies a wider world experienced weekly, monthly, annually or even once in a life time. The world beyond the everyday realm, presents a different set of opportunities and facilities from our home-based action space and this may be, in large part its very attractiveness to us. This outside world is special and exciting and is encountered occasionally during picnics or short distance tours. The focal places for amusement are important for contrasting breaks, holidays and day trips but they also follow hierarchical pattern which is directly proportional to the economic status. Outdoor leisure is again closely linked with income. The outside world is encountered occasionally by the lower income groups in the form of short term diversions like picnics or fairs and festivals. Car-borne mobility has encouraged day tourism and short distance tours among the middle and upper class residents. Such diversions are fast becoming frequent episodes among the middle class respondents, whose tight work schedules leave them exhausted and in need for quick respite. Moreover, these trips are less time consuming and economic too. Tourism, thus, appears as one end of broad leisure spectrum as tourism activities are an extension of leisure lifestyles reflecting the level of affluence of a society. As already mentioned, contrasting trends were represented in data on contemporary patterns. Home fosters inward-oriented usually individualised leisure activities, exerting a basically centripetal force on leisure distributions while cars encourage more centrifugal leisure momentum, since mobility enables and encourages widening leisure use of a range of more distant opportunities. These two divergent facets, one localised and the other, dispersed continue to generated a complex pattern of leisure participation among the urban folks.

References

Carr, Harvey, A. (1902). *The Survival Values of Play,* Boulder: University of Colorado.

Carr, Hugh, Charles (1902). *The Survival Values of Play.*

Collin's Essential Encyclopaedia. 1983. New York.

Dahl, G.H. (1971). *Time, Work and Leisure*. New York: Christian Century Foundation.

De Grazia, S. (1964). *Of Time, Work and Leisure*. New York: The Twentieth Century Fund.

Dumazedier, J. (1974). *Sociology of Leisure*. Amsterdam: Elsevier Scientific Pub. Co.

Henderson, et al., (2004). Theory in Recreation and Leisure Research: Reflections from the Editors. In *Leisure Sciences*, 26, Taylor and Francis Inc. pp. 411–425.

Iso-Ahola, S.E. (1989). Motivation for Leisure, in E.L. Jackson and T.L. Burton (eds.) *Understanding Leisure and Recreation: Shaping the Past, Charting the Future*. State Collage, Pa.: Venture Publishing.

Joblin, D. (1990). Leisure and the Infant: Giving Birth to the Saving Virtue of Hope. Paper Presented at the Fourth World Congress of the World Leisure and Recreation Association, Cardiff, UK.

Kaplan, Max. (1960). *Leisure in America: A Social Inquiry*. New York: John Wiley and Sons.

Mannell, R.C. and S.E. Iso-Ahola. (1987). Psychological Nature of Leisure and Tourism Experience. *Annals of Tourism Research*.14, pp. 314–331.

Miller, N.P. and D.M. Robinson. (1963). *The Leisure Age: Its Challenges to Recreation*. California: Wadsworth.

Modi, Ishwar. (1985). *Leisure, Mass Media and Social Structure*. Jaipur: Rawat.

Modi, Ishwar. (2010). Leisure: A Pathway to Human Happiness and Social Harmony, in I. Modi, Ma Huidi and Ning Zequn (eds.) *Leisure and Civilization: Interdisciplinary and International Perspectives*. China Travel and Tourism Press.

Pieper, J. (1952). *Leisure: The Basis of Culture*. New York: Pantheon Books.

Rojek, C. (1997). Leisure Theory: Retrospect and Prospect. In *Society and Leisure*. Vol. 20. Taylor and Francis online.

Rojek, C. (2005). *Leisure Theory: Principles and Practice*. Basingstoke, UK: Palgrave Macmillan.

Singh, Y. (1973). *Modernization of Indian Tradition*. Delhi: Thompson Press.

Stebbins, R.A. (1982). Serious Leisure: A Conceptual Statement. *Pacific Sociological Review*, 25.

Stokowsky, P. (1994). *Leisure in Society: A Network Structural Perspective*. London: Mansell.

Webster's Encyclopaedia. (1983). New York.

20

Global to Local Modernity in Bangladesh

Changing World Views of Rural Women

HABIBUL HAQUE KHONDKER

In recent years, Bangladesh has experienced significant progress in the transformation of traditional gender roles resulting in the empowerment of women. The achievement of key Millennium Development Goals (MAGS) relating to women in Bangladesh has been well received in the international community. This paper focuses on the impact of financial inclusion through microcredit on the attitudes and behaviours of women in rural Bangladesh. At the conceptual level we argue that the framework of individual modernity is in fact an aspect of global modernity, which is revealed in the changes of attitudes, behaviours and aspirations of the respondents. Individual modernity in this paper is used as a conceptual construct, a framework for understanding changes in the world views that comprise values, attitudes and aspirations of rural women. Modernity may be viewed as a social and cultural syndrome characterised by such characteristics as future-orientation, individualism, equity, tolerance of diversity, and rationality, a mark of which is a favourable attitude towards technology and science-based knowledge. This paper examines these trends towards modernity at the individual level and does not seek to establish causal relationships between variables or measure modernity on a psychological scale. This paper combines both qualitative and quantitative methods using a household survey of pre-selected samples mostly drawn from rural households in Bangladesh. Alongside the survey, the study relies on focus group discussions and use available secondary data. A variety of microfinance institutions have heavily impacted the rural society in Bangladesh. This paper postulates that the impact of modernity can be assessed through the changes in the values and attitudes towards future orientation and favourable views towards science and technology, educational aspiration and career of their female children. In all these indicators, the answers of the respondents indicate their individual modernity.

This paper uses the data collected by the author while affiliated with the Institute of Microfinance in Dhaka, Bangladesh in 2011. The author is grateful to the Institute and its staff for support. The author also wants to thank Aliya Khondker for editorial assistance. Paper written for the book in honour of Professor Ishwar Modi.

The borrowers of microcredit show a slightly higher educational aspiration for their daughters' education. In terms of beliefs in superstitions and other issues – another indicator of modernity – they are not indistinguishable from the non-borrowers. Our respondents, women of sampled households were future-oriented, had high aspirations for their children's education – both males and females – and were aware of the key developmental issues. However, when it came to their preference of age of marriage of their daughters, majority of the respondents chose age 16, which coincides with the high school graduation of their daughters. Often the respondents identified the problem of insecurity in the villages as a reason for marrying their daughters early. In other words, the paper signals both the positive modernisation outcomes as well as the challenges Bangladesh continues to face.

The respondents, rural women, had opinion about intrusion of new technology in their communities and they articulated their opinions on both the positive and negative impact of such technologies as satellite television (so-called dish television) and mobile phones. A large number of the respondents were not fatalists and believed that it was their actions and not a pre-determined fate that played the most important role in determining their future. These responses showed some underlying tendency towards rationalisation of their world views. Modern ideas seem to have affected the entire community of women both borrowers of microcredit as well as non-borrowers suggesting the influence of communication technology, which also has grown significantly in Bangladesh in the period between 2000 and 2015. Because of the wide availability of Internet-abled mobile phones, Internet users in Bangladesh reached 44.6 million in March 2015 which is 26.4 per cent of the population (www.internetworldstats.com/asia.htm#bd).

Theoretical Issues

In development and modernisation studies, there has been a shift of focus from growth oriented to well-being oriented approach to development. Correspondingly, there has also been a shift from mega-projects changing the entire nation or community at a macro-level to a more micro-level, individual-focused approach to development. Within the individual-focused approach it is now widely accepted that women-focused developmental approach yields more benefits to the society. Thus, the well-being of the women, in particular, has been identified as a goal of development with multiplier beneficial effects for the household and society. Financial inclusiveness, for example, through microfinance has evolved through ground-level experiences in Bangladesh and elsewhere and is now recognised as a useful tool for development. It is to be underscored at the very outset that microfinance is one of the many means of development and well-being and not equivalent to development itself.

At the very outset it may be useful to elaborate the concept of individual modernity. Since the concept of individual modernity has a lot of historical baggage it would be necessary to discuss the concept with as much care as possible. In the post-World War II period in the context of Marshall Plan and the emergence of Development Economics, sociologists, social psychologists and political scientists developed an intellectual field, which came to be known as modernisation theory or in the collective form, modernisation paradigm (in the sense of Thomas Kuhn). Modernisation process was conceived as social change that followed broader economic transformations. For example, as the developing countries were going through the process of economic rehabilitation and transformation, what were the social and cultural consequences of those changes? The priority or centrality of economic processes was accepted as a matter of course, which is best represented in the journal, *Economic Development and Cultural Change,* which was launched in 1952. Bert Hoselitz's question, 'Does economic development mean only a change in certain aspects of overt behaviour, notably the acquisition of new skills or the exercise of new forms of productivity, or is it accompanied by or contingent upon more basic changes in social relations and even the structure of values and beliefs of a culture?' (Hoselitz, 1952: 8) set the tone of the modernisation paradigm. Hoselitz asserted the importance of changes in values in order to entrench economic changes and he also emphasised the role of aspirations held in a society.

Modernisation was seen as social and cultural correlate of economic transformation. Sociologists, for example, argued that industrialisation resulted in breakdown of older family structures and created nuclear families. As large number of women entered the labour force, it led to an increase in their income paving the way for gender role transformation. Growing education and financial independence of women, was followed by women's empowerment. In developing the modernisation paradigm, sociologists (and other social scientists) drew upon the contributions of classical sociologists such as the works of Karl Marx, Max Weber, Alexis de Tocqueville and Emile Durkheim who in their own ways were grappling with the rise of the capitalist industrial society. Their focus was on different aspects of this social transformation. While Marx was preoccupied with the new social relations of exploitation and predicting a path towards an end of exploitation, Weber was concerned with the paradoxical consequences of Protestant transformation, Tocqueville was examining the social circumstances that gave rise to the democratic social order. Durkheim was the first systematic sociologist who examined the social and cultural consequences of the growing division of labour and specialisation in society brought in by industrialisation. That is, in their own ways, the major intellectual figures of the mid-19th and early 20th centuries were dealing with the key aspects of modernity. The main concern of sociology thus became an understanding of modernity. The master trends of modernisation were: a move towards equality (equalisation), administrative centralisation (emergence of state or state like organisations), industrialisation, urbanisation and rise of 'rationalised bureaucracy' (Weber, 1947).

In the post-World War II period, as sociologists turned their focus on social transformation often initiated by the state or a combination of market and state, they naturally drew upon the legacies of the forebears. As some of them examined the social consequences of economic development, others sought to explore the cultural and social institutional forces that stood in the way of economic development. By then, sociology came under the pressure of empiricism and a new epistemology. It is interesting to note that at the formative phase of sociology the founding figures such as Max Weber spent a considerable amount of intellectual energy on the epistemological and methodological questions.

As sociologists turned their attention on various social trends at a macro-level, there were others who wanted to examine changes at the individual level. The work of Alex Inkeles is illustrative. He and his associate embarked on a cross-national paper of individual modernity for which they, with the help of social psychologists, developed an individual modernity scale. They collected data from six countries that included what was then East Pakistan. Some of the main problems of those studies were that they were ethnocentric and used the West as the only modern society against which they measured the non-western societies. No concept has come under heavier attack than modernisation. Many critics have viewed it as a sign of the West's global dominance over the rest of the world, a form of cultural imperialism. Writers such as Andre Gunder Frank (1966), Samir Amin (1974) and others bitterly criticised the unilinear and ethnocentric modernisation theories.

In the 1970s, as a result of such critiques, modernisation theories as such fell into disrepute. Sociologists (Cardoso, 1977; Cardoso and Faletto, 1979) moved to analyse new problems such as Dependency and World-Systems theories of Immanuel Wallerstien and were even lured by fancier theories such as post-modernity in the 1980s and 1990s. This is not the place to dwell on the developments in various strands of sociological theories. In the closing years of the 20th century and the first decade of the present century, a new paradigm emerged under the banner of multiple modernities or alternative modernities. This development created a new ground in answering some of the seemingly ethnocentric views of the earlier theories and allowed for societies to pursue modernity in their own terms, in view of their cultural and social specificities. It also created possibilities for empirically examining the propositions of alternative and more reflexive modernities. The rapid economic development in the so-called Asian tiger economies – Singapore, Hong Kong, Taiwan and South Korea – brought back the subject of role of cultural values in economic development. Discussions of 'work ethic', high-savings, and entrepreneurial spirits often made reference to Max Weber's famous Protestant Ethic thesis (Weber, 1976).

A parallel stream in that intellectual context was a growing recognition of the role of women in economic development. The gendered aspect of development is widely recognised and is reflected in the development literature as well as in many development programmes. Gender refers to a complex system of power differentials played out in the different experience of women and men (Barriteau, 2001: 186–210). Feminist scholars adopted the concept to distinguish culturally specific characteristics associated with masculinity and femininity from biological features. Barriteau (2001) defines gender as complex systems of personal and societal relations through which women and men are socially created and maintained, and through which they gain access to, or are allocated, status, power, and material resource within society. Gender norms expressed within the household are reinforced and reflected in larger institutions of society. 'Gender relations are not confined to the domestic arena – although households constitute an important institutional site on which gender relations are played out – but are made, remade, and contested in a range of institutional arenas' (Kabeer, 1997). In other words, this is not simply a story of the household and its members, but about the shaping of gender identities by larger institutions, and the ongoing participation of family members in creating new gender norms.

According to Staveren (2001), finance and gender are closely related at various levels of economy. At the micro-level, women and men in households have different levels of savings and investments; this is mainly attributable to lower female incomes, and the fact that considerably less property is registered in women's names. At the macro-level, gender-based inequalities affect a country's gross domestic product (GDP), its levels of investment, its interest rates, and even the stability of financial markets (Staveren, 2001: 10).

The UNDP Human Development Report 1995, *Gender and Human Development*, recognises gender as a significant issue in development, especially to counteract the 'feminisation of poverty' in several least developed countries. Human Development Report 1995 estimated that 70 per cent of the populations living in poverty in the world are women (UNDP, 1995: 4). As many point out, behind the phenomenon of the feminisation of poverty, there are various aspects of gender inequity in terms of gender norms, the opportunity for education and remunerative jobs, the condition of reproductive health, and so forth (Miwa, 2005: 443).

A large number of studies exist on the linkage between microfinance and gender, the impact of microfinance on empowerment of women in general and female entrepreneurship in particular. Studies have examined the contribution of microfinance in the reduction of poverty and vulnerability, improved well-being of the borrowers, yet little attention has been given to the impact of microfinance on individual modernity. Sociological research has looked at individual modernity using national level data (Smith and Inkeles, 1966; Inkeles, 1977; Inkeles, Broaded and Cao, 1997; Inglehart, 2005) and some with comparative focus within the country between urban and rural cohorts (Zhang, 2003). Little research is available using household level data. Moreover, hardly any attention has been paid to examine individual modernity based on the in-depth paper of rural households in Bangladesh.

The social-psychological theories of modernisation may be seen as precursors to the philosophical perspectives of enhancement of individual capabilities and freedom expounded by Martha Nussbaum and Amartya Sen (1993) and Amartya Sen (1999). While for theoretical guidance it is worthwhile to look at the propositions of individual modernities and capability approach, for empirical reference a number of cross-cultural, PEW surveys, international Gallup polls and World Values Survey deserve attention. The World Values Survey of Ronald Inglehart of University of Michigan made significant contributions as a repository of comparative data [World Values Survey of Ronald Inglehart's (World Values Survey of 2005)]. Some of the questions used in our survey are adapted from the World Values Survey. Such cross cultural surveys shed valuable light but they are no substitutes for more in-depth studies that combine both survey methods as well as qualitative studies.

In development studies some ideas or propositions tend to assume dominant positions in certain contexts. In the last couple of decades there has been a shift of focus from growth oriented to well-being oriented approach to development. There has also been a shift from mega-projects to individual-focused studies. Within the segmented and individual-focused approach it is now widely accepted that women-focused approach yields more benefits to the society. Thus, the well-being of the women, in particular, has been identified as a goal of development with multiplier beneficial effects for the household and society. The idea of microfinance has evolved through ground-level experiences in Bangladesh and elsewhere and is now recognised as a useful tool for uplifting women's socio-economic situation. The present paper aims to understand the impact of microfinance, if any, on the transformation of traditional gender-role which may lead to individual modernity paving the way for societal modernisation or improvements in society.

By examining the impact of microfinance on the female borrowers, the paper explores whether there are tangible evidence of gender-role transformation and individual modernity as a result of the input of microfinance. Gender-role transformation is viewed as changes in the traditionally allocated unequal roles between males and females in the rural society to a relationship based on more gender equality and individual modernity is viewed as an increase in rationalism and individualism as reflected in the attitudes and opinions of the respondents. As cultural values change, individual members show an increase in rational thinking and belief in one's own individual ability to change a given situation. Human agency facilitated by a belief in individual ability gets prominence under conditions of modernity. In sociological discussion, individual modernity is seen as a result of 'exposure to, or participation in, certain kinds of social experiences and organisational context that promote the development of a coherent syndrome of modern attitudes and values' (Inkeles, Broaded and Cao, 1997: 31). In this paper, individual modernity is defined in terms of changes in the attitude and behaviour of a person where the individual accepts the idea that the individual has the agency, thus has the ability to transform her situation as she aspires to improve her life chances by honest, methodical and hard work. Her aspiration of higher living standard for herself, her family, and specially her children will also be used as criteria of individual modernity. In the early formulation of individual modernity, David Horton Smith and Alex Inkeles defined it as 'a set of attitudes, values, and ways of feeling and acting, presumably of the sort either generated by or required for effective participation in a modern society' (Smith and Inkeles, 1966: 353). They associated modernity with high level of industrialisation and urbanisation. There is an element of tautology in this formulation. Here, we argue that modern attitudes are neither limited to urban nor industrialised societies. In a world dominated by an increasing interconnectedness, people even in remote villages are touched and often affected by the forces of mass media and other agents of globalisation. In a study involving interviews of 6,000 men from six developing countries: Argentina, Chile, India, Israel, Nigeria and the then East Pakistan (Bangladesh), Alex Inkeles and David Smith (both of Harvard University) considered the following dimensions of individual modernity in the format of a scale. The paper was based on interviewing men betraying the bias of the researchers.

1. Openness for social change (new ideas, psychological dispositions, moving to another place, etc.).
2. Readiness for social change (changes in social organisation, changes in hierarchy, fuller opportunities for women).
3. Growth of opinion (disposition to form or hold opinions on a large number of issues (imagine themselves as Prime Minister, etc. and awareness of diversity of opinions).
4. Information – energetic in acquiring facts and information (active versus passive recipients of information).
5. Time (more present and future orientation than the past).
6. Efficiency (men can learn how to exert control over environment)
7. Planning (efficacy and time).
8. Calculability or trust (the world is calculable).
9. The valuing of technical skills.
10. Aspirations, educational and occupational (higher value on formal education).
11. Awareness of and respect for the dignity of others.
12. Understanding of production (how much he grasped the logic of production) – particularism, optimism.

Over time additional indicators such as kinship and family, women's rights, birth control or restriction of family size, religion, aging and the aged, politics, communication media, mass and non-mass, consumerism, social stratification (open or close) and work commitment were added.

The changes in gender relations in Asia as well as the rest of the world as a consequence of global social transformation in the 20th century and in the first decade of the 21st century show interesting and divergent trends. Worldwide women's literacy has increased, more women take part in non-household, paid employment and their overall social status has enhanced. In some countries women have achieved not only more civil rights and economic power, they have also gained political clout. Their achievements in education have been significant, their access to health services and legal rights mark clear gains. In some countries the progress is considerable, whereas in others the achievements have been insignificant and hardly noticeable. Although the gains that women in general have made are not always spectacular, they are not regressive. Afghanistan under the Taliban was an exception, which can be explained by that country's geo-political history and unfortunate entanglement in global confrontations. In Muslim majority countries, where the stereotyped views tend to see women as oppressed and enslaved, Muslim women have made significant achievements. In both economic and political realms, Muslim women's achievement has been noteworthy. For example, in the smaller Gulf countries, in both retailing business as well as corporate world, the presence of women is clearly visible. In South-East Asia encompassing, say, Buddhist Thailand and Muslim majority Indonesia or Malaysia, women are visible in the market place not only as buyers but also as sellers.

Despite tangible achievements in several areas, women as a group in South Asian countries remain vulnerable. This vulnerability is quite pronounced in India, Pakistan and Bangladesh. India has a sex-ratio of 933 according to 2011 Census data (http://www.censusindia.gov.in/Census_Data) accessed on 17 July 2011. Surely, in some key social indicators, Bangladesh has done better than the rest of the subcontinent, (Table 1) large number of South Asian women routinely become victims of human trafficking and enslavement and forced prostitution. The structure of South Asian society, a combination of economic, social and cultural forces slow, if not stagnate, the progress of women, severely restricting their life chances, and impeding their capabilities. The issues of women's equal rights are on the agenda of various NGOs. Here the role of a range of NGO and civil society initiatives continue to dent the traditional gender hierarchy, thus creating space for gender role transformation. Although conservative Islamic groups often target non-governmental organisations that are committed to the improvement of women's social and economic status, the NGOs show less sensitivity to such political threats and manipulations. In a number of cases, NGOs counteract by mobilising people at the grassroot levels against such regressive movements. Conservative religious groups for their alleged 'western' programmes have often targeted microfinance institutions.

Table 1

Gender and Literacy in SAARC Countries

Country	*Youth Literacy (Age 15–24) 2005–13 Male*	*Youth Literacy (Age 15–24) 2005–13 Female*	*Adult Literacy (Age 15 +) 2005–13 Male*	*Adult Literacy (Age 15 +) 2005–13 Female*
Afghanistan	62	32	45	18
Bangladesh	79	83	63	56
Bhutan	80	68	65	39
India	90	82	79	59
Maldives	99	99	98	98
Nepal	90	80	72	49
Pakistan	80	64	70	43
Sri Lanka	98	99	93	90

Source: Table 2.13 World Development Indicators: Education Completion and Outcomes, World Bank 2015. http://wdi.worldbank.org/table/2.13 (accessed on 27 November 2015).

It is interesting to observe that Bangladesh and Sri Lanka are the two countries in SAARC (South Asian Association of Regional Cooperation) that have seen marked improvement in female literacy. Bangladesh's success in increasing female literacy has been spectacular, 79 per cent male versus 83 per cent female. A similar pattern is also observed in the data of some of the Arabian Gulf states. For example, in the UAE female youth literacy is 97 per cent compared to male literacy of 94 per cent (World Bank, 2015).

Lessons from other countries (such as the Philippines and Thailand) where a marked improvement in women's capabilities – if not, complete gender-equality – has been achieved, both public policies and social mobilisations played important role. Economic development in itself is not a predictor of gender empowerment in the minimal sense of women gaining status in measurable social indicators. According to *The Global Gender Gap Report 2010* (Hausman, Tyson and Zahidi, 2010) published by the World Economic Forum, Philippines and Sri Lanka were ranked number 9 and 16 respectively of 134 countries in the overall score of gender empowerment. Gender empowerment index is composed of economic participation and opportunities, educational achievement, health services and political empowerment. Singapore's rank 56, Japan's 94, or Malaysia's 95 compared to Bangladesh's 82 clearly indicate that economic growth alone is not the only means of achieving gender equality or empowering women. In South-East Asia, Philippines and Thailand have done better in bridging gender gap compared to more economically prosperous Singapore or Malaysia (Khondker, 2009:2). The role of public policies and the women's movement must be considered as important variables in explaining women's empowerment. The improvement in the status of women is revealed in the declining infant mortality and maternal mortality in Bangladesh.

Table 2

Infant Mortality and Maternal Mortality in Bangladesh in Selected Years

Year	*Infant Mortality Rate (0–1 year) per 1,000 live births*	*Maternal Mortality per 1,00,000 live births*
1990	99.6	550
1995	81.0	440
2000	64.4	340
2005	50.9	260
2010	38.9	200
2013	33.2	130

Source: Financial Inclusion through Microcredit

The world-wide recognition of microcredit intervention is not only due to its innovative ideas but also because it touched the lives of millions of poor women, creating opportunities for improving their socio-economic situation. A plethora of studies have demonstrated the social and economic benefits of microcredit interventions (Wahid, 1993; Khandker, Khalily and Khan, 1995; Khandker, 1998). There are, however, critical studies (Rahman, 1999; Morduch, 1998) that point out some of the failures of microfinance as a tool of ending poverty. The present paper aims to understand the social impact of microfinance, if any, on the transformation of traditional gender role, which may lead to individual modernity. Our assumption is that durable societal modernisation or improvements in society is dependent to a large extent on changes in the values and attitudes of the people. The paper draws upon certain characteristics of individual modernity from sociological literature and investigates

Table 3

Educational Aspirations of Respondents (Mothers) for Their Daughters

Educational qualification of the respondent	*How far would you like to educate your daughter?*											
	complete primary level		*complete secondary level*		*complete college*		*complete university*		*don't know*		*total*	
	No. of res.	*%*	*Number of res.*	*%*	*Number of res.*	*%*	*Number of res.*	*%*	*Number of res.*	*%*	*N=*	*Row %*
No education	16	9.0%	90	50.6%	61	34.3%	8	4.5%	3	1.7%	178	100.0%
Non formal education and incomplete primary school	2	3.6%	19	34.5%	21	38.2%	13	23.6%	0	.0%	55	100.0%
complete primary school	1	1.9%	27	51.9%	17	32.7%	7	13.5%	0	.0%	52	100.0%
incomplete secondary school	3	5.4%	12	21.4%	28	50.0%	13	23.2%	0	.0%	56	100.0%
post secondary education	0	.0%	0	.0%	6	54.5%	5	45.5%	0	.0%	11	100.0%
Total	22	6.3%	148	42.0%	133	37.8%	46	13.1%	3	.9%	352	100.0%

whether those characteristics and trends are present in the rural society of Bangladesh. There are several factors that may have contributed to those changes. Impact of microfinance has been one such contributing factor.

In the case of Bangladesh, NGOs, especially, microfinance institutions have taken the lead in mobilising the women thus playing an important role in gender-role transformation and helping women attain what we call, individual modernity. In attaining individual modernity, financial inclusion through micro-credit has played an effective role. We do not want to establish a causal relationship between microfinance initiatives and improvement in women's status change. According to Wahiduddin Mahmud, 'It is not easy to identify the causal mechanism or 'triggers' behind the kind of social transformation that has taken place. For example, microcredit programs may have been a contributing factor by promoting social interactions and mobility for rural women in a traditional society characterised by female seclusion. Besides the economic impact of micro-credit on poverty, the mobilisation and functioning of women's credit groups can lead to non-economic gains through enhanced agency, empowerment, mutual support, etc. thus creating the social environment for other development interventions to work better. But, as mentioned earlier, changes in many of the social development indicators preceded the period of rapid expansion of the micro-credit programs in the 1990s. A plausible assumption is that social transformation that had started earlier was helped and extended by micro-credit which itself benefited from female membership' (Mahmud, 2008: 82).

Gender issues are entangled in class and traditional status hierarchy in South Asia. Women from the upper classes or middle-class women escape the harsh realities of subjugation that befall their rural counterparts. Sadly, many of the rural women continue to perpetuate the ideology of patriarchy. Their acceptance of patriarchy sustains a condition of their own vulnerability. A significant number of respondents in this paper were willing to accept gender inequality in terms of inheritance and were not ready to challenge the Sharia ordained distribution that privilege men. One of the recent changes in Bangladesh has been an increasing awareness of the importance of education not only of boys but also of girls. We asked our respondents on their educational aspirations for their daughters and sons. This question captures both their future orientation as well as their outlook insofar as gender equity is concerned. The following tables present the results.

We found that the high aspiration for children's education is near universal among the respondents regardless of their own education. For example, 44.3 per cent mothers who were uneducated themselves had aspiration to have their sons graduate from college. And 34.3 per cent mothers without education had aspiration to have their daughters to do the same. The percentage of respondents with no education who expected their sons to complete primary school (which entails five years of schooling) is about the same as those who wanted their sons to complete university education with 16 years of schooling. For the former it was 7.4 per cent and for the latter it was 6.8 per cent.

For the female children, the majority of women, 50.6 per cent, without education had expectation that their daughters would complete secondary level education. In our focus group discussions as well, the issue of the importance of education came up several times. One of the women, a widow, who participated in such a discussion, stated that she would like her daughter to complete medical school. The woman in question, who was unschooled and worked as a seasonal day labourer, wanted her daughter to be a physician.

Table 4

Willingness of Respondents of their Daughters' Employment

Educational qualification of the respondent	*Will your daughter(s) take-up non-household work?*					
	Yes		*No*		*Total*	
	Count	*Row %*	*Count*	*Row %*	*Count*	*Row %*
No education	107	60.5	70	39.5	177	100.0
Non-formal education	2	40.0	3	60.0	5	100.0
Incomplete primary school (class 1–5)	43	82.7	9	17.3	52	100.0
Complete primary school	38	73.1	14	26.9	52	100.0
Incomplete secondary school (class 6–10)	42	75.0	14	25.0	56	100.0
Complete secondary school	5	83.3	1	16.7	6	100.0
Incomplete higher secondary school (level 11th to 12th)	4	100.0	0	.0	4	100.0
Total	241	68.5	111	31.5	352	100.0

In table 4 we see that majority of the respondents, regardless of educational background, want their daughters to take up non-household employment. The only exception seems to be respondents who were self-taught or had non-institutional education. We also notice that women, with some education whether incomplete primary education or completed secondary education (both over 80%), prefer their daughters to take up non-household work. This is interesting, especially in the context of myths generated about the so-called traditional values of rural Bangladesh society that limited the participation of women in public sphere.

Table 4 points to changes that are taking place in rural Bangladesh. Part of this shift can be explained by growing poverty in the rural society but also a change in the outlook of the respondents, in part due to their exposure to MFIs and other NGOs. An increase in the number of women migrating overseas for work is another evidence of changes in gender role in Bangladesh.

Here too we find that a vast number of women prefer office work for their daughters. The only exception is respondents with incomplete secondary education many of whom aspired professional jobs for their daughters. Some respondents did not choose any career as such and wanted their daughters to grow up so that they can be autonomous and are able to run their families or households properly.

Table 5

Career Aspirations of Mothers for Their Daughters

Occupational Group	*Educational qualification of the respondent and aspiration for daughter's career*													
	No education		*Non-formal education*		*Incomplete primary school (class 1–5)*		*Complete primary school*		*Incomplete secondary school (class 6–10)*		*Complete secondary school*		*Incomplete higher secondary school (level 11th to 12th)*	
	Count	*Column %*	*Count*	*Column %*	*Count*	*Column %*	*Count*	*Column %*	*Count*	*Column %*	*Count*	*Column %*	*Count*	*Column %*
Office work	69	53.1%	1	50.0%	27	56.3%	21	55.3%	11	23.9%	3	50.0%	3	75.0%
Professionals	31	23.8%	1	50.0%	11	22.9%	16	42.1%	27	58.7%	2	33.3%	1	25.0%
To be autonomous	14	10.8%	0	.0%	3	6.3%	0	.0%	0	.0%	0	.0%	0	.0%
To be able to run their families	9	6.9%	0	.0%	2	4.2%	0	.0%	2	4.3%	1	16.7%	0	.0%
Technical personnel	3	2.3%	0	.0%	3	6.3%	1	2.6%	2	4.3%	0	.0%	0	.0%
Police	1	.8%	0	.0%	0	.0%	0	.0%	2	4.3%	0	.0%	0	.0%
To go overseas	1	.8%	0	.0%	0	.0%	0	.0%	0	.0%	0	.0%	0	.0%
Religious teacher	1	.8%	0	.0%	0	.0%	0	.0%	0	.0%	0	.0%	0	.0%
Agriculture/cottage	0	.0%	0	.0%	0	.0%	0	.0%	1	2.2%	0	.0%	0	.0%
To be just educated	0	.0%	0	.0%	0	.0%	0	.0%	1	2.2%	0	.0%	0	.0%
Don't know	1	.8%	0	.0%	2	4.2%	0	.0%	0	.0%	0	.0%	0	.0%

Table 6

Willingness of Microcredit Clients of their Daughters' Employment

Received microcredit?	*Educational qualification of the respondent*	*Will your daughter(s) take up non-household work?*			
		Yes		*No*	
		Count	*Row %*	*Count*	*Row %*
Yes	No education	98	60.5	64	39.5
	Non-formal education	2	40.0	3	60.0
	Incomplete primary school (class 1–5)	40	81.6	9	18.4
	Complete primary school	33	71.7	13	28.3
	Incomplete secondary school (class 6–10)	36	76.6	11	23.4
	Complete secondary school	5	100.0	0	.0
	Incomplete higher secondary school (level 11th to 12th)	4	100.0	0	.0
	Total	218	68.6	100	31.4
No	No education	9	60.0	6	40.0
	Non-formal education	0	.0	0	.0
	Incomplete primary school (class 1–5)	3	100.0	0	.0
	Complete primary school	5	83.3	1	16.7
	Incomplete secondary school (class 6–10)	6	66.7	3	33.3
	Complete secondary school	0	.0	1	100.0
	Incomplete higher secondary school (level 11th to 12th)	0	.0	0	.0
	Total	23	67.6	11	32.4

As we can see in Table 6, both clients and non-clients of microcredit showed striking similarity regarding their aspirations for their daughter's careers. To the question whether they want to see their daughters pursue an occupational career or take up jobs (the Bengali sentence captures both), 68.6 per cent of the clients and 67.6 per cent of the non-clients we interviewed responded in the positive. Considering the fact that the overwhelming majority of the respondents were Muslims, this finding puts the myth that religious value is an impediment for women's gainful employment to rest. Social change in the post-independence Bangladesh has seen participation of women of all socio-economic groups in various occupations. Here both the government and the non-governmental organisations have been equally supportive.

Perceptions and Awareness of Issues of Gender Inequality

On a question whether women are victims of injustice and repression, our respondents had the following answers.

There is hardly any difference observed in the responses between borrowers of microcredit and the non-borrowers. Over 87 to 90 per cent strongly agreed or agreed with the proposition that repression of women remains a serious problem and women are victims of inequality and injustice.

Table 7

Perception of Gender Inequality and Injustice

Inequality and injustice of women is a serious problem (Degree of agreement)	*Any member of the household borrowed micro credit*			
	Yes		*No*	
	Count	*Column %*	*Count*	*Column %*
Strongly agree	70	20.1%	10	29.4%
Agree	235	67.3%	21	61.8%
Neither agree nor disagree	28	8.0%	3	8.8%
Disagree	15	4.3%	0	0.0%
Strongly disagree	0	0.0%	0	0.0%
Do not understand	1	0.3%	0	0.0%

On the issue of whether women should get more opportunities, autonomy and power; we found a great deal of agreement among our respondents, as Table 8 indicates:

Table 8

Women Need More Opportunities and Power

		Micro credit status			
		Micro-credit client		*Non-client*	
		Count	*Column %*	*Count*	*Column %*
Girls and women need more opportunities and power	Strongly agree	130	37.2%	19	55.9%
	Agree	211	60.5%	15	44.1%
	Neither agree nor disagree	5	1.4%	0	0.0%
	Disagree	3	0.9%	0	0.0%
	Strongly disagree	0	0.0%	0	0.0%

On the question of equal income between male and female, our respondents were somewhat divided. Yet, majority in both groups wanted equal pay. One-third of our respondents who were women and micro-credit clients did 'agree' with the idea of same income for the same work between men and women rather than answering 'strongly agree' may indicate a sense of pragmatism in a culture where despite gains of women towards gender equality, age-old cultural values on gender differentiation and hierarchy continue to sway it influence.

Table 9

Equal Pay for Men and Women

The statement was: 'Salary should be same for both male and female for the same type of work'.	*Micro credit status*			
	Micro-credit client		*Non-client*	
	Count	*Column %*	*Count*	*Column %*
Strongly agree	224	64.2%	25	73.5%
Agree	122	35.0%	8	23.5%
Neither agree nor disagree	2	0.6%	0	0.0%
Disagree	1	0.3%	1	2.9%
Strongly disagree	0	0.0%	0	0.0%

On the issue of gender equality, i.e. that men and women should have equal rights, we see a negligible number do not want equality. In other words, on the issue of gender equality, there is a near-consensus among our respondents. Here too the difference between borrowers of microcredit and non-borrowers is negligible (Table 10).

Table 10

Gender Equality

Men and women should enjoy equal rights	*Micro credit status*			
	Micro-credit client		*Non-client*	
	Count	*Column %*	*Count*	*Column %*
Strongly agree	225	64.5%	25	73.5%
Agree	118	33.8%	8	23.5%
Neither agree nor disagree	3	0.9%	0	0.0%
Disagree	3	0.9%	1	2.9%
Strongly disagree	0	0.0%	0	0.0%

In Table 11, Not surprisingly, we find a strong consensus on the issue of gender equality from our respondents who are women.

On the question of whether they want to see more women in high positions in the government, they were fully in favour of seeing women in high positions.

Table 11

Should Women be Recruited in High Government Position?

Level of opinion	*Micro credit clients*		*Non-clients*		*Total*	
	Count	*%*	*Count*	*%*	*Count*	*%*
Yes	314	90.0%	33	97.1%	347	90.6%
No	34	9.7%	1	2.9%	35	9.1%
Don't Know	1	0.3%	0	0.0%	1	0.3%

Bangladesh has had female Prime Ministers since 1990. Majority of our respondents are supportive of the idea of a female Prime Minister. In recent years women have been appointed as cabinet ministers and high executive positions (Table 12).

Table 12

Do You Agree that a Woman can be Prime Minister?

Level of opinion	*Micro credit borrower*		*Non borrower*		*Total*	
	Count	*%*	*Count*	*%*	*Count*	*%*
Yes	289	82.8%	31	91.2%	320	83.6%
No	59	16.9%	3	8.8%	62	16.2%
Don't know	1	0.3%	0	0.0%	1	0.3%

Rational Thinking and Future Orientation

There is common sociological wisdom since Max Weber that a hallmark of modernity is the development of world views dominated by scientific rationality, which erodes beliefs in supernatural. Max Weber (1864–1920) one of the founders of modern sociology thus viewed rationalisation as 'de-magification'(Schluchter, 1989). He argued that even religious practices in modern society become rationalised. Howevcr, rationalisation does not mean that in modern societies, superstitions will completely disappear. However, there is a preponderance of rational think in modern society. In modern society, it is expected that the influence of superstitious beliefs will decline. Another important criterion of modernity is orientation towards future. Modern people tend to show a higher degree of orientation towards future. The following tables attempt to capture orientations towards future, belief in superstition and practice or behaviour guided by scientific rationality.

Table 13

Future Orientation with Housing Status

Do you think for your future?	*Nature of the residential house*					
	Permanent (pucca), semi pucca and tin shade houses		*Thatched houses*		*Total*	
	Count	*Column %*	*Count*	*Column %*	*Count*	*Column %*
Yes	164	100.0%	180	95.7%	344	97.7%
No	0	.0%	8	4.3%	8	2.3%
Total	164	100.0%	188	100.0%	352	100.0%

Table 14

Health Seeking Behaviour with Housing Status

What kind of treatment do you choose?	*Nature of the residential house*					
	Permanent (pucca), semi pucca and tin shade houses		*Thatched houses*		*Total*	
	Count	*Column %*	*Count*	*Column %*	*Count*	*Column %*
Allopath	130	81.3%	155	82.4%	285	81.9%
Homeopathic	30	18.8%	31	16.5%	61	17.5%
Exorcist	0	0.0%	2	1.1%	2	0.6%
Total	160	100.0%	188	100.0%	348	100.0%

We were also curious to see if belief in ghost or sighting of ghost had anything to do with use of modern amenities such as television, mobile phone, or electricity. There is a popular myth that electricity, a modern technology, killed ghosts. In our paper we found no such relationship. We conclude, based on the tables, following that it is not modern technology but modern scientific, rational thought that led to the decline in superstitions such as belief of ghosts.

Table 15

Access to Electricity with Future Orientation

Do you think about your future?	Electricity at home					
	Yes		No		Total	
	Count	Column %	Count	Column %	Count	Column %
Yes	255	97.7%	119	97.5%	374	97.7%
No	6	2.3%	3	2.5%	9	2.3%
Total	261	100.0%	122	100.0%	383	100.0%

Table 16

Access to Electricity with Belief in Supernatural (Ghost)

Do you believe in ghost?	Electricity at home					
	Yes		No		Total	
	Count	Column %	Count	Column %	Count	Column %
Yes	86	33.0%	41	33.6%	127	33.2%
No	175	67.0%	81	66.4%	256	66.8%
Total	261	100.0%	122	100.0%	383	100.0%

As far as the information in Table 16 is concerned, apparently there is no relationship between accesses to electricity and belief in ghost. Availability of a modern amenity itself is no guarantee against removal of superstitious beliefs. Presence of modern technology is not in itself may be a contributing factor for changes in beliefs and attitudes.

Table 17

Access to Electricity with Sighting of Ghost

Have you ever seen ghost?	Electricity at home					
	Yes		No		Total	
	Count	Column %	Count	Column %	Count	Column %
Yes	17	6.5%	5	4.1%	22	5.7%
No	244	93.5%	117	95.9%	361	94.3%
Total	261	100.0%	122	100.0%	383	100.0%

Table 18

Access to Electricity with Health Seeking Behaviour

What type of treatment do you choose?	Electricity at home					
	Yes		No		Total	
	Count	Column %	Count	Column %	Count	Column %
Allopath	208	80.9%	104	85.2%	312	82.3%
Homeopathic	48	18.7%	17	13.9%	65	17.2%
Exorcist	1	0.4%	1	0.8%	2	0.5%
Total	257	100.0%	122	100.0%	379	100.0%

One may consider the nature of health seeking behaviour as an indicator of one's belief in and a favourable disposition towards science. Modern, rational people are inclined to trust medicine based on scientific tests. This is not to say that modern society does not accommodate homeopathy or herbal medicines which are often treated as alternative medicine and considered as parts of holistic medicine. These alternatives are not treated as substitutes of modern medicine. In any case, in Bangladesh availability of electricity, which is an indicator of socio-economic status and thus exposure to modernity, does not seem to have any relationship with health seeking behaviour. Those who have access to electricity and those who do not have show similarity in health seeking behaviour.

Table 19

Access to Television with Future Orientation

Do you think of your future?	*Television at home*					
	Yes		*No*		*Total*	
	Count	*Column %*	*Count*	*Column %*	*Count*	*Column %*
Yes	175	97.8%	199	97.5%	374	97.7%
No	4	2.2%	5	2.5%	9	2.3%
Total	179	100.0%	204	100.0%	383	100.0%

Majority of the respondents in our study do not have television at home. This does not mean that they are not exposed to television. It is a common practice for many to go their neighbours' house to watch popular television shows in the rural areas of Bangladesh. Again having a television at home is not a factor in determining one's future orientation. An overwhelming majority of our respondents have future orientations. Whether they have television at home or not has almost no impact in this regard.

In the focus group discussion, a majority of the participants spoke against the adverse impact of mobile phone on the rural society. Many complained that it is eroding the moral values in the rural society. Illicit relationships are on the rise due to the wider availability of mobile phones.

Table 20

Access to Television with Belief in Supernatural

Do you believe in ghost?	*Television at home*					
	Yes		*No*		*Total*	
	Count	*Column %*	*Count*	*Column %*	*Count*	*Column %*
Yes	56	31.3%	71	34.8%	127	33.2%
No	123	68.7%	133	65.2%	256	66.8%
Total	179	100.0%	204	100.0%	383	100.0%

Table 21

Access to Television with Health Seeking Behaviour

What treatment do you choose?	*Television at home*					
	Yes		*No*		*Total*	
	Count	*Column %*	*Count*	*Column %*	*Count*	*Column %*
Allopath	144	80.9%	168	83.6%	312	82.3%
Homeopathic	34	19.1%	31	15.4%	65	17.2%
Exorcist	0	0.0%	2	1.0%	2	0.5%
Total	178	100.0%	201	100.0%	379	100.0%

Table 22

Access to Mobile Phone with Future Orientation

Do you think of your future?	*Do you have access to mobile phone*					
	Yes		*No*		*Total*	
	Count	*Column %*	*Count*	*Column %*	*Count*	*Column %*
Yes	270	98.2%	104	96.3%	374	97.7%
No	5	1.8%	4	3.7%	9	2.3%
Total	275	100.0%	108	100.0%	383	100.0%

Table 23

Access to Mobile Phone with Belief in Ghost

Do you believe in ghost?	*Have any mobile phone*					
	Yes		*No*		*Total*	
	Count	*Column %*	*Count*	*Column %*	*Count*	*Column %*
Yes	86	31.3%	41	38.0%	127	33.2%
No	189	68.7%	67	62.0%	256	66.8%
Total	275	100.0%	108	100.0%	383	100.0%

Table 24

Access to Mobile Phone with Health Seeking Behaviour

What treatment do you choose?	*Have any mobile phone*					
	Yes		*No*		*Total*	
	Count	*Column %*	*Count*	*Column %*	*Count*	*Column %*
Allopath	227	83.8%	85	78.7%	312	82.3%
Homeopathic	43	15.9%	22	20.4%	65	17.2%
Exorcist	1	0.4%	1	0.9%	2	0.5%
Total	271	100.0%	108	100.0%	379	100.0%

While some spoke in favour of television highlighting the educational programmes even mentioned National Geographic programmes, others were quick to point out the role of Dish Television that beam Bollywood movies, dance and music which attracts the young viewers. These television shows are offered in the tea-stalls in the villages. Some village elders and community leaders blamed such influence of television for the educational decline in the village. Students spend an inordinate amount of time watching television and do not study.

Social Values

A great majority of the respondents put religion as one of their most preferred values while asked to identify things they valued most. It came second to income and above family.

Table 25

Factor Considered Most Important by the Respondents

Factor	*N*	*Degree of importance*							
		Very important		*Rather important*		*Not very important*		*Not at all important*	
		Count	*Row %*	*Count*	*Row %*	*Count*	*Row %*	*Count*	*Row %*
Income	383	379	99.0%	2	0.5%	0	0.0%	2	0.5%
Religion	383	370	96.6%	13	3.4%	0	0.0%	0	0.0%
Family	383	365	95.3%	18	4.7%	0	0.0%	0	0.0%
Work	383	315	82.2%	68	17.8%	0	0.0%	0	0.0%
Education plan for son	383	309	80.7%	73	19.1%	1	0.3%	0	0.0%
Education plan for daughter	383	278	72.6%	101	26.4%	2	0.5%	2	0.5%
Health	383	257	67.1%	94	24.5%	32	8.4%	0	0.0%
Neighbour	383	120	31.3%	242	63.2%	21	5.5%	0	0.0%
Leisure period	383	60	15.7%	221	57.7%	67	17.5%	35	9.1%
Politics	383	7	1.8%	49	12.8%	83	21.7%	244	63.7%

Table 26

Freedom and Choice versus Absence of Freedom and Choice

Educational qualification of the respondent	*N*	*How much freedom of choice and control you feel you have over the way of your life*			
		Not at all		*Various degrees to 'A great deal of freedom'*	
		Count	*Row %*	*Count*	*Row %*
No education	193	21	10.9%	172	89.1%
Non-formal education and incomplete primary	66	9	13.6%	57	86.4%
Complete primary school	52	6	11.5%	46	88.5%
Incomplete secondary school	61	8	13.1%	53	86.9%
Post-secondary education	11	1	9.1%	10	90.9%
Total	383	45	11.7%	338	88.3%

One of the standard questions asked in various surveys measuring modernity, especially in the World Values Survey is the question of freedom versus lack of freedom. Freedom is viewed as freedom of choice of the individuals. So in our survey, we also asked the same question: 'Some people feel they have complete freedom of choice and control over their lives, while other people feel that what they do has no real effect on what happens to them. Please use this scale where 1 means 'no choice at all' and 10 means 'a great deal of choice' to indicate how much freedom of choice and control you feel you have over the way your life turns out to be.

Tolerance

On a question of who would they like to have their neighbours from a list of groups they responded as follows:

Table 27

Tolerance of the Respondents

Type of People	*N*	*Level of Tolerance*			
		No Problem		*Do Not Like*	
		Count	*Row %*	*Count*	*Row %*
People of other religion	383	255	66.6%	128	33.4%
Political leaders	383	193	50.4%	190	49.6%
People who have AIDS	382	87	22.7%	295	77.0%
People who are not religious	383	86	22.5%	297	77.5%
People who keep the environment dirty	383	40	10.4%	343	89.6%
Men who beat their wife	383	2	0.5%	381	99.5%
Thieves	383	0	0.0%	383	100.0%

Fatalism

When asked about fatalism, vast majority of the respondents did not agree with determinism of life by fate. However, while they were asked about the role of fate versus their own action in determining their future, the vast majority chose their own action.

Question was asked using the following: 'Some people believe that individuals can decide their own destiny, while others think that it is impossible to escape on which 1 means 'everything in life is determined by fate' and 10 means that 'people shape their fate themselves'.

Table 28

Fate is Pre-Determined versus Individual Shaping her Destiny

'Everything in life is determined by fate', or 'people shape their fate themselves'					
Fate is predetermined		*People shape their fate themselves*		*Total*	
Count	*Row %*	*Count*	*Row %*	*Count*	*Row %*
163	42.6%	220	57.4%	383	100.0%

Table 29

Fate is Pre-Determined versus Individual Shaping her Destiny by Microcredit Exposure

Type of Respondent	*N*	*'Everything in life is determined by fate, or 'people shape their fate themselves'*			
		Fate is predetermined		*people shape their own fate*	
		Count	*Row %*	*Count*	*Row %*
Micro credit borrower	349	150	43.0%	199	57.0%
Micro credit non-borrower	34	13	38.2%	21	61.8%
Total	383	163	42.6%	220	57.4%

Secular Values

A number of questions were asked about religious positions of the respondents. Although secularism is a huge topic some indicators of secularist tendencies may be captured in the following tables.

To the question: 'Those who do not believe in Allah (God), are not eligible for leadership position in society' the answers were following:

Table 30

Religiosity of the Political or Community Leaders

Degree of Agreement	*Micro Credit Borrower*		*Non Borrower*	
	Count	*%*	*Count*	*%*
Strongly agree	42	12.0%	2	5.9%
Agree	236	67.6%	24	70.6%
Neither agree nor disagree	10	2.9%	1	2.9%
Disagree	61	17.5%	7	20.6%
Strongly disagree	0	0.0%	0	0.0%

While religious in their beliefs, the rural women respondents in the study do not approve meddling of religious leaders in politics.

Religious leaders should not influence voters during the time of elections. The specific question was: 'Religious leaders should or should not influence the people while votes are being taken?'

Table 31

Political Role of the Religious Leaders (Ulemas, Moulavis, etc.)

Degree of Agreement	*Micro Credit Borrower*		*Non Borrower*	
	Count	*%*	*Count*	*%*
Strongly agree	30	8.6%	2	5.9%
Agree	216	61.9%	21	61.8%
Neither agree nor disagree	83	23.8%	8	23.5%
Disagree	19	5.4%	3	8.8%
Strongly disagree	0	.0%	0	.0%
Don't understand	1	.3%	0	.0%

To the question, 'It will be harmful or not for society if the leaders are zealots (religious extremists)?' the following answers were given.

Table 32

Religious Extremism and Politics

Degree of Agreement	*Micro Credit Borrower*		*Non Borrower*	
	Count	*%*	*Count*	*%*
Strongly agree	69	19.8%	4	11.8%
Agree	186	53.3%	24	70.6%
Neither agree nor disagree	79	22.6%	5	14.7%
Disagree	15	4.3%	1	2.9%
Strongly disagree Don't understand	0	0.0%	0	0.0%

Question was phrased: 'Since God has given us the stomach, He would also fill it Himself.' Respondents were given choices ranging from full agreement to complete disagreement.

Table 33

Divine Intervention versus Self-help

Level of Opinion	*Micro Credit Borrower*		*Non Borrower*		*Total*	
	Count	*%*	*Count*	*%*	*Count*	*%*
Fully agree	47	13.5%	5	14.7%	52	13.6%
Somewhat agree	165	47.3%	13	38.2%	178	46.5%
Disagree	115	33.0%	14	41.2%	129	33.7%
Fully disagree	13	3.7%	2	5.9%	15	3.9%
Don't know	9	2.6%	0	0.0%	9	2.3%

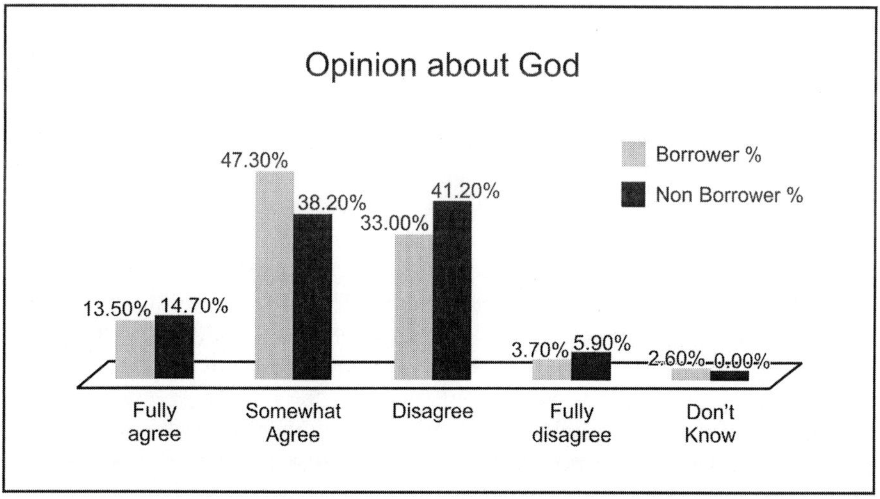

This is interesting because at a fundamental level, the respondents are expressing some doubt about the power of the almighty God. Nearly 40 per cent of the respondents have doubts about God's ability to satisfy our needs and by implication suggesting that one should take responsibility for one's own desire, and conduct and not expect a divine intervention.

Conclusions

In view of the framework and dimensions of individual modernity provided, it is quite clear that most respondents were experiencing changes in their world views under the rubric of individual modernity. The main findings of this paper are that women in rural Bangladesh are undergoing noticeable changes. They have achieved a great deal of individual modernity irrespective of their educational level and direct exposure to microcredits. Rural women are conscious of their overall circumstances, with views and opinions about the problems that impede social and economic changes of their communities and what is to be done. The problems they identify are similar to the problems that public intellectuals and researchers point out. They remain strong in their religious beliefs, yet they do not approve of religious interference in politics. They are in favour of women gaining more opportunities and power in public life.

It would be difficult to attribute all these positive changes to the micro-lending of microfinance institutions alone. Yet, it would be fair to say, that microcredits among other interventions of the government and NGOs have played a transformative role in the values and attitudes of rural women. They have become more confident and articulate. Their perceptions and attitudes in many respects are comparable to those in other South-East Asian countries. In the western development experience, changes in values and attitudes often emerged due to educational revolutions. Therefore, sociologists often identified education as the single most important factor in ushering in modernity. In the experience of the People's Republic of China, social mobilisation under the leadership of the Communist Party played the role. In Bangladesh, NGOs (MFIs included) seem to have played the role. In every focus group discussion, the participants mentioned BRAC and Grameen Bank in the same breath alongside government as they discussed changes in their communities due to interventions of NGOs and government.

It was also observed that the respondents were very aware of the problems affected their everyday life and they were emphatic about the lack of proper governance, red tape in the bureaucracy and dishonesty of the government officials. There was very low level of trust between the citizens and the government. They did not see the public officials as benefactors of society. Their suspicion has firm basis in reality. In focus group discussions, they repeatedly pointed out that the doctors at the rural clinics and hospitals were often absent or would come and go without providing services. They would demand fees although these were supposedly free clinics. Some respondents highlighted the importance of establishing local industries for creation of employment for village women. It was striking to see that they were more concerned about their employment and income and not necessarily dependent on either the income of their men folks or government subsidy. The focus on self-reliance was clearly evident.

In our focus group discussion, we found that our participants, comprising community leaders, NGO activists, schoolteachers, and the common people who were ready to share their opinions, articulated a clear understanding of the major issues affecting the development of Bangladesh. During our discussion, some of them highlighted the negative side of the NGOs, often a rehash of the left-leaning critique suggesting that NGOs were 'the agents of the western (imperialist) powers'. Some respondents pointed out the heavy-handed approach of some of the microfinance institutions (MFIs) in collecting their outstanding loans. Majority of our respondents in the focus-group discussions, in the end, recognised the overall positive contributions of the NGOs. They singled out the positive role of the MFIs in bringing about social changes in rural Bangladesh by making it possible for women to come out of their household roles into public domains. They also recognised that it was not the failure of the MFIs rather the failings of some individual borrowers who misuse the funds that bring misfortune to them and in the process tarnish the image of the Microfinance institutions. The ultimate responsibility lies with the individuals. Some of them used the loan for personal consumptions and even indulgences such as gambling; others made productive use of the funds to change their situation. In our in-depth interviews, we probed some of the cases of loan-default and the circumstances that led to it. Sometimes extreme poverty and vulnerability were causes of loan-default. It was the lack of social safety net and the extremely vulnerable existence that changed the lives of some villagers from poverty to destitution with a minimum shock, say, an illness in the family or a theft of their means of income.

Changes in the values and behaviours are of utmost importance for sustainable economic growth in Bangladesh. In the end, it is not just economic growth that should be the only concern of the policy makers and development experts. The key issue is to create an enabling environment for the people to grow by realising their own potential. The shifts in the development thinking from a narrow measurement of per capita income and other growth indicators and social conditions that help flourish the citizens despite the difficult circumstances they encounter.

References

Amin, S. (1974). *Accumulation on a World Scale: A Critique of the Theories of Underdevelopment*, New York: Monthly Review Press.

Baluja, K.F. (2003). *Gender Roles at Home and Abroad*, New York: LFB Scholarly Publications.

Barriteau, E. (2001). *The Political Economy of Gender in the Twentieth Century Carribean,* UK: Palgrave, Macmillan.

Broaded, C.M. Cao Z, and Inkeles, A (1994). 'Woman, Man and Construction of Individual Modernity Scales in China' *Cross-Cultural Research.* 28 pp. 251–286.

Cardoso, F.H. (1977). 'The Consumption of Dependency Theory in the United States', *Latin American Research Review*, 12 (9), pp. 135–176.

Cardoso, F.H. and Faletto, E. (1979). *Dependency and Development in Latin America*, Berkeley: University of California Press.

Frank, A.G. (1966). 'Development of Underdevelopment' *Monthly Review,* 18, pp. 17–30.

Gerschenkron, A. (1962). *Economic Backwardness in Historical Perspective: A Book of Essays*. Cambridge, MA: Belknap Press of Harvard University Press.

Hausmann, Ricard, Tyson, Laura and Zahidi, Saadia (2010). *The Global Gender Gap Report, 2010*, Geneva: World Economic Forum.

Hoselitz, B (1952). 'Non-economic Barriers to Economic Development', *Economic Development and Cultural Change.* 1 (1). pp. 8–21.

Inglehart, R. and Baker, W.E. (2000). 'Modernization, Cultural Change and the Persistence of Traditional Values', *American Sociological Review*, 65 (1), pp. 19–51.

Inglehart, R. (2005). *World Values Survey of 2005.* Center for Social Research, University of Michigan.

Inglehart, R. (1997). *Modernization and Postmodernization: Cultural, Economic and Political Change in 43 Societie,* Princeton, New Jersey: Princeton University Press.

Inkeles, A. (1977). 'Understanding and Misunderstanding Individual Modernity', *Journal of Cross Cultural Psychology*. 8 (2) pp. 135–176.

Inkeles. A and Smith, D. (1966). *Becoming Modern*, Cambridge, MA: Harvard University Press.

Inkeles, A, Broaded, C.M. and Z. Cao. (1997). 'Causes and Consequences of Individual Modernity in China', *The China Journal,* No. 37, January pp. 31–59.

Kabeer, N and Stark, A. (ed.) (2008). *Global Perspectives on Gender Equality*, New York: Routledge.

Khandker, S. Khalily, B. and Khan, Z. (1995). *Grameen Bank: Performance and Sustainability,* Washington, D.C.: World Bank.

Khandker, S. (1998). *Fighting Poverty with Microcredit,* Oxford: Oxford University Press.

Khondker, H. (2009). 'Socio-economic Development and Gender Empowerment in the ASEAN region.' *Gender Perspectives, 1 (2)*, pp. 1–3.

Khondker, H. (2011). 'Globalization and Transformation of Gender Relations in Asia', in N. Genov (ed) *Global Trends and Regional Development*, New York: Routledge.

Landes, D. (1983). *Revolution in Time: Clocks and the Making of the Modern World,* Cambridge, MA: Harvard University Press.

Landes, D. (1998). *The Wealth and Poverty of the Nations,* Cambridge, MA: Harvard University Press.

Lindsay, L. (2005). *Gender Roles: A Sociological Perspective*, Upper Saddle River, New Jersey: Pearson Prentice Hall.

Mahmud, W. (2007). 'Pathways to Social Development in Bangladesh: Surprises and Challenges.' *Indian Journal of Human Development*, 2 (1) 2008. pp. 79–92.

Morduch, J. (1998). 'Does Microfinance Really Help the Poor? New Evidence from Flagship Program in Bangladesh', pdf document.

Mullainathan, S. (2007). 'Psychology and Development Economics' in P. Diamond and H. Varitiainen (eds) *Behavioral Economics and Its Applications*. Princeton, NJ.: Princeton University Press.

Nussbaum, M. (2001). *Women and Human Development: The Capabilities Approach,* New York: Cambridge University Press.

Nussbaum, M. and Sen, A. (ed.) (1993). *The Quality of Life*, New York: Oxford University Press.

Rahman, A. (1999). *Women and Microcredit in Rural Bangladesh*, Boulder, CO: West View Press.

Staveren, I van (2001). *The Feminist Economics of Trade,* New York: Routledge.

Smith, David and Inkeles, Alex and David H. Smith (1966). 'The OM Scale: A Comparative Socio-Psychological Measure of Individual Modernity' *Sociometry,* 29 (4), pp. 353–371.

Valenzuela, J.S. and Valenzuela, A. (1978). 'Modernization and Dependency: Alternative Perspectives in the Paper of Latin American Underdevelopment', *Comparative Politics*. 10 (4) pp. 535–557.

www.internetworldstats.com/asia.htm#bd (accessed on November 30, 2015).

Wahid, A.N.M. (ed.) (1993). *The Grameen Bank: Poverty Relief in Bangladesh*, Boulder, CO: West View Press.

Wallerstein, I. (1974). *The Modern World-Systems*. New York: Academic Press.

Weber, M. (1947). *The Theory of Social and Economic Organization,* London: Collier and Macmillan.

Weber, M. (1976). *The Protestant Ethic and the Spirit of Capitalism,* London: Allen and Unwin.

Yunus, M. (ed.) (1982). *Jorimon of Beltoil and Others: In Search of a Future,* Dhaka: *Grameen Bank Publication.*

21

Leisure, Social Capital and Life Turns in Deviant Youth

FABIO MASSIMO LO VERDE

Three brief anecdotes, all coming from Sicilian common culture, clearly demonstrate how Sicilians picture their island. Two of them feature God and his relationship with Sicily, the third one concerns a cure for its problems.

The first tells about God deciding to play a bad-taste practical joke on someone. After having rotated his index finger in the air for several seconds he shouts 'You!', pointing his finger and deciding that this person will be born in Sicily.

God is also the protagonist of the second anecdote. After creating Sicily as an Eden-like land, he has to compensate for such an excessive perfection – so he creates Sicilians!

In the third tale an old man finally finds the remedy to Sicilian problems after unquantifiable meditation – the airplane! In fact there are many learned Sicilians who, having decided not to leave their land permanently by plane, remain in Sicily and assume a constantly laconic expression – sad or bad-humoured, annoyed or bitter – rarely happy. That is perhaps because they mix the heavy cultural load which they feel obliged to carry – and with which they collide – with the well known (at least in Italy) tendency to use the 'gattopardesque' categorisation of the supremacy of change to explain the static nature of Sicily.

In this brief note, I present a review of a quite important problem in the literature on the underdeveloped regions of Italy, that is the relation between leisure time and the construction of social capital. I also introduce a description of an ongoing research project about the 'turning points' (Laub and Samspson, 1993) in the biography of 40 Sicilian young adults (17–25 years old) who have decided to stop their deviant career as a consequence of a particular event (often an arrest), although in their social context it is more frequent that they continue this career. Can the young and intergenerational social capital built in leisure time be a barricade against deviant careers in Sicily too, like in other places of the world? Can this be a better solution than the airplane?

Leisure Time and Social Capital: A Short Review

Most of the literature on the creation of social capital within leisure time contexts refers to a notion of social capital in terms of 'relational goods' (Arai and Pedlar, 1997; Blackshaw and Long, 2005; Hemingway, 1999); such studies focus both on the availability of leisure time among people belonging to different social groups and on the relation between the amount of leisure time, its allocation and the construction of social capital in the community by means of the activities people do during such time (Rohe, 2004).

In a specific research dealing with the relevance of *leisure* within the literature on social capital, Glover and Hemingway (2005) – while criticising the insufficient attention Leisure Studies have paid to the concept of social capital – show how the study of the definitions and the practices of leisure, combined with the patterns of social capital construction, can contribute to bring to light some important aspects of contemporary sociality.

On the other side, one of the major scholar on *leisure*, Chris Rojek, states, 'Concretely, leisure is one of the main institutions which make it possible to accumulate social capital (2007: 324), since it is during this time and in its contexts that reciprocity dynamics can be activated, so supporting the strengthening of social ties and the improvement of community welfare' (ibid., see also Arai and Pedlar, 1997).

Such topic has also been widely treated by one of the best known works on social capital and its 'decline' in the United States (Putnam, 2004), which shows how sport associations and leagues – particularly those in the field of bowling – are an important context for supporting social cohesion. Rather than considering leisure time as a secondary field of social life or as a variable depending on other institutional fields of society, such as work, family, etc. Putnam considers leisure time as a field where the basis of the voluntary tendency to form associations and the subsequent social cohesion can be founded. In addition, leisure time is important not only in terms of recreation time, but also in terms of time dedicated to those forms of social exchange which support the construction of stronger ties and norms, shared values, opinions and statements on the world; moreover, Putnam argues that the disposition toward a 'lonely' consumption of free time is one of the causes of the 'erosion' of social capital in the industrialised societies.

This argument is supported also by other researchers (Hamermesh, 1999, 2000; Gershuny, 2000; Reyes-Garcia et al., 2008), who show that this trend of lonely consumption is raising in the developed societies. On the other hand, even in archaic societies there seems not to be a positive relation between the lonely consumption of leisure activities and well-being perceived in terms of satisfaction and good life quality (Reyes-Garcia et al., 2008: 4 and foll.). In fact, the research just mentioned proposes an estimation of the relation between well-being and the two ways of leisure time consumption, i.e. lonely and social, and shows how the latter in particular is able to jointly generate social capital and happiness.

After their analysis of the literature on the relation existing between social capital and leisure time, Glover and Hemingway (2005) argue that a notion of social capital as an extension of the individual involvement into formal and organised social structures, as well as informal associations[1] – where matters of high 'civic' content are treated – can be more easily found within leisure studies. In other words, it is within leisure studies that the second meaning of the concept of social capital – i.e. the 'civic' meaning – seems to prevail on the meaning of social capital as a structure of the resources, information, support, etc. that can be acquired through the individual participation in a social network.

Referring to this second meaning, Hemingway (1999), for instance, suggests that the amount of social capital that can be generated within leisure time is a function of the kind of leisure activities where the individuals are involved, and of the kind of leisure supply existing in different societies. Obviously, this fact influences the different forms of citizenship that can be generated (ibid., 154–61) and the subsequent forms of democracy and participation. Somehow this phenomenon would be related to the level of individual independence observed in the creation of a personal leisure rather than in a simple 'consumption' practice, and this fact would originate a wider possibility to increase individual 'capabilities', as Amartya Sen would say, and favour the creation and reproduction of social capital (Glover and Hemingway, 2005: 395). As the two scholars say, 'The question is not if leisure is associated with civically relevant social capital, but what kind of leisure in what kind of setting [...]' (ibid.). Therefore, Glover and Hemingway conclude that it seems obvious that leisure activities can help to increase and/or maintain social capital, but there can also be consumption practices that reduce rather than increase it, including several forms of passive leisure carried out especially through individual practices, as I argued elsewhere (Lo Verde, 2009; Dioguardi and Lo Verde, 2009).

In another study based on the data emerging from an English national survey[2] – which studied to what extent a greater consumption and variety of leisure activities could generate social capital – Warde and Tampubolon (2002: 163 and foll.) show the existence of a connection between the variety of leisure activities and the formal participation in membership groups, in the sense that the number of leisure activities seems to increase as the involvement in associative activities increases, including, of course, those activities directed towards the management of leisure services (sports clubs, recreation clubs, etc.)

As the authors argue, according to a view à la Putnam, the involvement in fun activities and hobbies seems to increase as individual social capital increases, even if the variation in the growth of such activities is positively related to education qualifications. People who are members of formal associations spend less time for each activity, since the number of the activities is greater; however, on the other hand, such people show high level of involvement, for instance, in terms of how frequently each activity is done. In addition, the growth of public and civic participation seems to be associated with the growth of the recreational activities practiced in private settings (ibid.: 166). According to these two authors, this would seem to disconfirm the theory by Hirschman (1983) that consumption and political activism are often conflicting. On the other hand, if we accept the theory that the total volume of participation in associations is strongly correlated with political activism, it would seem that whoever is politically active is simultaneously strongly involved in various forms of recreational activities. In the same study, Ward and Tampubolon analyse the relationship between friendship networks and the types of recreational activities practiced.

According to this research people who are members of caregiver associations tend to have a tendency to share different friends from themselves in terms of leisure choice, lifestyles and so on. As Ward and Tampubolon argue, 'This might imply that people take some notice of the classic agony aunt recommendation that if you are lonely or sad, and haven't got many friends, then join a club'. (ibid.: 169). However, people who generally have very different friends would also tend to have fewer friends. But this fact would reduce the participation in formal groups, far from the reverse situation. Relating to leisure, one is likely to decide to take part in formal groups if he/she cannot share activities with his/her friends. But it could also be plausible the reverse argument that the associations include very different people, in terms of age, gender, educational qualifications, etc. and this fact would consequently facilitate their mixing with other people who differ by nature.

According to the researchers there is no connection between all these things and the presence of social capital, since the embedding into friendship-based networks would seem to have weak effects on the participation in the activities within associations and, consequently, on a particular dimension of social capital, the civic one. In fact, the distance among friends is more sensitive to the number of activities that one can do than it is to their frequency. In other words, if one has friends who are so much like him/her, he/she will probably prefer to do more types of activities – perhaps because he/she shares them with such friends – than doing the same activity more frequently.

Social Capital and Leisure Time Among Young People

Our research question is how social capital among young people can be generated and, moreover, how it can be developed or eroded through their leisure activities.

Scholars point out that adults and policy makers usually consider leisure time among young people as an 'empty' time, and consequently – however without ever specifying this connection – as risky both for themselves and the adults they live within different communities. Equally often scholars argue that leisure time is important in the organisation and life of the community.

On the one hand, there are other studies focusing on youth participation in activities that can generate social capital, civic-mindedness, etc. (McFarland and Thomas, 2006; Helve and Bynner, 2007, Holland, 2009)[3] – such as activities like participation in voluntary associations. Also international organisations recognise the importance of leisure time in the development of communities (United Nations, 2004: 214ss.); on the other hand, however, little research has been carried out so far about the connection between the activities done by young people in their leisure time and the construction of trust networks that are fundamental for generating social capital. Mainstream studies predominantly deal with the lack of social capital and the relation between such lack and the diffusion of deviant behaviours (Mahoney, Stattin, 2000; Deuchar, 2009) or criminal ones (Hagan and McCarthy, 1997).

As some studies show, the analysis of how social capital can be generated among young people is important since those who participate in youth groups – and thus tend to generate a specific form of social capital – are more likely to maintain this practice in adulthood too. In addition, high levels of social trust among adults are positively correlated to high levels of social trust during their teen years (Stolle and Hooghe, 2004: 431). Briefly, according to Vesely (2006), the study of social capital among young people represents a 'window on the future' of societies, in spite of the problem of the low 'levels of stability' in the transition from one generation to another.

Finally there is a great amount of research on a particular kind of youth free/leisure time that can be defined as 'antisocial'. Such research includes, for instance, the studies dealing with the different kinds of gambling played by teenagers and young adults, or the 'normalisation' of drugs consumption (Parker, 1998; Griffiths, 1995). In general, these studies consider leisure time as a 'dangerous time', partially or entirely beyond the adults' control, with a high level of risk that young people may enter/stay in deviant groups, so generating deviant or illegal leisure (Rojek, 1999) rather than forms of pro-sociality coping.

One of these studies (Mahoney and Stattin, 2000) shows that the involvement of teenagers and young adults in 'more structured' activities[4] as well as the presence of an adult as a leader (coach, trainer, etc.) were negatively correlated to antisocial behaviours; whereas 'less structured' activities – such as joining youth community centres or watching television – were positively correlated to antisocial activities. In addition, adults who had taken part in less structured activities during their youth used to choose deviant individuals as their friends, have difficult emotional ties with their parents and get a lower support to their activities from operators (ibid.: 114ss).

Focusing on a 'criminological' view, Caldwell and Smith (2006: 399) have recently classified the studies about the relation between leisure and youth deviant careers into four lines of research:

(a) A line considers free/leisure time as time 'to be filled'. Therefore the time that 'is filled' with 'pro-social' activities cannot be filled with deviant ones.

(b) Another line of research looks at free/leisure time as connected with activities done with a deviant peer group: some activities have higher chances of generating deviant behaviours or are typical of deviant subcultures; therefore it is important to identify the genesis of such activities, to analyse the context where they were generated, etc.

(c) A further line analyses leisure time in connection with a higher or lower level of 'structured' activities: the time dedicated to those activities that are less organised, informal or with no supervision by adults is more likely to provide the context for deviant behaviours, unlike the time spent in activities that are supervised by adults or are more structured. There are opposite views especially in this case. For instance, many scholars agree that unstructured activities let people, especially teenagers, experience new roles, ideas and behaviours, hence supporting their social identity formation (Kleiber, 1999) as well as the development of an autonomous transition process to adulthood.

(d) Finally, a line of research looks at the interaction between the individual and the environment as a paradigmatic element: to have self-control and share norms and conventional activities prevent from adopting deviant behaviours.

Anyhow, in spite of the unsystematic, often fragmented and sometimes contradictory nature of the studies on the contribution that leisure activities and contexts can offer to the construction of social capital and to networks of shelter pursuing precautionary or rehabilitating aims (Williams and Walker, 2006; Williams, 2009), the topics on such contribution are partially treated also with respect to the biographies of young people and teenagers who are at risk of social exclusion or who already live in marginal contexts or environments; therefore these topics are usually covered by a literature looking at the importance of institutional 'networks', and no-profit organisations that benefit from the state intervention towards some social classes[5] or that live within re-educational institutions for teenagers outlaws.

Beyond the problems existing in data survey and data capture procedures on the different leisure activities (Gershuny, 2000), the fact is that a different amount of time is spent on different activities that have a higher sociability nature and this situation can be considered as a consequence of the way free/leisure time is institutionalised within different cultures. Nowadays such way is partially function of the supply, especially the supply of places and contexts for leisure time provided by the public sector, which is less and less capable of 'competing with' a private sector that tends to produce leisure services and goods to be experienced by single individuals in private places (Lo Verde, 2009).

As a temporary conclusion, it can be argued that leisure time can possibly be, under specific conditions, an important locus for social capital generation within peer groups and young adults. Togetherness and peer complicity, although more in a bonding rather than a bridging way, can be a supportive and relational resource for young individuals. Is it possible 'to trigger' life-turning decision in deviant young adults who spend their leisure time in occasional/frequent illegal practices? And how can this leisure time be turned from illegality to the construction of social integration?

In our still ongoing research we have focussed on two concepts, discontinuity and reflexivity, following Archer's typology of reflexivity (Archer, 2003). We want to know how the social relation system may contribute to a decision of discontinuity and what role reflexivity plays in this decision. We have interviewed 40 young adults aged between 17 and 25 years, asking them to narrate their decision of life change to see whether this decision was somehow related to some specific form of reflexivity. Moreover, we have compared these interviews with the opinions of social workers and teachers as expressed during three focus groups. We are currently working on the analysis of the data collected through such interviews and focus groups. From a first superficial analysis, there seems to be evidence that leisure time is a problematic dimension for these young adults (how and where to spend it, with whom, for how long, and so on). There also seems to be evidence that structured activities, daily engagements, the presence of an adult 'coach' or 'leader' or 'guide', the shifts or 'fractures' with the usual daily social context, may contribute to the reduction of the time spent in illegal leisure practices. Interestingly, this kind of evidence seems to bring Sicilian young adults much nearer to other global cities' young adults in the world. There is indeed room for new general hypotheses and research about leisure time, social capital and deviant young adults.

Notes

1. Among such informal associations the two scholars include the recent network of online discussion groups.
2. This survey is the *British Household Panel Survey* started in 1991.
3. About Italy see Bettin Lattes, 2001; Prandini, Melli, 2004, Cesareo, 2003, 2005; Donati, Colozzi, 1997; and IARD Reports (Buzzi, Cavalli e de Lillo, 1997, 2002, 2007).
4. The expression 'more structured activities' refers to those activities that need to be learned through socialization processes and that allow individuals to gain specific abilities, namely *serious leisure* activities (Stebbins, 2007; see also Caldwell, Smith, 2006: 402), such as the activities in the field of sport, music, art, handicraft, etc.
5. With reference to such interventions made in Italy, see Sanicola, Piscitelli, Mastropasqua (eds.), 2002.

References

Arai, S. and Pedlar, A. (1997). Building Communities Through Leisure: Citizen participation in a healthy communities initiative, *Journal of Leisure Research*, Vol. 29, No. 2, pp. 167–182.

Archer, M.S. (2003). *Structure, Agency and the Internal Conversation*, Cambridge: Cambridge University Press.

Bettin, Lattes G. (a cura di) (2001). *La politica acerba. Saggi sull'identità civica dei giovani*, Rubbettino: Soveria Mannelli (CZ).

Blackshaw T. and Long, J. (2005). What's the big idea? A critical exploration of the concept of social capital and its incorporation into leisure policy discourse, in *Leisure Studies*, Vol. 24, No. 3, pp. 239–258.

Buzzi, C., Cavalli A. De Lillo A. (a cura di) (2002). *Giovani del nuovo secolo. Quinto rapporto sulla condizione giovanile in Italia*, Bologna: Il Mulino.

Buzzi, C., Cavalli A. De Lillo A., (a cura di) (2007). *Rapporto giovani. Sesta indagine dell'Istituto IARD sulla condizione giovanile in Italia*, Bologna: Il Mulino.

Buzzi, C., Cavalli, A. De Lillo, A, (a cura di) (1997). *Giovani verso il Duemila. Quarto rapporto Iard sulla condizione giovanile in Italia*, Bologna, Il Mulino.

Caldwell, L.L. and Smith E.A. (2006). 'Leisure as a Context for Youth Development and Delinquency Prevention, in *Australian and New Zealand Journal of Criminology*, Vol. 39, No. 3, pp. 398–418.

Cesareo, V. (a cura di), *I protagonisti della società civile in Italia*, Rubbettino, Soveria Mannelli (Cs) 2003.

Cesareo, V. (a cura di), *Ricomporre la vita. Gli adulti giovani in Italia*, Carocci, Roma 2005.

Coleman, J.S. (1990). *Foundation of Social Theory*, Cambridge, MA: Harvard University Press.

Deuchar, R. (2009). *Gangs, Marginalised Youth and Social Capital*, London: Trentham Books.

Dioguardi, V. and Lo Verde F.M. (2009). Non solo 'quel che resta del giorno'. Un'analisi comparativa del consumo di tempo libero in Europa, in *Studi di Sociologia*, 4, pp. 345–381.

Donati, P. and Colozzi I. (a cura di) (1997). *Giovani e generazioni. Quando si cresce in una società eticamente neutra*, Bologna: Il Mulino.

Gershuny, J. (2000). *Changing Time: Work and Leisure in Post-industrial Society*, Oxford: Oxford University Press.

Glover, T.D. and Hemingway, J. (2005). 'Locating leisure in the social capital literature', in *Journal of Leisure Research*, Vol. 37, No. 4, pp. 387–401.

Griffiths, M. (1995). *Adolescent Gambling*, London: Routledge.

Hagan, J. and McCarthy B. (1997). *Mean Streets: Youth Crime and Homelessness*, New York: Cambridge University Press.

Hamermesh, D.S. (1999). *The Timing of Work Over Time*, in *The Economic Journal*, No. 109, pp. 37–66.

Helve, H. and Bynner J. (eds) (2007). *Youth and Social Capital*, London: Tufnell Press.

Hemingway, J. (1999). Leisure, Social Capital, and Democratic Citizenship, in *Journal of Leisure Research*, Vol. 31, No. 2, pp. 150–165.

Hirschman, A.O. (1983). *Felicità Privata, Felicità Pubblica*, Bologna: Il Mulino.

Holland, J. (2009). Young People and Social Capital: Use or Abuse, in *Young*, Vol. 17, No. 4, pp. 331–350.

Kleiber, D.A. (1999). *Leisure Experience and Human Development: A Dialectical Interpretation*, New York: Basic Books.

Laub, J.H. and Sampson R.J. (1993). Turning Points in the Life Course: Why Change Matters To The Study of Crime, in *Criminology*, Vol. 31, No. 3, pp. 301–325.

Lo Verde, F.M. (2009). *Sociologia del tempo libero*, Roma-Bari: Laterza.

Mahoney, J.L. and Stattin H. (2000). Leisure Activities and Adolescent Antisocial Behaviour: The Role of Structure and Social Context, in *Journal of Adolescence* No. 23, pp. 113–127.

McFarland, D.A. and Thomas, R.J. (2006). Bowling Young: How Youth Voluntary Associations Influence Adult Political Participation, in *American Sociological Review*, Vol. 71, No. 3, pp. 401–425.

Parker, H. (1998). *Illegal Leisure: The Normalization of Adolescent Recreational Drug Use*, London: Routledge.

Prandini, R. and Melli S. (2004). *I giovani e il capitale sociale dell'Europa futura*, Milano: Franco Angeli.

Putnam, R.D. (2004). *Capitale sociale e individualismo. Crisi e rinascita della cultura civica in America*, Bologna: Il Mulino.

Reyes-García, V., Godoy R., Vadez V., Ruíz-Mallén I., Huanca T., Leonard W., McDade T., Tanner S. (TAPS study Team), (2009). The Pay-offs to Sociality: Do Solitary and Social Leisure Relate to Happiness in Human Nature?. *An Interdisciplinary Journal with Biosocial Perspective*, Vol. 20, No. 4, pp. 431–446.

Roberts, K. (1983). *Youth and Leisure*, London: Allen & Unwin.

Rohe, W.M. (2004). 'Building Social Capital Through Community Development', in *Journal of the American Planning Association*, No. 70, pp. 143–144.

Rojek, C. (1999). *Deviant leisure: The Dark Side of Free-time Activity*, in Jackson E.L., Burton T.L. (eds.), *Leisure studies: Prospects for the twenty-first century*, Venture, State College PA, pp. 81–96.

Rojek, C. (2007). An Outline of the Action Approach to Leisure Studies, in Page S.J., Connell J. (eds.) (2007), *Leisure Studies*, London: Routledge, 4 Vol., Vol. I, pp. 321–335.

Sanicola, L., Piscitelli D., Mastropasqua I. (a cura di) (2002). *Metodologia di rete nella giustizia minorile*, Liguori, Napoli.

Stebbins, R.A. (2007). *Serious Leisure*, New Brunswick, New Jersey: Transaction Publisher.

Stolle, D. and Hooghe M. (2004). The Roots of Social Capital: Attitudinal and Network Mechanisms in the Relation between Youth and Adult Indicators of Social Capital, in *Acta Politica*, Vol. 39, No. 4, pp. 422–441.

Veselý, R. (2006). *Reproduction of Social Capital: How Much and What Type of Social Capital is Transmitted from Parents to Children?* Paper prepared for Trust, Reciprocity and Social Capital, The 2006 Ratio Colloquium for Young Social Scientists, Stockholm, August 25–26, 2006, publication in part in Ratio Working Papers No 105, from The Ratio Institute in http://econpapers.repec.org/paper/hhsratioi/0105.htm.

Warde, A. and Tampubolon G. (2002). 'Social Capital, Networks and Leisure Consumption, in *The Sociological Review*, Vol. 50, No. 2, pp. 155–180.

Williams, D.J. (2009). 'Deviant Leisure: Rethinking The Good, The Bad, and The Ugly', in *Leisure Sciences*, No. 31, 207–213.

Williams, D.J. and Walker, G.J. (2006). 'Leisure, Deviant Leisure, and Crime: Caution: Objects May Be Closer Than They Appear', in *Leisure/Loisir*, n. 30, pp. 193–218.

22

Leisure and Nishkam Karma

SHALINI MODI

One of the biggest dichotomies for students of 'leisure' is the distinction between work and leisure. For the layman, work refers to spending time and energy in pursuing a career in the hope of being better off in monetary terms or reputational reward. Alternatively, work is also done out of a sense of duty and obligation, for example housewives doing daily chores.

Comparatively, leisure suggests pursuing an activity of choice for the purposes of enrichment, without expectation of monetary gain or a sense of obligation.

This article contends that it is too simplistic to treat work and leisure as being two ends of the spectrum, or as being two unconnected and different concepts. One can as easily find work in leisure, as one can find leisure in work. This article focuses on the inter-connections between the two and how self-discovery is ultimately finding this state for oneself, transcending work and leisure as individual concepts.

There is also increasingly the pursuit of a mix between the two that has been coined as Serious Leisure by Stebbins (1982). He includes *Voluntarism* as part of Serious Leisure and reports enrichment and satisfaction as key takeaways for those who worked for the larger good of humanity. His research demonstrates that people who volunteered had great conviction in the cause for which they were working, albeit without money reward or award. So, they chose to do it in the spirit of leisure and with the seriousness of work.

The Bhagwad Gita is a handbook on how to live life consciously, mindfully and with awareness. It propounds the law of life that no one can remain inactive. It is in man's nature to work. Even as duty must be done according to one's circumstances and lineage, it suggests and extols that man should not be attached to the outcome of his actions. The sacred text cautions that the pursuit of work with the expectation of, and attachment to, outcomes leads to constant wavering of the happiness quotient. The battlefield discourse of Shri Krishna to Arjuna essentially spells out that the work performed without any expectation and attachment to rewards, provides freedom from the cycle of pleasure and pain. Alternatively, the text can be interpreted to be suggesting carrying out work in the spirit of leisure – Nishkam Karma (Action without expectation).

Maria Montessori, the first lady doctor from Italy, spent more than 50 years in researching the psychological development and needs of children across the world. She found that each child was unique and learnt at her own pace. Children learnt best when they worked towards their own development, without worrying about competing with others. From the moment a child was born, she worked incessantly to develop her body and mind, because she had a cosmic task to fulfil and become the person she was born to be!

Parent educator, Ruth Beaglehole, says that non-violent parenting, as opposed to parenting in the authoritarian style, though not an easy practice for parents, gives them the ultimate gift of truly seeing, hearing and knowing their children. It also gives parents the gift of truly seeing, hearing and knowing themselves. Given a safe and nurturing environment, children develop qualities of kindness, compassion, caring, generosity and experience the joy of growing and learning.

This essay reviews these apparently different teachings/propositions and seeks to find if the same philosophical thread underlies them all.

Leisure, Serious Leisure and *Nishkam Karma*

The definition of leisure suggests that there is a conscious choice in doing activities, which bring a sense of satisfaction, joy and enrichment. The motivation to do these activities is intrinsic and the doer is tireless and brimming with enthusiasm. Repetition of the activity brings perfection and therein lays its reward. It helps connect the doer to a spiritual source, which is a boundless ocean of *Advaita,* where dualities fade away and divinity is manifested.

Historical accounts refer to people spending their leisure time exploring and pursuing the arts and academia. There are references and instances of the State supporting talent, old and young, and the rulers taking pride in hosting and honouring the talented for their diverse crafts and acumen. Such recognition had the added benefit of inspiring the rest of the population to excel and realise their own potential, if not realise themselves.

The Romans and Greeks, or for that matter most ancient civilizations, appreciated people with special and unique skills and encouraged them to evolve their art forms. A famous lore is of King Akbar (16th century), who was a great lover of artists and intellectuals. His passion for knowledge and interest in learning from great minds attracted him to invite men of genius to his court. Nine of these courtiers were known as Akbar's *Navratanas* (Nine Jewels). One amongst them, in pride of place, was Tansena, the legendary musician. He was said to perform different ragas at different times of the day.

Kalidasa is widely regarded as the greatest poet and dramatist in Sanskrit language. He was one of the nine scholars who attended King Vikramaditya's court. His plays and poetry were primarily based on Hindu Puranas. Interestingly, and according to folklore, Kalidasa was not the most intelligent person to begin with, but was married to a bright princess. Challenged and humiliated by his intellectual wife, he studied poetry to become a poet. He will remain an example of one who out-did himself with sheer hard work, and proved his mettle.

Gurus were respected and *Gurukuls* were the centres of learning (akin to modern day universities), where children stayed and learnt life-skills. People went to great lengths to learn and develop their talents. The story of Eklavya, who sacrificed his thumb so that he could repay his teacher, is a story of pupil's extreme gratitude to his teacher, who did not even teach him directly. However, as the folklore goes, the pupil mastered the art of archery, by his relentless pursuit of excellence and by worshipping the Guru's statue. The stories of Arjuna and his Guru Dronacharya inspire children, students and sportspersons even today!

The satisfaction and enrichment from these higher values of life kept people less worried about commerce, trade and material wealth. There was less pressure 'to be', 'to reach' and 'to own' material and worldly good. The quest was for inner development and enrichment. Serious Leisure purports to similar principles where the motivation is intrinsic.

As time wore on, people started becoming more resourceful even as transportation by land and sea (and now air) became less challenging. Discoveries and innovations like the magnetic compass aided travel to far off lands and the more people saw, the more they seemed to want. Wars brought material wealth and wealth brought disparity. People had less and less time to appreciate beauty and art, as greed taught them to consume. They stopped seeking perfection in humanity and the beauty of simplicity. Technology and inter-connectedness only seemed to fuel desire, and not contentment.

People were busy trying to compete, and conflict took away most of the time that was earlier saved for leisure. Consumers became the new achievers. Comparisons egged everyone on to work more, display their images as larger than life, and conquer everything but their own need for self-gratification. The spirit of conflict and competition had its genesis in greed of wealth and power, so there was no peace of mind and salvation (Guru Rabindra Nath Tagore: *Spirituality and Human Values*).

Even as they had more and more, people felt lost and there was none of the peace that they had known before. Aggression and acquisition went hand in hand with development and brought with it industrialisation. Education for the masses meant there was little recognition of the individual's needs and unique talents, and assembly lines became the order of the day. Leisure changed meaning and reflection and introspection were more about outward issues than for dwelling within.

It was during India's fight for Independence that Mahatma Gandhi talked of *Nishkam Karma*. The British were displaying their greed to rule India and Gandhi decided to use non-violent resistance (*Satyagraha*) to halt them in their tracks. He galvanised people by motivating them to do their duty (*Swadharma*) and fight for their country's independence. The *Satyagrahi's* object was to convert, not coerce the wrong-doer (Gandhi: *Requisite Qualifications*, *Harijan* March 25, 1939).

He insisted that his people would not take revenge by resorting to violence. In his words: "I have also called it love-force or soul force. In the application of *Satyagraha*, I discovered in the early stages that pursuit of truth did not admit of violence being inflicted on one's opponent but that he must be weaned from error by patience and compassion. For what appears to be the truth to the one may appear to be error to the other. And patience means self-suffering. So the doctrine came to mean vindication of the truth, not by infliction of suffering on the opponent, but on oneself'.

His principled stand took the British by surprise. They had no idea how to respond and were at a loss. The entire country became united with the call of Quit India Movement, and people looked up to the Mahatma, who courageously stood for what he believed in. Freedom became their birthright. The courage to stand up to the British onslaught came from the absence of fear of loss, even as joy and satisfaction was intrinsic in performing their *Swadharma*. India may have been partitioned, but Mahatma Gandhi is still known and remembered as the 'Father of the Nation', essentially for espousing and practicing the means by which freedom was achieved.

Martin Luther King was also inspired by Gandhi's philosophy of non-violence. As he travelled throughout India for five weeks in early 1959, King reflected on the similarities and differences between India and the United States. He observed that although India was rife with poverty, overpopulation and unemployment, the country nonetheless had lower crime rates and stronger spiritual quality. In a radio address made on his last evening in India, King said: 'since being in India, I am more convinced than ever before that the method of non-violent resistance is the most potent weapon available to oppressed people in their struggle for justice and human dignity. In a real sense, Mahatma Gandhi embodied in his life certain universal principles that are inherent in the moral structure of the universe, and these principles are as inescapable as the law of gravitation' (Martin Luther King).

Nelson Mandela in South Africa and Aung San Suu Kyi in Burma, among others, have been strongly influenced by Gandhi's philosophy of non-violent resistance.

The *Bhagwad Gita's* emphasis on *selfless service* was a prime source of inspiration for Mohandas Karamchand Gandhi. The sun must shine and give warmth as that is its very nature, the river must flow, and similarly, fire must burn. If people do not want to receive the sun's warmth they have a choice to close their windows, but the sun continues to shine, fulfilling its duty. Interestingly, the sun does not shine because it needs the sunlight or the tree its shade. Human beings, too, cannot live without doing action (*Karma*). However, it is their choice to not be bound to the outcomes of their actions by having desires and attachment to their fruits.

> *'Karmanyevadhikaraste ma phalesu kadacana*
> *Ma karmaphalaheturbhurma te sango stvakarmani'*
>
> (Your right is in action only, never to the fruits; let not the fruit of your actions be not your motive nor let your attachment be to inaction.
>
> If you choose to remain idle, you putrefy and destroy yourself. Since you must act, perform the right action. You must learn to choose actions to fulfil your obligations and not merely to gain rewards and merit. Work for work's sake, knowing it will eventually take you to your ultimate goal. Work well accomplished is the joy of life.)

The Gita, Verse 47, Chapter 2

Gandhi said that whenever doubts haunted him and disappointments stared him in the face, and he did not see one ray of hope on the horizon, he turned to *Bhagwad Gita* and invariably found a verse to comfort him and put a smile on his face in the midst of overwhelming sorrow. 'Those who meditate on the *Gita* will derive fresh joy and new meanings from it every day.'

Today, with advancements in technology and globalisation making the world a really well connected place, Leisure has found place in people's lives again. With the time and inclination to read, explore, travel and connect, many avenues have opened up for new kinds of work, leisure and Serious Leisure.

Interestingly, the range of innovative thought and behaviour observed in leisure shows that it is the most fertile soil in modern society for the growth of new social and cultural forms. Serious Leisure is the systematic pursuit of deep satisfaction through an amateur, hobbyist or volunteer activity that participants find so substantial and interesting that, in the typical case, they launch themselves on a career centred on acquiring and expressing its special skills, knowledge and experience (Stebbins, 2001).

However, it is the volunteers, who willingly help others for a combination of personal and altruistic reasons. Volunteers, across the world, are working with tribal people, autistic children, the physically and mentally challenged, and in courts of law fighting for traumatised women and children from domestic strife. Students and adults look for opportunities, including travelling to less developed countries, to work for those less privileged, or to teach a language or sport to those teachers in institutes that do not have the wherewithal to get help professionally. People from all walks of life, especially young educated men and women join the 'Teach for India' movement. They spend two years of their lives' most productive years to be with under-privileged children and embellish their learning with joy so that they may not drop out of primary school. The same children could possibly become trailblazers as first generation learners. A lady, who went to a make-shift school for children at construction work-sites, reported how the children were keen to learn and said their ambition was to speak in fluent English like her.

Volunteers might invest their time and even money to make that little contribution to society. Planning, preparing, persevering consistently is part and parcel of their work so their successes and pitfalls don't weaken or harden them, but keep them passionate for the cause they work for.

> *'Tasmadasaktah satatam karyam karma samacara*
> *Asakto hyacarankarma paramapnoti purush'*
>
> (Therefore, always perform your actions (duties) without attachment to the fruit of your labour, and by doing so you reach the ultimate state of perfection.
>
> In this global world, leisure is multifaceted and varied. There are examples of people all who are working to better the lot of others and they are motivated by an inner force that drives them, making them persevere as if they would in a job. They are motivated from within and their reward is in the doing rather than in the fruits of their labour.)
>
> *The Gita*, Verse 19, Chapter 3

Serious Leisure, or more specifically, voluntarism, is something one chooses to do and persevere. One plans for it and puts in effort for a concerted period of time. Research shows that serious leisure contains its own disappointments and tensions, which the volunteer must deal with in some way (for summary see Stebbins). Interestingly, most volunteers experience self–enrichment, while other reported take-away is group accomplishment; followed by the twin rewards of self-enhancement and contribution to the maintenance and/or development of community.

To sharpen understanding of Serious Leisure, it is commonly contrasted with 'casual leisure' or 'un-serious' leisure, the immediately intrinsically rewarding, relatively short-lived pleasurable activity requiring little or no special training to enjoy it. These include play, relaxation, entertainment, sociable conversations and sensory stimulation. This is considerably less substantial and offers no career of the sort that can be pursued through serious leisure.

There are some philanthropists and generous people, the world over, who believe in working for the larger good and believe that by donating for the under-privileged, they are conduits and not doing a favour to anyone. True knowledge and conscious living are their *mantras*.

According to *The Gita*, this has always been a trend in our society.

'Karmanaiva hi samsiddhimasthita Janakadayah
Lokasangrahamevapi sampasyankartumarhasi'

(Just like the olden ruler, King Janaka who set an example by ruling his kingdom keeping in mind the larger good of the people, we should do our duties without any desire for recognition, fame or fortune.)

The Gita, Verse 20, Chapter 3

The Gita purports that it is man's innate nature to be happy and peaceful, and the only way to attain that is to work towards the benefit of the community (*lok-sangraha*). It has been argued that when people are engaged in serving the ignorant and suffering with love and compassion, one's own needs are lovingly and mystically taken care of by the Absolute.

Parenting, Childhood and *Nishkam Karma*

'The ability to say no to temptation comes from self-discipline or does self discipline come from saying no to temptation?'

Earlier there were few books or principles spelt out on how children could be parented. Everyone parented their children from their own experience. However, with changes in the family structure, emergence of nuclear families, migration to urban areas, working mothers and single child families, there has been felt need to re-look at parenting styles and what makes for holistic child development.

Many books have since been written on parenting, brain development and the parent's role in child development and in sculpting the child's brain. There are organisations that conduct weekly classes for parents and care-givers to emphasise the responsibility of their role and to understand child development. A whole host of daycare centres and individual crèches, with TV cameras to monitor, have come into vogue for those who can afford them.

The whole philosophy behind non-violent parenting is that a child should be treated with respect because he is an individual who has a mind of his own, which is very active and can think for itself. It talks about giving children choices. As per the tenets of non-violent parenting – rewards and punishments, bribes and shaming are said to be unnecessary, because the child is intrinsically motivated and dedicated to his own development (Ruth and Susan Beaglehole: *Non-violent Parenting*, 2008).

A group of feisty young women meet every week to take classes on being more aware parents. Their target audience is neighbourhood groups of mothers who can make time in the mornings when the children are at school. The group is now targeting corporate houses, private schools and even the local radio channels to broadcast their message to the public. All this is done for the love of the child and their commitment to make childhood joyful, possibly aided by the fact that some of them could not have it themselves.

As parents, we only have to believe in our children and be conscious role-models of the qualities we want them to assimilate. Amidst the lessons on empathetic communication, building inner discipline, emotional literacy, constructing the heart of the family, and setting limits, the underlying philosophy of parenting is to have no expectations from your children even as you continue to do your best for them. Once you have done your duty to the best of your ability, you have to let go.

To quote some lines from Kahlil Gibran (1961):

'Your children are not your children.
They are the sons and daughters of life's longing for itself…

You may give them your love but not your thoughts,
For they have their own thoughts…

You may strive to be like them, but seek not to make them like you.

For life goes not backward nor tarries with yesterday.
You are the bows from which your children like living arrows are sent forth…

For even as He loves the arrow that flies,
So He loves also the bow that is stable.'

The philosophy of *The Gita* talks of *Nishkam Karma,* which when performed with a relaxed and calm mind and with no hope of extrinsic reward, helps in alleviating sorrow and pain even in thought. Staying balanced and exploring age-old beliefs as part of social conditioning helps to attain the goal of being in a state of equipoise at all times (*Sthitpragya*).

A little child draws because he is driven by his need to express and not because he wants his mother's praise is a case in point. It is different that soon his mother's praise may limit him from outdoing what he has done earlier. *The Gita* clearly warns that reward and punishment are extrinsic motivators which give rise to more *kaam, krodh and lobh* (desire, anger and greed) and are therefore, best avoided.

The non-violent paradigm of parenting is based on unconditional love and is about nurturing a healthy relationship with the child. Non-violent parenting honours the connection with a child, respecting her core dignity as a full and complete person. This view insists on treating children not as disobedient children who need to be corrected, but as human beings who spend every minute of each day trying to meet their core, basic needs. The child's developing brain thrives with this emotional bonding, creating permanent positive effects on the brain's pathways and helping to develop the skills for creating and maintaining fulfilling life choices and relationships.

Violence is defined as more than physical abuse. It includes anything that hurts the heart, mind, body or spirit of a child. Violence includes corporal punishment no matter what it is called (a tap, swat, smack, spanking), emotional control techniques (the withdrawal of love, time-outs or forced rewarded isolation, shaming, threats and name calling), and manipulation (bribes, praise and rewards).

Parenting is all about reaching out and connecting. A child, who has experienced a responsive parent 'feel' for him, develops pathways over time that connects to the higher area of his brain. This is also known as the neo cortex, and it manages reason and rational thought, problem solving, creativity and imagination, kindness, empathy and concern.

> *'Yadyadacarati sresthastattadevetaro janah*
> *Sa yatpramanamkurute lokastadanuvartate'*
>
> (For the well-being of a state or institution or family, the head of that unit must lead the way. When the head works like a leader and sets an example people are encouraged and inspired to follow suit and even come to him for guidance.)
>
> *The Gita*, Verse 19, Chapter 3

Gandhian Principles and Montessori Philosophy

Maria Montessori met Mahatma Gandhi in London in October 1931. His practice of *Satyagraha* (non-violent resistance) had a profound influence on the development of Dr Maria Montessori's perspective on 'peace education'. He, in turn, was very happy that children so young were taught the virtue of silence in Montessori schools and wrote to Maria Montessori, requesting her to make her method of education available to children of the poor, in India, too!

She invited Gandhiji to Montessori Training College in London to speak where he said, 'You have very truly remarked that if we are to reach real peace in this world, we shall have to begin with children and if they grow up in their natural innocence, we won't have the struggle, we won't have to pass fruitless idle resolutions, but we shall go from love to love and peace to peace, which consciously or unconsciously, the whole world is hungering' (Gandhi: November 19, 1931).

Maria Montessori, in her understanding of the psychological development of the child, says that the unconscious powers in every child drive him from within to build himself up, reach out to others and help build a community of trust and brotherhood. Children brought up in a peaceful environment learn to appreciate others and themselves and realise their own inner potential.

The Gita echoes the same:

> *'Yogasthah kuru karmani sangam tyaktva Dhananjaya*
> *Siddyasisiddhyoh samo bhutva samatvam yoga ucyate'*

(Fix an ideal in life. An ideal envisages a noble cause, a common purpose, a higher goal beyond your personal likes and dislikes, the highest goal being self-realization. Pursue your goal without conclusion any attachment to the action or a craving for fruits thereof. You will then gain mental equanimity. Mental equipoise, balance and evenness of mind acquired through right action are yoga.)

The Gita, Verse 48, Chapter 2

This is what will lead and has so far led to social transformation! It talks of how we should do our best and not worry about the rest.

Conclusion

To conclude, happiness and peace and enrichment underlie the true spirit of Leisure, Serious Leisure, Parenting or educating children (as in the Montessori philosophy). The pursuit of *Nishkam Karma* becomes in itself a source of unending joy.

The lessons and conclusions are universal. Leisure adds life to years because the individual is doing something that they love to do and commit themselves to doing, without expectation of reward or recognition. It is about 'you' and choices 'you' make. *Bhagwad Gita's* core message is about doing your *Karma*, to the best of your abilities, without attachment and without expectation of fruits/outcomes. It essentially says that 'work in the spirit of leisure', and you shall be free from the cycle of pleasure and pain. Mahatma Gandhi talked of *Swadharma* and *Nishkam Karma* – as the way to achieve the purpose of life and to realise you. The underlying philosophy of Maria Montessori is that children *Love to Work*, for the sake of their own development, they want no rewards! They just want to reach perfection – they do this out of the joy of doing! The principles of Parenting – tell you to respect the child as an individual. It helps both the child and the parent in truly seeing, hearing, and knowing themselves.

Whatever *Karma* is done, it is done without any expectation of rewards. The detachment to awards and rewards makes every action a worship of the Divine. Once this is achieved, pleasure and pain become two sides of the same coin and man manifests his divinity in his equipoise (*Sthitpragya)*.

References

Gandhi, M.K. Requisite Qualifications, *Harijan,* March 25, 1939.

Gibran, K. (1961). *The Prophet.* New York: Alfred A. Knopf.

http://www.peace.ca/montessoriandgandhi.htm: Mahatma Gandhi meets Maria Montessori

http://peacemagazine.org/archive/v17n2p21.htm: The formative influences on Martin Luther King, Jr

King, M.E. (1999). *Mahatma Gandhi and Martin Luther King Jr: The Power of Nonviolent Action*. Paris: UNESCO.

Marshall B. Rosenberg, PhD. (2003). *Non Violent Communication,* A Language of Life.

Modi, Ishwar (ed.) (2000). *Human Values and Social Change*, Jaipur: Rawat.

Ruth Beaglehole and Susan Beaglehole Goldberg. (2008). *Non-Violent Parenting: A Parent Education Curriculum.*

Sinha, Dharmendra Mohan (2008). *Shrimad Bhagwad Gita – Jeevan Vigyan.*

Stebbins, R.A. (1982). 'Serious Leisure: A Conceptual Statement'. *Sociological Perspectives*, 25(2), pp. 251–272.

Stebbins, R.A. (2004). *Between Work and Leisure: The Common Ground of Two Separate Worlds,* New Burnswick: Transaction Publishers.

http://www.themontessoriplace.org.uk/011/message-from-mahatma-gandhi-to-maria-montessori/

Swami A. Parthasarathy. (2011). *The Complete Works including The Bhagwad Gita.*

23

Dialectics of Western Categories and Indigenous Understanding

Some Thoughts on Leisure

VINAY KUMAR SRIVASTAVA

The West has given us – the 'others', the communities of the developing world – the discipline of sociology, its concepts and analytical categories, its methods and the vagaries of thought. The result is that a long-drawn training in Western sociology hues the lenses of the non-Western sociologists. Becoming opaque to the nuances of the local reality, their own society, they start adjusting it to the typologies they have learned during their formal training, the tacit assumption being that the Western experience is the 'global experience'. What has happened in the West and what would happen therein in future is likely to occur in all parts of the world, although at different points in time. This was the summary of the evolutionary approach, and this was the underlying message of the famous speech that the former American President Harry Truman delivered in 1949 which inaugurated the idea of development in the international discourse. The West thought of converting the rest of the world in its cast. Erasing the differences that existed in different societies of the world was Western philanthropy; or the aid that came from the West for the non-Western world was believed to have the power to transform the latter in social and cultural terms as well.

The overwhelming impact of this thinking and training was that the concepts rooted in the Western experience were virtually imposed on alien contexts, often by the 'home scholars', the contexts on which they were imposed were their own, sometimes on their own initiatives, sometimes at the behest of their Western patrons, even if it was done with great unease and unconvincingly. By this the native researchers endeavoured to accomplish two objectives – they lent support to the idea of the universality of human experience notwithstanding the spatial and temporal contexts, and they also reposed confidence in the mighty scholarship of the Western scholars, and needless to say, also registered their loyalty to them, which of course over time was variously translated into tangible material gains, sometimes stupendous. The skein of this thought was often termed 'internationalism'; and it was preferred over any commitment to domestic scholarship or a dispassionate exploration of native ideas. This would explain why domestic journals received second-rate articles for publication as the best papers went to the foreign journals, or why brain-drain was justified and preferred.

Did the Western sociology expect an intellectual adulation from their non-Western counterparts? Perhaps not.

II

The story of the nineteenth century sociology, of classical evolutionism and apocalyptic theories, was different, for it tended to believe in the eventual homogenisation and merging of societies in a common whole. Differences would be wiped out in course of time, it was believed, for this would be the magic of evolution. If the nineteenth-century was the 'century of positivism', reinforcing an unshakeable belief in scientific methodology and the eventual levelling of the world, the early twentieth-century added cases on cases of societies and institutions vastly different from the West. Anthropologists studying them showed the function and the meaning of these practices, which also justified their existence, and also the fact that they had continued to exist even when the other parts of society were changing under the impact of colonialism. Against this backdrop, the protagonists of Western sociology expected to record the local perspectives on reality, that is a deviation from their views, which would eventually correct their understanding. This was expected to enrich the field of sociology; there would be, as a consequence, 'many sociologies', so to say, rather than one 'unified' picture of the discipline.

The twentieth-century Western sociologists wanted that to happen, for they knew of the enormous diversity of human society. They also knew the shortcomings of their perspective and anticipated that insights from other societies would provide viable alternatives. Intensively studying the simple societies in different parts of the world, anthropologists ably documented the ways of living in these societies that in many ways seemed to be, in terms of the value analysis, 'superior' to the Western ways of living. Just gauge the amazement of Sir E.B. Tylor, who said that in the Mexican countryside he had visited had no policemen, implying thereby that the society was free from any instance of criminality or any problem of law and order; or remember the work of Sir James Frazer who said that beliefs similar to those of the 'primitive people', which are described as bizarre, are found among the Europeans also, but there they are, rather paradoxically, not regarded as the signs of primitiveness. In this way, Sir James drew attention to the unity and similarity among human beings.

In fact, the studies of acculturation – which is invariably an asymmetrical process – showed that the contact of simple societies with the Western (or 'modern') in all cases was deleterious. Instead of appreciating the diverse ways of living, the outsiders ridiculed them, decimated their identity, forcibly imposed alien thoughts on them, mercilessly suppressed any opposition to their rule, and forced homogenisation of the cultures. However, anthropologists and sociologists stood by people, told the world the rationale of their practices, exposed the nefarious designs of the colonial rulers and the exploiters working at their behest, and in their own humble ways tried to protect the people's interests; and this was their unparallelled contribution to the triumph of plurality. Because of their pro-people stance, they were often the butt of anger of the rulers and the other powerful sections who wanted to usurp the local resources and convert the local populace into a battalion of serfs.

Thus, in a nutshell, after the decline of positivism and rebuttal of Victorian evolutionism, the Western sociologists were less confident about the ubiquitous application of their ideas, and welcomed alternative explanations based on the study of different societies. The native scholars also thought so, and so began the process of indigenisation, the aim of which was to privilege the local thoughts. The rise of the grounded theory method in sociology also placed 'research before theory', implying that the collection and understanding of facts would save one from the liability of the preexisting theories and the battery of the already given concepts. Although the intention was clear, some native scholars continued to apply the Western concept to understand the local reality, often with difficulty, often maneuvering the facts to suit the tenor of the theory. And this was an example of bad sociology.

III

Against the backdrop of these ideas, let us look at the concept of leisure. In many introductory texts in sociology, a chapter titled 'Work and Leisure' is invariably included, and the syllabuses in many universities often include a full paper on this topic. In these, however, as I have noticed, the concept of work receives larger attention than that of the leisure.

I remember, after my post-graduation in sociology (in 1976), I once sought an appointment with Professor André Béteille to discuss the research questions I thought I would like to pursue for my doctoral work. During discussion, Professor Béteille advised me to find an answer to the questions: 'Why in India people do not want to work?' and 'Why people consider work as onerous?'

It should not happen since the 'work' they did ensured their livelihood, their 'bread and butter'. Once out of work, their life chances were bound to be precariously thinned. Even when people knew this stark fact, they were still lax about work. A common observation about government offices those days was that the employees arrived late, spent double the time than what was earmarked for lunch, and during that time, they played cards or just slept on the floor of the office after having spread the leaves of newspapers, and left for home early, giving one lame excuse or the other to their superior staff. Female employees were infamous for bringing their knitting work, or popular magazines, to the office, and be devoted to those. Whilst the employees were in their seats, they abstained from carrying out quality work, or finishing the tasks for the day. No cajoling or threat by the superior staff or their clients would make them heed to work. Yes, ripples were joltingly produced when one of them was heavily reprimanded or put under suspension for being careless towards work. As a consequence, change would definitely be noticed in their degree of commitment, but all this would be grossly ephemeral. When people returned to their 'normal' schedule (which in fact is the 'dereliction of duty'), we would often say that it was because 'habits die hard'. We were so accustomed to this picture that when we found an employee working diligently, glued to his seat, we thought he was 'anomalous'.

'What is the meaning of work for these employees?' 'How "work culture" could be improved upon?' These were the additional questions enlisted in this research study. All through this discussion and later thinking, I was reminded of the hordes and hordes of employees playing cards in the circular parks near the Central Secretariat and in the park opposite the Department of Anthropology in the University of Delhi. For my research, fieldwork was expected to be conducted in a government office, spending hours and hours observing people at their work places.

What were the employees doing at their work places, where they were supposed to work but ironically were not working, or were unabashedly 'underperforming'? What was it if it was not work? What did these employees do in their houses, after the office hours were over and on holidays and vacations? Which concept should be used for the activities that were performed outside the 'work hours'? Could the word 'leisure' be used for them? The Western thought gave us the dichotomy of 'work' and 'leisure', and activities were defined simply by the method of elimination. When people were not working, they were at leisure; thus, the concepts of work and leisure were antithetically understood. I observed earlier that the concept of work received larger attention in comparison to that of leisure. Was it because the sociologists were less confident of the usage of the concept of leisure than work?

IV

The definition of the concept of work emerged out of the Western experience of industrialisation, where the work units were separated from the residences of the employees. Karl Marx provided a description of these units, which clearly pointed out that the earlier pattern of work (the feudal), where a handful of workers were attached to the farm of a lord, was changed with the emergence of these big units, because of which a large number of workers 'came under the same roof.' This was one of the reasons accounting for the emergence of a feeling of class consciousness among them. For the work they rendered, they were paid wages, and were free to leave the industry whenever they wanted. The employers were also free to terminate their workers, in some cases without assigning them a valid reason. The separation of the work place and residence went hand-in-hand with a decline in paternalistic ties between the lords and their vassals, the pattern found in feudal societies.

Work came to be defined in following terms and these parameters still continue: (1) it is an activity that takes place away from one's residence; (2) it is regulated by mechanical time and records; (3) for which the individual is paid in cash; and (4) the employment avenues and upward mobility of the workers are incumbent upon their levels of qualification and skill acquisition. Work schedule is time-bound; the individual is expected to work for a certain number of hours, and any deviation from this is monetarily evaluated. One loses wages when working for less hours and gains when one works 'overtime'. As industrialisation intensifies, the number of the self-employed workers is drastically reduced; Marx conveyed this idea using the expression: 'the big fish eats the small.' Such a situation further strengthens the concept of work as a wageful activity taking place away from residence.

What do people do after their work hours? When they are home, or on holidays, or when they are on vacation? The Western mode of thinking is of duality – if not *this*, then *that*. Here, the duality of 'work' and 'non-work' is of 'work' and 'leisure'. It was Thorstein Veblen's famous work of 1899 on the leisure class that popularised the concept of 'leisure'. The pooling of the capital of different individuals, who have control over the means of production, and emergence of the managerial class rendered the early capitalists 'work-less', bereft of any control they would exercise on the productive organisation. Absolved of the direct ruling power, the 'ruling class' would now become the 'economic class'; but because of its share in the capital, and the profit it would generate over time, even without working, it would be able to live affluently. In other words, even when one is not working, one's life chances are not slimmed. So, since it is not 'working', the leisure class, which is a product of the evolution of capitalism, indulges in an 'unproductive use of time'. And, this is the pithiest definition of leisure.

V

What does one do when one is in leisure? One relaxes, sleeps and eats; parking oneself before television, one watches all types of programmes, whether one likes them or not; one is free from the pressure of work and time, and the stresses concomitant with it; one plays, goes on holiday, gallivanting; leisure may comprise the 'time pass' or sheer 'waste of time' activities. In a nutshell, leisure is seen as an antithesis of work, as said previously. If work imposes a regime, schedule, discipline, and punctuality, leisure is liberated from all this. Since leisure relieves one from the demanding schedule, it is viewed as invigorating.

With the entry of the corporate world, the value of leisure has multiplied manifold. Since the corporation demands rigourous work, strenuous and arduous, of acute responsibility and commitment, as a kind of compensation, it legitimizes holidays, away from work, mobile phones, and a plethora of worries. The concept of 'paid holidays' has also come up. Life is seen as alternating between periods of 'lots and lots of work' and the 'periods of lots and lots of leisure'. The practice of 'working from home' is pursued by many organisations, for it cuts down on office expenses. This has important implications for the duality of work and leisure. In case of the fixed office working hours (what is popularly known as '9 to 5 schedule'), a person may be believed to be at leisure before the commencement and after the office hours, but when the 'house becomes the office' (the idea of 'employed elsewhere but working from home'), the distinction between work and leisure is blurred. When people work from home, they subscribe to the informality of their style, for instance, they are not dressed up the way they do when they are on way to their offices. Men may not change or shave; women may be in their night dresses. They may take sometime off from their work, attending to domestic duties. The work may extend to the time which may not be in the traditional sense the 'office hours'.

Commonplace ideas in 'leisurology' (the 'study of leisure', a term I heard Ishwar Modi using) are: (1) the cultural content of leisure varies from one context to the other, across regions, communities, states and nations; (2) each practice of leisure the people have is believed to have evolved over time; (3) the ways of 'leisuring' vary in accordance with gender, age, and strata, and intensive field studies may document them; and (4) the relationship between work and leisure is not uniform in different societies. It is to the last one that I intend to give a little more attention.

The problem with the dichotomous ways of looking at the world is that it does not permit us to explore some other categories, continuities, and blurrings that may coexist with the polarity. Well known is the criticism of the Western concept of work that deprecates the 'household engagement of women' (popularly known as "homemaker's work"), dubbing it as 'non-work', for it does not fit in the definition of work. Similarly, when self-employed workers lose their enterprise as it is engulfed by the 'big fish' and become 'work-less', do they lapse into the state of leisure? Suppose, after returning from office, I devote all my time to domestic duties, which besides the kitchen and cleaning tasks include helping my young children with their homework, driving my mother-in-law to her doctor, collecting the dry-cleaning, paying bills, etc. do I view them as 'leisure activities', since they take place outside my 'office hours', or do I regard them as another set of 'works' as important as is the 'office work'?

To take another example: after finishing my school, where I am employed as a teacher, I visit the houses of several boys and girls to impart them tuition classes for which each of my wards pays me on an hourly basis. According to the definition of work, after my school hours, I am on leisure, but from my perspective, I am always 'working', augmenting my income, and since my extra work does not conflict with my school schedule, I do not have any compunction about it nor does my institution raise any objection to it.

My last example comes from my profession, i.e. teaching. One of the severe criticisms of college and university teachers is that they work for a couple of hours a day and then are 'free' to pursue any other occupation or interest, which is believed to be their another source of income. And, there have been attempts to increase their working hours at their places of work, and some of these attempts have been successful in past despite resistance from teachers. The common tirade against the teachers is that they 'have little work'; if someone has one class a day, he is supposed to be working for fifty-five minutes a day, and for rest of the time, he is, according to the definition ingrained in our mind, 'leisuring'. What about the hours and hours he spends preparing his lectures; time spent each day marking the assignments of the students; solving the queries of the students after the class hours and on telephone; writing up research papers, for his promotion is dependent upon this output; and in addition, carrying out the administrative duties that his institution assigns to him. All that he does is certainly not 'leisure'; it is work. It is, therefore, myopic to confine work only to the time I spent in the class, for the success of my classroom teaching is greatly dependent upon the work I carry out beyond the class schedule. The academic administrators favouring the increase in the number of hours of work in the college suffer from a jaundiced definition of work, and are unable to realise that the academic work continues even beyond the so-called 'work hours'.

VI

My intention here is to expose the difficulty in keeping the distinction between 'work' and 'leisure', and to draw attention to, as has been done earlier as well, to the parochiality of the Western definition of work. In fact, a look at the traditional North Indian culture, which is still practiced in some quarters, will acquaint one to two words that come closest to the Western idea of leisure; they are *ārām* and *fursat*. The first means 'rest' – say, when one lies down after returning from the tiring office hours, it is often called *ārām*, and is used in Malinowski's sense of fulfilling the 'vital needs', which are essential for recuperation of the bodily strength. Thus, rest is not leisure; sleep is not leisure; and so is hospitalisation. Rather, they are physiological imperatives. When North Indians speak of *ārām*, they generally mean the 'state of lying down', 'watching television', 'indulging in pleasant chitchats'; it generally means 'carelessly lazing around', as the following couplet states:

> *kis kis ko yād kijeya, kis kis ko royīye; ārām badī chīz hai muhn dhak ke soyīye*
>
> [Whom to remember, whom to lament; rest is a big thing, cover your face and sleep.]

The 'unproductive use of time', to remember Veblen, that leisure is, is largely, rather reluctantly approved, for children. After the school-going children finish their examinations, they are permitted to laze around, as the following couplet points out.

> *nānī ke ghar jāyenge, dudh malaī khāyenge; motey ho kar āyenge*
>
> (After the examinations, we) shall go to maternal grandmother's house, (there we) shall drink milk and eat cream, (when we) return, we shall be fat.

Besides being permitted for children, leisure figures in moral messages as well. For instance, the idea that leisure breeds an 'unoccupied mind' is common, and such a mind is "devil's workshop" (*khālī dimāg shaitān kā ghar*). Or, the idea that God takes care of the needs of all is conveyed in a verse that uses the metaphor of leisure:

> *ajgar kare nā chākrī, panchī kare nā kām; dās Malukā kah gaye sab ke dātā Rām*
>
> (Neither does the python do any service, nor does the bird do any work; Ram [referring to God] takes care of all, that is, it provides them with food, so says the poet, Maluk Das [the sixteenth century devotional poet from Allahabad]).

To recapitulate, children are less willingly allowed to 'waste time', but still the elders compromise with their wards' 'simian' (or restless) nature and allow them to play and use time in an 'unproductive way'. However, any activity that might drive them to vagabondage is seriously curbed, or any company that might make them succumb to bad habits is closely watched. Gradually, the children are culturally ingrained with the idea that 'rest is unwarranted' (*ārām he harām*). 'One would be eligible for rest after one's demise' (*marne ke bād hī ārām milegā*), 'one notorious for rest earns ill-fame' (*jisne kiyā āram, who ho gayā badnām*), "[If you] study, [if you] write, you'll lead a life of affluence; [if you] play, you'll be bad [meaning, you'll be miserable]' (*padhoge likhoge banoge nawab, kheloge kudoge banoge kharāb*') – are the other adages that disapprove leisure. The adults are a product of this ideology, which throws the concept of leisure out of the door, and work acquires a cardinal place in individual lives.

VII

Work is divided into different categories. My office work is different from my domestic work – I return home after gruelling office duty; I am tired but the household work that had been waiting for me for hours invigorates me.

Mustering all energy I devote myself to domestic duties. For me, the distinction between 'work' and 'leisure' does not exist; what exists for me is 'work' and 'work' only. The specificity of one set of activities vis-à-vis the other distinguishes one type of work from the other. For years and years together, what engages me is work; in other words, the distinction between 'work' and 'leisure' is spurious for me, and the concept of 'leisure' is fake and unconvincing. I do not know what 'free time' (*fursat*) is, for I disdain wasting time. I am Protestant-like in my orientation; for me 'time is work', as for the Protestant 'time is money', for me, 'each moment I have must be put to work', in the same way as a Protestant spends each fraction of his time to 'bringing the glory of God on earth'. Guilt overcomes me when I waste time. The sentiments of the contemporary individual are beautifully expressed in an Urdu verse:

mujhe bhī bulātey hain zulfon ke sāye,
yeh gulshan, yeh manzar, yeh dilkash samān,
yeh izz-o-zar ke hisār-e-hasīn,
lipton mein inse yeah fursat kahān.

[The shades of tresses call me,
The gardens, the scenery, the bewitching environ,
The enchanting palaces of respect and wealth,
I have no free time to caress these.]

The spirit behind this is if a culture is seen from inside one would come across different relations between the concepts of 'work' and 'leisure'. On one extreme, we would find employees of the corporate world who make a clear distinction between these two concepts. They periodically go on vacations, switch off their mobile phones, for they want to shut themselves completely off from the world of the office. Holiday is seen as a 'medicine' to regain vigour and vitality to deal with the arduousness of work.

By contrast is the category of people for whom work and leisure collapse into one. For them, work gives them mirth; the more they work, the more happy they feel. Neither does the work give them ennui nor does it tire them out. Any 'unproductive use of time' is sin for them. They work all the time, in the office, outside it; all the waking hours are 'workful', 'productive', 'fulfilling', 'engaging', and 'salvational'.

VIII

The same orientation to work is discernible in the lives of homemakers in traditional Indian society.

Let me here be autobiographical and recall the work schedule of women in my traditional household, which had members of three generations living together. Women were homemakers; since the concept of domestic help was non-existent, all tasks, from sweeping and mopping the house to cooking food and cleaning pots and pans, from making various types of snacks and sweets to grinding grains, and from stitching clothes to washing and ironing them were woman-activities. Dependence on the market was only for the raw material, but processing of it was mainly at home, in which women played a predominant role. They were of course assisted by their children, particularly female, and that was how they learnt. As stated earlier, milk was processed at home to convert it into curd, and so were the sweets made at home; papadam (*pāpar*), lentil-pebbles (*barī*), potato chips (*alū kā lacchā*), were all home made, things which today are largely acquired from the market. Women enjoyed taking lead in these activities, trying to excel in their work. In between these activities, they also looked after their children. I remember learning the tables (*pahārā*) up to twenty from my mother whilst she would be engaged in one or the other household activity. At no time, I heard these women rueing of the pressure of work or demanding leisure or freedom from this. Yes, pressure on them increased when relatives used to come, but the interesting aspect was that the women accompanying them delightfully contributed to the household work. Often, when they were desisted from this, they would say: "Don't treat us like 'relatives' (*mehmān*), we are members of your house, allow us to work." Along with them, they would bring a number of gifts, household things. Of course, they were sent back with another set of gifts, but this gesture was always extolled and regarded as emulative. The visits of relatives were acculturative, for they rendered a priceless opportunity to learn new things, may be preparation of new dishes or new designs of knitting and weaving.

For these women, like the situation described earlier, work was leisurous. Whenever they got physically tired, they fell asleep soundly. I never heard my mother or my grandmothers ever complaining of lack of sleep or remaining awake for hours in bed. I also did not hear menfolk talking about it; the local expression for sound sleep was *ghorey bech kar sonā* ('to sleep after having sold the horses', which means 'sleeping unworryingly', 'sleep like a log of wood'). To recapitulate the point: rest here meant sleeping. 'A good sleep is a precursor to good work,' I learned this as a part of growing up in this culture.

Thus, if at all was leisure permitted, rather suspiciously, it was for children. Boys were allowed leisureful activities for longer number of years than girls, a fact showing gender-bias. The girls were inducted into household duties at a young age, to eventually become like their mothers and grandmothers in future. Like girls, the boys were also gradually withdrawn from playfulness, which constituted the bulk of their leisure, and were trained to devote them with full heart to work, the family occupation or to study; so they would become like their fathers and grandfathers. In this way, the family tradition was carried forward.

IX

The evolution was, therefore, from a life where leisure dominated to the one where leisure was suppressed, being regarded as a reckless squandering of time. The first phase was for children; it was often said: 'They are children, let them play' (*bacche haīn inhen khelne do*). During their socialisation, they gradually imbibed the value of time. 'Time never returns', 'time wasted is wasted forever', 'time flies like an arrow', 'time is not a boomerang, it does not return', 'time is invaluable', 'it is irreversible', 'God is kind to those who respect time, for He has created it' – these were the lessons that the children gradually internalised, through their interactions with the adults and listening to a myriad of folktales. As time rolled by, they came to value time by devoting them fully to work and equally, by shunning leisure.

A return to a leisurous life was expected after a person retired from active work schedule. In fact, many nearing retirement looked forward to a 'life of leisure' (*ārām kī zindagī*), life when they would have rest, but immediately after retirement, they took up one or the other work they liked, notwithstanding its financial returns. van Willigen and Chadha's study (1999) of the old people in Rana Pratap Bagh and Cohen's work (2000) on ageing amply showed that the retired people, unless they were challenged by a debilitating condition, were far more occupied in one or the other activity after their retirement than was the situation earlier. Against this backdrop, in one of my lectures at a Senior Citizens' Club (Greater Kailash-II, New Delhi), I proposed that one should seriously think in terms of a 'second career', especially those who work for time-bound jobs, where one retires at the age of sixty or sixty-five. Many such people start preparing for their retired life; some do an additional professional degree (such as in management, law, journalism and editing) so that after retirement they get into another profession, which would mark the beginning of another career. It is quite common to see many pensioners devoting themselves to social work and welfare commitments. The apparent reason is to keep oneself busy, for if not working one would be a nuisance at home, but the deeper reason lies in the subconscious rejection of the idea of leisure. Any waste of time is guilt-generating. It also amounts to setting a bad example for the young. The quality highly admired in a man is his 'devotion and immersion in work', the Sanskrit expression for which is to lead the life of a *karmayogi*.

X

By way of conclusion, my submission is that the analytical categories that had their origin in the Western experience are by means of universal applicability. This understanding of mine has been confirmed by many who have given the clarion call for the 'indigenisation' of sociology. It essentially means looking at the system from inside, trying to be as empathetic as possible. We have to liberate ourselves from the intellectual subservience to certain thoughts of thinking and analysis, and be prepared to examine them critically and question the established understanding. In this reflective paper, I have tried to grasp the life of people in the traditional North Indian society, and its continuity in contemporary times, against the backdrop of the distinction between 'work' and 'leisure', which emerged in the context of the Western industrial experience. My tentative submission is that in the categories of people I have in mind leisure is culturally negative. Work itself becomes the fountainhead of joy and fulfillment. I have sung the eulogy of work in this paper, for that is how I also think and live, and this is the 'work ethic' I want to inculcate in my progeny and students.

References

Cohen, Lawrence A. 2000. *No Aging in India: Alzheimer's, The Bad Family, and Other Modern Things*. California: University of California Press.

van Willigen, John and Narender K. Chadha. 1999. *Social Ageing in a Delhi Neighbourhood*. Connecticut: Bergin and Garvey.

Veblen, Thorstein. 1899. *The Theory of the Leisure Class*. New York: The Macmillan Company.

24

Why Public Sociology?

MICHAEL BURAWOY

As sociologists we find ourselves in a paradoxical situation: the world's problems require a sociological imagination for their solution but that imagination is losing ground as an academic discipline and as public knowledge. The struggle for public sociology is both an expression and an answer to this paradox.

What are the issues of today? Simply put the survival of the human race. As we plunder nature – whether it be land, water or air – for profit so we not only jeopardise long-term planetary existence (global warming, toxic waste, pollution of every sort), but displace enormous populations, dispossessing them of access to their means of existence, and thereby creating enormous reservoirs of labour. Wage labour becomes the privilege of ever fewer, themselves subject to ever greater insecurity. Instead of a proletariat we create an expanding, frightened precariat, rising into ever higher rungs of the socio-economic ladder. Unable to find consumers for the goods and services it produces, capitalism extends credit to all and sundry – individuals (mortgages, credit), communities (microfinance), nations (structural adjustment loans) – but when payments can no longer be postponed, the bubble bursts, bankruptcy follows upon bankruptcy and financial crises ensue, and ever more people are expelled onto the streets.

The commodifications of nature, labour and money are intimately related to one another, but in different ways in different countries. As sociologist we need to map out the interwoven patterns of market intensification and expansion. But each commodification is also connected to a more recent commodification, the commodification of knowledge. The extension of the market turns the university into a commercial enterprise, turning a public good into a private good. To finance itself the university sells the knowledge it produces, building close ties with corporations (cheap research) and the state (propaganda), charging for the dissemination and certification of knowledge (student fees), begging for funds from the rich and super-rich in exchange for symbolic capital. In some places the university becomes a shadow of its former self or simply withers away. The survival of disciplines within the university increasingly depends on their market value whether they render useful research for industry, ideology for the state or jobs for students. As the membrane separating the university and society becomes thinner, academics can no longer assume autonomy, so we have to decide whose side we are on, whose values we support.

Within the social sciences, economics – conventionally neoclassical but with notable dissenters – develops the technologies for new markets while providing the ideology that justifies the destruction of the planet. Political science, again with notable dissenters, is its accomplice, establishing the conditions of market expansion while contracting the meaning of politics, separating it from power, dispossessing people of control over their own lives. These are the social sciences that can make claims to pay their way – unlike sociology whose long-standing defense of civil society against market fundamentalism and state despotism is increasingly out of favour with the dominant forces in society.

There are states – fewer and fewer – that seek to contain the destructiveness of the economic tsunami, and even fewer that are successful. They include the welfare states of Northern Europe which still recognise the social dimension of problems and policies. Here sociological perspectives have legitimacy, particularly as a form of policy science. There are other states that erect barricades against the market, holding it at bay through authoritarian means. Here sociology's defense of an open civil society is seen as politically threatening and sociology's existence is precarious, as it is easily labelled an enemy of the state. Whether sociology survives at the national level will determine its survival at the global level – the level most critical to saving the planet for human habitation. A global sociology, not a false universalism, not a hegemonic projection of a singular, particular sociology, has to be our goal.

What is to be done? Sociology cannot insulate itself within the academy watching its support dwindle, but must advance into the public sphere and there excite debate about the direction of society, educate citizenry about the dangers of market commodification and political rationalisation. This can be done in two ways – as a traditional public sociology which uses various media – print, audio and visual – to stimulate conversation. This is never easy. Often, journalists have neither the patience nor the interest in critical commentary. Independent opinion pages are limited in space and readership. Television and radio are either carefully monitored or subject to arbitrary market criteria. Occasionally, a sociology text that links personal troubles to social issues captures the public imagination. Social media do provide an alternative outlet, but the competition is relentless, and so we have to be innovative in attracting attention. Whatever the challenges, even as a professional discipline, we cannot abandon the public sphere to conglomerate sponsors or to political propaganda.

There is a second way forward – organic public sociology. Here there is an unmediated relation between sociologists and their publics that can be social movements, social organisations, local communities. The publics concerned are active rather than passive, thick rather than thin, narrow rather than broad, counter rather than mainstream. Like traditional public sociology, organic public sociology requires enormous patience, eliciting the trust of others, resisting pressures to sacrifice intellectual autonomy, but also refusing a vanguardist role that condemns the subaltern voice to oblivion. Organic and traditional public sociologies are not mutual exclusive but complementary.

Public sociology has perhaps it greatest and most enduring potential in the classroom where most of us spend most of our professional lives. Indeed, just as public sociology is a form of teaching – in which the teachers are also the taught – so teaching can be a form of public sociology. It calls upon us to see students as a public with whom we can engage traditionally or organically, raising to a sociological plane their understanding of themselves and their connection to others.

Public sociology cannot be carried out in isolation. It has to be a conversation among sociologists about their conversation with publics, which are themselves involved in their own conversation. The lone public sociologist quickly gives up the mission, and retreats into cynicism or martyrdom. A collective esprit de corps is all the more necessary where public sociology is a matter of life and death as it has been in countries of Africa, Latin America and the Middle East. It requires collective support, collective imagination, and collective organisation. It cannot be a marginal moment of our discipline but integral to its very being, especially as the university is decisively inside society, buffeted by social, political and economic forces.

Very different from political activism, public sociology is accountable to the field of professional sociology, to its scientific norms and its accumulating body of research. As a discipline, sociology takes the standpoint of civil society (with all its warts), locating lived experience within its broader macro determinations, specifically state and economy – and to this scientific body of knowledge public sociology must be accountable. This is the body of knowledge that has to be translated into a language accessible for broader publics. Critical sociology is important in steering professional knowledge toward engagement with public issues, and its independence has, therefore, to be ferociously guarded.

Political activism, on the other hand, is accountable to the political field, to the logic of its institutions – legislatures, assemblies, parties, laws, etc. The trouble begins when the fields of the academic discipline and of politics overlap or in the worst case scenario when the latter envelopes the former. Here, independent of the will of the sociologist, public sociology becomes political activism or is defined as such by the state. Here the struggle becomes one of carving out an arena of professional and critical sociology independent of the political field, perhaps an underworld of dissidents, or daring the state to politicise scientific activity and thereby risking its own legitimacy. Without connection to a thriving professional sociology, public sociology is a lame duck.

Public sociology draws strength and inspiration from social movements, most recently those inaugurated by the Arab Spring of 2011, spreading cross the planet. From Tahrir Square to the Indignados (Greece, Spain, Portugal), from Nandigram (India) to Wukan (China), from the student movement to Occupy, these connected social movements are deeply ingrained with sociological perspectives. They are an expression of and a demand for a new sociology – propelled by an enduring commitment to values of freedom, equality, justice but increasingly concerned with human survival in the face of the Third World War declared by market and state on society.

Index